Present Dangers

Present Dangers

Crisis and Opportunity
in American Foreign and Defense Policy

edited by
Robert Kagan and William Kristol

Encounter Books
San Francisco, California

First edition published in 2000 by Encounter Books, an activity of Encounter for Culture and Education, Inc., a nonprofit tax exempt corporation.

Encounter Books website address: www.encounterbooks.com

Manufactured in the United States and printed on acid-free paper.

The paper used in this publication meets the minimum requirements of ANSI/NISO Z39.48-1992 (R 1997) (Permanence of Paper).

Library of Congress Cataloging-in-Publication Data

Kagan, Robert.
    Present dangers : crisis and opportunity in American foreign and
defense policy.
    p.   cm.
    Includes bibliographic references and index.
    ISBN 1-893554-13-9 (alk. paper)
    1. United States—Foreign relations—1989—Philosophy.   2. United
States—Military policy—Philosophy.   I. Kristol, William.   II. Title.

E840.K316   2000
327.7—dc21

                                                        00-034728

            10   9   8   7   6   5   4   3   2   1

Contents

Preface

This book is an outgrowth of an article we published in *Foreign Affairs* in 1996, "Toward a Neo-Reaganite Foreign Policy." We warned there of the growing threats to the American peace established at the end of the Cold War, and called for a foreign policy of "benevolent hegemony" as a way of securing that peace and advancing American interests and principles around the world. The article sparked controversy in the United States and abroad, and the question of American hegemony has become a principal focus of the foreign policy debate.

Events of recent years have given us no reason to change our fundamental view either of the emerging dangers or of the prescriptions for meeting these dangers. If anything, the trend of the past few years has proven more troubling than we anticipated. The emergence of China as a strong, determined, and potentially hostile power; the troubling direction of political developments in Russia; the continuing threat posed by aggressive dictatorships in Iraq, Serbia, and North Korea; the increasingly alarming decline in American military capabilities—all these and more suggest that the coming years may be critical in determining the fate of international peace and of the American hegemony on which that peace depends. The aim of this collection of essays is to provide a survey of these many dangers and to offer recommendations to American policy-makers on how to meet and overcome the challenges we face in the world.

As the reader will see, the authors in this book include some of America's leading foreign policy thinkers and practitioners of the past two decades. Paul Wolfowitz, Richard Perle, William Schneider, Elliott Abrams, and Peter Rodman have served at the highest levels of government. William Bennett, former secretary of education and drug czar, has been a leading commentator on the role of morality in American society and politics. Donald Kagan, Aaron Friedberg, and Nicholas Eberstadt are leading authorities in their respective academic fields. It is fair to say that all are conservative in their outlook. But what distinguishes them is that they are all conservative internationalists, with a strong commitment to vigorous American global leadership, to American power, and to the advancement of American democratic and free-market principles abroad. In this sense, they are the true heirs to a tradition in American foreign policy that runs at least from Theodore Roosevelt through Ronald Reagan.

The topics covered in these essays range across several broad themes. In our introductory essay, we argue that the world has, indeed, become a more perilous place after the squandered decade of the 1990s and that the "present danger" lies in America's hesitancy in maintaining its global hegemony against the many emerging challenges. James Ceasar then takes a broad look at the foreign policy debates of the past decade, and especially the debates among conservatives, offering an important analysis of what modern conservative internationalism is and is not.

Part Two deals with the main threats to American peace in the coming decade. First, Ross Munro and Peter Rodman address the challenges likely to be posed by two world powers, China and Russia. Munro contends that China is fast emerging as the greatest threat to American interests and that a serious conflict with China may come sooner than many would like to believe. Rodman argues that Russian leaders are moving toward a new realism in their foreign policy, one that offers both dangers and opportunities for the United States. The next three chapters consider the problem of "rogue states." Richard Perle warns that Saddam Hussein is on the verge of breaking free from the international constraints imposed on him at the end of the Gulf War, and that unless a concerted effort is made to remove him from power he will soon acquire weapons of mass destruction and fundamentally alter the strategic balance in the Middle East. Reuel Marc Gerecht cautions that the Iranian regime is not necessarily moving in a "moderate" direction, as many assume, and will continue to pose serious problems as a supporter of terrorism, a destabilizing influence in the Middle East, and a potential nuclear power. Nicholas Eberstadt argues that North Korea remains very dangerous and will remain so until the present regime in Pyongyang falls.

Part Three looks at America's resources for meeting these challenges: its allies and its military assets. Jeffrey Gedmin and Aaron Friedberg both discuss the question of America's alliances with the world's other great powers, in Europe and East Asia, arguing that these alliances, cornerstones of American leadership, have fallen into disrepair. Elliott Abrams describes the faulty logic that has driven American policy toward the Middle East for more than a decade, warning that the security of Israel, Turkey, and American friends in the Arab world may be jeopardized unless the United States shifts its focus toward strengthening friends and consolidating American influence in the region. The next two chapters assess the growing deficiencies in America's military capabilities as global threats multiply. Frederick Kagan provides an account of the reduction in the armed forces since the Gulf War and demonstrates that cuts in the defense budget have been driven not by a coherent strategy but by the political need to offer Americans a post–Cold War "peace dividend." William Schneider describes the breakdown of American efforts to prevent the proliferation of weapons of mass destruction and long-range missiles, as well as the disastrous inadequacy of American programs for building a missile defense system that can protect the United States, its troops stationed abroad, and its allies.

Part Four examines some broader issues of American foreign policy from a historical perspective. William Bennett makes a carefully reasoned defense of an American foreign policy based on principle, tracing the role of American principles in foreign policy from the Founding Fathers to the present. Paul Wolfowitz discusses the lost art of statesmanship and offers a long-time practitioner's perspective on the challenges to American foreign policy today. Donald Kagan stresses the vital importance of national will in the successful deterrence of war, offering examples of both success and failure from the past four centuries of European and American history.

In choosing these authors, we sought to find individuals who shared a common perspective on America's role in the world. We did not, however, insist on uniformity when it came to policy prescriptions. The reader may note that in the case of China, for instance, there is not complete agreement among Messrs. Wolfowitz, Friedman, and Munro on the exact policies to be pursued ‘on such matters as Taiwan or trade. Rather than viewing this as a problem, we think it is healthy. Within the broad strategy of conservative internationalism there will be more than one set of tactics.

We would also note that there are omissions in this collection. There is no essay on international economics, for instance, and no essay on Latin America, even though both issues are vitally important. We trust others will fill in the gaps we have left.

Finally, we wish to express our gratitude to a handful of people who made this book possible. Peter Collier at Encounter Books was a patient and steady hand throughout the process of putting this collection together, after having prompted us to make this effort in the first place. Karen Wright at the Project for the New American Century put in long hours and provided invaluable assistance throughout this process. Finally, we owe an enormous debt to Gary Schmitt, the Executive Director of the Project for the New American Century. Without his tireless efforts, his keen eye for detail, and his broad understanding of American foreign and defense policy, this book would not have been possible.

Robert Kagan
William Kristol
April 2000

I.

An Overview

Introduction:
National Interest
and Global Responsibility

A little over twenty years ago, a group of concerned Americans formed the Committee on the Present Danger. The danger they feared, and sought to rally Americans to confront, was the Soviet Union.

It is easy to forget these days how controversial was the suggestion in the mid- to late 1970s that the Soviet Union was really a danger, much less one that should be challenged by the United States. This was hardly the dominant view of the American foreign policy establishment. Quite the contrary: prevailing wisdom from the Nixon through the Carter administrations held that the United States should do its utmost to coexist peaceably with the USSR, and that the American people in any case were not capable of sustaining a serious challenge to the Soviet system. To engage in an arms race would either bankrupt the United States or lead to Armageddon. To challenge communist ideology at its core, to declare it evil and illegitimate, would be at best quixotic and at worst perilous. When the members of the Committee on the Present Danger challenged this comfortable consensus, when they criticized détente and arms control and called for a military build-up and a broad ideological and strategic assault on Soviet communism, their recommendations were generally dismissed as either naive or reckless. It would take a revolution in American foreign policy, the fall of the Berlin Wall, and the disintegration of the Soviet empire to prove just how right they were.

Does this Cold War tale have any relevance today as Americans grapple with the uncertainties of the post–Cold War era? The Soviet

Union has long since crumbled. No global strategic challenger has emerged to take its place; none appears visible on the horizon; and the international scene at present seems fairly benign to most observers. Many of our strategists tell us that we will not face another major threat for twenty years or more, and that we may as a consequence enjoy a "strategic pause." According to opinion polls, the American public is less interested in foreign policy than at any time since before World War II. Intermittent fears of terrorist attack, worries about the proliferation of weapons of mass destruction, distant concerns about the possible outbreak of war in the Taiwan Strait or in the Balkans—all attract attention, but only fleetingly. The United States, both at the level of elite opinion and popular sentiment, appears to have become the Alfred E. Newman of superpowers, with its national motto being, "What, me worry?"

But there *is* today a "present danger." It has no name. It is not to be found in any single strategic adversary. It does not fit neatly under the heading of "international terrorism" or "rogue states" or "ethnic hatred." In fact, the ubiquitous post–Cold War question—where is the threat?—is misconceived. Rather, the present danger is that the United States, the world's dominant power on whom the maintenance of international peace and the support of liberal democratic principles depends, will shrink its responsibilities and—in a fit of absentmindedness, or parsimony, or indifference—allow the international order that it created and sustains to collapse. Our present danger is one of declining military strength, flagging will and confusion about our role in the world. It is a danger, to be sure, of our own devising. Yet, if neglected, it is likely to yield very real external dangers, as threatening in their way as the Soviet Union was a quarter century ago.

ooooo

In fact, beneath the surface calm of world affairs today, there has already been an erosion of the mostly stable, peaceful and democratic international order that emerged briefly at the end of the Cold War. Americans and their political leaders have spent the years since 1991 lavishing the gifts of an illusory "peace dividend" upon themselves, and frittering away the opportunity to strengthen and extend an international order uniquely favorable to the United States.

It is worth reviewing the record of the past ten years, if only to show how great is the opportunity we have wasted and the dangers that may await us in the future as a result.

The 1990s, for all their peace and prosperity, were a squandered decade. The decade began with America's triumph in the Cold War and its smashing victory over Iraq in Desert Storm. In the wake of those twin triumphs, the United States had assumed an unprecedented position of power and influence in the world. By the traditional measures of national power, the United States held a position unmatched since Rome dominated the Mediterranean world. American military power dwarfed that of any other nation, both in its war-fighting capabilities and in its ability to intervene in conflicts anywhere in the world on short notice. There was a common acceptance, even by potential adversaries, that America's position as the sole global superpower might not be challenged for decades to come. Meanwhile, the American economic precepts of liberal capitalism and free trade had become almost universally accepted as the best model for creating wealth, and the United States itself stood at the center of that international economic order. The American political precepts of liberal democracy had spread across continents and cultures as other peoples cast off or modified autocratic methods of governance and adopted, or at least paid lip-service to, the American credo of individual rights and freedoms. American culture, for better or for worse, had become the dominant global culture. To a degree scarcely imaginable at mid-century, or even as late as the 1970s, the world had indeed been transformed in America's image.

Our country, in other words, was—or could have been—present at another creation similar to the one Dean Acheson saw emerge after World War II. For the first time in its history, the United States had the chance to shape the international system in ways that would enhance its security and advance its principles without opposition from a powerful, determined adversary. A prostrate and democratizing Russia had neither the ability nor the inclination to challenge the American-led international democratic order. Though it turned toward harsh repression at home in 1989, China had barely begun to increase its military capabilities, and rather than thinking about launching a challenge to American dominance in East Asia, China's military leaders stood in awe of the military prowess and technological superiority America had exhibited in the Gulf War. The world's strongest economies in Europe and Japan, meanwhile, were American allies and participants in the international economic and political system, with the United States at its center. The newly liberated nations of Eastern and Central Europe yearned for membership in the American-led North Atlantic alliance. In the Middle East, the defeat of Saddam's armies, the liberation of Kuwait, and the waning of Soviet and then Russian influence seemed to open a new era of American influence.

ooooo

The task for America at the start of the 1990s ought to have been obvious. It was to prolong this extraordinary moment and to guard the international system from any threats that might challenge it. This meant, above all, preserving and reinforcing America's benevolent global hegemony, which undergirded what President George Bush rightly called a "new world order." The goal of American foreign policy should have been to turn what Charles Krauthammer called a "unipolar moment" into a unipolar era.

The great promise of the post–Cold War era, however, began to dim almost immediately—and even before Bill Clinton was elected. The United States, which had mustered the world's most awesome military force to expel Saddam Hussein from Kuwait, failed to see that mission through to its proper conclusion: the removal of Saddam from power in Baghdad. Instead, vastly superior U.S. forces stood by in March 1991 as Shi'ite and Kurdish uprisings against Saddam were brutally crushed and the Iraqi tyrant, so recently in fear of his life, began to re-establish his control over the country. Three months later, Yugoslav President Slobodan Milosevic launched an offensive against the breakaway province of Slovenia, following up with a much larger attack on Croatia. In the spring of 1992, Serb forces began their bloody siege of Sarajevo and a war of ethnic cleansing that would cost the lives of 200,000 Bosnian Muslims over the next three years. In the second half of 1992, meanwhile, American intelligence learned that North Korea had begun surreptitiously producing materials for nuclear weapons.

Saddam Hussein, Slobodan Milosevic, and the totalitarian regime of North Korea, each in their own way, would be the source of one crisis after another throughout the remainder of the decade. Each of these dangerous dictatorships appears certain to survive the end of the twentieth century and go on to present continuing risks to the United States and its allies in the new millennium. And their very survival throughout the 1990s has established a disturbing principle in the post–Cold War world: that dictators can challenge the peace, slaughter innocents in their own or in neighboring states, threaten their neighbors with missile attacks—and still hang on to power. This constitutes a great failure in American foreign policy, one that will surely come back to haunt us.

But these were not the only failures that made the 1990s a decade of squandered opportunity for American foreign policy. The past decade also saw the rise of an increasingly hostile and belligerent China, which had drawn its own conclusions about U.S. behavior after the Gulf War. While every other great power in the world cut its defense budget throughout the 1990s, China alone embarked on a huge military buildup, augmenting both its conventional and its nuclear arsenal in an effort to project power beyond its shores and deter the United States from defending its friends and allies. China used this power to seize contested islands in the South China Sea, to intimidate its neighbors in East Asia, and, in the most alarming display of military might, to frighten the people of Taiwan by launching ballistic missiles off their shores. Throughout the 1990s, moreover, the Chinese government continued and intensified the repression of domestic dissent, both political and religious, that began with the massacre in Tiananmen Square. The American response to China's aggressive behavior at home and abroad has, with but a few exceptions, been one of appeasement.

In the face of the moral and strategic challenges confronting it, the United States engaged in a gradual but steady moral and strategic disarmament. Rather than seeking to unseat the dangerous dictatorships in Baghdad and Belgrade, the Clinton administration combined empty threats and ineffectual military operations with diplomatic accommodation. Rather than press hard for changes of regime in Pyongyang and Beijing, the Clinton administration—and in the case of China, the Bush administration before it—tried to purchase better behavior through "engagement." Rather than confronting the moral and strategic challenge presented by these evil regimes, the United States tried to do business with them in pursuit of the illusion of "stability." Rather than squarely facing our world responsibilities, American political leaders chose drift and evasion.

In the meantime, the United States allowed its military strength to deteriorate to the point where its ability to defend its interests and deter future challenges is now in doubt. From 1989 to 1999, the defense budget and the size of the armed forces were cut by a third; the share of America's GNP devoted to defense spending was halved, from nearly 6 to around 3 percent; and the amount of money spent on weapons procurement and research and development declined about 50 percent. There was indeed a "peace dividend," and as a result, by the end of the decade the U.S. military was inadequately equipped and stretched to the point of exhaustion. And while defense experts spent the 1990s debating whether it was more important to maintain current readiness or to sacrifice present capabilities in order to prepare for future challenges, the United States, under the strain of excessive budget cuts, did neither.

Yet ten years from now, and perhaps a good deal sooner, we likely will be living in a world in which Iraq, Iran, North Korea and China all possess the ability to strike the continental United States with nuclear weapons. Within the next decade we may have to decide whether to defend Taiwan against a Chinese attack. We could face another attempt by a rearmed Saddam Hussein to seize Kuwait's oil fields. An authoritarian regime in Russia could move to reclaim some of what it lost in 1991.

Other, still greater challenges can be glimpsed on the horizon, involving a host of unanswerable questions. What will China be in ten years: a modernizing economy peacefully integrating itself into the international system, an economic basket case ruled by a desperate dictatorship and a hypernationalistic military, or something in between? What will Russia be: a struggling democracy shedding its old imperial skin, or a corrupt autocracy striving to take back some of what it lost in 1989 and 1991? And there are other imponderables that derive from these. If Japan feels increasingly threatened by North Korean missiles and growing Chinese power, will it decide to rearm and perhaps build its own nuclear arsenal? What would Germany do if faced by an increasingly disaffected, revanchist, and bellicose Russia?

These threats and challenges do not exhaust the possibilities, for if history is any guide we are likely to face dangers, even within the next decade, that we cannot even imagine today. Much can happen in ten years. In 1788 for instance, while Louis XVI sat comfortably on his French throne, French philosophers preached the dawning of a new age of peace based on commerce, and no one had ever heard of Napoleon Bonaparte. Ten years later, a French king had lost his head and Napoleon was rampaging across Europe. In 1910, Norman Angell won international acclaim for a book, *The Great Illusion,* in which he declared that the growth of trade between capitalist countries had made war between the great powers obsolete. By 1920, the world had suffered through the costliest war in human history, fought among the world's great capitalist trading powers, and had seen a communist takeover in Russia, a development that was literally unimaginable a decade earlier. In 1928, the American economy was soaring, Weimar Germany was ruled by a moderate democrat, and Europe was at peace. Ten years later, the United States was struggling to emerge from the Great Depression, and Neville Chamberlain was handing Czechoslovakia over to Adolf Hitler.

While none of this argues that the world *must* become a vastly more dangerous place, the point is that the world *can* grow perilous with astonishing speed. Should this happen once more, it would be terrible to have to look back on the current era as a great though fleeting opportunity that was recklessly wasted. Everything depends on what we do now.

No "Return to Normalcy"

Contrary to prevailing wisdom, the missed opportunities of the 1990s cannot be made up for merely by tinkering around the edges of America's current foreign and defense policies. The middle path many of our political leaders would prefer, with token increases in the defense budget and a more "humble" view of America's role in the world, will not suffice. What is needed today is not better management of the status quo, but a fundamental change in the way our leaders and the public think about America's role in the world.

Serious thinking about that role should begin by recalling those tenets that guided American policy through the more successful phases of the Cold War. Many writers treat America's Cold War strategy as an aberration in the history of American foreign policy. Jeane Kirkpatrick expressed the common view of both liberal and conservative foreign policy thinkers when she wrote at the decade's start that, while the United States had "performed heroically in a time when heroism was required," the day had passed when Americans ought to bear such "unusual burdens." With a return to "normal" times, the United States could "again become a normal nation."[1] In the absence of a rival on the scale of the Soviet Union, the United States should conduct itself like any other great power on the international scene, looking to secure only its immediate, tangible interests, and abjuring the broader responsibilities it had once assumed as leader of the Free World.

What is striking about this point of view is how at odds it is with the assumptions embraced by the leaders who established the guiding principles of American foreign policy at the end of World War II. We often forget that the plans for world order devised by American policy-makers in the early 1940s were not aimed at containing the Soviet Union, which many of them still viewed as a potential partner. Rather, those policy-makers were looking backward to the circumstances that had led to the catastrophe of global war. Their purpose was to construct a more stable international order than the one that had imploded in 1939; an economic system that furthered the aim of international stability by promoting growth and free trade; and a framework for international security that, although it placed too much faith in the ability of the great powers to work together, rested ultimately on the fact that American power had become the keystone in the arch of world order.

American leaders in the early to mid-1940s believed, in fact, that the "return to normalcy" that President Harding had endorsed in 1920 was the fatal error that led to the irresponsible isolationism of the 1930s. Franklin Roosevelt said in 1941 that "We will not accept a world, like the postwar world of the 1920s, in which the seeds of Hitlerism can again be planted and allowed to grow."[2] Men like James Forrestal and Dean Acheson believed the United States had supplanted Great Britain as the world's leader and that, as Forrestal put it in 1941, "America must be the dominant power of the twentieth century."[3]

Henry Luce spoke for most influential Americans inside and outside the Roosevelt administration when he insisted that it had fallen to the United States not only to win the war against Germany and Japan, but to create both "a vital international economy" and "an international moral order" that would together spread American political and economic principles—and in the process avoid the catastrophe of a third world war.[4] Such thinking was reflected in Roosevelt's Atlantic Charter and, more concretely, in the creation of the international financial system at Bretton Woods in 1944 and of the United Nations a year later.

Thus, before the Soviet Union had emerged as the great challenge to American security and American principles, American leaders had arrived at the conclusion that it would be necessary for the United States (together, they hoped, with the other great powers), to deter aggression globally, whoever the aggressor might be. In fact, during the war years they were at least as worried about the possible re-emergence of Germany and Japan as about the Soviets. John Lewis Gaddis has summarized American thinking in the years between 1941 and 1946 thus:

The American President and his key advisers were determined to secure the United States against whatever dangers might confront it after victory, but they lacked a clear sense of what those might be or where they might arise. Their thinking about postwar security was, as a consequence, more general than specific.[5]

Few influential government officials, moreover, were under the illusion that "collective security" and the United Nations could be counted on to keep the peace. In 1945 Harry Truman declared that the United States had become "one of the most powerful forces for good on earth," and the task now was to "keep it so" and to "lead the world to peace and prosperity." The United States had "achieved a world leadership which does not depend solely upon our military and naval might," Truman asserted.[6] But it was his intention, despite demobilization, to ensure that the United States would remain "the greatest naval power on earth" and would maintain "one of the most powerful air forces in the world." Americans, Truman declared, would use "our military strength solely to preserve the peace of the world. For we now know that this is the only sure way to make our own freedom secure."[7]

The unwillingness to sustain the level of military spending and preparedness required to fulfill this expansive vision was a failure of American foreign policy in the immediate aftermath of the war. It took the Iron Curtain and the outbreak of war in Korea to fully awaken Americans to the need for an assertive and forward-leaning foreign policy. But while the United States promptly rose to meet these challenges, a certain intellectual clarity was lost in the transition from the immediate postwar years to the beginning of the Cold War era. The original postwar goal of promoting and defending a decent world order became conflated with the goal of meeting the challenge of Soviet power. The policies that the United States should have pursued even in the absence of a Soviet challenge— seeking a stable and prosperous international economic order; playing a large role in Europe, Asia and the Middle East; upholding rules of international behavior that benefited Americans; promoting democratic reform where possible and advancing American principles abroad—all these became associated with the strategy of containing the Soviet Union. In fact, America was pursuing two goals at once during the Cold War: first, the promotion of a world order conducive to American interests and principles; and second, a defense against the most immediate and menacing obstacle to achieving that order. The stakes surrounding the outcome of that latter effort became so high, in fact, that when the Cold War ended, many Americans had forgotten about the former.

Leadership

But the collapse of the Soviet empire has not altered the fundamental purposes of American foreign policy. Just as sensible Americans after World War II did not imagine that the United States should retreat from global involvement and await the rise of the next equivalent to Nazi Germany, so American statesmen today ought to recognize that their charge is not to await the arrival of the next great threat, but rather to shape the international environment to prevent such a threat from arising in the first place. To put it another way: the overarching goal of American foreign policy—to preserve and extend an international order that is in accord with both our interests and our principles—endures.

Certainly, the dramatic shift in international strategic circumstances occasioned by the Soviet collapse requires a shift in the manner in which this goal is pursued. But it is not a shift to "normalcy." In the post–Cold War era, the maintenance of a decent and hospitable international order requires continued American leadership in resisting, and where possible undermining, rising dictators and hostile ideologies; in supporting American interests and liberal democratic principles; and in providing assistance to those struggling against the more extreme manifestations of human evil. If America refrains from shaping this order, we can be sure that others will shape it in ways that reflect neither our interests nor our values.

This does not mean that the United States must root out evil wherever and whenever it rears its head. Nor does it suggest that the United States must embark on a crusade against every dictatorship. No doctrine of foreign policy can do away with the need for judgment and prudence, for weighing competing moral considerations. No foreign policy doctrine can provide precise and unvarying answers to the question of where, when and how the United States ought to intervene abroad. It is easy to say that the United States must have criteria for choosing when to intervene. But it is a good deal harder to formulate those criteria than simply to say they must exist. Henry Kissinger writes in *Diplomacy* that what is most needed in American foreign policy are "criteria for selectivity."[8] But he does not venture to suggest exactly what those criteria might be. Yet if one admits that closely linked matters of prestige, principle and morality play a role in shaping foreign policy, then rigid criteria for intervention quickly prove illusory. As Kissinger well knows, the complicated workings of foreign policy and the exceptional position of the United States should guard us against believing that the national interest can be measured in a quasi-scientific fashion, or that areas of "vital" national interest can be located, and other areas excluded, by purely geopolitical determinations. Determining what is in America's national interest is an art, not a science. It requires not only the measurement of power but also an appreciation of beliefs, principles and perceptions, which cannot be quantified. That is why we choose statesmen, not mathematicians, to conduct foreign policy. That is why we will occasionally have to intervene abroad even when we cannot prove that a narrowly construed "vital interest" of the United States is at stake.

It is worth pointing out, though, that a foreign policy premised on American hegemony, and on the blending of principle with material interest, may in fact mean fewer, not more, overseas interventions than under the "vital interest" standard. Had the Bush administration, for example, realized early on that there was no clear distinction between American moral concerns in Bosnia and America's national interest there, the United States, with the enormous credibility earned in the Gulf War, might have been able to put a stop to Milosevic's ambitions with a well-timed threat of punishing military action. But because the Bush team placed Bosnia outside the sphere of "vital" American interests, the resulting crisis eventually required the deployment of thousands of troops on the ground.

The same could be said of American interventions in Panama and the Gulf. A passive worldview encouraged American leaders to ignore troubling developments which eventually metastasized into full-blown threats to American security. Manuel Noriega and Saddam Hussein were given reason to believe that the United States did not consider its interests threatened by their behavior, only to discover that they had been misled. In each case, a broader and more forward-leaning conception of the national interest might have made the later, large and potentially costly interventions unnecessary.

The question, then, is not whether the United Sates should intervene everywhere or nowhere. The decision Americans need to make is whether the United States should generally lean forward, as it were, or sit back. A strategy aimed at preserving American hegemony should embrace the former stance, being more rather than less inclined to weigh in when crises erupt, and preferably before they erupt. This is the standard of a global superpower that intends to shape the international environment to its own advantage. By contrast, the vital interest standard is that of a "normal" power that awaits a dramatic challenge before it rouses itself into action.

Tools and Tactics

Is the task of maintaining American primacy and making a consistent effort to shape the international environment beyond the capacity of Americans? Not if American leaders have the understanding and the political will to do what is necessary. Moreover, what is required is not particularly forbidding. For much of the task ahead consists of building on already existing real strengths.

Despite its degradation in the last decade, for example, the United States still wields the strongest military force in the world. It has demonstrated its prowess in war on several occasions since the end of the Cold War—in Panama in 1989, in the Persian Gulf in 1991, and most recently in the air war over Kosovo. Those victories owed their success to a force built in the Reagan years. This is a legacy the United States has lived off for over a decade, an account it has drawn too far down. Today the United States spends too little on its military capabilities, in terms of both present readiness and investment in future weapons technologies. The gap between America's strategic ends and the means available to accomplish those ends is growing, a fact that becomes more evident each time the United States deploys forces abroad.

To repair these deficiencies and to create a force that can shape the international environment today, tomorrow, and twenty years from now will probably require spending some $60 billion to $100 billion per year above current defense budgets. This price tag may seem daunting, but in historical terms it represents only a modest commitment of America's wealth to defense. And in a time of large budget surpluses, spending a tiny fraction on defense ought to be politically feasible. For the United States to have the military capability to shape the international environment now and for the foreseeable future would require spending about 3.5 percent of GDP on defense, still low by the standards of the past fifty years, and far lower than most great powers have spent on their militaries throughout history. Is the aim of maintaining American primacy not worth a hike in defense spending from 3 to 3.5 percent of GDP?

The United States also inherited from the Cold War a legacy of strong alliances in Europe and Asia, and with Israel in the Middle East. Those alliances are a bulwark of American power and, more important still, they constitute the heart of the liberal democratic civilization that the United States seeks to preserve and extend. Critics of a strategy of American pre-eminence sometimes claim that it is a call for unilateralism. It is not. The notion that the United States could somehow "go it alone" and maintain its pre-eminence without its allies is strategically misguided. It is also morally bankrupt. What would "American leadership" mean in the absence of its democratic allies? What kind of nation would the United States be if it allowed Great Britain, Germany, Japan, Israel, Poland and other democratic nations to fend for themselves against the myriad challenges they will face?

In fact, a strategy aimed at preserving American pre-eminence would require an even greater U.S. commitment to its allies. The United States would not be merely an "offshore balancer," a savior of last resort, as many recommend. It would not be a "reluctant sheriff," rousing itself to action only when the threatened townsfolk turn to it in desperation. American pre-eminence cannot be maintained from a distance, by means of some post–Cold War version of the Nixon doctrine, whereby the United States hangs back and keeps its powder dry. The United States would instead conceive of itself as at once a European power, an Asian power, a Middle Eastern power and, of course, a Western Hemispheric power. It would act as if threats to the interests of our allies are threats to us, which indeed they are. It would act as if instability in important regions of the world, and the flouting of civilized rules of conduct in those regions, are threats that affect us with almost the same immediacy as if they were occurring on our doorstep. To act otherwise would make the United States appear a most unreliable partner in world affairs, which would erode both American pre-eminence and the international order, and gradually undermine the very alliances on which U.S. security depends. Eventually, the crises *would* appear at our doorstep.

This is what it means to be a global superpower with global responsibilities. The costs of assuming these responsibilities are more than made up by the benefits to American long-term interests. It is short-sighted to imagine that a policy of "keeping our powder dry" is either safer or less expensive than a policy that aims to preclude and deter the emergence of new threats, that has the United States arriving quickly at the scene of potential trouble before it has fully erupted, that addresses threats to the national interest before they have developed into full-blown crises. Senator Kay Bailey Hutchison expressed a common but mistaken view last year when she wrote that "a superpower is more credible and effective when it maintains a measured distance from all regional conflicts."[9] In fact, this is precisely the way for a superpower to cease being a superpower.

A strong America capable of projecting force quickly and with devastating effect to important regions of the world would make it less likely that challengers to regional stability would attempt to alter the status quo in their favor. It might even deter such challengers from undertaking expensive efforts to arm themselves in the first place. An America whose willingness to project force is in doubt, on the other hand, can only encourage such challenges. In Europe, in Asia and in the Middle East, the message we should be sending to potential foes is: "Don't even think about it." That kind of deterrence offers the best recipe for lasting peace; it is much cheaper than fighting the wars that would follow should we fail to build such a deterrent capacity.

This ability to project force overseas, however, will increasingly be jeopardized over the coming years as smaller powers acquire weapons of mass destruction and the missiles to launch them at American forces, at our allies and at the American homeland. The *sine qua non* for a strategy of American global pre-eminence, therefore, is a missile defense system that can protect all three of these targets. Only a well-protected America will be capable of deterring—and when necessary moving against—"rogue" regimes when they rise to challenge regional stability. Only a United States reasonably well shielded from the blackmail of nuclear, biological or chemical weapons will be able to shape the international environment to suit its interests and principles.

With the necessary military strength, strong and well-led alliances, and adequate missile defense, the United States can set about making trouble for hostile and potentially hostile nations, rather than waiting for them to make trouble for us. Just as the most successful strategy in the Cold War combined containment of the Soviet Union with an effort to undermine the moral legitimacy of the Moscow regime, so in the post–Cold War era a principal aim of American foreign policy should be to bring about a change of regime in hostile nations—in Baghdad and Belgrade, in Pyongyang and Beijing, and wherever tyrannical governments acquire the military power to threaten their neighbors, our allies and the United States itself.

Regime Change

The idea, common to many foreign policy minimalists and commerce-oriented liberals alike, that the United States can "do business" with any regime, no matter how odious and hostile to our basic principles, is both strategically unsound and unhistorical. The United States has in the past worked with right-wing dictatorships as a bulwark against communist aggression or against radical Muslim fundamentalism. It has at times formed tactical alliances with the most brutal regimes—with Stalin's Soviet Union against Nazi Germany, and with Mao's China against the Soviet Union. But these should properly be viewed as tactical deviations from a broad strategy of promoting liberal democratic governance throughout the world, the result of circumstances in which our security was immediately threatened or where there was no viable democratic alternative.

Relationships with tyrannical regimes, moreover, are inherently difficult to sustain. The problem is not merely that such relationships become distasteful to Americans. More important, in today's environment American interests and those of tyrannical regimes inevitably clash. For the force of American ideals and the influence of the international economic system, both of which are upheld by American power and influence, tend to corrode the pillars on which authoritarian and totalitarian regimes rest. To bolster their legitimacy, such regimes therefore resort frequently to provocation, either with arms buildups designed to intimidate both the United States and its allies, as in the case of China and North Korea, or by regional conquest, as in the case of Iraq and Serbia. With no means of acquiring legitimacy for their domestic policies, they, like the Soviet rulers described by George Kennan, seek the nationalist legitimacy that comes from "standing up" to an external enemy. Hence, the Chinese government knows there can be no real "strategic partnership" with the United States. The North Korean government knows there can be no true "normalization" with South Korea and the West. Saddam Hussein knows he cannot simply give up the struggle and try to live peaceably with his neighbors and with his own people. Slobodan Milosevic knows that he cannot truly integrate himself into the European community. The price of such accommodations would be loss of power.

When it comes to dealing with such regimes, then, the United States will not succeed in persuading them to play by the existing—which is to say American—rules of the game. We cannot expect to limit their acquisition or sale of dangerous weapons by relying on their voluntary adherence to international nonproliferation agreements. We cannot hope to stem their aggression by appealing to their consciences and asking them to accept the "norms" of the civilized world. For those "norms" serve as obstacles to their ambitions and even threats to their existence. They have, and will continue to have, a clear and immutable interest in flouting them.

Here we would do well to cast another glance backward, for this is hardly the first time we have confronted the question of how to manage relations with dictatorial adversaries. During the 1970s, the view of U.S.-Soviet relations promulgated by much of the American foreign policy establishment was that the key to peace and stability lay in an effort to reach mutual understanding with Moscow. The way to deal with the threat of apocalypse posed by the Soviet and American nuclear arsenals was through mutual arms control. The way to cope with Soviet adventurism abroad was to bind Moscow's leaders into a "web of interdependence" and thereby compel them to recognize the advantages of responsible international behavior. But these measures proved futile, as Soviet leaders would not and probably could not fulfill their side of the proposed bargain without undermining their rule at home. The source of confrontation between the two sides was not mutual mis-understanding, a lack of interdependence, or the military arsenals amassed by both sides. It was the nature of the Soviet regime. When that regime came to an end, so did the arms race, so did Russian aggression beyond its borders, and so did the Cold War. This lesson can be applied to the post–Cold War era. The most effective form of nonproliferation when it comes to regimes such as those in North Korea and Iraq is not a continuing effort to bribe them into adhering to international arms control agreements, but an effort to bring about the demise of the regimes themselves.

To be sure, the United States cannot simply wish hostile regimes out of existence. The United States would not dispatch troops to topple every regime we found odious. An American strategy that included regime change as a central component would neither promise nor expect rapid transformations in every rogue state or threatening power. But such a strategy would depart from recent American policy in fundamental ways. Instead of ending the Gulf War in 1991 after the liberation of Kuwait, an American strategy built around the principle of regime change would have sent U.S. forces on to Baghdad to remove Saddam Hussein from power, and it would have kept U.S. troops in Iraq long enough to ensure that a friendlier regime took root. Such a strategy would not only have employed ground forces in Kosovo last year but would have sent sufficient NATO forces to Serbia to topple the Milosevic regime. Those who believe such efforts would have been impossible to implement, or who caution against the difficulties of occupying and reforming such countries, or who insist that the removal of one man provides no solution to a problem, may wish to reflect on the American experiences in Germany and Japan—or even the Dominican Republic and Panama. In any case, if the United States is prepared to summon the forces necessary to carry out a Desert Storm, and to take the risks associated with expelling the world's fourth-largest army from Kuwait, it is absurd, and in the event self-defeating, not to complete the job.

Tactics for pursuing a strategy of regime change would vary according to circumstances. In some cases, the best policy might be support for rebel groups, along the lines of the Reagan Doctrine as it was applied in Nicaragua and elsewhere. In other cases, it might mean support for dissidents by either overt or covert means, and/or economic sanctions and diplomatic isolation. These tactics may or may not succeed immediately and would constantly have to be adjusted as circumstances in these regimes changed. But the purpose of American foreign policy ought to be clear. When it comes to dealing with tyrannical regimes, especially those with the power to do us or our allies harm, the United States should seek not coexistence but transformation.

To many the idea of America using its power to promote changes of regime in nations ruled by dictators rings of utopianism. But in fact, it is eminently realistic. There is something perverse in declaring the impossibility of promoting democratic change abroad in light of the record of the past three decades. After we have already seen dictatorships toppled by democratic forces in such unlikely places as the Philippines, Indonesia, Chile, Nicaragua, Paraguay, Taiwan and South Korea, how utopian is it to imagine a change of regime in a place like Iraq? How utopian is it to work for the fall of the Communist Party oligarchy in China after a far more powerful and, arguably, more stable such oligarchy fell in the Soviet Union? With democratic change sweeping the world at an unprecedented rate over these past thirty years, is it "realistic" to insist that no further victories can be won?

If anything, we ought to be fairly optimistic that such change can be hastened by the right blend of American policies. The Chinese regime, for example, shows many signs of instability. The inherent contradiction between its dictatorial rule and its desire for economic growth so preoccupies the Beijing government that it feels compelled to crack down even on nonpolitical, semi-religious sects like the Falun Gong. The United States and the West can either make it easier or more difficult for the People's Republic of China to resolve these contradictions. Our policy in this instance ought to be the latter, so that we can hasten the day when the conflicting currents of Chinese society prove beyond the capacity of its dictatorial government to manage.

But as disturbing as recent developments in China are, a strategy aimed at preserving American pre-eminence cannot and should not be based on the threat posed by any single nation. We need not go searching for an enemy to justify the requirement for a strong military and a strong moral component in our foreign policy. Even if the threat from China were to disappear tomorrow, that would not relieve us of the need for a strong and active role in the world. Nor would it absolve us of the responsibilities that fate has placed on our shoulders. Given the dangers we know currently exist, and given the certainty that unknown perils await us over the horizon, there can be no respite from this burden.

It is fair to ask how the rest of the world will respond to a prolonged period of American dominance. Those regimes that find an American-led world order inhospitable to their existence will seek to cut away at American power, will form tactical alliances with other dictatorships and "rogue" states for the common purpose of unsettling the international order, and will look for ways to divide the United States from its allies. China's proliferation of weapons and selling of weapons technologies to Iran, its provision of financial support to Milosevic, its attempt to find common ground with Russia against American "hegemonism"—all represent opportunistic attempts to undercut American dominance. Russia can similarly be expected to search for opportunities to weaken U.S. political, diplomatic and military preponderance in the world. Even an ally such as France may be prepared to lend itself to these efforts, viewing a unified Europe as a check on American power and using the UN Security Council as an arena for forging diplomatic roadblocks, along with China and Russia, against effective U.S.-led international action, whether in the Balkans or in the Persian Gulf.

All this is to be expected as part of the price for American global pre-eminence. It does not, however, add up to a convincing argument against preserving that pre-eminence. The main issue is not American "arrogance." It is the inescapable reality of American power in all its many forms. Those who suggest that these international resentments could somehow be eliminated by a more restrained American foreign policy are deluding themselves. Even a United States that never again intervened in a place like Kosovo or expressed disapproval of China's human rights practices would still find itself the target of jealousy, resentment and in some cases even fear. A more polite but still pre-eminently powerful United States would continue to stand in the way of Chinese ambitions in East Asia, would still exist as a daily reminder of Russia's vastly diminished standing in the world, and would still grate on French insecurities. Unless the United States is prepared to shed its real power and influence, allowing other nations genuinely to achieve a position of relative parity on the world stage, would-be challengers of the international order—as well as those merely resentful at the disparity of power—will still have much to resent.

But neither should Americans fear that any effective grouping of nations is likely to emerge to challenge American power. Much of the current international attack on American "hegemonism" is posturing. Allies such as the French may cavil about the American "hyper-power," but they recognize their dependence on the United States as the guarantor of an international order that greatly benefits France. (Indeed, it is precisely this recognition that breeds French resentment.) As for Russia and China, the prospect of effective joint action between those two nations against the United States is slight. Their long history of mutual mistrust is compounded by the fact that they do not share common strategic goals—even with regard to the United States. While Chinese leaders consider the United States an enemy, a sporadically democratizing Russia has a more ambivalent view. Post-Soviet Russia seeks inclusion in an American-led West, both for economic and ideological reasons.

As a practical matter, as William C. Wohlforth has argued, it will be very difficult for other nations to gang up on the United States precisely because it is so powerful.[10] But the unwillingness of other powers to gang up on the United States also has something to do with the fact that it does not pursue a narrow, selfish definition of its national interest, but generally finds its interests in a benevolent international order.[11] In other words, it is precisely because American foreign policy is infused with an unusually high degree of morality that other nations find they have less to fear from its otherwise daunting power.

Our Inheritance

At the beginning of this century, Theodore Roosevelt worried that Americans had become so "isolated from the struggles of the rest of the world, and so immersed in our material prosperity," that they were becoming "effete."[12] Roosevelt implored Americans to look beyond the immediate needs of their daily lives and embrace as a nation a higher purpose in the world. He aspired to greatness for America, and he believed that a nation could only be great if it accepted its responsibilities to advance civilization and improve the world's condition. "A nation's first duty is within its borders," Roosevelt declared, "but it is not thereby absolved from facing its duties in the world as a whole; and if it refuses to do so, it merely forfeits its right to struggle for a place among the people that shape the destiny of mankind."

In appealing to Americans to support a robust brand of internationalism, Roosevelt possessed the insight to appeal to their sense of nationalism. It was a nationalism, however, of a uniquely American variety: not an insular, blood-and-soil nationalism, but one that derived its meaning and coherence from being rooted in universal principles first enunciated in the Declaration of Independence. Roosevelt was no utopian; he had contempt for those who believed the international environment could be so transformed as to rid the world of war, put an end to international conflict, and, indeed, put an end to the notion of nationhood itself. Roosevelt was an idealist of a different sort. He did not attempt to wish away the realities of power, but insisted that the defenders of civilization must exercise their power against civilization's opponents. "Warlike intervention by the civilized powers," he insisted, "would contribute directly to the peace of the world."[13]

Americans should once again embrace a broad understanding of the "national interest," one in keeping with Roosevelt's vision. In recent years, many American foreign policy thinkers, and some politicians, have come to define the "national interest" as consisting of a grid of ground, sea lanes, industrial centers, strategic chokepoints and the like. This was a definition of interests foisted upon our foreign policy establishment by "realists" in the middle of the century. It is not a definition that would have been welcomed by previous generations of Americans. If someone had asked Alexander Hamilton what the "national interest" was, he would have cited prosperity and security, but he would also have invoked the need to lift his young country into a place of honor among the world's great powers. Past American presidents and statesmen would never have imagined that the national interest, a term that can encompass a people's noblest aspirations, would come to possess such a narrow and limited meaning as many American thinkers give it today.

Honor and greatness in the service of liberal principles used to be understood as worthy goals of American foreign policy. In insisting that the "national interest" extended beyond material security and prosperity, and in summoning Americans to seek honor as a nation, Theodore Roosevelt echoed the views of the American Founders. And almost fifty years after Roosevelt, Reinhold Niebuhr insisted that America's "sense of responsibility to a world community beyond our own borders is a virtue," and this virtue was in no way diminished by the fact that this sense of responsibility also "derived from the prudent understanding of our own interests."[14] Common wisdom holds that Americans do not care about their nation's role in the world. But it has been a long time since any of their leaders asked them to care, or made an appeal to the elevated patriotism that joins interest and justice, which has characterized the American republic from its beginning.

The American-led world that emerged after the Cold War is a more just world than any imaginable alternative. A multipolar world, in which power is shared more equally among great powers—including China and Russia—would be far more dangerous, and it would also be far less congenial to democracy and to individual liberties. Americans should understand that their support for American pre-eminence is as much a strike for international justice as any people is capable of making. It is also a strike for American interests, and for what might be called the American spirit. George Kennan wrote more than fifty years ago that the American people should feel a

> certain gratitude to a Providence, which by providing [them] with this implacable challenge, has made their entire security as a nation dependent on pulling themselves together and accepting the responsibilities of moral and political leadership that history plainly intended them to bear.[15]

The "implacable challenge" facing Americans has, of course, changed. Our fundamental responsibilities have not.

The Great Divide:
American Interventionism
and its Opponents

A merica in the last decade has reached the zenith of its military power in relation to the rest of the world. Yet interest in foreign affairs, whether among the public or its politicians, has seldom been lower. Bill Clinton won the presidency in 1992 by deliberately signaling his lack of concern for foreign affairs; that was clearly the gist of his campaign promise to focus on the economy "like a laser beam." Matters were not much different in 1996, when foreign policy played only a minor role in the presidential campaign. Although events have since proven that an American president cannot really escape the demands of conducting foreign policy, it remains the case today that most presidential candidates choose to address this realm only when they appear at a school of international affairs or when bidden to do so by some earnest journalist. The idea of proposing a project for America on the stage of world politics that would serve as the centerpiece of a national agenda seems the furthest thing from the concerns of either of our political parties.

The mismatch between America's position of power in the world and Americans' interest in world affairs finds its parallel in the name that students of international relations employ to designate the present period: the post–Cold War era. A "post" label in whatever field is a certain indication of an awareness that something has been left behind, while nothing genuinely new has been created to take its place. Just as we live in a "postmodern" era in art and philosophy because no new theme has replaced "modernist" ideas, so we live in a post–Cold War world because no new foreign

policy has been developed for our age. The inability or unwillingness to articulate such a project is clearly a bipartisan failure. Neither Democrats nor Republicans—or, if one prefers, liberals or
conservatives—have been able to agree among themselves on a
coherent approach. Each party is often split on foreign policy questions, and neither ideological label any longer identifies a clear
position.

The liberal approach to foreign affairs over the past two decades
has been Janus-faced. A rejection of the use of American force was
in the ascendancy throughout the eighties, culminating in the overwhelming liberal opposition to the use of American force in the
Gulf War in 1991. Yet the crusade for human rights was always just
beneath the surface, and liberals criticized American foreign policy—from China to Bosnia–for not doing enough to ensure a respect
for universal moral principles. Such universal norms should be
enforced, liberals preached, although who should do the enforcing and by what means were matters covered by such vague rhetor-
ical platitudes as "let sanctions work" or "the United Nations must
take vigorous multilateral action." A doctrine of Immaculate
Enforcement was sufficient for an opposition, but confronting the
reality of having to conduct the nation's foreign policy has forced
liberals to make choices.

The new liberalism of the nineties has begun to show its internationalist face. While it has become clear that in practice this
entails a vigorous use of American national power and military
might, the older liberal reservations remain strikingly evident in
the half measures, the fecklessness, and the unwillingness to assert
decisive American leadership that have characterized foreign policy in this decade. After eight years of liberal direction of America's foreign policy, who can feel confident that this form of timid
internationalism could withstand a major challenge, or indeed that
liberals have taken the minimal steps toward preparedness to sustain it in the future? Having miraculously pursued their internationalist policy thus far without loss of American life—except in
Somalia, where the response was immediately to cut and run—
can liberals be trusted, especially if they should be in opposition,
not to begin tacking back toward their anti-militarist and anti-
nationalist position?

Turning to conservatives, what can be said of their approach to
foreign affairs? Conservatives today are split between two camps

of conviction on America's role in the world. On one side are the conservative isolationists. They promise to keep America armed and ready as the "Arsenal of Democracy," but would restrict the use of military force to instances of direct threat to our physical or economic security. Isolationists oppose becoming too deeply involved in the world and its problems, fearing that constant meddling will bring a loss of lives and treasure, and will damage the delicate balance among the political institutions of what they fondly refer to as our "old republic." Many isolationists are also wary of unrestricted international trade because of its adverse effect on wages and on the stability of working communities.

On the other side are the conservative internationalists. They stand ready to employ American influence to help shape a stable world order and promote fundamental American principles. Internationalists too are in favor of maintaining a strong military—stronger perhaps than the isolationists—but not just for deterrence or for being placed in a storehouse. Internationalists regard military force as an instrument of foreign policy to be called upon when necessary to achieve our goals. A bit more abstractly, but no less importantly, internationalists find worth and dignity in the nation committing itself to this kind of enterprise; it allows America to pursue a noble purpose on the stage of world history, one that our Founders intended that it should serve.

Between conservative isolationists and internationalists floats a third group, the "realists," who could never be mistaken for constituting a camp of conviction. Depending on the issue at hand, realists side sometimes with the isolationists and sometimes with the internationalists. Above all they pride themselves on avoiding the excesses of what they call "ideology." Realists are therefore most at ease while questioning and dissecting what others do. They base their thinking on the touchstone of the "national interest," a concept which they purport to be uniquely able to understand.

The division of isolationists from internationalists has been one of the most alarming developments within the Republican Party in the last decade. Small signs of the division surfaced during the Gulf War, when a few isolationists gathered together in a Saddam corner to decry the whole venture. The conflict became more evident in the responses to America's use of force in Somalia, Haiti, and Bosnia, and, in the economic realm, to the treaties proposing American participation in the North American Free Trade

Agreement (NAFTA) and the expansion of the General Agreement on Tariffs and Trade (GATT). Matters came to a head, however, during the war in Kosovo, when the extent of the penetration of isolationist thinking in the party became clear. Although positions on the war often varied according to individual judgments of a complicated situation—and what is more complicated than a Balkan conflict?—the most fundamental division reflected the opposing views of isolationists and internationalists. Within every segment of the party—its presidential candidates, its congressional delegation, and its intelligentsia—were found both the strongest critics of the war and its staunchest defenders, including the leading voices urging a much firmer military effort. The GOP's big tent in foreign policy had to be pitched wide enough to shelter everyone from Patrick Buchanan to John McCain.

The split between conservative internationalism and conservative isolationism has deep historical roots. It can be traced back to the aftermath of World War I, when many conservatives, reacting against Wilson's crusade for the League of Nations and fearing the subordination of America's sovereignty to international bodies, adopted a more isolationist stance. This position gained a wider following as disillusionment over the accomplishments of the war set in. Contrary to expectations victory had raised, it was discovered that the world had not fundamentally changed. The new isolationists appropriated the label of "Americanism," which until just a few years before had designated the Republican Party's policy of vigorous internationalism. The isolationists implicitly disowned the positions championed by William McKinley and Theodore Roosevelt, who had led the nation into the Spanish-American War and insisted on staying the course in the Philippines

Democrats were then the more isolationist party, with a slightly pacifist orientation. Woodrow Wilson ran his 1916 presidential campaign still appealing indirectly to some of these sentiments, famously accusing the Republicans in one of his campaign speeches of "outspokenly declaring that they want war." Wilson's particular form of internationalism, as some have pointed out, was in a sense a response to his party's isolationist tendencies. Wilson proclaimed America's universal principles, but he did so in a way that promised to end international politics as we knew it. The hope of replacing the power politics of national interest with a new system of international relations, more than anything else, merits the label of "idealism." This approach is reminiscent of the policy of Thomas Jefferson, who, by means of an embargo (rather than war), believed he could overcome the old system and permanently transform the character of international affairs.

It is thus completely false to claim, as so many do, that American internationalism began with Woodrow Wilson and that its only form has been "idealistic." American internationalism existed long before Woodrow Wilson. Indeed, its spirit can arguably be traced right back to the Founders and their frequent assertion that the American Revolution and founding were of interest not just to the United States but to "the whole human race," although they understood full well the nation's limitations of strength at the time. What distinguishes Wilsonian or liberal internationalism from some of the more conservative variants is not its commitment to promoting universal principles—almost all American internationalists have shared this objective—but its insistence on changing the nature of international affairs and somehow overcoming a reliance on the unit of the nation-state. Conservatives never imagined dispensing with the primacy of the nation in the conduct of foreign affairs. Theirs has always been an internationalism with a realist face, based on national power and national resolve. It has been the kind of internationalism that might look forward, in Alexander Hamilton's words, to a time when America would be "able to dictate the terms of the connection between the old and the new world."

The rift between conservative isolationists and internationalists re-emerged in the 1930s in the dispute over America's potential involvement in World War II. On one side was the America First Movement, the most important organization in behalf of what was known as the "non-interventionist" cause. The movement included for a time a fair number of Democrats and pacifists, but its leading figures were Republican conservatives. As in the 1920s, the conservative variant of isolationism was committed to military preparedness and to the national idea—views at odds with the more humanitarian sentiments of liberal isolationists, who eventually made their way to other organizations. On the other side were the so-called "interventionists," who in one way or another saw that war was coming and that America would eventually have to take part in it. Conservative internationalists did not just march to the beat of Franklin Roosevelt's drum, as Wendell Wilkie eventually would, but set forth their own more nationalist view of the future. It was the conservative interventionist Henry Luce who gave internationalism its most potent slogan, calling on his fellow countrymen to make the twentieth century not just (as is widely thought) "the American century" but "the first American century." Luce asked America to lead a free alliance of nations to help spread the universal principles of free government and guarantee a new order. In his vision, the promotion of an improved world would depend on the continuing will of the nation, not on any supranational arrangement.

The attack on Pearl Harbor in 1941 put an end to this division, and all parts of the party fell into line behind the war effort. There was never a "peace wing" within the Republican Party during World War II. But the two groups shortly began to disagree again over postwar strategy on such issues as America's participation in NATO, the extent of the Marshall plan, and the United Nations. The "old nationalists," as they were sometimes called, were led by Mr. Republican, Senator Robert Taft of Ohio, who is celebrated by conservatives of all stripes for offering some of the most forceful critiques of liberal internationalism. As for his own views, Taft was somewhat isolationist, and in particular he questioned getting involved in any kind of "policing of the entire world by the Anglo-Saxon race." While confident of America's own principles, he was doubtful that they could be transferred to the various "Hottentots" inhabiting the world. Taft frequently attacked Henry Luce—not to mention Franklin Roosevelt—for his imperialism, militarism and do-gooderism. He believed that internationalism, whether of a conservative or liberal kind, would lead to overextension and threaten American democracy and freedom.

Beginning in the mid-1950s most of the old isolationist camp joined the internationalists in a common battle against communism. For the duration of the Cold War, their old dispute was placed in deep freeze. Together, these two camps within the Republican Party tended to join in resisting the more accommodating or détentiste policies favored by many realists. During the Vietnam War, the size of the internationalist contingent among Republicans was enlarged when a group of neoconservative refugees left the Democratic Party in response to its growing isolationist and pacifist positions. Stronger than ever before, the full corps of conservatives bonded together in support of Ronald Reagan in 1980, going so far as to risk the opprobrium of polite society by trying to make anti-communism respectable. In the end, the conservatives even managed to drag the party's realists along, slightly embarrassed and apologizing all the while.

Common action for more than thirty years led many to think that these two groups had become indistinguishable. But after the collapse of the Soviet Union the old division began to reappear, and in historical perspective it is now clear that the pact between them was only a temporary truce. In looking back on Ronald Reagan's foreign policy and their own support of internationalism at the time, isolationists today argue that Reagan's internationalist themes were tactical, representing not his deepest views but a way to defeat Soviet communism. Once this strategy proved successful, it could be abandoned. With communism now defunct, except in China and Cuba, isolationists argue that America can "come home" and return to normalcy. Isolationists today view conservative internationalists as not just dangerous idealists in their own right, but dupes of a new form of liberal internationalism. Just as Woodrow Wilson managed to trick conservatives into going along with him in an ill-fated universalist crusade, so Bill Clinton has made fools of conservative internationalists today by enlisting their help to carry his water.

By contrast, conservative internationalists view the victory in the Cold War as one moment, albeit surely a most significant one, in the pursuit of America's broader aims. But in no sense does the end of the Cold War mark the end of history. Its conclusion on terms so favorable to America sets the stage for the next phase in further extending the benefits of free government to "the whole human race." In looking back to Reagan's foreign policy, internationalists regard his position not just as an expedient to fortify the West in its resolve against communism—although that was certainly its immediate objective—but as a powerful restatement of the tenets of conservative internationalism. And contrary to the view of many today, that policy cannot rightly be described as simply "Wilsonian." Indeed, it marks a terrible poverty of thinking to claim that any foreign policy that goes beyond asserting concrete economic or immediate strategic interests—any policy that mentions "values"—becomes ipso facto "idealistic" or "Wilsonian." This view reduces all invocations of values to the same category; it conflates the promotion of principles backed by military power and

national resolve, with the vaguest expressions of "values" uncon-
nected to any serious plan for securing them. Nursed by an odd
coalition of realists and isolationists, this notion is designed to
obscure the distinctive ground on which conservative internationalism stands.

ooooo

The division of isolationists from internationalists is clearly uncomfortable for Republicans, as their reaction to the war in Kosovo
showed. Differences among them ran so deep that many Republicans have since wished to forget that the war ever occurred. Yet
a policy of amnesia cannot succeed. Patrick Buchanan's defection
from the party on the issue of foreign policy shows that the issue
cannot be avoided—nor does it settle matters within the party. A
public airing of some of the issues in dispute will obviously not
resolve everything, but it could change the opinion that dominates
the broad center of the party, and that will inform the thinking of
the next administration, should it be Republican, or otherwise, of
its opposition. The presidency is pre-eminently an office that deals
with foreign affairs, and one way or another a president must
decide on what direction he (or she) wishes to take the party and
the nation.

There is reason to believe that many Republicans are not nearly
as far apart as they may think. Whether tending toward an isolationist or an internationalist position, they share many of the same
sentiments about foreign affairs, but political circumstances during the Kosovo war obscured this agreement, as has happened at
other points during the twentieth century. As fate has had it, liberal internationalist presidents have been in office at the beginning of most of this century's major wars. This is not to assert
causality, along the lines of Robert Dole's unfortunate remark about
"Democrat wars" during the 1976 vice-presidential debate, but simply to state a fact. With the Republican Party in the opposition, its
isolationists were generally in the better position to score rhetor-
ical points. As pure opponents, they could speak in the clear language of a ringing NO and boil matters down to a simple proposition: criticize liberal internationalism as a way of rejecting
internationalism outright. They could use the common property
of doubts about liberal internationalism and antipathy to the presiding president to push the party further in an isolationist direction

than it might naturally go if left to its own inclinations. By contrast, conservative internationalists have been forced to speak in more ambiguous terms and use the awkward language of "Yes, but." They have supported the immediate policy of the opposition's president, but for somewhat different reasons. They have been in the difficult position—like John McCain during the war in Kosovo—of trying to argue for the third option of another kind of internationalism, which they are at the time in no position to put into effect.

The depth of the Republican rift on foreign affairs is thus in part a function of their being in the opposition. When Republican presidents of an internationalist disposition have been in office, conservative isolationism has not come close to winning the hearts of most in the party. Dwight Eisenhower thwarted the isolationists during his first administration, and isolationism made little headway against George Bush during the Gulf War in 1991. Evidence that the problem Republicans confront here is partly due to circumstance can be seen by turning the matter around and observing the opposite case, when Democrats have been in the opposition and have had to face conservative internationalist presidents. In these instances, liberal isolationists in the Democratic Party—the pacifist elements—have enjoyed far more success than their conservative counterparts and have generally managed to become the party's dominant voice. They were able to put the Democratic Party in Congress on record against the Vietnam War (a war that a Democratic administration had begun) during the Nixon-Ford years, against President Reagan's support for the Contras, and against the Gulf War, when huge majorities of Democrats in the House and in the Senate voted to deny President Bush authorization to launch a ground attack.

Republicans therefore have good reason to look past current poll numbers and consider how party members will respond once they control the presidency rather than being the opposition. Candidates for president can begin by reminding party members of the beliefs that Republicans share in foreign affairs, which include many points of disagreement with liberal internationalism. These were all in evidence during the Kosovo war. To begin with, there was Tony Blair's claim, picked up by liberal internationalists on both sides of the Atlantic, that Kosovo was the first "progressive war." This fanciful idea served to give a clean conscience to many of the progressives who had deplored every previous use of military force since the 1960s and who had opposed procurement of the sophisticated military weaponry that allowed so painless a victory against Serbia. For liberal internationalists, past wars either were wrong in principle (instances of so-called American imperialism like Vietnam) or were tainted by economic interests (protecting access to oil during the Gulf War). "Progressive" rhetoric was heard from almost all of the "Third Way" leaders. Slobodan Milosevic, the lifelong communist, suddenly became a "right-wing" fascist—as if ethnic cleansing had not been a policy of communism, practiced on a massive scale by the Soviets. And has anyone heard of Tibet? The progressives seemed to wish to forget what no conservative can ever forget: that the barbarisms of the twentieth century derived no less from a fanatical universalism (the extreme of the left) as from a warped particularism (the extreme of the right).

Conservatives also share a deep uneasiness at the liberal internationalists' constant questioning of the idea of the nation. Since American conservatives identify proudly with the American nation, they can see no reason—all things being equal—not to respect national pride elsewhere. They have no trouble in condemning ultranationalism, as it manifested in Serbia for example, but they are aware that nationalism in Lithuania, Poland, and Slovenia provided a source of particular attachment that proved essential in resisting communist empires. In any case, conservatives well know that nationalism, even in its ethnic varieties, is a fact of life that cannot be wished away; and they wonder how the right of national self-determination that was once the core of liberal internationalism for Woodrow Wilson can be so easily dismissed in favor of a universal multi-ethnic future in the liberal internationalism of Bill Clinton.

The issue here is not the worth of such ideals so much as whether they can serve as the foundation for a practical foreign policy. And in Clinton's case, conservatives cannot help but suspect that his universalistic multiculturalism is a way also to promote his domestic agenda. At a minimum, he often seems to see the foreign and domestic through the same prism, with the Kosovo war sometimes justified in language paralleling his calls for hate-crime legislation. For the traditional American principle of rights based on nature, the president has substituted a respect for groups based on a tolerance of diversity, replete with fashionable postmodern references to the "other": "If we want to go—from Northern Ireland to the Middle East, to Kosovo and Bosnia, to Central Africa—and ask people to lay down their hatreds; to no longer fear the other; to see diversity as a source of interest and joy that makes life more exciting, but in no way undermines our common humanity ... we must do good at home and always become better." Or take President Clinton's statement at his victory press conference following the war that "the young people of America are likely to live in a world where the biggest threats are not from other countries but from horrible racial, ethnic and religious fighting." Somehow or other, the nation as the central unit of international affairs has been removed from the scene and replaced by the management of race and ethnic group conflict.

Conservatives also mistrust a mood in liberal internationalism that has been growing for some time now, which aims at the internationalization and legalization of the conduct of foreign affairs. It favors the subordination of the will of nations to international enforcement regimes and to norms interpreted by international bodies and judges. On the face of the matter, conservatives' concern on this point seems wholly misplaced in relation to the Kosovo war. As is well known, the war could not be fought under the auspices of the United Nations because no consensus existed there. Another forum had to be found, and the war was prosecuted by the alliance of the Western democracies. The lesson to be drawn from this event—or so one would think—is almost the antithesis of the hopes of liberal internationalism: the war proved the need for a benevolent power, supported by allied nations, acting in concert to protect right.

Yet to hear the way many liberals defend the war, there has been much embarrassment at using a particular national force to protect a universal idea of rights; this method is seen as, at best, an embarrassing step along the way to a more advanced universal mechanism of enforcement. Conservatives have been dismayed at the double talk going on here. The power of the United States is used to enforce order at the same time that liberal internationalists speak as if the world were somehow moving beyond the idea of the nation-state. The end has been mysteriously detached from the means, a little difficulty placed in the often-invoked progressive category of "in the process of being overcome." Even when the United Nations serves as the instrument of enforcement, as in the Gulf War, no one should be under any illusion that it can proceed in any significant case without American support. What looks like—and in a strict sense is—multilateral action nonetheless ultimately requires the approval and backing of one particular nation. For other nations, multilateralism means choosing to engage in an action along with the United States; for the United States, it means assuming the primary responsibility in any major engagement. There are no doubt very good practical reasons for downplaying this fact, but it is dangerous to allow the gentle fictions of modern diplomacy to penetrate too deeply into our own way of thinking. The whole system depends on the national resolve of the United Sates, and this resolve cannot be maintained over the long run without a strong sense of national purpose.

Some conservatives have also wondered at the liberal internationalists' easy dismissal of the principle of sovereignty. Under the new banner of humanitarian intervention, liberal internationalists made the Kosovo conflict a war to end sovereignty. Of course sovereignty has been compromised and violated from the very moment it was enshrined as a foundational principle; it nonetheless tended to be honored in the breach by elaborate legal explanations pretending that it was being respected. With the Kosovo war, however, many on the left openly proclaimed that the principle of sovereignty must yield to a higher god. Some conservatives have worried about such arguments, not so much because conservatives have traditionally been more solicitous of the general principle of sovereignty than liberals, but because they suspect that the current campaign for limiting sovereignty is meant eventually to be applied to the United States. And it could very well be, if we submit to some of the new "regimes" of liberal internationalism that aim to weave a web of institutions and ideas to control American power.

What conservatives sense here, without articulating it as well as they might, is pressure from a new argument for liberal internationalism, or at any rate an argument coming from a new source. Formerly, the primary energy for promoting liberal internationalism derived from some of our own thinkers and statesmen. Americans took the lead in preaching the gospel of idealism, which tended to be resisted by Europeans, who were inveterately tied to the idea of the nation. American conservatives could always count on Europeans, especially European conservatives, to provide intellectual support in resisting schemes of abstract internationalism. The situation today, however, is characterized by the fact that Europeans—and this includes many European conservatives—often pay court to the ideas of liberal internationalism, and for quite understandable reasons. While our allies recognize that they need American military power, they also see that it is so disproportionate to their own (or any other nation's) that it is beyond being balanced. Nothing is gained for these nations by defending the concept of the nation. For many in Europe the rhetoric about the end of sovereignty, while it is clearly directed in the first instance at outlaw or offending nations, also has a secondary target in the United States. It is designed to contain the United States, to control Gulliver. Europeans are trying to defend their sovereignty by doctrines that deny sovereignty.

Europeans have another reason today to distance themselves from the idea of the nation: they are, in fact, rapidly denationalizing. The major European states—Russia, of course, excepted—are in the midst of forming the European Union, a necessary corollary of which is an alteration of the status of the nation-state as it has been known for centuries. Europe's leading statesmen accordingly often talk of the need to overcome "nationalism" and "the idol of state sovereignty," as if these were crude relics of the past. Europeans, we must remember, invented the modern nation-state system and supplied the concepts and vocabulary for modern international relations; they can therefore be excused if they think that by altering their own situation, they are changing the meaning of these concepts. But indulgence for this mistake should not lead us to take their local views as normative for the United States.

ooooo

The rank and file in the Republican Party, which consists mostly of people of conservative temperament, are in agreement in their concern for the nation and are wary of a watery internationalism that seeks to move beyond it. This concern has, from the beginning, been the key element in conservatives' opposition to liberal internationalism. Yet how to maintain the nation while constructing an effective foreign policy has led conservatives in two different directions.

For the isolationists, the best way to safeguard the nation is to reject internationalism, root and branch. If liberal international-ism involves—as it has—the proclamation of universal principles, then it must be a good thing to reject universal principles. The iso-lationist interpretation of the American experience is driven by the imperative to fit this conclusion. The United States, it is said, is as particular as any other nation; and its founding principles, although supposedly based on universalist ideas, are no more than its own particular tradition. Or in another version, America's claim to be founded on universal principles is simply ignored, and the United States is said to be held together, like any other country, by its "cul-ture." This last notion can easily degenerate—as it sometimes has—into a view of the American nation as a tribe or race, which is rem-iniscent of a sort of nationalism found in so many other countries.

To buttress their position further, isolationists now often adopt realist notions of the national interest, where the premises of what constitutes the national interest appear to be drawn from the clas-sic era of the European state system. Isolationists thus speak of such principles as "off-shore balancing," as if the world of 2000 were the same as that of 1900. Isolationists seem to believe that if the world could return to a system of nations acting as particular entities, then the dangers of internationalism could be avoided. Not that the world would be characterized by peace and harmony—conservative isolationists have never been partial to sentimental ideas of lions lying down with lambs; but it could become again a place of largely traditional conflicts, in which our superior power would enable us to protect our own interest. For isolationists, the order of the international system is no single nation's particular responsibility, and is in any case beyond the influence or control of any individual nation. Behind this policy of laissez faire, how-ever, seems to lie the shadow of a belief that a tolerable interna-tional order is likely to form naturally on its own. Isolationists are more favorable to the idea of the invisible hand than they care to admit.

Conservative internationalists, by contrast, see no difficulty in squaring the assertion of universal principles with a belief in the nation and the national purpose. What is more an expression of the particular mission of *this* nation, they ask, than to give voice to the universal principles on which it was founded? To renounce this element of the American founding in the name of avoiding internationalism would mean, ironically, to reject the foundation of our own nationalism. It would be to relinquish our own specificity. The fact that America rests on a different foundation from that of most other nations—that the American people become one by adhering to certain principles as well as sharing certain cultural features—is surely no reason to abandon what is our own. A good nationalist should rather proudly assert it.

It is on this point—on the relationship of a particular nation (America) to the upholding of universal principles—that the conservative internationalist is most often challenged. How is it possible, many ask, to cherish the nation and yet also take a stand by principles that are said to extend beyond the nation, being universally valid? Surely, the latter would tend to dissolve the former. Yet for the conservative internationalists, this conflict is more in the minds of the objectors than in the facts. As a practical matter, the world has no way of protecting universal principles except through the nation. And theoretically, there is no reason to think that universal ideas are better realized through international agencies of interpretation or enforcement than through being lived and articulated by distinct communities. The experience of trying to "internationalize" such principles in some of the international charters of human rights adopted over the years demonstrates how easily they can become distorted and watered down. It is not that our own understanding is always right or best, but that the principles are best maintained when they derive from the experience and traditions of different nations and when they are embraced by the free consent of nations. We know from experience that when acting for universal principles as we understand them, we can often count on the support of many allies who have come to share the same fundamental views, not because they are American ideas but because they have a rational claim to universal validity.

Recognizing the importance of universal principles for our own national identity, however, is obviously not sufficient to establish that we should act to promote them by a strong internationalist foreign policy. Whether to adopt such a policy must take account of basic circumstances, such as our own power and the situation in the world. Conservative internationalism is not based on a so-called ethics of intention according to which America must act to fulfill certain universal ideals regardless of the consequences to itself or others. It considers results, as any sensible approach must, and therefore allows for different forms according to the basic context. When commentators try to make a case against conservative internationalism by citing George Washington's Farewell Address ("It is our true policy to steer clear of permanent alliances with any portion of the foreign world"), they are engaging in the height of folly. It is not just that Washington himself signaled that he was speaking in the context of America's prevailing situation of power ("the period is not far off when . . . we may choose peace or war, as our interest, guided by justice, shall counsel"), it is also that no sensible person would expect the particular policy prescriptions of a statesman from the eighteenth century to dictate what is best policy for the twenty-first.

Conservative internationalists do not therefore oppose acting in the national interest but, denying that realists have an exclusive lien on the concept, they offer their own view of it. Their understanding of national interest begins with the obvious point that our power relationship to the rest of the world has changed dramatically in the last decade. As the only nation in the world able to exert significant power beyond its own immediate geographical location, America now has the opportunity to enforce an order in all theaters where the local powers are not very great. If this opportunity exists, so too, arguably, does an interest in doing so, for having a decent order in the world is clearly to our benefit. Unlike isolationists, with their implicit faith in spontaneous order, conservative internationalists tend to think that world order is highly fragile and must be cultivated; it is maintained either by a situation of balance or by the superior might of an active power. If so many of our statesmen in the nineteenth century publicly denied this view, especially with regard to any potential benefits we accrued from the order established by the British Empire, this was for reasons of our own particular interest at a time when we were a secondary power.

The conservative internationalist views the role of the nation— at least *this* nation—as being at the core of international relations today more than ever before. The world may be divided, not geographically but conceptually, into two "zones": one in which our power is clearly superior to that of any local force, and one in which, in a local theater, we would be challenged to our limits. In the first zone, America can assume the role of leader in guaranteeing a general order, as we did in Kuwait and Kosovo. Any decision to use force within a local theater cannot be made except by us, and that action will always be a national decision. This does not mean that we will generally act alone. Active support and participation by others provide added legitimacy to any venture, making the exercise of our power more acceptable to the world. But which forum we use for action—the United Nations, NATO, or some ad hoc alliance—is a matter of prudence, not principle.

When scholars today speak of America's exercise of power in this zone, they often refer to an "imperium" or a "hegemon." Although these terms are considered to be purely descriptive and neutral, in fact they carry strong connotations of dominion and empire. They are accordingly best avoided today, not just because they may give offense, but because they do not describe the kind of enterprise in which the nation is engaged, which is not directly to rule others, but to maintain a civilized world order and allow the benefits of free government to become known. A term like leadership is better suited to the circumstances.

Another linguistic problem is that some speak of "globalization," as if a vast and general process were afoot that obviated the need for the nation. There is a clear sense, of course, in which nations today—especially those in the zone of order—are increasingly connected in the realms of economics, mass communications, and culture. But interconnectedness in these areas does not necessarily translate perfectly to the realm of security or the capacity to exercise military power jointly. One suspects that the term "globalization" has been adopted by many to soften or obscure the reality of power relationships. Military power has not become globalized, but rather more concentrated in one nation.

What has changed, accordingly, is not the importance of the nation for *us*, but its importance for others. Other nations do not bear the primary responsibility for maintaining a world order; when they engage in action under our umbrella they are less likely to use a national rhetoric and more apt to speak in terms of enforcing an international norm. At the same time, therefore, that we must think more nationally than ever before, we must accept that others will be thinking more internationally. Our understanding of the nation must be different from others' because our power and responsibilities are different. We must be prepared to make appropriate demands and claim appropriate prerogatives for the nation—this nation, at any rate—even when others oppose or condemn them. This is what it means to be alone on top. The challenge we face is to learn how to command, and no challenge is harder for a democratic people.

In the other zone of the world, where the power of others would be a match for our own in any local confrontation, the dangers of the loose talk about globalization are even more readily apparent. The "classic" form of international affairs has not changed very much in this zone. It is still a world of states—now typically continental superstates like China, India and America—where terms like the nation or sovereignty do not have to be parsed; they are fully understood, as is the possibility of conflict. The fact that this does not describe the situation among the states of Europe does not mean that "international relations" does not exist, but only that these nations are no longer players in the way they once were. In our efforts to accommodate the sensibilities of nations within the first zone—where there is all the talk about the obsolescence of the nation and of humanitarian interventions—it is important that we not allow ourselves to forget the potentially harsh character of traditional relations among states; for we continue to live in a state system.

The United States, then, is in the unique position of being the only nation actively engaged in both zones. It is the leader within the first zone and the most powerful actor in the second. The other nations that are part of the first zone of order are scarcely involved any longer in classic state-to-state security relations, while the other superstates in the zone of classic security relations are not involved in guaranteeing any kind of world order. Only the United States is in a position to have a genuinely global horizon consistent with the reality of the era of international affairs that we are now entering. This position, while it enjoins upon the United States a general obligation to maintain the basic peace and order of the world, does not lessen its chosen responsibility to promote political regimes based on respect for individual rights and democratic rule.

Conservative internationalists, or at least the more prudent among them, are aware that this objective must not be pursued dogmatically, inflexibly, or without regard to the zone in which the nation is operating. America is not under a mission to transform every nation in the world. There are obvious distinctions to be made, for example, between settled and indigenous traditional orders and outright tyrannies, between nations that are leaving others alone and nations that are threatening their neighbors. All this said, the experience of the past half-century, dating back to the occupation of Germany and Japan, and then through the effect we have had on nations as different as Korea, the Philippines and Nicaragua, gives the lie to the notion that the elements of free government cannot be transferred to others. Of course, success cannot be assured in all cases, but this is no reason to shun commitment to a general policy that has proved its plausibility.

Conservative internationalism purports to speak to this reality. It appeals to sentiments that are shared in inchoate form, almost as a matter of instinct, by a large number of Americans, and not just those in the Republican Party. But when it comes to moving beyond vague sentiments to a coherent articulation of a political project for action embraced by a large number of political leaders, conservative internationalists are struck by how much ground has been lost. Our university campuses today scarcely even conceive of the subject of international relations in these terms. In the political arena, our politicians tend to judge each case of intervention as a discrete issue rather than as one part of a much broader strategy. The military, still worried about the fecklessness of our politicians, has developed no strategic vision to support this project. For conservative internationalism to be viable, we will need statesmen of a new breed.

II.

The Mounting Threat

China:
The Challenge of
a Rising Power

However history judges William Jefferson Clinton, the assessment of how his administration dealt with a rising China is certain to be harsh. As Clinton prepares to leave office, America faces a China much more dangerous than it was when he arrived in 1993—to a significant degree due to his administration's policies and actions.

Granted, no president this past decade could have eliminated the danger posed by China as long as it continued to be ruled by an aggressive and fundamentally anti-American dictatorship that seeks ultimately to dominate Asia. But a strategically minded president would have treated such a regime with profound wariness while he affirmed both American interests and values by building stronger ties with our democratic friends and allies on China's periphery. The Clinton administration did neither; in fact, it did the opposite by attempting to appease and placate the Beijing regime and by negligently allowing relations with our natural, democratic partners in Asia to deteriorate. Betraying American values, President Clinton courted China's dictators while slighting democratically elected governments in Tokyo, Taipei and New Delhi. This emboldened China but disturbed and dismayed our Asian friends and allies. So the Clinton administration's legacy in Asia has been to weaken America's standing, and to make China a greater danger to its neighbors and to the United States than it would otherwise have been.

Virtually every serious strategic thinker in the United States today agrees that China, if current trends continue, represents a greater potential danger in the long term than any other nation in the world. Many analysts go considerably further: We are convinced that the danger is not just potential and long-term, but here and now, real and present. It is the proximity of the threat, in fact, that constitutes one of the most serious indictments of current policy.

If the Clinton administration had only failed to take seriously the danger that China may pose to the United States in the long term, we could at least comfort ourselves with the prospect of a future, strategically minded president repairing the damage and reversing the trends that President Clinton set in motion. But the administration's strategic obtuseness and its policy of appeasement has emboldened China to the degree that the next few years could well prove to be an extremely dangerous period in U.S.-China relations.

Flashpoint Taiwan

No issue in U.S.-China relations today is more volatile, or more charged with immediate danger for the United States, than Taiwan. Primarily because of the Clinton administration's ineptitude, the possibility of another military confrontation between China and Taiwan has risen dramatically over the past year. Such a confrontation would immediately present the United States with a dilemma much more serious than it faced in 1996, when it was necessary to dispatch two U.S. naval aircraft carrier task forces to waters near Taiwan to convince China to end its threatening military actions against the island republic. Although still enjoying clear-cut military superiority, U.S. forces would have to weigh the threat posed by Russian-built anti-ship missiles and other advanced new weapons that the People's Liberation Army has deployed since 1996.

If there was a confrontation and the United States delayed or avoided coming to Taiwan's assistance, the result would prove catastrophic for U.S. interests. Taiwan is not just an old and democratic friend of the United States; it is also, despite its relatively small size, an essential factor in counterbalancing an increasingly powerful China. If the United States failed to assist Taiwan, Asian countries would conclude that we were no longer committed to supporting a balance of power in Asia or to supporting our allies in the region. Led by Japan, our friends would scurry to make concessions to China, possibly including closing their ports and airfields to U.S. armed forces. Our days as a true Asian power would be numbered. On paper, our military strength might still dwarf China's. But American credibility in Asia would be shattered because we would have revealed that we lacked the political will to use that military power when the stakes were high.

The heightened possibility today of a China-Taiwan military confrontation, with its grim implications for the United States, can be traced back to the previous Taiwan crisis. The U.S. Navy's intervention in the 1996 crisis, after China had bracketed Taiwan with missiles, concretely demonstrated America's commitment to maintaining stability in East Asia and to preventing China from using military force to settle the Taiwan issue. It seemed, at the very least, that the United States had bought several years of stability before China would feel militarily strong enough to seek a new confrontation with Taiwan.

But the Clinton administration squandered its success almost immediately. Unnerved by having to make this show of force and face the possibility of a real conflict with China, the administration began to tilt its cross-strait policy toward China and to pressure the Taipei government into making concessions to Beijing. Naturally, this only whetted China's appetite for more concessions, not less, and tensions between China and Taiwan were visibly rising by 1998.

That is when President Clinton, in his visit to China that summer, became the first U.S. president to endorse publicly the "Three No's": declaring that the United States would not support an independent Taiwan, nor a one-China/one-Taiwan policy, nor membership for Taiwan in any international organization that required sovereign statehood. The president thereby indirectly but effectively endorsed Beijing's stance that Taiwan is merely a province of China. Underscoring that this was a concession, was the fact that Clinton made his statement in a question-and-answer session stage-managed by his hosts. His performance was a stunning blow to the leaders of Taiwan and the voters who elected them democratically. Nearly all Taiwanese believe that, at a minimum, Taiwan is a legal, sovereign and distinct state whose people have the right to determine democratically whether and when they will become part of "one China." The Clinton White House then followed up the president's statement by pressuring Taipei later in 1998 and in 1999 to reach "interim agreements" with Beijing that put Taiwan on a negotiating path toward reunification and ultimately Chinese rule, despite the overwhelming opposition of Taiwan's people to moving in this direction.

Concerned about the increasing tendency of the administration to accept the PRC's version of "one China," Taiwan's President Lee Teng-hui had little choice except to attempt to create political and diplomatic room for Taiwan by declaring in the summer of 1999 that, in the future, Taiwan would negotiate with China only on a state-to-state basis: in other words, as an equal. By its diplomatic blundering—appeasing Beijing and pressuring Taipei—the Clinton administration had done the nearly inconceivable: it had induced both China and Taiwan to harden their stands.

The administration's reaction was to denounce Lee's "provocative" statement, while the PRC put on a show of mobilizing its military forces on China's east coast opposite Taiwan. Yet President Lee didn't budge. In the March 2000 presidential election, the three major candidates to succeed him, although offering different formulations, all stuck to Lee's basic position: Taiwan is a separate and sovereign entity that will talk to China only as an equal. And they reinforced this stance after the Chinese government issued an official white paper transparently designed to intimidate Taiwan's voters, threatening to take military action if Taiwan's leaders indefinitely delayed negotiation on reunification. By making this threat official policy, the Beijing regime substantially escalated the conflict with the island. Previously, the core of Beijing's policy had been to threaten military action if the Taipei government declared an independent Republic of Taiwan. Even though a few U.S. officials and Sinologists predictably attempted to downplay the shift, the Clinton administration felt compelled to denounce Beijing's move officially.

Beijing's issuance of the white paper also failed in its main aim of reversing the growth in support among Taiwan's voters for Chen Shui-bian, the presidential candidate of the Democratic Progressive Party, which had been founded with the aim of declaring an independent Taiwan Republic. Chen seemed "safe" to a plurality of Taiwan's voters because he had moderated his stance on independence so that it was effectively the same as that of his two major opponents. With the independence issue neutralized, Chen then won a plurality because of his reputation as a "clean" leader who stood out from the competent but corruption-plagued ruling Kuomintang (KMT) party.

Clinton administration envoys and other officials have been almost rapturously praising Beijing for its "restrained" and prudent response to Chen's election. But Beijing's declaration that it will "watch and wait" does not reflect moderation; it reflects shock and indecision in the wake of Chen's victory. The regime's threats are still official policy. Thus, the United States must be prepared for an increase in tensions for many months, if not years, and the eruption of armed conflict over the island.

What American and Chinese leaders alike have only begun to absorb is that Chen's victory will almost certainly strengthen American commitment to intervene militarily to help Taiwan defend itself if China attacks. For years, the opposite was predicted: that the emergence of a government in Taiwan under the DPP, long an advocate of independence, would prompt Washington to increase its distance from Taipei. But the U.S. commitment to Taiwan is actually stronger today than it was six months ago because the peaceful and democratic transfer of power from the long-ruling KMT to Chen confirms Taiwan's standing as a vibrant and genuine democracy. Taiwan's latest election has given millions of people in China a potent example of such an ideal. As for the United States, it's clearer than ever that we cannot abandon Taiwan without abandoning our core principles. Our obligation to Taiwan is even stronger because of the restraint and moderation that Chen has been displaying in the face of crude threats and bullying by China.

One troubling possibility is that Beijing will conclude that it must act before Clinton leaves office. China's hawks are well aware that a Republican in the White House is more likely to intervene militarily on Taiwan's behalf than the current chief executive. Indeed, the Chinese can't even count on a new Democrat in the White House to staff his administration with so many officials as sympathetic to China as the present one.

Judging by what they are saying today both publicly and privately, Clinton's China hands still do not understand that they bear primary responsibility for the crisis over Taiwan, even though the issue has virtually exploded in their faces. Because of their naive misreading of China's intentions toward Taiwan, they have convinced themselves that Taiwan is first and last a symbolic issue rooted in Chinese nationalism. Clinton's China hands believe that if Taiwan would only make some legal and token concessions to the mainland, then the China-Taiwan relationship could stabilize while little would actually change in Taiwan itself. In other words, they expect that China would be satisfied with a face-saving compromise. But the writings of China's strategic thinkers make clear that Beijing doesn't see reunification with Taiwan as an end in itself. However much they wrap the Taiwan issue in nationalistic rhetoric for domestic and foreign consumption, China's political and military leaders view Taiwan as a strategic target. They must acquire Taiwan if they are to achieve their goal of dominating Asia. So the sorts of concessions that the Clinton administration is pushing Taiwan to make will, instead of satisfying the Chinese leadership, only whet its appetite for actual control of the island.

Weakened Alliances

It is not just democratic Taiwan that has been alienated by Clinton administration policy. The inescapable corollary of a policy of courting China has been neglect of vital relationships with most of America's friends, allies and fellow democracies in the region. The United States depends on ties with countries such as Japan, South Korea, and Taiwan to help maintain a balance of power in Asia and to prevent any other, potentially hostile nation from upsetting that balance.

President Clinton did his worst damage to America's Asian alliance structure during his official visit to China in 1998. Not only did he undercut Taiwan's bargaining position, as we have seen, but he also snubbed our key ally in the region, Japan, at Beijing's request. In talks about the arrangements for Clinton's visit, Chinese officials insisted that the president not visit any other countries while he traveled to and from China. In effect this meant eliminating the U.S. president's usual stopover in Japan as part of a China visit—an event which, however brief, had always symbolized that Washington saw its alliance with Tokyo as the linchpin of U.S. policy in the region. Clinton's China hands, seemingly oblivious to the fact that one of Beijing's key goals is to weaken U.S. ties with Japan and our other Asian allies, acceded to China's request. Japanese officials publicly insisted that the change was unimportant, but privately they were shaken.

While he was in Beijing, moreover, Clinton joined Chinese leader Jiang Zemin in a formal joint statement excoriating India for testing nuclear weapons. The statement had troubling strategic implications. It implicitly endorsed a strategic role for China in South Asia, and, since China has long possessed nuclear weapons, it had a U.S. president effectively endorsing a permanent Chinese nuclear advantage over India. The statement also ignored the fact that Pakistan had also "gone nuclear" only because of China's substantial assistance. Unlike their Japanese counterparts, Indian officials did not hide their anger and anxiety over what they rightly saw as the United States siding with China in the competition between Asia's two giants.

Although India is not a U.S. ally, it is a democracy that shares with the United States an interest in counterbalancing China's growing power. Indeed, many U.S. strategic thinkers outside the Clinton administration believe that developing closer ties with India should be a much higher priority for the United States than it has ever been since relations began with India's independence in 1947. But Clinton's blunder in Beijing added to India's mistrust of the United States.

India, Japan and Taiwan were all more alarmed than they otherwise might have been by Clinton's slights because they all occurred under the umbrella of a U.S.-China "constructive strategic partnership." In many Asian eyes, the United States appeared to be making a major strategic shift, tilting in China's favor and pulling back from the traditional U.S. military commitment to maintaining a balance of power. Equally sobering, they feared that Clinton was signaling to Asian countries that they too should accommodate themselves to China's growing power and depend less on the United States.

Not surprisingly, Clinton's actions in China prompted our Asian friends and allies to reassess U.S. Asian policy and to wonder about the extent to which they can depend on the United States. Ever since Clinton's China visit in 1998, our Asian allies have stepped up "hedging" actions prompted by concerns that the United States is not as reliable a long-term ally as it once was. For instance, Southeast Asian countries are increasingly discussing economic and security arrangements that would exclude the United States. Japan's Prime Minister Keizo Obuchi announced early this year that Japan is putting more emphasis on developing stronger ties with Europe and the rest of Asia. South Korea is hedging by attempting to strengthen its relations with China itself. In November 1999, in what could prove to be the beginning of a strategic shift in Asia unless a future U.S. president moves to repair the damage, ASEAN leaders conferred with the heads of state of Japan, South Korea and China in a meeting that excluded the United States.

Chinese Missiles: A Homegrown Threat

An even more concrete risk than compromised alliances for the United States in any future confrontation over Taiwan, or any other issue, is China's arsenal of increasingly accurate and destructive missiles aimed at us and our friends. Some of those missiles owe much of their improved accuracy and greater destructive power to technology stolen from or negligently transferred by the United States during the Clinton era.

During the course of the 1990s, as China continued to accelerate its military buildup, the Clinton administration worked hard to minimize its significance. While it is true that China's overall military capabilities remain well below that of the U.S., this fact misses the point that China's military leaders have focused much of their effort on developing and deploying various missiles that threaten democratic Taiwan and U.S. naval forces in Asia, as well as the U.S. itself. In one of the most plausible scenarios for a future crisis, China strikes Taiwan with missiles, provoking panic on the island, while deploying newly acquired naval craft, armed with state-of-the-art Russian anti-ship missiles, to threaten U.S. naval forces should they move toward the strait in an effort to help defend Taiwan. China might also threaten to fire missiles at American cities, as it did just before the 1996 crisis and most recently in the wake of the white paper, if the United States intervened. Although this might be a bluff, such threats would make the United States hesitate before attacking targets on the Chinese mainland, such as coastal missile bases, that would have to be eliminated before an attack on Taiwan was crushed.

China's missile arsenal already constitutes a more credible menace than anyone would have predicted in the early 1990s. Largely because of the corrupt, anything-goes atmosphere that pervaded the White House, especially in 1995–96, U.S. corporations whose executives were leading financial supporters of the president felt free to share guidance and other high-tech missile technology with China. Meanwhile, thanks to the lax security standards that prevailed before and during the Clinton era, China acquired some of our most secret nuclear warhead technology.

In recent months, there has been an effort by Sinologists and administration apologists to minimize these losses and to question the competence of those, like Congressman Chris Cox, who have sounded the alarm bells. But it is difficult to dispute Aaron Friedberg's analysis of the harm done to the security of the United States and its friends when he wrote that the theater-range rockets and ICBMs that China is now building and deploying are "more accurate and more reliable and more destructive because of technology obtained in various ways from the United States."

Danger's Catalyst: Beijing's Insecurity

The force that exacerbates these dangers and makes them more immediate for the United States and its friends and allies is the mounting crisis of legitimacy in which the Chinese regime finds itself today. Since the early 1980s, the Communist Party dictatorship has favored two main tools for holding on to power: economic growth (the "you never had it so good" argument that rang true for most Chinese until recently) and political repression (necessary, the one-party regime argues, to maintain the order and stability required for continued economic growth). Ordinary Chinese have generally accepted political repression—manifested in Chinese officials' everyday arbitrariness and corruption—as long as their living standards keep improving and they are largely left alone when it comes to their private lives.

However, most independent economists are now convinced that a major economic downturn or financial crash is likely after seven consecutive years of slowing economic growth, and the Chinese regime is running scared. Repression is increasing, as witnessed by the regime's surprisingly severe crackdown on the Falun Gong sect, which seemingly poses little threat with its apolitical regimen of exercise and spirituality. But increased repression ultimately won't be sufficient for the regime to remain securely in power if the economic downturn is severe, and so the PRC elite is turning increasingly to a chauvinist and expansionist version of Chinese nationalism in its efforts to hold onto power.

While Bill Clinton has come close on more than one occasion to hailing Jiang as China's future great democratizer, a Chinese Gorbachev, Jiang himself has made it clear in recent months that he has no such goal. Instead, his propagandists are declaring that Jiang wants history to recognize him as China's great unifier—a euphemism for saying that his primary goal is to conquer Taiwan. Put another way, it means Jiang intends to draw on and reinforce Chinese nationalism to stay in power. China's escalating threats against Taiwan, its increased military activity in the South China Sea, the growing number of verbal attacks on the United States as "hegemonist," and the increasingly explicit anti-American character of China's cooperation with Russia on global issues all point in this direction.

China as a Rogue State

Given China's inherent instability and the insecurity of its leadership, it is possible that the world's most populous nation will evolve into a rogue state. It's a chilling prospect but one we must face, if only because Chinese leaders themselves have made it clear that they don't rule out this option. Clinton administration officials confirm that Chinese officials have recently been threatening once again, albeit sotto voce, to destabilize Southwest Asia and the Middle East by sales of missiles and other advanced weaponry to rogue regimes as a quid pro quo for U.S. sales of advanced defensive weapons to Taiwan. China would benefit to a modest extent financially, but the transfers would also serve China's strategic interests by allowing second- and third-rung countries to tie down and preoccupy the United States.

The Central Intelligence Agency has identified China as "the principal supplier of weapons of mass destruction to the world." And China has a history of supplying weapons and conducting business with states like Iraq and Iran, as well as others that are among the most odious on earth, such as Myanmar (Burma) and Sudan. Not surprisingly, it is now on cordial terms with Slobodan Milosevic's Yugoslavia.

That China's ruling elite considers rogue-state tactics a valid option was demonstrated by the recent publication in China of *Unrestricted War*, written by two Chinese army colonels. In order to fight the powerful United States, the book argues, relatively weak

China must consider using terrorism, drug trafficking, environmental degradation and computer virus propagation. *Unrestricted War* is part of a large body of Chinese military writing today that asserts China can defeat the much stronger United States by carefully selecting its weapons and its tactics and by possessing greater political will.

The Roots of the Current Conflict

To understand how this picture of an armed and dangerous China developed, we must return to the early 1990s. Entire books have been written about how America has "misperceived" China over the years, but never were U.S. perceptions and policies toward China more disconnected from reality than they were in this period.

When Bill Clinton was running for president in 1992, American attitudes toward China were still determined by the television images of Chinese tanks crushing young protesters in Tiananmen Square in June 1989. The mainstream view of Sinologists was that the regime had so disgraced itself that it would never recover sufficient legitimacy to rule effectively, let alone restore the vibrant economic growth of the 1980s. As for China's armed forces, discussion centered not on the accelerating military buildup but on how demoralized the army was after being forced to suppress the Tiananmen demonstrators. Indeed, many China hands, most notably Winston Lord, then Clinton's top China adviser, were predicting the regime probably wouldn't survive after Deng Xiaoping's death.

In short, most Americans who thought about U.S. China policy at all viewed it then as largely a one-dimensional issue: how to respond to an illegitimate and doomed regime's repression of the human rights and political freedoms of the Chinese people. Few skeptical voices were raised, therefore, when candidate Clinton promised in 1992 that he would never coddle "the butchers of Beijing" or when President Clinton followed through in May 1993 by pledging to raise punitive barriers against imports from China unless the Beijing regime substantially eased its repressive practices within twelve months.

Clinton's ultimatum came precisely when the confidence of the Beijing regime was not only recovering from the aftermath of Tiananmen but hitting new hubristic heights: China's leaders had survived and taken measure of the world's ineffectual attempts to isolate them. Indeed, given their mood those days, China's leaders were almost eager to defy Clinton's ultimatum. China's economy in 1993 was in its second year of hyper-growth thanks to a new wave of deregulation and a virtually open door to foreign investment. Recognizing that the greatest economic takeoff in history had resumed, the world's CEOs were eager to kowtow to the regime's leaders, throwing their investment dollars at almost anything Chinese, and telling their leaders back home not to spoil relations with those running the world's fastest growing economy. China's rulers immediately grasped what enormous leverage the prospect of doing business in China gave them with the governments of the world's leading industrial powers.

Even more significant from a strategic perspective than China's economic takeoff was the country's unanticipated windfall from the total unraveling of the Soviet Bloc in 1989–91. Initially, Beijing had worried that the collapse of the communist regime in Moscow would be contagious and that chaos in the newly independent Central Asian republics would infect China's Muslim minorities. By 1993, however, the regime had come to see the Soviet crack-up as constituting a huge strategic bonanza. China was now unchallenged in continental East Asia. All of its land neighbors, not just in East Asia but in South and Central Asia as well, were seeking a rapprochement or at least a modus vivendi with their giant neighbor next door. This included former parts of the Soviet Union, such as Kazakhstan and neighboring Central Asian republics, and the one-time Soviet satellite Mongolia, as well as Vietnam and India, both once strategic allies of the USSR. China was free to re-deploy the massive military resources it had devoted to securing its borders with Soviet bloc countries.

The ramifications of the Soviet Bloc collapse for China proved to be profound. For the first time in two centuries, China was not only unchallenged on the land mass of East Asia, it faced no significant military threat from any country on earth. Without fighting a single battle, China found its relative military strength in Asia skyrocketing. Yet China's generals allowed no pause in their military buildup; if anything, it accelerated. That was one of the first concrete signals that China had adopted an ambitious and aggressive new grand strategy for Asia.

China Seeks Hegemony

By late 1993, flush with its economic success and its gain in relative military strength, the Chinese regime concluded that it could attain the goal of all the great Chinese dynasties: primacy in East Asia. That meant not only continental East Asia, already slipping into the Chinese sphere of influence, but maritime East Asia as well: Japan, the Korean Peninsula, Taiwan, the Philippines, Indonesia, Singapore and the rest of Southeast Asia northward to Myanmar and Vietnam.

Beijing made it unmistakably clear that, if necessary, it intended to conquer Taiwan and the South China Sea militarily—two conquests that together would be more than sufficient to swing the Asian balance of power decisively in its favor. As for the other countries, China had little desire to invade and occupy them. Instead, Chinese strategists instinctively turned to what they viewed as the only positive model in the history of China's international relations: the "tributary states system" of the imperial era when China's neighbors, ranging from Japan to Burma, regularly sent "tribute" to the emperor in Beijing. In return for China's tolerance of their separate existence, they pledged to do nothing China deemed to be against its strategic interests.

China's goals in Asia, voiced with increasing frankness during the 1990s, amount to a program for domination of the region. China has openly declared that it aims to occupy Taiwan and control the South China Sea, to end the U.S. military presence in Asia, to break all U.S. military alliances with Asian countries, and to force Japan into "permanent strategic subservience" without the right to a full-fledged military. What China wants is an Asia where no country could oppose its will.

For China's leaders, the goal of restoring China to its glory days of unquestioned dominance over its neighbors gives them a sense of pride and purpose, something they had lost with the crumbling of Marxist-Leninist ideology. After effectively admitting that Marxist economics doesn't work, the Communist Party dictatorship needed further justification for one-party rule beyond the argument that stability was necessary for economic growth. The Chinese leaders' dilemma was that they could not come right out and declare their ambitions without forcing Asian and U.S. leaders to confront the threat they posed. So they have tried to square this circle with general assurances that they do not seek hegemony in Asia, while actually pursuing a set of specific goals that amount to precisely that.

China's goal to dominate all of Asia was only the first part of the consensus on a new grand strategy that emerged in Beijing in 1993–94. The second part was identifying the United States as China's long-term strategic foe.

Intense but inchoate anti-Americanism has always been rife in Communist China. The dictatorship has regularly displayed an instinctive fear of the messages conveyed by the free and democratic politics and culture of the United States. But in the post–Cold War era, there is more reason than ever for the Chinese elite to see America as the enemy.

For more than a century, it has been a goal of the United States to prevent the domination of East Asia by a potentially hostile power. Unlike their American counterparts, Chinese strategists recognize that their own goal of regional dominance has put China on a collision course with the United States. Since 1994, virtually all general strategic writings in China have identified the United States as China's adversary, the country with which Chinese military forces will one day probably clash. Every major foreign policy speech by China's leaders contains a denunciation of the evils of "hegemony," universally understood as code for American policy. While often absent from bilateral U.S.-China meetings, the attack on "hegemony" is typically featured in the official Chinese media when senior U.S. officials visit China, to remind the population and officials at all levels that, despite brief displays of amity, China's long-term strategic view of the United States as the enemy has not changed.

During 1993–94, Beijing shifted not only its strategy towards the United States, but its tactics as well. While Deng had urged that China avoid provoking or antagonizing the United States, we know now that by late 1993 his failing health had largely put him on the sidelines. A younger generation of political and military leaders, brimming with confidence in Chinese power, discarded Deng's cautious approach to the United States. They reasoned that they could adopt confrontational tactics with the United States—in this instance, openly defying Clinton's May 1993 ultimatum for reform—by enlisting the help of U.S. corporations lusting to get a piece of China's unprecedented economic boom. The story of how China then helped mobilize U.S. business to form a pro-China lobby has been told in detail elsewhere.[1] Here it is worth noting that China's leaders were so sure they had discovered the skeleton key to the U.S. political system that, by March of 1994, they were contemptuously rebuffing the administration's pleas for even a gesture or two that President Clinton could then characterize as "progress" on democracy and human rights.

So, in the spring of 1994, the Clinton administration found itself completely out of sync with the ambitious, self-confident men who now dominated the Beijing regime and viewed the United States as the enemy. The administration was also out of sync with the U.S. business community, which lobbied on behalf of China's leaders because it so coveted the mythic China market. Clinton folded, completely abandoning any linkage of trade with human rights and democracy. After that, Clinton never recovered his credibility with the Chinese. Indeed, the Chinese now believed they had hit pay dirt with his presidency, and that rolling Clinton on issue after issue was a near certainty.

The Folly of "Engagement"

Events in 1994 did not destroy the long-standing myth, first propagated by Christian missionaries in the nineteenth century, that "we can change China." Even after abandoning a policy of "linkage"—the threat of closing America's markets to Chinese exports to induce Chinese reforms—Clinton did not abandon the myth but instead reformulated it as "engagement." At the core of this new policy was the dubious proposition that if the United States helped China grow economically, mainly by trading with and investing in it, this would lead inexorably to a market economy, a middle class, civil society, rule of law, pluralism and, ultimately, democracy. What's more, China would become a responsible member of the international community, restrained by its dependence on trade and investment from acting aggressively in the world.

"Engagement" was a masterstroke by a master political phrasemaker. After the term's adoption, the Clinton administration and its defenders defined critics of its China policy as opponents of "engagement" and therefore in favor of "isolating China." Engagement also served as a politically palatable screen for hiding the administration's surrender of China policy to the new China lobby of U.S. business interests who had successfully derailed linkage and had then begun to press the administration to suspend or eviscerate restrictions on exporting high technology to China. From 1994 on, the Clinton administration did not make a single major decision regarding China that was opposed by the pro-China business lobby.

Packaging China policy as "engagement" may have been a domestic political success, but it was still in conflict with American national interests. In the long term, of course, there is a correlation between economic development and democratization, but far from 100 percent, and it has little relevance to the matter of U.S. policy towards China in the present. Consider that in 1900, one could have argued that Germany's and Japan's level and rate of economic development guaranteed that both countries would become democracies integrated with the world community. Yet both subsequently suffered under ruthless regimes that launched three horrendously destructive major wars between them; and that reality, not long-term prospects, was what Western democracies had to deal with.

In China, a transition to democracy could take many decades, and is by no means guaranteed. Per capita income in predominantly Chinese Singapore today surpasses most industrial democracies, yet Singapore remains essentially a one-party authoritarian city-state, however benign it might be. Indeed, China itself grows richer yearly, yet there is probably less political freedom today than a decade ago. In fact, since Clinton's 1988 visit, a new wave of political repression has continued into the new century.

Clinton's policy of engagement owes much of its remaining public credibility to a cohort of China specialists in and out of government who have fervently argued throughout the 1990s that China's armed forces are weak and backward and therefore pose no significant military threat to the United States. Members of this "weak China" school insist that those who argue otherwise are alarmists who exaggerate China's military capabilities. Their analysis is simplistic; but it is the subtext that is truly dangerous: even if China's goal is to dominate Asia and even if China views the United States as the enemy, there is still no need to be alarmed because China is so far behind us militarily. We have plenty of time, they say, to wait for Clinton's engagement policy to work and for China to "evolve" before we should worry about this alleged "China threat."

In the real world, there are many reasons to worry about the Chinese military threat right now. Many elements of China's military, including most of its land forces, are indeed quite backward. But China's strategy for building up its military is shrewdly focusing its limited resources on a few advanced weapons programs and a limited number of military units that can inflict maximum damage on the United States and its Asian partners, especially Taiwan. Chinese strategists are not trying to match the U.S. gun for gun. Instead, they are looking for those weapons that can give China an asymmetrical but decisive advantage in any conflict.

We have already seen, for instance, how China's missile arsenal today poses a threat to U.S. interests. While the "weak China" school often comes close to suggesting that we needn't worry about China's Navy until it acquires a "blue water" capability in Asia comparable to ours, the Chinese don't think that way at all. They are mounting anti-ship missiles not just on new, Russian-built Sovremenny-class destroyers but also on small naval craft, making it potentially very costly for the U.S. Navy to mount even a show of force in the next Taiwan crisis. China is also investing heavily in information warfare and space warfare as a relatively inexpensive way of countering some of our most advanced military technology. And since Chinese authorities recently permitted publication of *Unrestricted War*, U.S. war plans must take into account the possibility that China will also use weapons ranging from terrorism to an engineered financial panic against us.

Not that China isn't spending in more traditional areas as well. Thanks in part to the huge trade surplus it is running with the United States, China can afford to pay the Russians at least one billion dollars a year for warplanes, submarines, and other advanced weapons, including even its best multiple-warhead missile technology.

Recently the leaders of both China's air force and its navy have confidently announced a shift in their military posture from defensive to offensive. Put another way, China is developing "power projection" capabilities that will enable it to fight wars increasingly further from the mainland. This means an increased Chinese threat to Taiwan, to the Philippines and other littoral states of the South China Sea, and ultimately to Japan as well. The United States should be comparing Chinese capabilities not to our own but to those of our friends and allies that are China's neighbors. Not only

Taiwan but also Japan and maritime Southeast Asian nations such as the Philippines increasingly view China as a military threat, especially as confidence in the U.S. will and capacity to meet Chinese ambitions erodes.

While the United States and other major powers have been reducing military expenditures, China's official defense budget has been rising for the past eleven years at an average annual rate of more than 10 percent and, for the past two years, at a rate of 13 percent.[2] The "weak China" school is fond of emphasizing that China's official military expenditures remain far behind those of the United States. But the official defense budget may represent only a fraction of China's actual military expenditures if one counts secret programs and spending for weapons procurement (which isn't counted in the official defense budget) and then adjusts for the differences in costs between China and the United States. And in making this comparison, the "weak China" school ignores the fact that America's defense expenditures are intended to support a global, not just a regional, set of requirements.

The "weak China" school reflects an arrogant complacency about the world's most populous country with the world's fastest growing military budget. After all, even relatively small and backward Vietnam and Iraq both challenged us with forms of military aggression that were not easy to counter. This arrogance seems even greater given the emphasis that traditional Chinese strategy places on using deception and surprise to defeat a stronger enemy. To assume that we know all the significant military capabilities of a secretive China is foolish indeed.

Engagement Becomes Appeasement

In 1994, when he unveiled his policy of engagement, Clinton pledged that his administration would approach each bilateral issue individually, guided only by U.S. national interests. Military proliferation or trade issues, for instance, would not be linked with human rights issues but would be negotiated on their own, separate merits. On the surface, this had immense common-sense appeal; but once again, the president was being disingenuous. Stuck with its own 1994 cave-in to China and to China's corporate allies in the United States, the Clinton administration was loath to stand up to Beijing on almost any issue. In one instance after another, the administration has given China much more than it has received in return, a syndrome that has only emboldened China, making it more dangerous and more difficult to deal with.

The following failures summarize the Clinton administration's record on China:

Failure to halt the rise of China's trade surplus: Since Clinton disavowed linking trade with human rights and democracy in 1994, the U.S. trade deficit with China has grown every year. China uses a panoply of mercantilist devices to indirectly subsidize its exports to the United States and to restrict the import of U.S. goods and services. For seven years, amid the unprecedented U.S. economic boom, the Clinton administration did almost nothing directly to reduce the soaring trade deficit, now more than $60 billion. This inaction alone amounted to a massive concession to China.

The Clinton administration claimed all along that it was addressing this problem by negotiating with China for its entry into the World Trade Organization. In late 1999, the United States and China finally announced agreement on the terms of China's entry into the WTO. For months these terms remained classified. But in some respects, the nitty-gritty details of the agreement are not as important as the fact that China has no intention of abiding by the spirit of the agreement. As Willy Wo-lap Lam, perhaps Hong Kong's most respected China watcher, reported right after the agreement, "various [Chinese government] departments are already trying to erect roadblocks to slow the influx of goods, services and ideas that is expected into China after the WTO accession."[3]

All this has great strategic significance that mocks the theory underlying engagement. Chinese policy-makers loathe the idea of permanent economic interdependence. They are openly seeking to build an economically powerful and technologically self-reliant China that depends as little as possible on the outside world. China's imports today tend to be in one of three categories: raw materials and commodities; components that will be processed or assembled and then re-exported; and high technology that China intends to learn how to produce itself.

Chinese mercantilist policies are designed to amass large foreign exchange reserves. It is worth recalling that the original mercantilists urged nations to amass gold (the equivalent of today's foreign exchange reserves) not as an end in itself but in order to raise armies and wage wars of conquest that would increase national wealth and power. Today, Russia always demands U.S. dollars from China for weapons systems originally designed by the Soviets to be used against the United States.

Chinese mercantilism has imposed another price on the United States and its friends in Asia that has gone largely unnoticed by Americans. China's often subsidized exports have stolen U.S. market share from allies and other friendly countries of Southeast Asia. Indeed, the Asian economic crisis of 1997 was precipitated (although not primarily caused) by the sudden halt in the growth of exports from Southeast Asia because of China's increasing penetration of U.S. and other western markets.

Failure to effectively counter Chinese espionage against the United States: We have already noted the loss of some of our most valuable nuclear and missile technology during the Clinton era. What still isn't fully appreciated is that this loss occurred as part of a larger pattern of negligence that prevailed throughout this administration, thanks in part to the symbiosis between its engagement policy and the "weak China" argument. Another contributing factor was the corrupt atmosphere in the White House that facilitated access for suspected Chinese agents who had made contributions to the Democrats or to the Clintons' legal defense fund. During the Clinton administration's first term, for instance, the Federal Bureau of Investigation substantially reduced its budget for "counterintelligence." Two federal employees informed me that counterintelligence operations against China were particularly hard hit—a disaster considering the huge investment of man-hours that must be made (particularly given the language difficulties) to build up institutional memory and operational expertise. Inevitably the price of those cutbacks is being paid in recent and future intelligence losses.

Failure to counter Chinese military adventurism in Asia: We have already looked at how, after the 1996 Taiwan crisis, the Clinton administration abetted Beijing's attempts to gain the upper hand against Taipei. But the administration had also assisted Chinese adventurism in East Asia before then. After Clinton's 1994 concession to the Chinese, his administration was slow to criticize, let alone counter, aggressive Chinese rhetoric and actions. After Washington protested China's transfer of missiles and nuclear weapons technology to Pakistan, for instance, the president nevertheless later gutted the prescribed sanctions against Beijing by issuing waivers that allowed sensitive U.S. technology to be sold to China.

In 1995, after Chinese troops disguised as fishermen seized Mischief Reef in the South China Sea from the Philippines, a U.S. ally, the Clinton administration said and did virtually nothing for five months, and then issued a mushy expression of concern. The statement tried to sidestep the issue of the forceful seizure of the reef by focusing on the legitimate, but long-term, issue of the international right of free and unimpeded passage of ships through the South China Sea. This hesitation and ambiguity could only have emboldened the Chinese in their later moves against Taiwan.

It was on the question of Taiwan that the Clinton administration was at its most inept prior to the 1996 crisis. With its troops no longer tied down on its land borders, China's military buildup on its central east coast opposite Taiwan was going full steam ahead by 1994. That same year, China mounted its first serious exercise in decades aimed at preparing for an invasion of Taiwan. But Washington failed to issue any serious warning or to press for an explanation, even though a commitment to a peaceful resolution of the Taiwan issue is enshrined in U.S. law.

Even when China first began organizing large and threatening military exercises on and near the Taiwan Strait in the summer of 1995, rattling its sabers over the visit of Taiwan's President Lee Teng-hui to Cornell University in the United States, the Clinton administration reacted slowly and ambiguously. Worse, President Clinton responded to China's threats by attempting to appease Chinese leader Jiang Zemin with a secret letter declaring the administration's opposition to Taiwan's independence under any conditions.[4]

In late 1995, Chinese officials and operatives began an obviously concerted effort to determine whether the United States would respond with military force to a Chinese attack on Taiwan. A key exchange occurred in Beijing when a senior Clinton administration official described the U.S. position—far too ambiguously—as "you don't know and we don't know." Coming in the wake of repeated demonstrations of the administration's timidity in the face of Chinese assertiveness during the preceding two years, this could only have encouraged the Chinese to continue escalating their threatening military exercises, which they explicitly announced were aimed at intimidating Taiwan.

Several other U.S. missteps followed, all betraying the Clinton administration's hesitation and lack of will in the face of the accelerating Chinese military buildup opposite Taiwan. Only when China announced it was lobbing missiles into Taiwan's air and sea space in March 1996 did Clinton finally order an aircraft carrier task force into the area. With China showing no sign of backing down, the U.S. Congress was about to demand formally that the president order a second task force to the area. Only then, when he was on the verge of losing control of his own military, did Clinton do so. Soon thereafter China halted its military provocations against Taiwan, but was saved from a loss of face, let alone a humiliating lesson, by the timorous policies that the administration then adopted.

Looking Ahead

As Clinton's final year in office began, it was difficult to get a consistent and coherent account of current U.S. China policy from the various administration officials involved. The argument that economic engagement will lead inexorably to a freer and more democratic China is heard less and less these days. Nor do administration officials voluntarily use the term "strategic partnership" any longer to describe the U.S.-China relationship. It was remarkable to hear the president during his final State of the Union speech downplaying, after several years of inflated rhetoric, the impact that U.S. policy might have on China's future liberalization.

In trying to formulate a new and effective China policy—one designed to recover the ground lost over the past eight years—the United States faces a dilemma: There is actually little the United States can do directly to bring an end to dictatorship in China, while it is largely because it's a dictatorship that China constitutes a danger to the United States. On an ideological level, the very fact that they are dictators makes China's rulers hostile to a United States that represents and promotes democracy and individual rights as well as an open, market economy that nobody controls. Seeking to prolong their rule, China's rulers are turning to a chauvinist and expansionist nationalism to legitimize their leadership. That nationalism is today manifested in the Beijing regime's grandiose goal to dominate all of Asia as did the great Chinese dynasties of the past. That in turn constitutes a direct threat to Taiwan and China's other democratic neighbors—and to America's vital interest in a balance of power in Asia.

For the past decade, the debate over U.S. China policy has focused primarily not on the strategic threat that China poses to the United States but on the repression of basic human rights that is one of the main tools that the Beijing regime uses to stay in power. But the United States can do very little directly to reduce the regime's domestic repression. Ultimatums have been tried and failed. The "inevitable evolution" argument—that U.S. trade and investment will foster Chinese economic growth, which in turn will, at a minimum, force the regime to ease its repression and eventually to make way for democracy—has less and less credibility. For good reason: after more than two decades of rapid economic growth, China today is regressing, not progressing, in the area of human rights and political freedom.

Yet while there is little the United States can do directly to replace dictatorship with democracy in China, there is an enormous amount we can do indirectly to undermine the dictatorial regime in Beijing, and simultaneously advance concrete U.S. economic and military interests. *First,* we can counter the Beijing leadership's chauvinist and expansionist foreign and military policy—and the way the regime waves the flag of Chinese nationalism to rally popular support—by containing those aspirations through reinvigorated alliances in the East. The *second* thing the United States can do is confront Chinese mercantilism—the dictatorship's frantic attempts to keep afloat an increasingly distorted economy, in part by manipulating trade relations with the United States and other large market economies. And, *third,* the United States can get its own house in order by taking seriously the strategic problem presented by the rising ambitions and power of China.

Asian Alliances
Perhaps the single most effective thing we can do for freedom and democracy in China is support the free and democratic countries to China's east and south in resisting Chinese domination. If these countries succeed with our help in standing up to the bullying of their giant neighbor, that alone will significantly undermine the Beijing regime. To be exposed as an ineffectual bully can be disastrous for a dictatorship.

Already most of these countries are our friends and allies, but the Clinton administration has neglected them. We must strengthen these relationships by once again making it utterly unambiguous, in both word and deed, that our first commitment in Asia is to Japan and other democratic countries. It is here that our concrete interests and our most important values coincide. As we stand by these countries and work closely with them, we are not only supporting free democracies, we are firming up the balance of power in Asia that is vital to our future as a world power.

Of all our relationships with Asian democracies, the most important to be protected is with Japan. Its economic power and military potential are so great that if Japan were to shift to an opportunistic, neutral stance vis-à-vis the United States and China or, worse, effectively accept Chinese domination of Asia, it would be a disaster for us. With the stakes so high, we must solidify our long-term strategic relationship with Japan. That means both countries must discard what remains of the "protectorate psychology" of the post-war period. Indeed, the U.S.-Japan alliance won't be completely stable until we agree that the long-term goal of the alliance is to make Japan an equal partner of the United States in Asia, with shared responsibility to maintain the balance of power in the region.

If our relationship with Japan is the most important strategically, our relationship with Taiwan is the most pressing morally. The first order of business of a new administration would be to reverse the Clinton administration's view of Taiwan as a liability. Instead, Taiwan should be viewed as an asset, a de facto ally that is not only a democracy but also a key to maintaining a benign balance of power in Asia. As long as Taiwan remains independent, China will find it almost impossible to achieve its goal of dominating Asia.

What's more, the very existence of Taiwan as a separate, democratic and prosperous entity stands as a daily rebuke to the regime in Beijing, which claims that democracy and rapid economic development are incompatible. Jiang Zemin has declared that his most important mission is "reunification" with Taiwan. If the United States can frustrate his attempts to achieve that, we will be undermining the declared raison d'être of China's dictatorship.

Given President Clinton's efforts since 1996 to distance the United States from Taiwan, the next president must move quickly to strengthen U.S.-Taiwan ties. Above all, we must bring an end to any ambiguity about our commitment to intervene on Taiwan's behalf if China moves against the island militarily. We must also tell Beijing that we will view as a hostile act any attempt to set a timetable or a deadline for resolution of the Taiwan issue, as its recent white paper declared China might do. Any such attempt would amount to a thinly veiled threat to use military force against Taiwan.

We can reduce the chances of war even further by giving Taiwan the weapons systems it needs now to deter a Chinese attack. And, we must ensure that Taiwan has at least enough military capability to resist until the United States has time to mobilize and position its forces.

The WTO Trap

The second front we should open against China is economic. Clinton has fled from the fight against Chinese mercantilism throughout his presidency. The agreement that his administration reached with Beijing last fall over terms for China's entry to the World Trade Organization is not, given all we know about China's trade practices, going to result in a new era of opened Chinese markets. Clinton hailed the agreement with characteristic hyperbole by declaring that China had "embraced" the world trading system. Granted, there are a few, not very influential Chinese reformers who sincerely want a genuinely open and pluralistic economy. But the consensus in China today is that the WTO is a good thing because it will guarantee Chinese access to the U.S. and other industrial markets while China continues to find all kinds of informal and bureaucratic means to preclude reciprocal access. The Chinese are already making the Japanese of the 1970s look like Teddy bears by devising new barriers to imports of goods and services that will replace the barriers they've agreed to dismantle. In short, the WTO agreement is shaping up as a huge and damaging concession to China.

By approving permanent normal trade relations with China, Congress surrenders the most important nonmilitary leverage that the United States possesses against China. To retain that leverage, Congress needs to find some way to continually review trade relations with China and to impose high tariffs when, as is virtually inevitable, the current regime reneges on its WTO commitments. The WTO is an organization dedicated to a liberal economic order whose effectiveness turns on the support of the globe's leading democracies. China is neither dedicated to those economic principles, nor a democracy grounded in the rule of law. Either the

WTO will bend to Chinese behavior, or the WTO will try—but fail—
to bend China's current regime to its strictures. In either case, Congress must be prepared to review this issue.

The Home Front
A third front against China must be opened within the U.S. government itself. We need an entire change of mindset, starting at
the top. In foreign and military affairs at least, William Jefferson
Clinton was America's least strategically oriented president in many
decades. A new strategically minded president, focused long-term
on the national interests of the United States, will by definition
view China with great wariness.

The U.S. military must also be reoriented. Too much of our military planning and resource allocation is still Eurocentric, even
though no major or significant challenges to our vital national
interests loom in the European theater. The most likely wars, affect-
ing vital U.S. interests, that the United States will fight in the foreseeable future will be in the Asia-Pacific region. And we're not
ready.

Intelligence and counterintelligence also need shaking up. With
the partial exception of the Pentagon, the U.S. intelligence community sometimes seems almost blasé about the Chinese threat.
At best, the wariness level is far too low, and that helps explain
some of China's successes in recent years. Counterintelligence
directed at China, after being gutted, needs to be rebuilt.

China could collapse in economic and political disarray in a year
or two, but we cannot base China policy on that assumption any
more than we can base it on the assumption that China will
inevitably evolve into a market democracy. If we are going to prevail, we must be ready for a long, difficult period whose challenge
will be quite unlike that of the Cold War.

We have to find a new vocabulary for this conflict. George W.
Bush's declaration that China is our "competitor" and not our "strategic partner," as President Clinton claimed, is a good start. To that
end, officials in the new administration must be frank with the
American people and tell them that, while we are willing to work
with the Chinese to help them take their seat at the council of
nations, we have no interest in doing so if they continue on a path
whose goal is to challenge an international and regional security
order that is friendly to American principles, interests, and power.

This is not a new cold war. But the United States is once again on the right side of a serious and significant international competition. We stand for democracy and freedom. And we stand for a balance of power that can bring both prosperity and peace to Asia.

Russia:
The Challenge of
a Failing Power

During the Cold War, many in the West exaggerated the power
and durability of the Soviet Union and, particularly in its
later years, missed the signs of decay and overextension that led
the Soviet empire to its collapse. These days, we must guard against
the opposite mistake. As post-communist Russia has suffered
through its long economic and political ordeal, ruled for most of
that time by a seeming bumbler, it has been tempting to dismiss
it as an insignificant factor in international politics. But, as Tal-
leyrand once warned, Russia is never as strong—or as weak—as
it appears.

Russia under Vladimir Putin now presents a new face to the
world. Even in its reduced condition, Russia remains inescapably
a major power. Stretching over eleven time zones, possessing over
20,000 nuclear weapons and a veto in the UN Security Council,
exerting influence in such vital regions as Europe, the Middle East,
South Asia, and East Asia, and presiding over a vast economic and
technological potential that only awaits a more coherent government policy to realize it, Russia will be a preoccupation of American foreign policy now and in the decades to come. The recent
Chechen war only dramatized the problem. The Clinton administration's Russia policy, in which it invested so much political and
emotional capital, lies in shambles—including its assumption that
Russia was America's "strategic partner" in international affairs.
The next president of the United States will surely have to deal
with Russia, but with open eyes and a firm hand on his wallet.

Dashed Hopes

When Soviet communism fell apart a decade ago, the world was filled with awe at the historic transformation. The Red Army's brutal postwar occupation of Central and Eastern Europe abruptly ended. The global ideological thrust of a Leninist foreign policy, which had sustained radical movements from Latin America to Africa to the Middle East to Southeast Asia, collapsed. The USSR itself broke apart, liberating Ukraine, the Baltic states, and a dozen other republics. And Russia itself was launched on an unprecedented course of democratization.

Whatever problems may now exist in our relations with Russia, therefore, no one should ever doubt the profound change that has taken place. Whatever dark forces may tear at the fabric of Russian society today, a return to the communist past is probably the least likely path of its internal evolution. Post-Soviet Russia, for all its turmoil and uncertainties, has turned a new page in Russian—and world—history.

Yet, nothing could be clearer than that Russia has failed to live up to the high hopes once held out for it in the United States. Our faith in democracy led many Americans to expect that the triumph of true democracy in Russia was inevitable and irreversible. After a period of transition, Western-style political and economic institutions were expected to emerge, and Russia would evolve into a country looking much like the boring parliamentary democracies of Western Europe. Even more important, many also assumed that such a democratic Russia would be a natural friend of the United States. America, a nation whose very existence embodies the capacity of human beings to transcend history, expected that Russia too would transcend its past. It is not mean-spirited to observe, more than eight years after the dissolution of the USSR, that the reality of Russia's post-communist evolution has been a rude disappointment.

Genuinely democratic and pro-Western forces were indeed in the ascendant in Russia in those euphoric early years, but since then the picture has changed. While a private economy is developing, Russia's economic and political institutions are many years away from being normalized by Western standards. Russia may remain for some time in an anomalous and turbulent condition that is *sui generis,* neither a law-based market democracy on the

Western model nor a reversion to the past. In foreign policy, Russia has adapted to its reduced status and stifled the global ideological impulses that had so often led to trouble—for us or for itself—in the Soviet period. What is left, however, is a classical Russian foreign policy governed by economic and other geopolitical interests, and also by historic—and sometimes raw—nationalist reflexes. With the rapid rise of Vladimir Putin, former KGB operative, to the presidency, the near-comical image of Boris Yeltsin has given way almost overnight to something quite different: a more capable and vigorous leadership, more effective in its governance and more purposefully nationalist in its policies.

Even the Clinton administration's most prominent Russophile, Deputy Secretary of State Strobe Talbott, has betrayed a certain nervousness about possible future outcomes in Russia, "some of which are as ugly and dangerous as its past." Russia is a "work in progress," Talbott observed a few years ago, with many crucial questions still unanswered about its political culture, economic prospects, and relations with its neighbors.[1] The very unpredictability of Russia's near-term future argues against Western complacency about either its internal evolution or its foreign policy.

Thus, the starting point of any successful policy toward Russia is to shed illusions and to replace them with a dose of realism— realism about where Russia may be heading as a nation, realism about our relationship with it, and above all realism about how the United States can best serve its own interests in the world as Russia heads down its own rocky path.

We can start by facing some basic facts.

Russia's Faltering Reform

It is hard for Americans to conceive of a country that doesn't have enough lawyers. Yet that is Russia today. In the broadest sense, the rule of law is the missing component in both the economic and the political spheres. Dismantling of the Communist Party, state, and economy was a necessary condition for a free society. But it was not sufficient. The anarchic quality of much of Russia's public life today is a vivid demonstration of the philosophers' truth that law is what makes freedom possible.

This is true, literally, in the economic realm. In Western economies, businessmen rely on a foundation of legal principles and institutions that can enforce them. Those who try to do business in Russia these days can rely on neither. To this day, there is not a firm legal basis for private property, especially in land, or a reliable law of contracts or commercial code. In the jungle of the Russian business world, contract enforcement has too often become a function of organized crime groups, operating in their own inimitable style, rather than one of law.

These weaknesses in Russian institutions have combined with other endemic problems inherited from the Soviet era to produce an economic disaster. In the period 1991–1994, according to official statistics, Russia's gross domestic product (GDP) and per capita income declined by some 50 percent while prices increased 1200 percent.[2] While a "gray economy" undoubtedly took up part of the slack, this was a crisis far exceeding in both depth and duration the Great Depression of the 1930s in the United States. The social costs have been devastating. Demographic analyses show catastrophic declines in public health as measured by the resurgence of infectious diseases, the rise in infant mortality, and a decline in life expectancy—compounded by a horrific legacy of environmental degradation left over from unaccountable government in the Soviet period.[3]

While more recent figures suggest that the Russian economy may be slowly turning a corner—aided in part by high oil prices—the prospects for sustained recovery are still not bright. Unemployment in 1998–1999 was about 18 percent and inflation about 50 percent, lower than in past years but hardly comforting to the average Russian. Meanwhile, much of the economy operates on a barter system instead of cash transactions; the failure of tax collection perpetuates a governmental budgetary and financial crisis; and capital flight since 1987 is estimated at somewhere between $150 billion and $300 billion.[4] In August 1998 the ruble collapsed on international markets. A food shortage is expected this year; the need to tap into currency reserves to import grain could depress the currency again and trigger a new round of inflation. And (as Leonid Brezhnev found out), spikes in oil prices don't last forever.

Some of the structural weakness of the Russian economy is a product of how the "reform" process was conceived and undertaken. The good news is that privatization has successfully transferred 70 percent of Russia's GDP from state control into private hands. The bad news is that privatization has been conducted in a way that has made millionaires out of favored members of the old *nomenklatura* and created a new privileged class of oligarchs.[5] This new class emulates the predatory habits of America's 19th-century "robber barons" but without their constructive qualities. America's "robber barons" built railroads and industry, and later even discovered philanthropy; their capital accumulation was not all the result of governmental financial favors, and it was not all immediately transferred to Swiss bank accounts.

Russia's economic failures are directly related to its political failures. As former Prime Minister Sergei Kiriyenko has admitted, the Russian economic problem "is a political problem, namely, a basic weakness in the government's real power and authority. Most of the simple and natural prescriptions for reviving the Russian economy have come up against this important political weakness."[6]

The corruption and power of the new oligarchy are one symptom of the failure of Russia, so far, to develop a healthy civil society in the wake of totalitarianism's collapse. This is the fundamental weakness underlying the political system. Perhaps over time a healthy civil society will grow. But the oligarchs are entrenched. The true (noncorrupt) reformers remain a small minority, easily outmaneuvered in the political process.

In the meantime, the political system has suffered from other distortions. The vacuum of governmental authority cited by Kiriyenko has been, institutionally speaking, a function of the breakdown of relations between the executive and legislative branches. The requisite laws—the laws that might have created the foundation for normal economic life—never got passed by a Russian legislature dominated by communists and ultranationalists. Yeltsin then attempted to impose some of the reforms by decree—which deprived the reforms of democratic legitimacy. Democratic politics are never easy to manage, but in a society so desperately in need of decisive policies this paralysis of the political system has been a historic disaster.

It is no help that Russia has lacked a stable and functioning party system, such as can be found in the newly liberated democracies of Central Europe. In the early 1990s, Yeltsin had an opportunity to create a parliamentary party for himself, but he failed to do so, considering it beneath his presidential dignity. This was a fatal political blunder. A political party is the transmission belt of governmental authority. Especially in a system that separates the executive and legislative branches, a president cannot govern without a large bloc of troops loyal to him and his programs. As we know in our system, even if the president's party lacks a majority in the legislature, it gives the president some leverage over the process—and can provide political allies, as well, in regional power centers across the country. Not until the Duma elections of December 1999 did a significant pro-government bloc begin to take shape.

Sad to say, the memorable image of executive-legislative relations in the Yeltsin era was the picture of tanks lobbing shells into the parliament building in October 1993 (giving new meaning to the phrase "government shutdown"). While the reactionary views of the Supreme Soviet in those days led many (including the Clinton administration) to take Yeltsin's side in that confrontation, the setback to the evolution of normal constitutional practices in Russia may have been a fateful price to pay.[7]

Boris Yeltsin deserves history's everlasting gratitude for the role he played in destroying the communist system. Mikhail Gorbachev undermined the Soviet empire by mistake; Yeltsin resolutely drove the stake through its heart. Throughout his tenure, Yeltsin retained a remarkable moral clarity on a number of key issues: presiding at the re-interment of the Romanov bones to express his society's remorse; urging the removal of Lenin from his shrine in Red Square; forthrightly condemning anti-Semitism whenever it reappeared. Yeltsin's glaring inadequacy, of course, was as a builder of new institutions. Fortunate is the society whose founding leaders have both the vision and the decisiveness to create lasting institutions of democratic legitimacy—the framers of our Constitution; Konrad Adenauer and Charles de Gaulle; David Ben-Gurion. Russia's tragedy is that—again, unlike the Central Europeans—it has squandered the past decade in a swamp of corruption and the pettiest kinds of political warfare.

Did We "Lose" Russia?

A "strategic alliance with Russian reform" is how President Clinton described his partnership with Yeltsin in 1993.[8] Unfortunately, to many Russians, "reform" has become synonymous with semi-authoritarian and corrupt government, and U.S. advice and assistance over the past few years have become linked to failure in Russian minds. The assertiveness with which we proffered our help—and the reality of the disproportionate economic leverage that we (and our surrogate the International Monetary Fund) enjoyed—only fostered the impression that we shared responsibility for the dismal results. It was a short step from that to the belief, now held by an amazing 80 percent of Russians, that it was all a deliberate American plot to keep Russia weak.[9]

This is a canard. The Clinton administration's good intentions cannot be denied—only its judgment. It embraced individuals whom it identified with enlightened "reform," and who turned out to be deeply flawed if not venal, including leaders as prominent as economic adviser Anatolii Chubais and Prime Minister Viktor Chernomyrdin.[10] When the bad news started to come in, the administration went into denial. Russian authorities lied blatantly to the IMF in 1996 and 1998 about the state of the economy in order to keep loans coming—"we conned them," Chubais has admitted—but the lending continued, with the fig leaf of supposedly stricter "conditionality."[11] When the U.S. embassy and the CIA received information about corruption in the highest places, the White House made clear such reporting was not welcome.[12] In the fall of 1999, the corruption problem metastasized into a massive scandal involving offshore money laundering and reaching as high as Boris Yeltsin's family and entourage.[13] Then, and only then, did senior administration officials warn the Russian government to start cleaning up its act or face a cut-off of Western loans.

This is not a matter of "Who lost Russia?" since Russia was never ours to lose. Whatever the administration's mistakes as an enabler, the fundamental cause of the disaster has been the failure to build the institutions that would make a normal economy and political system possible. That was not our doing.

What can be said, however, is that the Clinton administration has fallen short of its own stated goal of helping bring genuine reform to Russia. In its unwavering embrace of Yeltsin and his advisers as the embodiment of all hopes, it strove to further *their* interests within the Russian political maelstrom. In so doing, the Clinton administration not only lost the good will of the Russian people; it too often lost sight of *America's* interests and even sacrificed those interests in pursuit of its illusory "strategic partnership."

The Emerging Contours of Russian Foreign Policy

If the direction of Russia's future political and economic evolution is today uncertain, ironically the direction of Russia's foreign policy has become much clearer. Having abandoned Marxist-Leninist ideology as the basis for their external relations, Russians have gone through an intense introspection about their nation's new place in a world dominated by the West. But that period of reassessment is now over. Yeltsin declared proudly in 1998, "Russia is demonstrating in practice that it has to be reckoned with."[14]

The firing of Foreign Minister Andrei Kozyrev in January 1996 and his replacement by Yevgenii Primakov was a watershed. A shift in the direction of Russian foreign policy had, to be sure, occurred earlier; Kozyrev had long since been unable to sustain domestically the close association with the West with which he was identified. But with Primakov's appointment, the shift toward a less sentimental approach to the U.S.-led West was complete.[15]

The guiding principle of Russian global policy today is not to welcome the American embrace but to keep America at arm's length. In fact, in the "unipolar" world of American "hegemony," Russia sees its prime goal as restoring "multipolarity" to the international system—that is, to build counterweights against American dominance. As Primakov stated in his address as foreign minister to the UN General Assembly in September 1996, one of the conditions for a durable peace was

> the emancipation from the mentality of "those who lead" and "those who are led." Such a mentality draws on illusions that some countries emerged as winners from the Cold War, while others lost it. But this is not the case. Peoples on both sides of the Iron Curtain jointly got rid of the policy of confrontation. Meanwhile the mentality of "those who lead" and "those who are led" directly paves the way for a tendency to establish a unipolar world. Such a world order is unacceptable to the overwhelming majority of the international community.[16]

"The time has come," Yeltsin warned, "to understand that in the present-day world, particularly in the twenty-first century, no state, however strong, can impose its will on others."[17] "Russia was and will remain a great power," asserts Vladimir Putin. "It is preconditioned by the inseparable characteristics of its geopolitical, economic and cultural existence."[18] Former Prime Minister Kiriyenko recently said he expected the United States to take Russia's interests into account only where Russia was in a position to defend them. Russia had to build up its economic strength, "and in this, no one will help us. . . . The illusion that someone will bother with our national interests is gone. Each [country] defends its own interests."[19]

Russia's independence, and even its re-emergence as a great power, are not intrinsically a threat to the United States. Nonetheless, Russo-American relations ought today to be viewed by Americans without the sentimentality of the early post-Soviet years— just as they are now clearly viewed by Russians. Where the Clinton team has imagined a Wilsonian affinity between a "progressive" American administration and the forces of "reform" in Russia, Russians themselves are thinking in more classical terms about how to define their national interests in the extraordinary circumstances in which they now find themselves. Resisting American dominance is and will continue to be a main part of that definition.

In the summer of 1998, then–Foreign Minister Yevgenii Primakov delivered a revealing lecture at the Russian foreign ministry on the 200th anniversary of the birth of Prince Aleksandr M. Gorchakov, Russia's distinguished statesman of the mid-nineteenth century who served as foreign minister after Russia was defeated in the Crimean War. As Primakov noted pointedly, "many at that time thought they were present at a funeral for the Russian Empire, or at any rate witnessing its turning into a second-rate power."[20] Some thought the country had no choice but to "resign its great power status, quit the international scene, and . . . accept the rules of the game the victors forced on the conquered." Gorchakov chose a different course: advocating internal reforms to restore Russia's strength, coupled with a "vigorous foreign policy to guarantee better conditions for internal renewal." Over the next thirty years, Gorchakov achieved these goals far better than anyone could have imagined.

Primakov drew from Gorchakov's historical example five lessons for Russian foreign policy today.

First, Gorchakov demonstrated that for a weakened Russia, an active foreign policy was not only a possibility but a necessity. "Foreign policy abhors a vacuum." Only an active foreign policy could ensure that Russia preserved its independence and its hopes for recovering great-power status. Gorchakov was able to maneuver successfully to help prevent an international system in which "any one power [could] rise above the others and gain dominating positions."

Second, Russian foreign policy could not be "limited to some single direction." It ought to foster relations with all international players, big powers and small, in all regions of interest to Russia.

Third, Gorchakov never doubted that Russia had "enough strength to play the part of a leading state on the international scene." Modern Russia, Primakov added, had more than enough geopolitical and material potential to do this.

Fourth, while Russia's scale and weight objectively gave it an important world role, in present circumstances this was enhanced by "the unquestionable unwillingness of the vast number of states to agree to a world order determined by one power."

Fifth, Gorchakov was wrong (in Primakov's view) to pursue shifting alliances in Europe's balance of power. Far better to work consistently for a "multipolar democratic world" in partnership with "all the emerging world poles" of power.

Primakov concluded that Russia today should seek "equal and mutually beneficial partnership" with the West, but not sacrifice its national interests; that Moscow should forswear any dream of reconstructing the "Empire and the Soviet Union," but that economic reintegration with its immediate neighbors was "becoming one of the most important tasks of the Russian foreign policy of today"; that Russia had to come to terms with the changes in its position in the past decade, but a narrow localism in its foreign policy would "unjustifiably constrain Russia's interests, which are of world proportion in some parameters."

"There are no constant enemies," Primakov pointed out, "but there are constant interests"—a bit of classical wisdom that would find no parallel in the more romantic rhetoric of the Clinton administration. Not to mention the nearly obsessive objection to American dominance that runs through the entire Primakov thesis and has become the central theme of Russian policy, and which similarly finds no acknowledgement in Clinton administration discussions of Russia.

This philosophy today inspires Russian foreign policy in ways that are troublesome for the United States on such vitally important issues as China, Iran and Iraq, Europe, and strategic arms control.

Russia and China

The rapprochement between Moscow and Beijing goes back at least to Mikhail Gorbachev. Under his aegis, what China labeled the "three obstacles" to normalized relations—the Soviet occupation of Afghanistan, the Vietnamese occupation of Cambodia, and the Soviet military threat along the Chinese border—were all resolved or substantially eased. The Sino-Russian breakthrough was symbolized by Gorbachev's visit to Beijing in May 1989, coinciding (in one of history's little ironies) almost exactly with the upheaval in Tiananmen Square, which struck a blow to the Sino-American relationship from which it has not yet recovered. Thus was the "strategic triangle" wrought by Nixon and Kissinger essentially reversed.

Yeltsin continued and institutionalized what Gorbachev began. Putin announced that he intended his first foreign visit to be to China. The pattern is now an annual summit of presidents, semiannual meetings of prime ministers, and more frequent meetings of foreign ministers, punctuating a burgeoning cooperation in the economic and military fields. They have finalized an agreement on delineating the 4,000-kilometer Sino-Russian border, resolving a century and a half of disputes and eliminating the problem that generated violent clashes in the 1960s—the same clashes that prompted the Sino-American rapprochement in the first place.

Most important, Russia and China have made common cause in the grand project of restoring "multipolarity" to the global system. When Chinese Premier Li Peng met with Yeltsin in Moscow at the end of December 1996, their joint communiqué declared this to be the purpose of their "strategic cooperation": the two sides agreed that "a partnership of equal rights and trust between Russia and China aimed at strategic cooperation in the 21st century ... promotes the formation of a multipolar world."[21] When Yeltsin visited Jiang Zemin in Beijing in April 1996, the rhetoric on both the Russian and Chinese sides was extraordinary in its bluntness. The two leaders came close to branding the United States a threat to peace. "[T]he world is far from being tranquil," they declared. "Hegemonism, power politics and repeated imposition of pressures on other countries have continued to occur. Bloc politics has taken up new manifestations."[22] Yeltsin warned of an attempt by unnamed countries to "dominate" the world and celebrated the fact that "Russia and China are [as] one in creation of a new world order, in which no one will aspire to a monopoly in world affairs."[23] On Yeltsin's last visit to Beijing, in December 1999, he and Jiang repeated the catalogue of complaints against American impositions and spoke openly of their own "strategic partnership" and foreign policy "coordination."[24]

The two countries have found common ground on a wide range of key issues, all contrary to American preferences. China has endorsed Russian policy in Chechnya and supported Russia's opposition to NATO enlargement. Russia has endorsed China's policies in Taiwan and Tibet. Both have vigorously opposed NATO's military involvement in the Balkan crises, seeing the new Western doctrine of "humanitarian interventionism" as a blank check for American global ambitions. Both are eager to constrain U.S. deployment of missile defenses. Both have denounced Washington's attempts to use its economic leverage for political ends. The Chinese are especially pleased by Russia's stance on human rights in China. "Russia," one Chinese scholar has noted, "unlike some Western countries, has refrained from attempting to interfere in the internal affairs of China."[25]

The Russians, of course, have economic incentives for cozying up to China. As Russia's defense budget declines, as the Russian military shrinks, and as Russia's defense industries consequently starve from lack of domestic procurement, Russia profits from having China as a big-time paying customer for weapons and other defense production. According to Russian sources, arms exports finance more than 50 percent of the country's military production, and the largest portion of this comes from China.[26] The military-industrial complex continues to wield disproportionate clout in Russia's turbulent politics—and also views cooperation with China as having strategic value in countering the United States. One Russian military commentator, for example, was pleased to note that the "active promotion of Russian armaments in the Asia-Pacific Region is leading to a new balance of power taking shape there, in which the United States will no longer play the decisive role."[27]

"The stronger China becomes, the more peace and stability in the region will benefit," Primakov proclaimed categorically in

1996.[28] Thus, it is a combination of commercial and strategic calculation that accounts for the extraordinary expansion of Russian arms sales to China, by which the latter has obtained some of Russia's most advanced equipment. This includes state-of-the-art anti-ship weapons designed to sink American ships, as well as Russia's most modern aircraft (Su-27 jet fighters and Su-30 fighter-bombers).[29] As one observer put it, Russia has become the "Toys R Us" for Chinese military supply.[30]

To be sure, some prominent Russians worry that their government is playing with fire. Fears are sometimes vented in the Russian popular media that China is more of a threat to Russia than a partner. The hundreds of thousands, perhaps millions, of legal and illegal Chinese immigrants pouring into the Russian Far East raise a specter in some Russian minds of Chinese penetration if not eventual annexation of the area.[31] In the context of Yeltsin's 1996 visit to Beijing, Russian officials took pains to reassure an anxious parliament and public that China "does not pose any threat to Russia in the foreseeable future."[32]

So it is not 1950 all over again. The Sino-Russian relationship today lacks the global scope and ideological impetus of the alliance period and, even more than that alliance, contains the seeds of its possible future undoing. As that Sino-Soviet alliance fell apart because of Chinese fear of Soviet power, this "strategic partnership" is vulnerable because of Russian fears of growing Chinese power.

It is in the West's interest that the door always be open to Russia to reverse course. Russia must always have a Western option. But having a Western option should be at least as important to Russia as it is to us. Policies that exacerbate the West's major strategic problems (such as arming China) do not help keep that door open. If Russia wants to keep a Western option, the price for it must be respect for the West's vital interests. The Clinton administration's obliviousness to this principle has been one of the most disturbing elements of its Russia policy.

Russia and Iran

Similar problems exist with respect to Russia's relations with Iran. Russia is one of Iran's principal foreign suppliers of conventional weapons, as well as nuclear assistance. The conventional arms relationship is reflected in the supply of modern jet fighters, bombers, tanks, helicopters, and submarines. The United States has formally protested Russia's sale to Iran of parts and know-how for the construction of Iran's Shahab-3 and Shahab-4 missiles. (The Shahab-3 will have a range of 1,300 kilometers with a 700-kg warhead.)[33] Russia has also been selling Iran, at bargain-basement prices, some of its most advanced anti-aircraft missiles, including shoulder-fired SA-18's, and with the knowledge that Tehran planned to transfer several of them to Hizbollah terrorists.[34] Russian-Iranian nuclear cooperation, enshrined in a January 1995 agreement between the two countries' atomic energy organizations, involves the supply of a thirty- to fifty-megawatt light-water reactor and of two thousand tons of natural uranium to the Iranian nuclear power plant at Bushehr, plus a contract for training Iranian nuclear scientists at Russian academic institutions.[35] Russia reportedly has been paid more than $6 billion for the weapons since 1992 and will receive $3–4 billion for the nuclear project.[36] The missile transfers have long been a bone of contention with the United States and have resulted in U.S. sanctions against Russian companies that persist in the activity.

What are Russia's motives for selling conventional arms, missiles, and nuclear technology to Iran? As with China, the commercial benefits are obvious, especially as others among Russia's traditional Middle East customers (like Iraq and Syria) are cash-strapped or debt-ridden or otherwise unable to pay for significant arms purchases. Bureaucratic pressures, such as from the Russian Ministry of Atomic Energy, are undoubtedly real, and administrative controls over the frenetic arms sales may have broken down in general. But it would be a serious error to assume that Russia's commercial motivations conflict with its policy preferences. When then–Foreign Minister Primakov visited Tehran in December 1996, he hailed the two countries' "converging viewpoints on many international issues."[37]

The Russians have aligned themselves with Iran's diplomatic positions on a number of key Persian Gulf issues: that Iran should not be excluded from regional security arrangements, that the U.S. naval presence in the Gulf is "unnecessary," that territorial disputes between Iran and the Arabs over small islands in the Gulf should be handled as Iran prefers, etc.[38] Primakov denounced the U.S. Fifth Fleet in the Gulf as an "alien presence,"[39] and went out of his way to defend Islamic fundamentalism as a noble force in the world, not to be equated with extremism as the West is wont to do.[40]

Russia's cooperation with Iran serves a variety of geopolitical purposes. For one thing, Russia's historical and natural concern with the security of its frontiers leads it, in this day and age, to worry about Islamist influence in Central Asia and the Caucasus. Coopting the Islamic Republic of Iran is an element of its strategy.

It is surprising how smoothly this has gone. With ideology a less intense force in both Russia and Iran, national interests come to the fore. And these interests today point to mutual accommodation. Thus, Iran has kept a low profile so far in the ex-Soviet Muslim republics, emphasizing economic and cultural links rather than overt Islamist agitation. Both Moscow and Tehran oppose the Taliban in Afghanistan. Iran offered its diplomatic mediation in Moscow's Tajik war. Nor has there been a peep out of Tehran criticizing the brutality in Chechnya. There is a modus vivendi in a region that could have become a focus of conflict between Russia and Iran. The two countries have seen a common interest in blunting Turkey's influence and in dividing up the territory when it comes to energy resources in the Caspian Basin.[41]

But one of the most important geopolitical purposes on both sides has to do with the United States. For Russia, it is an opportunity to fill a vacuum—to make inroads in a strategic Middle Eastern country that the United States has ostracized and to make common cause against U.S. "hegemony." Andranik Migranyan, a prominent academic and occasional adviser to Yeltsin, told *Iran News* that in many areas "Iran can be a good and strategic ally of Russia at [the] global level to check the hegemony of third parties and keep the balance of power." While trying "not to damage our relations with the West," Migranyan declared, Russia would "not let the West dictate to Russia how far it can go in its relations." Russia would continue to "cooperate with Iran as a big regional power."[42] A nationalist Russian writer summed up the relationship in even blunter terms in early 1995:

Cooperation with Iran is more than just a question of money and orders for the Russian atomic industry. Today a hostile Tehran could cause a great deal of unpleasantness for Russia in the North Caucasus and in Tajikistan if it were to really set its mind to supporting the Muslim insurgents with weapons, money and volunteers. On the other hand, a friendly Iran could become an important strategic ally in the future.

NATO's expansion eastward is making Russia look around hurriedly for at least some kind of strategic allies. In this situation, the anti-Western and anti-American regime in Iran would be a natural and very important partner. Armed with Russian weapons, including the latest types of sea mines, torpedoes and anti-ship missiles, Iran could, if necessary, completely halt the passage of tankers through the Strait of Hormuz, thereby dealing a serious blow to the haughty West in a very sensitive spot.[43]

The Russian-Iranian connection is thus unmistakably a strategic one. A Western observer might suggest that here too, as with China, Russia is playing with fire in the longer run—especially by helping Iran's nuclear program. On the other hand, Russia has been playing the "Great Game" in this part of the world for centuries, and Russian leaders are confident they know what they are doing. The relationship serves too many obvious strategic purposes on both sides.

Unfortunately, Russian-Iranian cooperation comes at America's expense, in another region where U.S. interests can truly be called vital. Yet the Clinton administration, imagining still that Russia is *its* strategic partner, has responded too little and too late, pressuring Russia only when pressured to do so by Congress.

Russia and Iraq

Russia's support of Iraq's Saddam Hussein has been another problem. The Russian-American consensus that so remarkably characterized the 1990–91 Gulf crisis is no more—another casualty of the nationalist turn in Russian foreign policy. In recent years, as Saddam has thwarted efforts to dismantle his programs for weapons of mass destruction and attempted to break out of the isolation imposed on him in the settlement of the Gulf War, Russia has increasingly taken his side. Russia has led diplomatic efforts to ease UN sanctions and vigorously opposed U.S.-British efforts to punish Iraq's violations by force. Clearly, Russia has been champing at the bit to resume at least part of its earlier patron-client relationship with Iraq. Iraq policy thus serves as yet another issue on which Russia can foster "multipolarity" and demonstrate its "independence" from the United States.[44]

A typical example was Foreign Minister Primakov's conduct during the Iraq crisis of November 1997. Following Saddam's expulsion of American UN weapons inspectors, Primakov demonstratively convened a meeting of the foreign ministers of the five Security Council permanent members at 2:00 A.M. in Geneva with the aim of heading off any U.S. effort to build a consensus for the use of force. A flimsy accord was put together readmitting the inspectors. (It didn't last long.) The Russian press hailed Primakov for having "demonstrated the ability that Russia still has in world affairs, even in its current very weakened state."[45]

Russia's eagerness to see UN sanctions lifted or eased is often attributed to the $7 billion prewar debt that Iraq owes Russia. But there must also be a residual temptation to resume a profitable relationship from the time when Moscow was a major arms supplier. Iraq's oil minister visited Moscow in May 1999, moreover, to discuss the Russian oil giant Lukoil's possible exploitation of Iraq's West Qurna oil fields. Russian Foreign Minister Igor Ivanov took the opportunity to assure him of the "active steps" that Russia was taking in the UN Security Council to create a more lenient system of UN arms monitoring and easing of sanctions.[46] Meanwhile, the Russians vigorously denied reports in the London *Sunday Telegraph* in February 1999 claiming that Iraq's transport minister, on a recent trip to Moscow, had signed contracts worth over £100 million by which Russia would re-equip the Iraqi air force and air defense systems.[47] If true, this would be a blatant violation of UN sanctions.

Russia and Europe

In Europe, Russia's foreign policy has been more circumspect. If Russia's assessment of its national interest leads it to behave as a status quo power in Europe, this would augur well for Russia's relations with the West in what was, after all, the central theater of the Cold War. Not coincidentally, Europe is the region where the West has been more assertive of *its* interests.

Russian leaders have insisted that Moscow accepts the independence of all the new states born from the rubble of the Soviet empire. "The present reality," Primakov declared in his 1998

Gorchakov lecture, "is such that the sovereignty of the ex-USSR republics should not be subject to whatever doubt."[48] Boris Yeltsin deserves particular credit for the statesmanship with which potentially explosive conflicts with Ukraine were avoided—over the Black Sea fleet, control of the Crimea, and the status of the large and rambunctious Russian-speaking minority in Ukraine. While NATO's admission of Poland, Hungary, and the Czech Republic was the subject of considerable Russian bluster, in the end Moscow acquiesced, content to extract a host of reassurances and commitments from an (overly) anxious U.S. administration.

Disputes with the West have persisted in other areas, however. The crises in both Bosnia (1994–95) and Kosovo (1998–99) led to tensions as Russia reacted bitterly to NATO bombing. In the end, Russia acquiesced in NATO actions it could not stop, but serious differences of perspective, philosophy, and interest remain. The sources of these differences are many: a traditional Russian sympathy for fellow Orthodox Serbs; a sense of strategic humiliation that NATO, its old adversary, continued to expand its sphere of influence eastward, barely a year after effusively assuring Moscow of the alliance's purely defensive character; and a broader strategic fear that the cause of human rights is being used by the West as a formula for global interventionism free of any restraints by institutions, like the UN Security Council, in which Russia has a veto. Foreign Minister Ivanov put the issue this way in a June 1999 article:

> Attempts to justify the use of force without the consent of the UN Security Council, as by citing some kind of "right to humanitarian interference" do not stand up to criticism. Such use of force becomes a hostage to the political predilections and biased interpretation of events. No one has the right—without a mandate from the international community—to judge who is right and who is wrong and how to punish a culprit. That is a direct road to anarchy and chaos in the world. Russia condemns the violation of human rights and international humanitarian law by whoever and wherever they are committed. At the same time we are convinced that these phenomena can only be combated on the solid foundation of international laws.[49]

The status of the three Baltic states remains another potential problem. Russia's bullying of Latvia, in particular, over allegations of mistreatment of the Russian minority only serves to keep the question of NATO protection for these countries on the agenda. There are two separate issues: whether the Baltic states owe their Russian-speaking citizens full rights (which they clearly do), and whether bullying tactics by Russia raise a larger question of its behavior as an "evolved" modern nation. The fact that the Balts were formerly part of the USSR cannot be an excuse for infringements of their sovereign independence: the Molotov-Ribbentrop Pact is no longer operative. The West will need to decide how best to deter Russian pressures on the Baltic states, and a variety of options are available, of which NATO membership is one. But the West is bound to view Russia's conduct in this matter as a litmus test of its commitment to peace in Europe—and as another test of the compatibility of its interests with ours.

Strategic Arms Control

So far, the Reagan- and Bush-era U.S.-Russian strategic arms reduction treaties (START I and START II) have continued to represent a significant mutual interest. The same is true of cooperation in containing the problem of "loose nukes" on ex-Soviet soil. The West has a strong stake, as well, in Russian adherence to the limitations on conventional armed forces in Europe. But a large gap now exists between Russian and American perceptions of post–Cold War strategic realities. And that gap is growing—masked though it is by the intellectual confusion of the Clinton administration.

The new reality is that America's strategic problems can no longer be addressed simply by arms control agreements with Moscow. During the Cold War, the bilateral U.S.-Russian relationship alone defined American strategy. Today, however, American leaders have the duty to defend the United States, its forces abroad, and its allies from attack by rogue states with weapons of mass destruction; and they need to plan for the gradual emergence of China as a major nuclear power. The West has accordingly accelerated its pursuit of ballistic-missile defenses, to which the Russians object and against which they invoke the bilateral U.S.-Soviet Anti-Ballistic Missile (ABM) Treaty of 1972.

The Russians, to be sure, are schizophrenic when it comes to missile defense. The virtues of missile defense, after all, have been a staple of Soviet and Russian strategic doctrine for decades. Some of the threats to which the West is responding—rogue states and China—are potential threats to Russia, too. (The Russian defense ministry agrees.)[50] But the Russians are congenitally afraid of American technological breakthroughs—*especially* in a field like missile defense, which they strongly believe in.

Since the motivation for U.S. missile defenses today is not anti-Russian, it makes sense for any American administration to start by talking to Moscow about the ABM Treaty. There are two possible ways for an American government to approach this. It could seek to carve out some understandings with Russia giving both sides greater freedom of action to develop the needed missile defenses against a common challenge. If the Russians proved obstructionist in their talks—too eager to limit technical capabilities that the United States and its allies needed to protect themselves—the United States would always retain the option of withdrawing from the Treaty. That was the Bush administration's approach: In June 1992, President Bush and Boris Yeltsin agreed to pursue a limited global missile-defense program jointly, by implication agreeing to carve out whatever freedom of action was necessary under the ABM Treaty.[51] (In fact, this was originally Yeltsin's idea.)

The Clinton administration, however, has deliberately pulled the Russians in the opposite direction. Whereas Richard Nixon and Henry Kissinger, architects of the ABM Treaty, long since concluded that the Treaty had outlived its purpose,[52] the Clinton arms controllers hate strategic defense out of liberal doctrinal passion and therefore continue to worship the ABM Treaty as "a cornerstone of stability."[53] Thus, with their priorities totally backwards, they have been willing to sacrifice American technological capabilities in order to preserve the sanctity of the Treaty. Alas, the Russians have been more than willing to seize the opportunity handed them to constrain U.S. technological development.

The administration has compounded the error in its attempt to bribe the Russians into a comprehensive agreement on further reduction of offensive weapons (START III) together with (very constrained) deployments of missile defenses. The American side has been considering new, lowered ceilings on strategic offensive weapons (perhaps as low as one to two thousand). That might be fine if the only challenge we faced were Russia. But such low ceilings can only tempt the Chinese to redouble *their* missile buildup.

By the end of the decade, the Chinese are expected to deploy a MIRV'd mobile ICBM,[54] which will surely affect our future strategic requirements (and the Russians' too). It is folly to pursue bilateral U.S.-Russian arms reductions without regard to the China factor.

Chechnya

The brutal suppression of Chechnya has illuminated yet again the dark side of Russian policy. It was a depressing close to the Clinton administration's long effort to bring post-communist Russia into the moral mainstream of the West.

It cannot be Western policy to seek the breakup of the Russian Federation. Nor was it obvious what the West could have done to change Russia's policy. The crackdown in Chechnya was, above all, *popular* in Russia; it triggered a resurgence of nationalism in the country that transformed Russia's domestic politics. As we saw in both December's Duma election and Putin's rapid ascendancy, Chechnya strengthened nationalist forces and weakened many moderate and more genuinely pro-Western and reformist political groupings.

At the very least, however, the Chechnya war should serve as a wake-up call to the West. It is a case study in Moscow's political clumsiness and casual resort to force, an indicator of what Russian nationalism, even of the democratic variety, can look like. Moscow's pressures on Georgia (in connection with the alleged harboring of Chechen rebels) are a harbinger of a tougher Russian policy in its "near abroad." It would have been useful to make Russia pay some political price, if only to discourage its resort to force in future conflicts with neighboring countries. Chechnya, in short, is a reminder that Russia could get back on its feet geopolitically long before it gets back on its feet economically.

U.S. Policy after Clinton

Of all the elements of unpredictability in a very fluid post–Cold War world, the uncertainty of Russia's domestic evolution is one of the most glaring. Putin's Russia seems precariously poised between democracy and authoritarianism, between stagnation and economic revival, between resentment of the West and eagerness to keep ties with it. Yet, as already noted, the great paradox is that, with all this domestic uncertainty, the thrust of Russia's foreign policy is already clear. History and geography give Russia a keen sense of its natural sphere of influence and its imperative of maintaining stability around its periphery. Its power, potential if not actual, gives it an aspiration to be treated as an equal by the West, and its present weakness gives it a strategic interest in blocking what it sees as American political and economic dominance. Whether Russia evolves more toward democracy or away from it, what we see now is probably the real center of gravity of Russian foreign policy.

Conflict between Russia and the United States is certainly not foreordained. There are many converging or parallel interests, especially if Russia demonstrates that it indeed respects the sovereign independence of all its neighbors. China looms large, as noted, as a long-term factor over which Russia may ultimately choose to reverse course and tilt toward the West.

The Clinton administration deserves credit for getting a number of things right. It proceeded with NATO membership for Poland, Hungary, and the Czech Republic (after Republican prodding); and it has been forward-leaning with respect to possible NATO membership or other security guarantees for other countries newly liberated from the Soviet empire. The administration has shown good strategic judgment in extending material as well as political support to bolster the independence of Ukraine, Georgia, Azerbaijan, and other ex-Soviet republics, including the new grouping nicknamed "GUUAM" (comprising Georgia, Ukraine, Uzbekistan, Azerbaijan, and Moldova). It has also been correct in preferring oil and gas pipeline routes that would enable newly independent Central Asian and Caucasus republics to avoid either Russian or Iranian dominance.

But on other matters, the administration has tripped up. The absurd doctrinal fetish it has made of the ABM Treaty has been discussed. Its timidity about making American goodwill conditional on more sensible Russian policies toward China, Iran, and Iraq is another lapse of strategic judgment. This bespeaks a sentimentality toward Russia, an unwillingness to assert major American strategic interests and impose a penalty for harm done to them, lest the poor Russians feel hurt. This is not serious foreign policy, and it must invite contempt from the Russians (and Chinese,

Iranians, and Iraqis). This posture is of a piece with the blind eye turned to corrupt economic "reforms" and lying to the IMF.

Paternalism of this kind is ultimately insulting to the Russians. It treats them as children who must be indulged, lest harsh responses upset or alienate them. A policy of realism, in contrast, would pay the Russians more respect, even as it championed American interests. It would treat Russia as a serious power responsible for its actions; it would foster more realistic expectations by linking our goodwill to those Russian actions that are compatible with our interests, instead of to personalities whom we are then driven to romanticize. We do the Russian people no favor by glossing over the glaring anomalies in their country's domestic evolution, and we do ourselves no favor by turning a blind eye to the negative trends in Russia's foreign policy. Realism would be a basis for steadiness and consistency in our own policy, cushioning it against disillusionment.

The leaders of post-communist Russia have already reached this state of maturity; they have arrived at a reasonable definition of their strategic interests in new conditions. It is time the American side did the same.

Iraq:
Saddam Unbound

In the summer of 1999, the leaders of the U.S. Congress, including Senators Joseph Lieberman and Trent Lott, sent a sharply worded letter to the Clinton administration to express their dismay over "the continued drift in U.S. policy in Iraq."[1] The letter complained about the administration's refusal to help the Iraqi opposition free their country from the totalitarian vise of Saddam Hussein's regime.

The question of how to deal with Iraq has caused a remarkable division between the Clinton administration and a bipartisan majority of both houses of Congress. Congress has understood that Saddam Hussein threatens American interests in the Gulf to a degree that cannot be overcome by diplomatic accommodation. The Clinton administration—its occasional rhetoric to the contrary notwithstanding—has been content to leave Saddam in power. Not since the Cold War, when the issue was whether to accept the permanence of the Soviet Union and find ways to get along with it, or challenge its legitimacy and develop policies to bring about its demise, has Washington seen two such starkly different approaches to a foreign country.

Congress has authorized and voted funds to begin a program to replace Saddam by uniting and supporting Iraqi freedom fighters.[2] The Clinton administration, despite having signed the Iraq Liberation Act into law, has opposed any such plan and has sought to undermine even those steps the Iraqi opposition has taken on its own to fulfill Congress's more assertive policy.

The direction of the administration's policy can be seen in the use it has made of the resources Congress has appropriated to assist the Iraqi opposition. At the beginning of the year 2000, the administration had spent a mere $20,000 of the more than $100 million (in funds and equipment) appropriated over eighteen months earlier to aid the opposition to Saddam Hussein. More- over, administration plans for aiding the Iraqi opposition consisted of little more than proposals to ship office furniture and obsolete computers from the Department of Defense to opposition group headquarters in London. The Iraqi National Congress, the princi- pal umbrella group uniting opposition organizations, has scoffed at the administration's claim to have a detailed program to sup- port the opposition. Graduate students will one day write doctoral theses on this case study in how an administration can frustrate the intent of Congress by pretending to implement legislation it is determined to vitiate.[3]

The Clinton administration policy toward Iraq, which leaves Saddam in place while claiming to have him "contained," is bound to fail. It ignores the increasing strength of Saddam's position and the accelerating decline of our own. It depends on a continuation of ever-weaker sanctions to obscure the decisive victory Saddam will achieve when the sanctions are eventually lifted. It ignores the deterioration of the coalition once arrayed against Saddam, and the emergence of France, China and Russia as opponents of tough measures against Saddam and advocates of lifting those sanctions still in force. It leaves to the next administration a legacy of weak- ness and vacillation: pinprick military strikes that served princi- pally to bolster the myth of Saddam's invincibility; endless nego- tiations aimed at restoring United Nations inspections on terms acceptable to Saddam and his friends on the Security Council; and a willingness to accept Saddam's rule in Iraq which has demoral- ized his opponents and undermined resistance in the region.

Current policy fails to comprehend the fundamental nature of Saddam Hussein's regime as well as the likely consequences of his removal from power. This failure springs from deep within the institutions charged with setting and implementing policy in the Mideast, and from the adoption of the view of the Departments of State and Defense and the Central Intelligence Agency by an admin- istration that came to office with neither knowledge nor experi- ence of the region.[4] It seems obvious that current policy toward Iraq—cling to the sanctions and hope for the best—cannot protect

American interests in the Gulf region or the world. As support for the sanctions now in force has diminished, the embargo by which the United Nations has tried to regulate the flow of goods and services into Iraq has become increasingly porous, and is now routinely circumvented. Oil exports from Iraq are currently at or near their pre–Gulf War level, and the goods and services flowing into Iraq go far beyond the "humanitarian" imports allowed by the United Nations.[5] With UN inspectors having been expelled from Iraq, we no longer know how far Saddam's program to acquire weapons of mass destruction has progressed. It is simply a matter of time before the combination of televised images of hungry Iraqi children, the opposition of three of the five permanent members of the UN Security Council, and the obvious inefficacy of the sanctions leads to their abandonment. Yet the Clinton administration appears indifferent to this troubling prospect. It is hard to escape the conclusion that it is mainly concerned with getting past November's presidential election without further trouble from Iraq.

Several flawed ideas have led the administration into an Iraqi policy marked by passivity and drift. The most important of these have to do with (a) a fixation on the issue of stability in Iraq and the Gulf region, (b) a mistaken belief that turbulence in Iraq would strengthen Iran, and (c) the stubborn insistence that Saddam can only be brought down by a Sunni coup from within the regime and not by a politico-military strategy of support to the Iraqi opposition. Particularly when it comes to supporting the Iraqi opposition, as the Congress has urged, there is a pervasive fear in the Clinton White House that the opposition would get into trouble and have to be rescued by the United States. I call this particular administration obsession the "Bay of Pigs syndrome" because administration officials frequently compare the Iraqi opposition to the anti-Castro force that was trapped on a Cuban beach in 1962.

The Question of Stability: The Clinton administration, even more than the Bush administration before it, has elevated an American interest in "stability" to the central focus of U.S. diplomacy. In Haiti, Bosnia and Kosovo, the restoration of "stability" became a principal rationale for American military intervention. In North Korea, "stability" has made a totalitarian regime the largest recipient of American foreign aid in Asia. In Iraq, "stability" has kept the Clinton administration from taking the risks involved in waging a campaign to remove Saddam from office.

The obsession with "stability" has inevitably led the administration to regard Saddam's repression as a tolerable price to pay for maintaining it. But the idea that a stable Iraq requires a strong, repressive leader like Saddam (or some Ba'athist successor, ideally chosen by the United States), or that an Iraq led by such a leader is certain to be more stable than a freer, but perhaps less unified Iraq, is highly questionable. A new leadership preoccupied with domestic affairs, and ready to abandon the drive for weapons of mass destruction, would surely be preferable to Saddam—or yet another military dictatorship—even if the process required to bring about such a change carries some risk of Iraq breaking up. Moreover, as the conflicts raging through the former Yugoslavia have shown, territorial integrity is not synonymous with stability: where centrifugal forces are strong enough, central control achieved through force may actually lead to heightened instability.

The Question of Iran: Influenced by the Departments of State and Defense, the Central Intelligence Agency and the National Security Council (the Iraq Policy Group), the administration has accepted the idea that a "strong" Iraq—or, at the very least, an Iraq that is not in the throes of an internal conflict carrying a risk of political disintegration—is essential to "contain" Iran. Moreover, the architects of the Clinton administration policy seem to believe that the revolutionary Shi'ite government of Iran will be the inevitable beneficiary of any successful internal opposition to Saddam in which the Shi'ites of Iraq play a role. It has wrongly regarded the Shi'ites of Iraq as mere ancillaries—tools, even—of the Shi'ites of Iran. Even before the Gulf War, the Department of State believed that strong Sunni control in Baghdad was essential to offset Iran's influence among Iraq's Shi'ite majority. But the evidence suggests that the Shi'ites of Iraq are far more independent than the State Department supposes. For instance, despite a strong effort, Iran could not persuade Iraqi Shi'ites to change loyalties during the Iran-Iraq War. And Iran did nothing to help them during the massive uprising against Saddam immediately after the Gulf War. As a consequence, its influence over the affairs of Iraqi Shi'ites remains marginal. In any case, the Clinton administration's concern with Iran's possible influence in Iraq is not sufficient to justify accepting a unified Iraq ruled by Saddam Hussein. On the contrary, if an Iraq without Saddam Hussein would best serve our interests, efforts to remove him should not be affected by fear of Iran's influence.

The Question of the Opposition: The Clinton administration's policy is marked by an unwarranted pessimism about the Iraqi opposition. The White House appears to have accepted the view of the Iraq Policy Group—reinforced by the CIA, which has long believed that only Iraqis *inside* the government really matter—that only a Sunni coup from within can bring Saddam down. They have imagined a broad Ba'athist military elite in Baghdad becoming Iraq's salvation by taking matters into its own hands and overthrowing Saddam, despite the evidence of several failed coups. At the same time, they dismiss Iraqi opposition forces outside Iraq as so removed from Iraqi society and culture as to have no visible following nor anything in common with Iraqis still under Saddam's control.

Even before the Gulf War, the Iraq Policy Group believed that effective power in Iraq was in the hands of Ba'athist military officers with whom they had established contact while assisting Iraq during its war with Iran. In fact, they wrongly believed that this covert relationship with the top levels of the Ba'athist military had been established independently of Saddam himself and constituted a separate center of power in Iraqi policy-making. So confident were they of the potential of these covert relationships with the Iraqi military, that they continued to place faith in them even after they had failed to be of consequence during the Gulf War. This helps explain our readiness to cooperate with any Iraqi military officer who signaled an intent to conspire against Saddam.

Unfortunately, the Iraq Policy Group—especially the CIA—was wrong. There was no U.S.-Iraqi relationship except the one tightly controlled by Saddam.[6] He alone mattered, and he filled his senior military slots with officers who understood that. All contacts with the Americans were controlled to serve his agenda. These relationships, even those which disguised themselves as coup plotting, were managed by Saddam for *his* purposes. Repeatedly outmaneuvered, the CIA went from failure to failure in a vain effort to recruit from within the Baghdad elite the plotters who would bring Saddam down.

The belief that there are residues of influence from these relationships has persisted since the Gulf War. U.S. policy-makers continue to be as surprised at the failure of coup attempt after coup attempt as they were in 1991 by the Ba'athist military's continued loyalty to Saddam, even after his crushing defeat. Even if there are "insiders" who wish to bring down Saddam's regime, they appear utterly unable to conspire, least of all when the U.S. is involved. Those who place hope on military dissent within the regime will wait a long time; and visible popular dissent inside Iraq is even less likely. Everyone either grovels or remains silent under Saddam's rule. A policy based on the hope of a coup is a policy of wishful thinking. Saddam is more wily, brutal and conspiratorial than any likely internal opponent the United States might mobilize against him.

The inescapable conclusion is that only Iraqis *outside* of Iraq can form a potentially effective opposition to Saddam. Only they can operate freely abroad and in the northern Iraq safe haven, away from Saddam's brutal and omnipresent security apparatus. Only they can safely plan and act upon their antipathy toward Saddam. It is a mistake to dismiss the external opposition as ineffective, as so many of the region's specialists have done, because it musters little visible support inside Iraq. How could it be otherwise? It is as impossible for Iraqis inside Iraq openly to express support for any external liberation movement as it is to mobilize internal opposition.

To dismiss the potential of external opposition forces because evidence of support for them within Iraq is lacking—as the Clinton administration has done—misses the key point about Saddam's Iraq: his reign of terror is so complete and comprehensive that any visible opposition within the country is suicidal. And even if it were not—even if open opposition to Saddam were merely dangerous and not fatal—there would be little motivation for Saddam's opponents within Iraq to make themselves known. After all, there is no organization in place that could make effective use of expressions of opposition. There is no sign of external support that might give heart to Saddam's opponents. Within Iraq, public denunciation of Saddam, or declarations of support for his opponents, are quite pointless, especially without an external opposition to give them focus and meaning.

The Bay of Pigs Syndrome: Within the Clinton administration there has been a widespread fear that the Iraqi opposition, even if it were well organized and capable of mounting military operations against Saddam, would somehow be maneuvered into a situation where it would face annihilation unless U.S. forces were rushed to the rescue. The fear that support for an insurgency to rid Iraq of Saddam might force us to secure and possibly defend additional safe havens has paralyzed us and reduced our policy to little more than fantasizing about a coup. Yet there is no reason why support for an Iraqi opposition must inevitably lead to a fiasco like the Bay of Pigs. No one who argues that the U.S. should support the Iraqi opposition also argues that the opposition should mount a military offensive against the strongest elements of Saddam's remaining loyal troops. Strategies that would entail far less risk are clearly preferable. Only through a poor choice of strategy would the opposition place itself in a situation where it would require an American rescue mission.

For several years now, we have limited our military actions against Saddam to air strikes carried out against buildings known to be empty, including one attack against the vacant headquarters of the secret police. To Iraqis the meaning has been clear: we do not wish to do serious damage to one of the instruments of Saddam's power. We have half-heartedly played at damaging his communications and badgering his personal security detachment. We have reacted irregularly to Iraqi activity in the no-fly zones by dropping bombs against local targets with minimal effect. In the last year or so we have dropped a great many bombs, the principal effect of which has been to demonstrate Saddam's apparent invincibility. Consistent with a weak and uncertain policy, we have not tried to damage his overall *fighting* capability, especially the Special Republican Guard.

The problem of Saddam Hussein and his regime cannot be allowed to linger indefinitely in the state of resignation into which the administration now seems to have descended. Time is not on our side. Because of our behavior, our friends in the region are increasingly convinced that Saddam is there to stay. They can see no benefit in continuing to isolate him. Support for nearby bases in the event of new hostilities has eroded, raising uncertainty and narrowing our options. The inspectors who once searched out elements of Saddam's multiplicity of programs for the development and production of weapons of mass destruction have been expelled from Iraq for periods long enough to allow secret installations to be relocated and programs to be hidden in new locations.

Even in the immediate aftermath of Iraq's defeat in the Gulf War, when Saddam was under strict sanctions and the United Nations made a determined effort to ferret out and destroy these weapons, he still forged ahead with his programs to develop biological and chemical munitions. With the passage of time and the repeated, prolonged disruption of inspection activities and expulsion of the UN inspectors, the situation has grown much worse. The data base for inspections, which is degraded whenever periods of non-inspection allow new hiding places, is far less useful than it once was. Moreover, Iraq has learned a great deal about the sources and methods used by inspectors in the past—information it will use to defeat inspections in the future. Finally, Saddam has become much more aggressive in controlling the rules by which inspectors operate, and the United Nations has tended to acquiesce in his demands.[7] The result of all this must be a collapse of confidence in the inspection regime aimed at unearthing Saddam's ongoing programs to acquire nuclear, biological and chemical weapons. Iraq is one of the few countries to have ever used such weapons, against Iran and against its own people. It must be assumed that Saddam would be willing to use such weapons again.

If we do not develop a strategy for removing Saddam now, we may be unable to do so later. Once he is in possession of sophisticated weapons of mass destruction, our options will have narrowed considerably. It is clear that the dangers his regime poses cannot be eliminated as long as our objective is simply "containment" and the means of achieving it are limited to sanctions and exhortations. The static policy of containment has already led to serious erosion in our efforts to isolate Saddam. Major actors along Iraq's border, such as Syria, ignore the consequences of violating sanctions. Even Iraq's long-time enemy Iran has been actively helping it to circumvent UN restrictions on oil shipments clandestinely. The quantities and sophistication of equipment allowed to enter Iraq under the humanitarian aid provisions of the sanctions regime has increased markedly, and almost certainly includes a stream of nominally prohibited items. Put simply, Saddam is again a growing, rather than only a continuing, problem.

The record of the last few years also has made it clear that efforts to constrain Saddam Hussein through diplomacy (agreements to which he is a party) or arms control will fail. Any agreement with him is worthless and will be circumvented when he finds it useful to do so. The agreement with Kofi Annan in February 1998 to solicit Iraqi cooperation for continuing the UN weapons inspection efforts, for instance, was bound to collapse, as collapse it did. Arguably, this might have served as a pretext for a shift to a more aggressive effort against Saddam. But even were this the intent of the Annan agreement—and there is no evidence it was—it was a risky and problematic device. The very act of negotiation with Saddam, especially over inspections, conferred legitimacy upon him as the head of Iraq, when it should be the aim of any coherent and meaningful policy to deny him that legitimacy. Unfortunately, the administration did not intend to use the Annan agreement as grounds for embarking on a more forceful policy, but rather as a way of getting Saddam off the front pages. It was followed by State Department and White House actions to undermine an aggressive inspection program so as to avoid an immediate confrontation, which would have confirmed how empty Saddam's promises were.

The administration's policy of sacrificing a tough inspection regime rather than confronting Saddam Hussein was exposed by Scott Ritter's resignation from UNSCOM and by the release of test results showing traces of chemical agents on Scud warheads recovered from Iraq. The revelation that Saddam was indeed hiding an ongoing chemical weapons program was a major factor in congressional demands that the United States go beyond containment and develop a serious program to remove him from power.

As long as the administration failed to formulate a broader strategy to remove Saddam, it had little choice but to retreat. More forceful action, even an extensive air campaign, would have been ineffective if it were not part of a comprehensive strategy to remove Saddam from power. When the Clinton administration finally did undertake a bombing campaign against Iraq in December 1998, it did so not in the service of some larger strategy but because the failure to act was becoming a political problem. Not surprisingly, the December 1998 bombing had no lasting effect. It did not restore inspections. It did not weaken Saddam, and it did nothing to contain his continuing program to acquire weapons of mass destruction. It was, by any measure, a very expensive failure.

So what should be done? First, it is clear that the current administration will leave office before Saddam does, and so any policy initiative toward Iraq will come from its successor. If the next administration is to protect America's interests in the Gulf and help bring about the conditions for long-term stability in the region, it must formulate a comprehensive political and military strategy for bringing down Saddam and his regime. This can only be done by supporting the external opposition. That strategy, which was put forward by the Iraqi National Congress in the early 1990s, has now secured bipartisan support in a series of laws, the most important of which was the Iraq Liberation Act of September 1998.

At the center of this strategy is the recognition that Saddam Hussein's regime is so discredited, deceptive and dangerous that it no longer can be considered a legitimate government, and that the opposition, which is forced to operate outside Iraq, holds a greater claim to legitimacy. Accordingly, the United States should move to recognize a provisional government of Iraq based on the principles and leaders of the Iraqi National Congress (INC), which is representative of all the people of Iraq. A number of policy initiatives follow from this:

- The sanctions should be lifted in liberated areas under INC control. Sanctions are instruments of war against Saddam's regime, not against Iraqis as a people; those who have freed themselves from Saddam should also be free from the sanctions imposed on Saddam's Iraq.
- The safe haven in northern Iraq should be restored and enhanced to allow the provisional government to extend its authority there. A zone in southern Iraq, from which Saddam's ground forces would be excluded, should also be established.
- The oil resources and other products of the liberated areas should be used to help fund the provisional government's activities and humanitarian relief for the people of liberated Iraq. At the same time, Iraq's frozen assets—which amount to at least $1.6 billion in the United States and Britain alone—should be released to the control of the provisional government.
- Laws should be enacted against entering into any active or provisional agreements with Saddam's regime; businesses which do enter into such agreements should be barred from the U.S. market.
- Saddam's regime should be delegitimized by, among other things, indicting him and his lieutenants for war crimes, and by challenging his credentials to fill the Iraqi seat at the United Nations.

Such a political strategy will set the stage for an eventual military strategy, which can be planned now and executed as the political strategy matures. It would have several elements: First, the United States can expand liberated areas of Iraq by refocusing its continuing bombing campaign against important targets such as the Special Republican Guard divisions and the Fedayeen forces, which prop up the regime, and the military infrastructure that sustains it. These bombings would be a response to violations of the no-fly zones, which now take place daily.[8] There is no reason, in logic or law, why retaliation for violations of the no-fly zones should be limited to forces within the zones. Bombing attacks on Iraq must be linked to a coherent military strategy on the ground, which relies on Iraqi opponents outside of Saddam's clutches.

In this context, the United States should also consider each confrontation as another opportunity to torment Saddam and endanger his regime's survival—for example, by extending safe havens into areas where they would deny him oil and thus revenue. Saddam's grip on the regular army and those forces furthest out on the periphery has always been tenuous. In 1991, it was clear that after substantial bombing of regular army units, most would rather surrender or defect at the first opportunity.

Had the December 1998 bombing been coordinated with opposition forces on the ground, a southern safe haven might have come into being. That four-day bombing, known as Desert Fox, focused on damaging Saddam's personal security forces as well as severing communications between Baghdad and southern Iraq, suggesting that the administration hoped a "spontaneous" revolt would erupt in the south among the Shia. The operation, however, was neither deep nor long enough to have such an effect. Most importantly, the administration failed to coordinate its operation with opposition forces in southern Iraq, leaving them neither warning nor time to plan and execute such a revolt. A serious attempt at severing southern Iraq from Saddam's control—which would deny him access to most of his oil—would require an operation coordinated and planned in advance with the opposition.

Of course there can be no guarantee that even a well-conceived plan for Saddam's removal will succeed or that the Iraqi opposition, even if supported properly, will be able to prevail. As a last resort, and as a visible insurance to those who will fight on the ground, we should build up our own ground forces in the region so that we have the capacity to protect and assist the anti-Saddam forces in the northern and southern parts of Iraq.

The United States Congress has demonstrated bipartisan support for this plan. In the Iraq Liberation Act, it took the unprecedented step of actually voting authority for the administration to transfer U.S. military equipment to the opponents of Saddam Hussein, in order to give them, if they can organize themselves, some means with which to oppose his regime. The Congress also voted a small, but extremely important amount of money for radio broadcasting by the opposition into Iraq. Yet the Clinton administration continues to resist putting these resources to use or even examining seriously the prospect of mobilizing the opposition to Saddam. And the administration will continue to do so, either genuinely accepting or hiding behind the judgment of the intelligence community that an effort along these lines will fail, while an effort by the much tried and frequently failed approach of organizing a coup is more likely to succeed.

The Clinton administration has consistently displayed more resolve and ingenuity in denying support to the Iraqi National Congress than in trying to get rid of Saddam. It refuses to spend more than a minuscule amount of the money intended for the Iraqi opposition under the Iraq Liberation Act, and it continues aggressively to sabotage efforts of the Iraqi opposition to hold meetings which would send a meaningful signal to those inside Iraq who oppose Saddam.[9] At the same time, the administration pours cold water on any suggestion that it would even consider supporting a lethal insurgency—this despite ample evidence that most Iraqis oppose their regime and would be willing to do something about it if they had meaningful American support.

Our flailing, ineffectual policy has by now seriously damaged both our diplomatic and our military position with respect to Iraq. Much work will need to be done to develop a credible strategy for dealing with Saddam; after years of drift and weakness, it will take a major effort to assemble a coalition of regional states to support an appropriately aggressive policy. It is a heavy burden for the next American president.

Iran:
Fundamentalism and Reform

The Near East Bureau in the Department of State lives for the "three I's": Iraq, Israel, and Iran. After January 7, 1998, when CNN broadcast President Mohammad Khatami's "dialogue-of-civilizations" interview, Iran quickly became the land of diplomatic promise; neither Iraq nor Israel was then offering much hope. To most observers, Iran's president was clearly a "moderate" cleric, promisingly different from Ali Khameneh'i, the country's revolutionary leader, and Ali Akbar Hashemi-Rafsanjani, Khatami's predecessor.

Iran-watching American diplomats privately echoed some of the more optimistic press and academic assessments of the former Minister of Islamic Guidance, who had unexpectedly won the presidency in a landslide in May 1997. The hard-line Khameneh'i was still a large obstacle in the way of friendlier relations, but since Khatami had done the CNN interview—widely seen as a bold, symbolic act—he obviously wanted to change the status quo between the two countries. After all, a cleric who admired the Pilgrims and had read Alexis de Tocqueville couldn't really detest the United States.

Given his decision to talk about a "dialogue" with America—the thorniest political issue in Iran—in his first major international TV address, Khatami appeared to many Iran-observers to have the will and just possibly the domestic political leverage to talk directly with the United States. With Khatami as president, reopening the U.S. embassy in Tehran was, remarked an American diplomat, "distinctly conceivable."

The Clinton administration, which had hitherto often described clerical Iran as a "rogue" or "terrorist state," now instructed U.S. officials at home and abroad to shy away from such language. In particular, mentioning possible Iranian culpability for the 1996 terrorist attack against the Khobar Towers in Saudi Arabia, where nineteen U.S. servicemen were killed, became untoward speculation. The Central Intelligence Agency's favorite, Usama bin Ladin, became, especially after the embassy bombings in Africa, a more palatable and probable suspect. "Dual containment," the Clinton administration's official U.S. policy toward Iran and Iraq since 1993, also became passé. Though the two-target strategy was dead by January 1998—the administration killed it and the 1996 Iran-Libyan Sanctions Act (ILSA) by refusing to sanction French, Russian, and Malaysian oil companies for an Iranian oil deal in July 1995—the State Department still occasionally pretended in press conferences that ILSA's secondary boycott against Iran's energy sector could have teeth. After Khatami's CNN interview, however, "dual containment" and ILSA, too, became awkward subjects.

America's Persian-language broadcasting to Iran also became a sensitive issue. The State Department and the National Security Council didn't like the idea of a new, Congressionally mandated Persian radio service. The Iranian government (seconded by the *New York Times*) was already describing future Radio Free Europe–Radio Liberty Persian broadcasting as "propaganda," and so the still-to-be-born service was obviously counterproductive to U.S.-Iranian relations. Washington needed to put its best face forward, thought the administration's foreign policy-makers, and Radio Free Europe–Radio Liberty, with its CIA roots and Cold War associations, could complicate relations between the two countries. Unfortunately for State and the NSC, President Clinton hadn't vetoed the radio's birth. Congress would allow the administration to change the radio's name ("Radio Free Iran" became simply the Persian service of RFE-RL), but the broadcasts would go forward.

The birth pains of "Radio Liberty"—the name the Iranians use for RFE-RL's service—reveal how badly the Clinton administration has misunderstood the Islamic Republic. This should have been regarded as one of the more effective ways for the United States to help reforming forces in Iran. The Persian service, unlike the Voice of America's broadcasts, are supposed to be substitutes for censored local radios, providing listeners with richly detailed news. In its heyday, RFE-RL was on the cutting edge of the defense of human rights behind the Iron Curtain.

The more the clerical regime complained about the radio broadcasts, the clearer it should have been to the administration that the still-to-be-born service was hitting pay dirt. Iranians would not tune out Radio Liberty because the Iranian government and the *New York Times* had called it CIA " propaganda"; rather, they would listen precisely because it had been so labeled. In Iran, the truth is always *posht-e-pardeh,* hidden behind the curtain, and the shadowy Central Intelligence Agency, according to Iranian geopolitical mythology, is much more likely to know it.

The State Department's derailing of Radio Liberty would not have made Khatami's government respect the United States more. Quite the contrary. It would have proven the hard-liners' contention—which reflects a general Persian understanding of the way their usually despotic world works—that kindness and consideration reflect weakness, not strength.

In its actions toward "A Dialogue of Civilizations" and the radio service, and in its general response to Iran after the election of Khatami, the Clinton administration essentially accepted the view that the clerical regime's politics were sufficiently evolutionary to allow a possibility for direct dialogue with the United States. Knowingly or not, the Clinton administration had bought the line of the Iranian "left": that America, not Iran, was "behind the times" and preventing a thaw in U.S.-Iranian relations. Influential unofficial commentators—former National Security Advisors Zbigniew Brzezinski and Brent Scowcroft, former Assistant Secretary of State Richard Murphy and the Mobil Oil Corporation on the op-ed page of the *New York Times*—amplified the views often heard inside the administration. Mutual mistrust, misapprehension, and U.S. domestic politics—read the "Israeli-Jewish lobby"—needed to be overcome before Washington and Tehran could reach a modus vivendi. At least on the American side, ideas were no longer the fundamental causes of the enmity separating the two countries.

The policy first cogently voiced in 1993 by the then assistant secretary of state for the Near East, Edward Djerejian—that radicalism, not Islamic fundamentalism per se, posed a problem for the United States—had evolved into the hope that clerical Iran and the Islamic revolution no longer necessarily had to be damningly anti-American. Jimmy Carter's former NSC director on Iran, Gary Sick, put it succinctly in the *Washington Post* on March 28, 1999: Iran had changed; we had not. Confidence-building measures, the leitmotif of "conflict resolution," needed to be at the forefront of American diplomacy. Washington needed to be patient, conciliatory, and sympathetic. Hard-ball politics—tough rhetoric backed by sanctions—were ineffective and counterproductive.

With good intentions and hope shaping their analysis, many Western Iran-watchers listened to Khatami's words about "the dialogue of civilizations," "liberty," and "the rule of law," and heard a progressive cleric essentially free from radical Islamic ideals. They divided the ruling regime conveniently into two sides—the reformist Khatami vs. the "conservative" revolutionary leader Ali Khameneh'i—and concluded that the president's coalition in principle and practice was decidedly more pro-Western. The excitement at this discovery became a wish-fulfillment for many Western Iran-watchers impatient with the twenty-year stalemate, particularly those who like or love Iran (a natural response for anyone who tastes just a little of the culture, language, and playfulness of the Iranian people).

Guilt, too, perhaps plays a part in Western attitudes toward the new regime. On April 12, 1999, President Clinton felt Iran's pain in a rambling but probably sincere expression of sympathy. "Iran has been," Mr. Clinton extemporaneously reflected in a White House gathering, ". . . a subject of quite a lot of abuse from various Western nations. . . . It's quite important to tell people: look, you have a right to be angry at something my country or my culture or others that are generally allied with us today did to you 50 or 60 or 100 or 150 years ago. . . . So I think while we speak out against religious intolerance we have to listen for possible ways we can give people the legitimacy of some of their fears, or some of their angers, or some of their historical grievances, and then say . . . now can we build a common future?"

On March 17, 2000, Secretary of State Madeleine Albright further defined and advanced the president's conception of foreign policy as apologia. In a speech at the American-Iranian Council, she regretted America's participation in the 1953 coup d'état which downed the oil-nationalizing Prime Minister Mohammad Mosaddeq and returned Shah Mohammad Reza Pahlavi to power. She questioned America's subsequent support to the Shah and the "shortsightedness" of the Reagan administration's aid to Iraq during the first Gulf War. (Was this a reference to the U.S. photographic reconnaissance given to Iraq when Ayatollah Khomeini's legions threatened to crack Iraqi lines and "march to Jerusalem through Baghdad"? Or to the U.S. Navy's reflagging and escort operations that prevented Iran from paralyzing Persian Gulf oil shipments? Mrs. Albright doesn't say.)

It isn't hard to find journalists, academics, Persian-service radio directors, and even Foreign Service officers who also harbor such feelings, which have until recently been more or less counterbalanced by an awareness of revolutionary Iran's political incorrectness. As the French scholar Olivier Roy has remarked, the Iranian revolution would have received much more support from the American and European left had it not attacked women's rights and the author Salman Rushdie. Now, with Khatami seen as a champion of women and an opponent of the Rushdie *fatwa*, the pendulum was freed to swing back. Liberal guilt about the Shah and a general uneasiness with a perceived American heavy-handedness in the region naturally meld well with the traditional American desire to be liked and to make friends with just about anyone.

But feelings, no matter how sincere and well-founded, aren't particularly helpful in crafting foreign policy. Knowing how people think, which is not at all the same as knowing how people feel, is essential to diplomacy.

Iran's people and politics are often a contradictory maze. Yet Iran is not Iraq. Iranians loudly argue among themselves. Even in the tight-knit clerical circles, which have become noticeably less fraternal since Khomeini's death, the truth often pours out. The tricky part of analyzing Iran isn't obtaining information; it is cutting through the commotion, the noise, the often wide gulf between private views and public statements, and through the strong American impulse to label Iranians as we label ourselves. If we can get metaphorically close to the *darun,* the quiet inner chamber of a Persian home where Iranians more clearly speak their minds, we have a chance of separating friend from foe and answering the most pressing policy questions.

The central questions are three: Can clerical Iran peacefully evolve into a democratic nation, where a nonclerical opposition has a chance of survival, let alone winning? Is Mohammad Khatami the cleric to lead Iran away from the Islamic revolution? And most important for us—and perhaps for the Iranians themselves—can clerical Iran ever make peace with the United States?

The Khatami Factor

If one listens carefully to Mohammad Khatami, it is hard to be optimistic. The Islamic revolution with its anti-American core, though dead for the vast majority of the Iranian people, is still very much alive for the clergy, be they "right-wingers," "leftists," "moderates," or "conservatives."

This is not to say that U.S. officials have mislabeled the Iranian president. Mohammad Khatami *is* a moderate cleric. But so, too, depending upon the context, is Hashemi-Rafsanjani, the first Iranian president to try to channel and control the revolution's zealots. And in foreign policy, context is everything.

Khatami's election was—as Ayatollah Ali Montazeri, Iran's preeminent and most feared dissident cleric, put it—"a second revolution." The country is at a historical crossroads; and the United States, clerical Iran's *bête noire*, will inevitably have a ring-side seat in the nation's continuing political struggles. The unexpected election of Khatami clearly revealed to Iran's ruling clergy, as well as to the outside world, that the Iranian people had had enough of the oppression, corruption, poverty, and boredom that defined the Islamic revolution after twenty years. Khatami, the little-known establishment mullah who ran as a reforming outsider, captured the nation's frustration and won 69 percent of the vote. Most Iranians hoped that Khatami, with people-power behind him, would lead the ruling clergy, kicking and screaming no doubt, to a more civil, "post-Islamist" society.

But Khatami's call for "a dialogue of civilizations" does not mean that he wants to end the confrontation between the United States and Iran. If one looks at the president's speeches, his campaign pamphlets, the commentary of his clerical and university friends and mentors, and, perhaps most important, his books—*Fear of the Wave* and *From the City-World to the World-City*—one doesn't find his intentions friendly. Khatami, like so many Islamic reformers before him, wants to borrow from the West so that Muslims can stand tall and defy the West's, especially America's, seemingly unstoppable cultural and economic power. He wants to give faithful Iranians more spiritual maneuvering room in the modern age so that they can compete and triumph. He wants, perhaps above all else, to show that "liberty," properly defined and applied to a Muslim, can launch the Islamic world into a new renaissance. With an Islamic-Iranian renaissance, Muslims throughout the world might no longer be seduced by the West's increasingly immoral and atheistic use of individual freedom.

Being a good Muslim, Khatami sees history as evolutionary. Morally dilapidated and senile as it may be, America is still—unquestionably in Khatami's view—the dominant civilization. But, *inshallah*, it won't last, and every Muslim can and ought to borrow the good, which Khatami usually translates as the useful, from American civilization. Khatami is struggling with the conundrum that has dogged faithful Muslims ever since the Ottoman Empire went into decline: How can it be that the recipients of God's final revelation have fallen so far behind the civilization of Jews and Christians?

It can be a truly unsettling question for a believing Muslim. The answer for Khatami lies in the application of reason. Perhaps following the lead of his one-time academic friend, Professor Javad Tabataba'i, who has written about the failure of Islam to successfully nurture its "Greek roots," Khatami can't stop talking about the need for a more productive marriage of reason and faith. He steers far from any comparative study of monotheisms, seeing reason, and its by-product, the individual's quest for liberty, as essentially disconnected from any religious background and identity. In other words, Khatami is searching for a nonreligious means of borrowing from the West.

V. S. Naipaul once remarked that Iran's Islamic revolution was, in part, a scream against the cultural baggage that came with the Industrial Revolution. According to Naipaul, if you build a flashlight, you'd better be prepared to endure the cultural forces that originally led to its invention. Khatami disagrees with the author of *Among the Believers*. He doesn't see—or doesn't want to see—all of the interconnectedness and causality. He will concede some of the blowback, but not all. For him, reason and liberty, and everything else that flows from these two forces, can and must be checked by divine revelation. The early Islamic empires unashamedly borrowed from Byzantium and Sassanid Iran to create superior societies; Khatami sees no reason why the Islamic Republic—and all Muslims—cannot do likewise with the modern West.

For Khatami, this is the essence of "dialogue." Its motivation is historical and sociological; it isn't moral. Khatami's highly intellectual "dialogue" with American civilization explains why Iran's revolutionary leader Ali Khameneh'i, and Khatami's erstwhile patron, former Iranian president Ali Akbar Hashemi-Rafsanjani, didn't veto the CNN interview (and there is no question that they could have). When Iran's lively (though not free) press started speculating about the possibility of diplomatic contacts between U.S. and Iranian officials, Khameneh'i, his supporters, and Khatami himself came forward to state explicitly that "dialogue" did not mean that Tehran and Washington were going to talk.

A Persian-speaking European friend of mine visited Tehran soon after Khatami's CNN interview and met several Westernized, pro-Khatami types in the ministries of Foreign Affairs and Islamic Guidance. The officials had all become noticeably more anti-American. The Tehran rumor mill, which voraciously feeds on itself as well as on the closely monitored foreign press, had gone wild with stories about contacts between Washington and Tehran. The Iranian officials wanted my friend to know that they should not be viewed as pro-American just because they were pro-Khatami. In their own minds, not just publicly among their peers, their identity as revolution-loyal Iranian Muslims had been challenged by all the talk of a rapprochement with the United States.

This is not to say, however, that the same individuals have an eternal enmity for America. In all probability, they do not; on the contrary, they probably would love to put an end to the Islamic revolution and restore relations with the United States. Both positions, although seemingly contradictory, are sincere. For many Iranians, the "truth" depends on time and place. And anytime Washington tries officially to draw closer to Tehran is the wrong time, in the wrong place.

It is amusing to remember how much gossip there was in Iran and the West in 1997 and 1998 about discreet, serious discussions taking place between the United States and the Islamic Republic in multilateral forums. Yet it should have been obvious that no such post-CNN "dialogue" had occurred, since President Clinton, Madeleine Albright, and Undersecretary of State Thomas Pickering kept trying quite openly to elicit just a "hello" from the mullahs.

For Iran's ruling clerics, "the dialogue of civilizations" isn't just about the transmission of ideas, cultural sensitivity, and religious self-defense. Without a dialogue with the West, there are no foreign bank loans or export credits. No foreign investment and expertise to develop Iran's life-sustaining energy sector and transportation system. No foreign agricultural credits for the importation of foodstuffs. No communications technology with which to buttress the principles and propaganda of the Islamic Republic. And no nuclear technology, which the ruling mullahs see as the key to trumping any military threats from Iraq, Pakistan, Turkey, and, perhaps most important, Israel and the United States. Khameneh'i, Rafsanjani, and Khatami—the clerical big three—are unquestionably united on the desirability of nuclear weapons.

Dialogue with America, as opposed to the West in general, is of course not essential to such trade. Iran's corrupt, capricious, command economy—not any threat of sanctions by the Clinton administration—is what really has deterred foreign investment and aid. But softening America's resistance to trade with the Islamic Republic is helpful in soliciting more deals with European, and especially Japanese, businessmen. Khameneh'i, Khatami, and Rafsanjani—but not all revolutionary clerics—don't appear to have an insurmountable problem with soliciting foreign investment, particularly if it allows them to thumb their noses at the United States. And Khatami's mild-mannered charm and his promises to work for a "civil society" under the "rule of law" have definitely helped Iran obtain more foreign credit and commerce.

Khatami's offer of a "dialogue," deftly backed by an outreach effort to the American Iranian community, has certainly sown doubts in the present administration, not to mention the American business community, about the wisdom of a hard-line approach to Iran. This summer's arrest of thirteen Iranian Jews on charges of espionage and the violent suppression of student demonstrations throughout the country have caused some disquiet and uncertainty in Washington about Khatami since he ignored the Jews' plight and reprimanded the students who had been among his most loyal and essential supporters. The State Department's assistant secretary for the Near East, Martin Indyk, publicly wondered how the Jewish persecution could be compatible with Khatami's "rule of law." But the afterlife of the CNN interview continues. The administration still hopes for a dialogue with the Iranian president and remains averse to criticizing him. After the February 2000 parliamentary elections, where "moderates" routed "conservatives,"

Madeleine Albright again appealed to Tehran to begin an official dialogue with the United States. Despite the secretary's apologies for 1953 and for U.S. aid to Iraq during the first Gulf War, Tehran refused, suggesting that Washington needed first to drop all its sanctions and ameliorate its hostility toward the Islamic revolution.

Immediately after the CNN interview, a consensus developed among many Iran-observers that President Khatami had in fact become the number one cleric in Iran's clerical hierarchy since he'd tackled the nation's most sensitive issue: relations with the United States. As explained above, this view was wrong because it misapprehended what Khatami meant by "dialogue," and thus why Khameneh'i, Rafsanjani, and others did not initially object to the interview.

Nor was Khatami letting loose a trial balloon, as some have suggested, cleverly designed to see if the moment was right to take U.S.-Iranian relations one step farther. On CNN, Khatami said nothing about the United States that he hadn't said before. Rafsanjani would never have backed him for the presidency, and Khameneh'i would never have allowed him to be approved as a presidential candidate (in clerical Iran, most presidential candidates are disqualified on technical or ideological grounds) if they were threatened by Khatami's views on cultural dialogue and the United States. Also, in elite clerical circles, where everybody is related to everybody else by marriage or mentor, word gets around.

For Khatami, talking about "the dialogue of civilizations" is not bold. Having a serious discussion about Iranian society and internal politics would be courageous, which is one of the reasons that Khatami is more vague on this subject than he is about the United States. What Khatami means by "civil society," *jame'eh-ye madani* in Persian, the key phrase that propelled him to victory in the presidential elections, isn't clear. Khatami, unlike Ayatollah Khomeini, isn't a man of explicit manifestos. He is a man of many parts: a cleric, a student of Western political philosophy and sociology, a mullah-bureaucrat for nearly two decades, and an intellectual child of Ali Sha'riati, *the* intellectual force behind the Iranian revolution, who blended together a dizzying array of Western, Iranian, and Islamic ideas.

Khatami often shows in his prose and speech the diversity of his intellectual formation. Depending upon the audience and the news current in the headlines, he can sound either hardcore or soft: backing to the hilt Khameneh'i and his regime-saving paramilitary forces one moment, lauding women's rights or anti-regime intellectuals the next. This probably is not primarily a politician's duplicity or a nonconfrontational man's vacillation—though Khatami is not without guile and does not like conflict. His vagueness is a natural reflex for an eclectic—a Westerner might say confused—mullah.

"Civil society" in Khatami's mind appears to mean that after twenty years of hard-nosed clerical rule, a little less would be more. He certainly understands that the Iranian people define "civil society" in an increasingly Jeffersonian manner: they want the Islamic Republic out of their daily lives. Or as a Tehran academic more pithily put it: *"jame'eh-ye madani* means one thing: f—k off!" A fun-loving, mirthful, indulgent, somewhat naughty people, Persians are tired of the regime's moral police and ubiquitous corruption, as well as its insulting inclination, which mirrors and amplifies that of the last Shahs, to view the entire Iranian population—clerics excepted, of course—as juveniles.

Khatami, who values the Iranian clergy as a vanguard to guide and protect the faithful, is well aware of the people's rampant cynicism toward the regime, and wants to check it by instituting a more transparent, accessible justice system. He never explains the details of his "rule of law"—what law? whose rule?—but the clear connotation is that some checks and balances ought to be introduced into the Islamic Republic.

Khatami may understand how interconnected domestic and international politics are in his country. If he does, it is likely that he doesn't want to push the discussion to its logical conclusion. The ideological rigidity necessary to maintain anti-Americanism in Iran after twenty years of Islamic revolution is the same ideological rigidity that fights the expansion of democracy. Whenever freedom and justice are discussed in Iran, no matter how you try to limit the debate by redefining the terms, the United States is inevitably going to enter the conversation. Khatami knows that "liberty" once unleashed instinctively and unceasingly gnaws at traditions. And America, for Khatami, is the ultimate expression and reference point for liberty in the modern age.

The Revolutionary Clergy and the West

For Khatami, no less than for Khameneh'i, the tension and confrontation between the West—in particular the United States—and Islam is inevitable. The traditional Muslim division of the world into the *dar al-harb* and the *dar al-Islam*—the House of War and the House of Islam—still loudly echoes in both men's words about "them" and "us." The two gentlemen differ over how clerical Iran should specifically respond to the American challenge. "Know thine enemy" might be Khatami's guiding motto while "We know enough already!" would be more apposite for the revolutionary leader, who is more of a revolutionary pragmatist than the Western press's "conservative," "hard-line," or "staunch traditionalist" labels usually make him appear. There are many in Khatami's camp—and one should include here the majority of the Iranian people who voted for the cleric—who would dearly like to end Iran's cold war against the United States. But few of the ruling clergy are in this camp. For most revolutionary mullahs, even those who are "Khomeini lite," anti-Americanism and the veil, the cloaking of women in either a chador or a head scarf, are the only two revolutionary principles left that can legitimize their rule. Believing that the Islamic Republic can still annoy, if not thwart, the United States is one of the few *frissons* open to the ruling clergy, who have otherwise failed so miserably.

To adequately capture how difficult it is for the clerical regime to conceive of restoring diplomatic relations with the United States, it is only necessary to try to imagine the revolutionary leader Ali Khameneh'i standing next to Madeleine Albright on a tarmac listening to the "Star Spangled Banner." The image is a little less absurd if Khatami is substituted for Khameneh'i—but it is still too far-fetched to be an objective of American foreign policy.

Ali Akbar Hashemi-Rafsanjani, the former president, and arguably the most powerful man in Iran after Khameneh'i, is easiest to visualize on the tarmac because he is so profoundly corrupt. Personal corruption in a failing revolutionary society is a sure sign of realism, and Rafsanjani is, accordingly, the ultimate pragmatist. He is also much bolder than Khameneh'i (Khatami, who has never been known for his intestinal fortitude, isn't in the same league). It is just possible to imagine him, the *Gorbeh,* the clever cat, trying to reverse the clergy's well-grounded fear of America's cultural seductiveness by co-opting America's popularity among the Iranian people. Through restoring diplomatic relations with Washington, he might steal America's awe and prestige, rare qualities among Iran's discredited clergy. By dropping sanctions against the importation of Iranian pistachios, the Clinton administration has certainly shown kindness to Rafsanjani, whose family dominates Iran's pistachio industry.

But Rafsanjani is not stupid. Opening the door to the United States would inevitably start a chain reaction of questions, doubts, and accusations among the mullahs. In the eyes of the Iranian people, the Islamic Republic is a wreck—the nationwide student demonstrations in July 1999 are only the most recent, and the most violent, sign that the young, once the bedrock of Iran's revolutionary movement, have grown tired of clerical rule. Restoring diplomatic relations with the United States would only provoke their questioning, cynicism, and appetite for freedom. For good cause the revolutionary clergy—Khatami included—can't stop talking about America's "cultural invasion" of Iran.

As the revolutionary ethos has waned in Iran—deflated by the eight-year (1980–88) Somme-like war with Iraq, the death of Ayatollah Khomeini in 1989, and the boredom and poverty of Iran's fundamentalist society—the seductive aura of America, the forbidden land at the center of the revolutionary mind, has intensified. As the school instructor shouts in the Iranian film, *Gabbeh*, "Life is color!" And America is *the* full palette. For mullahs who see themselves as the vanguard of the revolution, it is an unbearably perverse situation. They are pinned by the past, defined at the clergy's insistence by reference to the "Great Satan," and by the high-tech future, defined again, as the clergy constantly warn, by the United States.

They are also pinned by the very technology that Khomeini so successfully used in 1978 from his exile in France: direct-dial telephone. Owing in great part to the telephone system the Shah installed, Iran remained a relatively open country even in its darkest revolutionary days. Unlike Saddam Hussein's Iraq, where information is regulated in a truly Orwellian fashion, outside news has always made it into the Islamic Republic. Telephone calls and family visits abroad have kept Iranians at home regularly in touch with the diaspora. Hundreds of thousands of Iranians now live in the United States. And they are by no means only from the privileged classes who fled Iran in the revolution's early years. Iranians from all walks of life have escaped to the Promised Land. In general, they have not yet been atomized by America's mobile, free society. Devotion to family and love of the homeland are still strong. At no other time in history has the ruling elite of one nation damned its enemy as "the Great Satan" or "the World Arrogance" only to have the aspersions daily belied by thousands of direct-dial telephone calls from its own exiles. Though they have been slow to realize their influence, Iranian émigrés in the U.S. and Western Europe have helped fuel the intellectual civil wars at home.

And these wars are inevitably going to get hotter. The July 1999 student demonstrations—the largest, most violent street demonstrations since the early days of the revolution—are a foretaste of what is likely to happen in the next few years. Iran has been trying in spurts to develop some kind of a democratic system for nearly one hundred years; only Turkey has a more substantial commitment to institutionalized democracy in the Muslim Middle East. This movement continues.

The Islamic revolution not only empowered Ayatollah Khomeini, the most reserved, charismatic messiah of totalitarianism in the twentieth century, it also advanced the practice of democracy. The two opposing forces are enshrined in the Islamic Republic's constitution, which gives ultimate authority to the *rahbar*, the revolutionary leader, but bases the government, however distorted in practice, on the consent of the governed. The Iranian parliament, like the presidency, has real power, even if all the candidates for office have been vetted by the political clergy. The extreme tension between theocracy and democracy was held in check so long as Khomeini lived—the undeniable awe in which he was held neutralizing Iran's burgeoning democratic ethos. But Khomeini's successor, Ali Khameneh'i, is devoid of charisma and clerical accomplishment. He is a politicized mullah, *pur et dur*. He rules because the state's instruments of repression—the Revolutionary Guard Corps, the Intelligence Ministry, and the Basij, a mobilized force of increasingly thuggish young men—remain loyal.

Those Iranians who clamor for real democratization now have the philosophical high ground, and the clerical establishment knows it. The clergy itself, ironically, has been a prime mover of the democratic process. The traditional clerical establishment, which did not care for Khomeini and his theocratic pretensions, is a consensual community raised on a diet of legal disputation in the Socratic manner. The revolutionary clergy is a different creature, in mentality and pedagogy closer to the *nomenklatura* of a communist party. But the old ethos is by no means dead among them. Profoundly affected by Western values, the radical clergy cannot divorce the idea of lawful government from the legitimating consent of "the people." The need for debate among politicized clerics, if not among the ordinary people, is still seen, more or less, as natural and healthy. There are limits, and the semi-secret Special Clerical Court, which tries and punishes recalcitrant mullahs, has been very busy ensuring that independent-minded clerics don't go too far.

The clerical power struggle, the so-called Khatami vs. Khamene-h'i tug-of-war, is a product of the traditional love of disputation mixed with the Western idea of democracy; it is also, to a great extent, the revenge of the have-nots against the haves. Many of Khatami's clerical and lay allies are from the revolutionary "left," who not so long ago were among Khomeini's most ferocious supporters. The "Students Following the Line of the Imam" (a.k.a. the hostage-takers) and the Combatant Clerics Association (the *Ruhaniyun*) were, a few years back, among the hardest of the hard core. They are now followers of Khatami's line. The one woman in Khatami's cabinet, Masumeh Ebtekar, was even the spokesman for the hostage-takers. Ali Akbar Mohtashemi-pur, Iran's former ambassador to Syria who was in the 1980s a key player in Hizbollah-Iranian terrorism launched from Lebanon, regularly aligns himself with the Khatami camp. Mehdi Karrubi, a strong backer of the embassy-seizing "students," a violence-loving revolutionary and a founder of the Combatant Clerics Association, is a staunch backer of the president. So, too, Mohammad Mosavi-Kho'iniha, a real fire-breather who was Ayatollah Khomeini's representative to the Islamic pilgrimage to Mecca and in that capacity engaged in nonstop troublemaking. Mr. Kho'iniha was the publisher of the now-banned *Salam*, one of the more iconoclastic revolutionary papers, and is counted in the "moderate" camp.

There is also Sa'id Hajjarian, the editor in chief of *Sobh-e Imruz* and a politically savvy alter ego for Khatami, who was seriously wounded in an assassination attempt on March 12, 2000. As a former deputy minister of intelligence (he was purged by Rafsanjani), it is likely that Hajjarian oversaw, at least in part, the Intelligence Ministry's domestic or its foreign assassination teams, which have been an integral part of this ministry's mission since the first years of the Islamic Republic. Hajjarian, who has publicly alluded to these domestic hit-teams, was in all likelihood not gunned down by "rogue" forces in the regime but by authorized officers-*cum*-

thugs of the security forces, which wanted to apply the ultimate sanction to a "rogue" ex-intelligence officer who had violated his trust.

The list of "hard-liners" turned "reformers" could go on and on. Indeed, Khatami himself was the Minister of Islamic Guidance (1982–92) during that ministry's ugliest, most vicious period. According to university acquaintances, Khatami was intellectually transformed between 1991 and 1993, and shed his previous hard-core predilections. He resigned from his position in 1992 owing to criticism in the Iranian parliament about his "liberalizing" tendencies.

The "right wing," too, has been redefined by both Westerners and Iranians. Just a few years back, the Combatant Clergy Association (the *Ruhaniyat*), led by Ayatollah Mohammad-Reza Mahdavi-Kani, was seen by many analysts as a relatively pragmatic counterweight to the "radical" *Ruhaniyun*. Mahdavi-Kani, who was one of the first prominent revolutionary clerics to warn about too much clerical involvement in politics, now usually gets labeled as a "hard-liner" or a "conservative."

In the late 1980s and early 1990s, the Iranian "left" lost numerous battles against the "conservatives," "hard-liners," or "pragmatists" (which label depends on time, place, subject matter, and the Western journalist covering the story). Perhaps more than any other pragmatic cleric, Rafsanjani outmaneuvered the "left." A flexible and rich fellow, Rafsanjani has, however, managed to maintain his connections to both the "left" and the "right," often using one, then the other to maintain his agenda, position, and prerogatives. In the 1997 presidential elections, his support for Khatami, for example, was not unqualified. Like everybody else, he really didn't expect Khatami to win. As Rafsanjani's undemocratic power base has been weakened by the Khatami landslide, it's likely that the former president—easily the greatest mullah-politician of the Islamic revolution—has had second thoughts about his indispensable early assistance to the mullah he helped pluck from near obscurity.

The whole governing clerical class, indeed, can be fluid; and figuring out and accurately labeling the shifting coalitions isn't easy. For example, the "left" can merge with the "traditionalists," "conservatives," or "hard-liners" on economics since most are deeply suspicious of foreign investment. On the other hand, a noted "conservative" like Khatami's election rival, Ali Akbar Nateq Nuri, the speaker of Iran's parliament, is far more of a free-marketeer than the Iranian president, who retains his leftist sympathies for social justice over free enterprise. Suspicious of foreigners in general, traditional clerics, which Nateq Nuri manifestly is not, tend however to be Iran's most devout guardians of home-grown, small-scale capitalism, following age-old understanding of Islamic law and custom.

It is natural that the Iranian left would evolve; there's nothing like being on the losing end of a rigged game to make you value a more open system with rules. Far more open to Western ideas than the traditional clergy, lay and clerical leftists have accordingly both hated and loved the United States more intensely. And Iran is a topsy-turvy country, where people and their ideas can change quickly and profoundly.

But change may not be all that it appears. Khatami's inner circle of advisers can spend endless hours among themselves talking about "freedom," as if the repetition of the word can realize the idea. We should be very cautious in judging the motivations of Khatami's allies. Some are unquestionably real progressives; some are intellectual juveniles, consuming ideas as if they were candy; others are probably wolves in sheep's clothing, mouthing slogans about democracy and free speech while waiting for an opportunity to gain the upper hand. It is very much an open question whether Khatami has the desire, the political savvy, and the stamina to meld together a winning leftist coalition, whatever its legislative and international objectives.

The real threat to clerical rule doesn't come from clerics, like Khatami, who want, more or less, to keep but improve the present system. It comes from Iranians who no longer believe in the basic tenets of the Islamic Republic. The true children of clerical Iran are the secularists. They do not often call themselves such—the word grates against the Iranian Muslim ear; but they nonetheless seek the de facto, if not de jure, separation of church and state. Pick up any reformist Iranian newspaper and one can see secularist arguments trying to break free from both traditional and radical Islamic strictures and language.

Iran's pre-eminent public intellectual, Abd al-Karim Sorush, has been ever more openly dividing church from state in his writings and speeches. A philosopher of unimpeachable revolutionary credentials who is also an admirer of Karl Popper, Sorush now emphasizes the spirituality of Islam, not its public practice sanctified by the Holy Law or the revolutionary leader. Indeed, Sorush's writings leave no room for a *rahbar,* a revolutionary leader, in a just society. Accordingly, he has been attacked, in print and in person, by the regime's thugs. Fearful of his influence abroad, the regime has tried on more than one occasion to stop him from traveling. But Sorush's influence continues to grow on university campuses across the country.

In the religious schools and in universities, clerics like Mohammad Mojtahed-Shabestari, Mohsen Kadivar, and even Khomeini's one-time successor Ali Montazeri undermine in their writings and speeches the supremacy of clerics over the will of the people. Montazeri, who is not a secularist, advocates the election of the revolutionary leader and demotes the entire function of the office. One may justifiably wonder whether Montazeri, who more or less played Trotsky to Khomeini's Stalin, would be so animated in his attacks on the *rahbar* if he had inherited the position. Nonetheless, traditional clerics throughout Iran now echo his criticisms. For him, and for Kadivar, clerics should at most supervise the moral functioning of government, never run it. The ballot box, not the opinions of religious judges, must be the final arbiter of public policy. Kadivar's and Montazeri's views directly violate the Islamic Republic's constitution, which Khatami has publicly pledged to support.

Abdallah Nuri, Khatami's impeached interior minister, is also in the Montazeri camp. A protégé of both Montazeri and Khomeini, Nuri has gained prominence because of his trial and conviction, in the Special Clerical Court, for revolutionary apostasy and defamation of Khomeini's and Khameneh'i's names. Though Nuri devoutly defends his revolutionary Islamic credentials, his message carries an increasingly nationalist tone, echoing the voices of Mehdi Bazargan, a founding father of Iranian nationalism and the Islamic Republic, and Mohammad Mosaddeq, the prime minister downed by the 1953 coup d'état. Mosaddeq, whom Khomeini loathed, has re-emerged in the revolutionary pantheon as the left searches for a nationalist icon who is not royal, who has anti-American credentials, and who (in a somewhat contradictory twist in the myth), if he had not been politically martyred, might have led the way to a democratic society unscarred by an Islamic revolution and clerical rule.

The hard-core political clergy is profoundly fearful of Nuri because he appears to be a true firebrand, a progressive mullah willing to turn on his own class even if it provokes a clerical collapse. The court slammed him with a five-year sentence—a tough ruling against a member of the brotherhood—because his popularity and his bold, mocking manner suggested he might have inherited Montazeri's popular touch and his mentor's go-to-hell attitude toward brother clerics. Since Nuri, a long-time clerical "leftist," appears to be in an intellectual free fall, it is difficult to say how religion, nationalism, liberty, and democracy have now melded in his mind. Though he does not appear yet to have evolved into a secularist, his courtroom exegesis of the philosophical and legal roots of the Islamic revolution cannot help but advance the legitimacy of a more secular nationalism.

More boldly than Khatami, Nuri is trying to grapple with an observation made by Tocqueville. The Qur'an contains "not only religious doctrines, but political maxims, civil and criminal laws, and theories of science," the Frenchman noted, while "the Gospel speaks ... only of the general relations of men to God and to each other, beyond which it inculcates and imposes no point of faith. This alone ... would suffice to prove that the former of these religions will never long predominate in a ... democratic age." How to make Islam democratic without robbing it of its law-bound beauty is a question, however, that Nuri has not yet answered. Perhaps no Muslim cleric can without forfeiting the essence of his faith and training.

Yet Mojtahed-Shabestari does try, taking the arguments of Kadivar, Montazeri, and Nuri toward what a Westerner might call a reformation. Like Sorush, he moves Islam into the spiritual realm away from the public square and calls into question the eternal validity of the Holy Law. With an audacious reinterpretation of Islamic history, he suggests that church and state have always in theory and in fact been separate in Islam. Thus, secularism is not an affront to a Muslim, but a natural, unavoidable political state.

Sorush, Shabestari, Kadivar, Montazeri, and other "dissident" intellectuals and clerics aren't writing and speaking for a small, inconsequential audience. The student populations in the universities and the clerical schools have grown enormously with the revolution. Standards for admission may have fallen, but the Iranian dream of higher education has never been stronger. And Iranian students read. So, too, do the public sector's thousands of bureau-crats, as well as the soldiers in the Iranian army and the Revolu-tionary Guard Corps. There is so little recreational fun in the Islamic Republic that books, even extraordinarily dense ones by Sorush, get read and discussed throughout the country. And the ruling regime is very sensitive to intellectual debate. Clerics, including the mullahs-turned-bureaucrats, have devoted much of their lives to the written word. Even those who have give up the revolution-ary mission and sold out for graft can easily be sparked into ani-mated arguments about subjects such as *Whither Idealism?*

The clerical regime has long known that universities are perni-cious incubators of Western ideas. The proper Islamic attitude is an important academic criterion for both students and faculties. Purges in Iranian higher education have been common. And lib-eral intellectuals outside universities have been regularly jailed and killed by the regime's intelligence service, to send a message that regime-challenging dissent, particularly by intellectuals who too openly embrace Western ideas, will not be tolerated. But as the 1999 student demonstrations-turned-riots revealed, ideas like free speech, limited and representative government, and due process can send Iranian young into the streets. Though the ruling clerics handled the student demonstrations exceptionally well, quickly applying just the necessary level of violence to cow the demon-strators, the ideas themselves persist.

As the scholars Farhad Khosrokhavar and Olivier Roy have writ-ten, the intellectual opposition in clerical Iran is not yet searching for a means to take power by a violent revolution. Unlike the cler-ical regime, it doesn't say that it knows the way to heaven. All it wants is a little breathing room, an open public space where men and women can argue freely without being accused of treason.

But the hard core in the clerical regime are forcing them into a different direction—hence the student demonstrations that esca-lated and turned violent. The next large-scale confrontation will almost certainly be more bloody. Yet it's hard to blame the hard-core clerics. They know how ideas, once unleashed, have a will of their own. They know how quickly things can go awry in Iran when weakness is shown. They remember the Iranian revolution.

The February 2000 national elections in Iran are likely to increase public frustration with Iran's cleric-led political system. The Khatami government and the new reformist majority in Parliament, torn between statists and free-marketeers, are very unlikely to restructure significantly Iran's highly centralized, socialist economy. Even if the price of oil skyrockets, Iran's poor will likely grow faster. With a clerical leadership deeply divided and confused about the meaning and advisability of a more "civil society," it is unlikely that Iran's youth, particularly university-educated young men, will control their frustration with a government perpetually making vague promises that, at best, produce small, easily-revoked freedoms. At any time, public anger could start to boil over into the streets. With or without riots, the political discourse in Iran will coarsen and the pressure will build on Khatami to try to do *something* to open up the system. Whether he intercedes on behalf of the people or, more likely, stands by and does nothing, Iranian politics will become much uglier.

Clerical Sins and U.S. Policy

How should the United States deal with the rapidly changing, potentially explosive, situation in the Islamic Republic? If we understand how contradictory and frustrating are Iran's internal dynamics—that it is impossible for the clerical regime to make peace with the United States even though an overwhelming majority of Iran's people would dearly love to—can we design a better Iran policy than that followed by the current administration? What do we really want from the country that has for twenty years been our *bête noire* in the Middle East?

The Clinton administration, following in its predecessor's footsteps, sees five principal problems with the Islamic Republic: Iran sponsors terrorism; opposes the Middle East peace process, providing financial aid, if not terrorist training, to radical Palestinian groups; gives spiritual and material comfort to Islamic militants throughout the Muslim world; regularly abuses its own citizens; and, worst of all, seeks to acquire weapons of mass destruction. All of these charges are of course true. Khatami's election has quieted public discussion of these issues, but his presidency has not yet eliminated the contentious points. As the Islamic Republic's hard core continues to question, if not lose, its grip on power, some of these concerns could become even worse. Yet with the exceptions of terrorism and nuclear weaponry, they do not necessarily compel us to strong action.

First Sin: Sponsoring Terrorism

The Islamic Republic has had a twenty-year love affair with terrorism. It is ideal for striking against threatening expatriates who
live abroad, or against stronger enemies, like the United States or
Israel, who are too dangerous to face in open confrontation. For
a revolutionary movement nurtured by conspiracy and "behind-
the-veil" politics, terrorism is a natural way of doing business, its
pro's and con's dictated largely by an amoral calculation of national
and clerical interests.

Tehran has unquestionably killed Americans in its cold war
against "the Great Satan." The Iranians probably have not engaged
in much terrorism against the United States since the 1980s, with
the probable exception of the June 1996 bombing of the Khobar
Towers in Saudi Arabia. Though the Saudis have not been helpful, we have known since the summer of 1996 that Arab Shi'ites
from eastern Arabia were involved in the bombing. Neither the
Saudi terrorist Usama bin Ladin nor other dissident Saudi Wah-
habi fundamentalists are ecumenical: they hate Shi'ites, probably
as much as they hate either the Saudi royal family or the United
States; perhaps more. The same is true for the principal player in
bin Ladin's Middle Eastern network, the Egyptian Islamic Jihad.

We know that Saddam Hussein, who would gladly bomb us wherever he could, has not developed a significant "illegals" network
beyond the contact and control of his intelligence service based in
his embassies and consulates. When the Western powers shut down
Iraq's official diplomatic facilities during the second Gulf War, no
bombs went off. Nor has Saddam been particularly adept at killing
Iraqi oppositionists, though he has certainly tried. By comparison,
Iran's clerical regime, which has worked much harder and more
effectively to develop an illegals network, has an impressive record
of assassinations against its expatriate opposition. There is no indication that Saddam has built a lethal, unofficial, clandestine network among the Shi'ites or even the Sunnis of eastern Arabia.
Forming such a network was an essential first step for the bombing at Khobar.

We know that Tehran has long tried to build ties, and occasionally foment insurrections, among the Shi'a of eastern Arabia. We
have long known that Iranian intelligence and the Revolutionary
Guard Corps have trolled for volunteers among the Arab Shi'ite
pilgrims to Syria and Iran. It strongly appears that among the

suspected Arab Shi'ites, at least one made very suspicious visits to Damascus. Indeed, according to knowledgeable Saudi intelligence sources, part of the bombing team escaped to Iran after a flight to Damascus (which, of course, didn't put Syria's dictator, Hafiz al-Asad—"an indispensable player" in the Arab-Israeli peace process—in a very good light).

If Arab Shi'ites were involved in the bombing, it is unlikely that bin Ladin's people, or those loosely associated with him, or any other Sunni radical group in Arabia were the masterminds. It is possible that an autonomous Arab Shi'ite group, home grown in the sands of Arabia, nourished by hatred of the oppressive anti-Shi'ite royal family and its principal foreigner backer, might have executed the bombing. But it isn't likely. The nature of the attack, the munitions used, the known organizing efforts of the Iranians in eastern Arabia, the travels of certain suspects, the revolutionary Iranian clergy's undiminished antipathy for the Saudi royal family, and the real fear Tehran had repeatedly expressed about a permanent, large U.S. ground presence in the Persian Gulf all point to Iranian inspiration, if not tactical control.

Indeed, according to individuals with long-standing connections to Saudi intelligence, Riyadh had gathered damning intelligence against Tehran within three months of the bombing. The Saudis refused to share this information with the American investigative team primarily for two reasons. First, the Federal Bureau of Investigation, which was the lead agency in the investigation, wasn't "culturally sensitive" in its work. Ham-fisted and weak in Arabic-speaking officers, the Bureau seriously annoyed the conservative Saudi Interior Ministry, which effectively shut down the U.S. part of the investigation.

As important, Riyadh had serious doubts about the Clinton administration's reliability. One reason: in the summer and autumn of 1996, Washington abandoned, or relocated to Guam, the Arab and Kurdish Iraqi oppositionists allied with the American-supported Iraqi National Congress. In August, Saddam Hussein had challenged them with a mechanized column; the White House responded by refusing to provide air support to the insurgents. Although National Security Advisor Anthony Lake did not see the INC-Kurdish rout as a U.S. defeat, Arabs, Turks, and Iranians unequivocally did. And when Saddam Hussein had tried to assassinate George Bush in April 1993, President Clinton's reprisal was

PRESENT DANGERS

to attack empty buildings with cruise missiles. The general Middle Eastern reaction to this act of retribution was not particularly impressive.

With the most flexible backbones in the Middle East, the Saudis were not keen to test Washington's resolve again with an enemy they truly feared. They believed that if Washington pin-pricked Tehran, or even hit harder, they more than the Americans would have to confront the aftermath. They also hoped that Tehran would recognize and honor the debt it now owed them. Nineteen dead U.S. servicemen did not matter by such *realpolitik*.

And Americans haven't been the only victims of the dark side of Tehran's foreign policy. The clerical regime has also gone after Israelis and, it strongly appears, non-American Jews, usually through employing their most zealous disciples, the Lebanese Hizbollah—though whenever the Hizbollah are culpable, Iranian inspiration may have to take a second seat to Syria's on-the-ground control. Lebanon's grim proconsul, Hafiz al-Asad, could, if he were so inclined, effectively cut off Iranian aid and discourage the Hizbollah from anti-Israeli attacks.

If the Israelis believe they've got the goods on the Iranians—for example, finding convincing evidence linking them to anti-Israeli/anti-Jewish bombings abroad—then they should by all means retaliate as directly as possible. And Washington should do nothing to discourage an Israeli response, but rather let it be known that the United States will aid the Israelis in any way possible to exact vengeance on terrorists. The more the Iranians believe they might be the victim of a pinpoint, satellite-assisted bombing raid, the less likely they are to misbehave in the first place. In one hundred hours, America's armed forces did to Saddam Hussein what the Iranians had dreamed of doing for eight years.

If Washington catches the Iranians in a terrorist act, then the U.S. Navy should retaliate with fury. And the Khobar incident ought not to go unpunished. Unless the White House can make a convincing case against Tehran's culpability—and the original CIA brief against bin Ladin is not convincing—then Washington at a minimum ought to state publicly that the evidence strongly suggests that Tehran is culpable. Rafsanjani and Khameneh'i ought to be mentioned by name—no terrorist attack would have occurred without both clerics' approval. Since the Clinton administration likes to treat terrorism as if it were a criminal proceeding in a U.S.

court, then the White House ought to seek the equivalent of an international subpoena against Rafsanjani, Khameneh'i, and the former Iranian intelligence chief, Ali Fallahiyan. If a German judge could do the equivalent in response to a considerably less lethal Iranian attack against Kurdish-Iranian dissidents resident in Germany, then Washington ought to be able to muster the will to avenge U.S. soldiers. At a minimum, the three men should be worried about ever traveling again outside Iran's borders.

And if Washington has in its possession new evidence buttressing the pre-existing case against Tehran—which may well be the case—then the United States ought to strike the Islamic Republic militarily. If Tehran knows that we know the truth and have chosen to do nothing, we are asking to be hit again. We will not split the "moderates" from the "hard-liners" on the issue of terrorism against the United States. And the hard-liners won't fail to note that they can neutralize America by playing the "Khatami card"— that the promise of internal Iranian reform turns Washington's cheek. If we attack, U.S. armed forces must strike with truly devastating effect against the ruling mullahs and the repressive institutions that maintain them. That is, no cruise missiles at midnight to minimize the body count. The clerics will almost certainly strike back unless Washington uses overwhelming, paralyzing force.

A counterstrike against clerical terrorism probably would not damage reform inside Iran. Quite the contrary. By turning the temperature up—by clearly letting Iran's fractious ruling class, not to mention the Iranian people, know that Khameneh'i and Rafsanjani have provoked the United States to strike, endangering the nation and the clerical status quo—Washington will accelerate the internal debate about the morality and competence of Iran's leadership. The Iranian people, at least most of them, are not going to rally long around the flag in defense of the people and institutions they detest most. Underneath any initial flurry of righteous indignation at America's actions will be seething anger at the clerics who put Iran on a collision course with the United States, a nation whose allure has skyrocketed in large part because its culture and power are considered inimical to the Islamic revolution.

As the clerical regime falls apart, it isn't unlikely that the Iranian hard core may return to terrorist attacks against the United States. At the first whiff of any new Iranian mischief, we should make it clear to Tehran through back channels that X number of clerical homes will be struck with cruise missiles. Seriously threatening clerical Iran for nefarious behavior is, also, perhaps the most effective way to get the Iranians into a face-to-face dialogue with U.S. officials.

Iranian terrorism, however, should not be a paralyzing issue for Washington, preventing us from having any dealings with Tehran. We have areas of important mutual interest that can be pursued discreetly through the use of third parties. Though it's a cultural point that is often difficult for Americans to grasp—it would seem particularly difficult for certain officials in the State Department— the clerics will be much more likely to work with us privately if we are seriously following a hard-line policy against them publicly. Such a byzantine approach is natural in Iran, where the fiercest enmities do not necessarily prevent useful temporary alliances.

Iran needs help dealing with both Saddam Hussein and Afghanistan's Sunni Taliban, who have replaced the Iranians as the godfathers of the Muslim world's most virulent anti-American (and anti-Shi'ite) fundamentalism. The United States urgently needs to find a means to end Saddam Hussein's rule and check the lethality, if not the growth, of Taliban/bin Ladin–style Islamic radicalism in Afghanistan and Pakistan. A tacit Iranian-American alliance could provide decisive help to the Iraqi opposition and significantly strengthen the anti-Taliban forces in northern Afghanistan, who remain the best hope of eventually fracturing Taliban power, expelling bin Ladin's growing army of proselytes, and deflating the spirit and ambitions of the pro-Taliban Pakistani fundamentalists. Such U.S.-Iranian "cooperation" in Iraq and Afghanistan would not, of course, necessarily improve official relations between Washington and Tehran.

Concerning sanctions, we can keep them on the clerical regime for its terrorist track-record—and terrorism alone is certainly heinous enough to invoke U.S. sanctions—but we should realize that we are engaging in shadow-boxing. Sanctions have never stopped the Iranians from bombing us; they never will. They lack the requisite immediacy and comprehensiveness to concentrate the clerical mind on its own misbehavior. And once the Clinton administration refused to confront the Europeans and Russians in 1996, energy-related sanctions lost most of their punitive value. Furthermore, if the United States is instituting sanctions against the Islamic Republic for aiding and abetting terrorism, then we should probably be bombing, not boycotting, them.

Second Sin: Supporting Islamic Militants Throughout the World
The clerical regime has certainly tried to do this, but so what? Saudi Arabia and Pakistan have done a far better job—they both probably should share the credit for Usama bin Ladin. As the Islamic revolution has aged, the Iranians have proven to be less and less ecumenical. Shi'ites, a small minority in the Muslim world, not Sunnis, have received the bulk of their affections and aid. Islamic radicalism in the Sunni world hasn't turned out the way Iranians had hoped. When Sunni militants gain strength, they tend to kill Shi'ites. Pakistan and Afghanistan, Iran's neighbors, have murdered an ever-increasing number of Shi'ites—both Iranian and the home-grown variety—as their politico-religious cultures have radicalized. With the possible exception of the Hizbollah, it is difficult to find a single radical Islamic movement that would be significantly less menacing if Iranian aid were cut off. Hamas and Islamic Jihad in the West Bank and Gaza would feel the pinch, but neither group would probably become less lethal to the Israelis or the PLO.

Third Sin: Denouncing the Peace Process and
the Very Existence of Israel
True again. But so what? Much of the Arab world—Yasser Arafat included—condemns the peace process and the existence of Israel when not directly in front of an American television camera. Iran's support to anti–peace process radicals in Jordan, the West Bank, Gaza, and Lebanon is certainly annoying—and for the Israelis perhaps a legitimate reason for lethal counterattacks—but it does not at all alter the peace process's fundamentals.

Fourth Sin: Violating Human Rights
Iran's human rights record at home has been awful—toward the Baha'is and now the Jews, truly awful. But compared to the Saudis or Syrians, are the Iranians beyond the Middle Eastern pale? The modern Middle East is an ugly place, where individuals constantly get sacrificed on the alter of nationalism, regional stability, and faith.

Of course, the clerical regime's violations of human rights should not be downplayed: Iran is neither Syria nor Iraq nor Saudi Arabia. Iran considers itself, in most ways, superior to its neighbors. Human rights are an extremely critical issue inside Iran not because their violation offends American standards but because most Iranians are deeply ashamed of the revolution's violence and incivility. Indeed, a loud defense of human rights is perhaps America's foremost *realpolitik* weapon against the clerical regime. The Clinton administration, unfortunately, doesn't realize this, preferring to see Khatami and the "reformist" clerical class as an avatar of a gradual, peaceful democratic evolution. Defending human rights too strongly—in other words, questioning Khatami's commitment to defending civil liberties—is thus, for the Clinton administration, counterproductive. Fortunately for Iranians, U.S. officials probably cannot significantly delay the inevitable expansion of civil liberties in Iran by sending the wrong signals.

Fifth Sin: Seeking the Bomb

Tehran certainly wants nuclear weapons; and its reasoning is not illogical. Iran was gassed into surrender in the first Persian Gulf War; Pakistan, Iran's ever more radicalized Sunni neighbor to the southeast, has nuclear weapons; Saddam Hussein, with his Scuds and his weapons-of-mass-destruction ambitions, is next door; Saudi Arabia, Iran's most ardent and reviled religious rival, has long-range missiles; Russia, historically one of Iran's most feared neighbors, is once again trying to reassert its dominion in the neighboring Caucasus; and Israel could, of course, blow the Islamic Republic to bits. Having been vanquished by a technologically superior Iraq at a cost of at least a half-million men, Iran knows very well the consequences of having insufficient deterrence. And the Iranians possess the essential factor to make deterrence work: sanity. Tehran or Isfahan in ashes would destroy the Persian soul, about which even the most hard-line cleric cares deeply. As long as the Iranians believe that either the U.S. or Israel or somebody else in the region might retaliate with nuclear weapons, they won't do something stupid.

A nuclear-armed Islamic Republic would of course check, if not checkmate, the United States' maneuvering room in the Persian Gulf. We would no doubt think several times about responding to Iranian terrorism or military action if Tehran had the bomb and a missile to deliver it. During the lead-up to the second Gulf War, ruling clerical circles in Tehran and Qom were abuzz with the debate about nuclear weapons. The mullahs of the *Ruhaniyun* and *Ruhaniyat* agreed: if Saddam Hussein had had nuclear arms, the Americans would not have challenged him. For the "left" and the "right," this weaponry is the ultimate guarantee of Iran's defense, its revolution, and its independence as a regional great power.

Trying to stop clerical Iran from developing nuclear weapons is, therefore, a worthwhile U.S. foreign policy. Iran will one day have the bomb—the technology behind weapons or the weapons themselves *always* proliferate—but it would be much better to delay the inevitable as long as possible, particularly since the clerical regime might fall in the not too distant future.

And in fact, the United States could do more than what the Clinton administration has done to delay Iranian nuclear plans. Washington could more harshly sanction Russia and North Korea, the two principal suppliers of the technology and the materiel that allows Iran's nuclear industry and missile program to move forward. Allowing Russia and North Korea, in particular, to prevent significant punitive actions by repeatedly playing their respective "chaos" cards ties the United States to the status quo, where the Iranians advance and we do nothing. Instead, we should answer their challenge. Beijing, too, has been helpful in developing Tehran's conventional and unconventional missile capacity. Tougher, targeted sanctions against all these states are a good idea. We should be under no illusions, however, about the chances for long-term success in thwarting Iran's nuclear ambitions. We should assume that the clerics will soon have the bomb, and plan accordingly.

A New U.S.–Iran policy

Despite the Clinton administration's flaccid follow-up to its tough sanctions rhetoric and its naive, just-one-more-appeal-and-apology approach to Khatami and the clerical regime, the United States is not in a weak position vis-à-vis the Islamic Republic. Though American concerns about Iran are real and, in the cases of terrorism and proliferation, serious, they are manageable. They require us essentially to be restrained and even cold-hearted, fighting only those battles that enhance, not diminish the awe in which we are held—our most prized asset in Middle Eastern politics.

Concerning sanctions, fate again has been relatively kind to us. A significant mistake made by the Clinton administration was to raise the ante on U.S. sanctions and then walk away as soon as the French oil company Total challenged them. This made the United States seem weak and the Iranians, undeservedly, strong.

If the Clinton administration wanted to take a pass on sanctions—and it is definitely an arguable point whether Iran's sins are meaningfully countered by across-the-board unilateral sanctions—it should have vetoed the 1996 Iran-Libya Sanctions Act or publicly abandoned it upon Khatami's election, a tactical move that was judiciously advanced by Patrick Clawson of the Washington Institute for Near Eastern Policy. The White House could have proclaimed a new beginning in U.S.-Iranian relations. This would have been a lie, of course. The Iranians and others would have seen this move as a U.S. defeat, but we would have had some cover-for-action. And we could have loudly described the clerical regime as backwards and culturally retrograde, scared of renewing diplomatic relations with the United States.

Sanctions as a policy tool make sense if Washington's real objective is to weaken the clerical regime in the hope that it will, through a combination of external and internal pressures, eventually collapse. Sanctions make sense if the objective is to deny clerical Iran the cash to produce or buy conventional weaponry. Since the clerics are determined to obtain unconventional weapons of mass destruction, which are comparatively cheap to produce and certainly within the range of Iran's oil revenues, sanctions, realistically, will not greatly degrade the Iranian effort to develop or steal such arms.

However, using sanctions as leverage to encourage better clerical behavior—the stated objective of the Clinton administration—makes no sense and betrays the administration's ignorance of Iranian politics. For those who believe in it—and Khatami, Khameneh'i, and Rafsanjani certainly do—the Iranian revolutionary identity just isn't negotiable. No economic sanction, for example, will deter Tehran from a terrorist action that the ruling clergy believes is in the national interest.

This is not to say that dropping energy-related sanctions would have helped the diplomatic dialogue. The ruling mullahs want our money; they don't want a U.S. embassy in downtown Tehran. There is no "confidence-building measure" that can seduce them into eliminating the life-sustaining psychological support of anti-Americanism. No diplomatic or commercial carrot would convince them to allow American diplomats and spies into direct contact with the country's innumerable dissidents. Clerics were indispensable to the American-assisted 1953 coup d'état that put the Shah back into power. Conspiracy-obsessed, they would not want history to repeat itself.

And keeping unilateral sanctions now doesn't really carry much cost. The Iranian economy is so fouled up, Iranian rules regarding foreign investment are so hostile, and the security of foreign investment is so politically precarious that the United States has essentially got, thanks to the mullahs, what sanctions were supposed to deliver—a clerical regime strapped for cash, unable to invest heavily in armaments. U.S. businesses are, no question, losing out to foreign competitors in Iran; but we're not talking *that* much money. The French company Total is satisfied, though not ecstatic, with its investment in the Persian Gulf. The "post-sanctions" great Iranian oil and gas bonanza hasn't happened. Other contracts have been signed, but the market remains wary. If the price of oil keeps rising, the Iranians will of course be in better shape. But it's doubtful that they will benefit from a stampede. Iran is not Iraq. Oil isn't bubbling out of the ground: increasing Iranian oil production is an expensive, long-term affair. And oil aside, given the nature of clerical Iran, where politics and business become personal quite quickly, it's perhaps best that there are no U.S. business personnel in the country. Iranians are not averse to making false arrests and using hostage businessmen for higher purposes.

U.S. sanctions often get hit with another false charge: that if it were not for U.S. pressure, the Islamic Republic would have contracted for oil and gas pipelines from Central Asia to the Persian Gulf. American energy companies that invested massively and perhaps prematurely in Central Asia would then not be in such an awful bind trying to find a cost-effective way of transporting the region's oil and gas to Western and Asian consumers.

In fact, the threat of U.S. sanctions has provided the Iranians with a superb excuse in a politically and economically awkward situation. Why would they want to allow Central Asian oil and gas onto the world market? They want the price of oil to go up, not down. They desperately need more foreign investment in their energy sector, and attracting it has so far proven more difficult than they had hoped. Why divert foreign investment toward Central Asia and toward a pipeline which would provide transship-ment revenues far less than what newly developed Iranian oil fields would bring? The Iranians need to develop a realistic pricing structure for internal gas development and distribution (the cler-ics essentially give away gas free on the domestic market) rather than allow foreigners to forgo developing the Iranian market alto-gether. And why would they want to annoy the Russians, from whom they buy military and nuclear technology, by bypassing the Russian-controlled pipeline from Central Asia? U.S. oil companies who have invested heavily in Central Asia may think Iran is the promised path for a pipeline; Tehran does not.

There really isn't a good reason for the U.S. to reverse course now on sanctions. There is no need to make a public issue out of a losing cause. And we know from the clerical regime's constant whining about U.S. sanctions that they are not without effect. There can be no doubt now that the sanctions approach originally designed by Patrick Clawson and the Bush administration's Zal-may Khalilzad has financially hurt the clerical regime at minimal cost to the United States. If the Clinton administration walks away from sanctions now, the Iranians will neither say "thank you" nor change their behavior. Tehran will just crow that Washington is weak, unable to resist the allure of Iranian oil. Whether the next administration should want to keep the exact same sanctions is, however, a debatable point.

U.S. trade is a live wire in Iran, provoking vitriolic debates among the country's hard core. This is all for the best: the more we can corrode the revolutionary spirit, the better. Obviously, sanctions against Iran's military industries should remain in place. The Clin-ton administration's decision to allow Iran to export carpets, caviar, and pistachios to the United States is, for the most part, a harm-less, insignificant action. (Enriching Rafsanjani, the pistachio king, who unquestionably has authorized the killing of Americans, is an ugly, if unintended, consequence of the administration's "little car-rot" approach.) Concerning the rest, it might be best to downplay the situation if possible, lift all restrictions on the export of U.S. cultural and consumer goods (which enter the country in any case through the United Arab Emirates), politely, quietly, but firmly dis-courage U.S. companies from making major investments, and allow the Iranians to destroy their own economy.

There is arguably no more important issue for the United States in the Middle East than to see the Islamic revolution put to rest by the Iranian people. If the Iranians can do it, and replace the clerical regime with some kind of functioning secular democracy, then the Middle East will be forever altered. To borrow from the Princeton historian Bernard Lewis, Kemalism will have triumphed over Khomeinism, and Muslims will have shown, to an often dismissive and condescending West, that they, too, have earned the right to demand and enjoy the liberties of free men. If the Turks and Iranians, the two most powerful Muslim peoples of the Middle East, can maintain secular democracies, then the Arab world and Central Asia will have models that will be hard to ignore. The success of the Arab-Israeli peace process in comparison is a minor issue.

As the clerical regime comes apart, the United States ought to remain essentially a bystander. A few things, however, might be done. Enterprises such as Radio Liberty should be expanded; Iran in the year 2000 has moved beyond radio. Even in the slums of south Tehran, television has become the lingua franca. We should ensure that Radio Free Europe–Radio Liberty and the Voice of America deliver hard-hitting news that the ruling clergy cannot squelch. Delivering news and entertainment and advancing human rights—not reconciliation or the dream of opening bureaus in Tehran—ought to be the only objectives of America's Persian broadcasting.

We should, in general, eschew quiet diplomacy with the clerics. If the mullahs jail or murder dissidents and minorities, we should protest loudly and continuously. We should understand that the moral debate isn't between us and them, but among Iranians themselves. When we talk about injustices in Iran, we sustain and provoke discussions in Tehran, Qom, Isfahan, and elsewhere. And a loud diplomacy doesn't prevent us from quietly pursuing points of common interest.

As the Clinton administration has promised, we should eliminate the time-consuming and needlessly offensive visa procedures that diminish the flow of Iranian visitors to the United States. Iranian terrorism was a far greater threat to the United States in the 1980s than it is today, yet in the 1980s, visa procedures were simpler and more efficient. There is no good security reason why we can't go back to the procedures we had in, say, 1985, when consular officers in the field, not officials in Washington, could determine whether to issue a visa within twenty-four hours. American-educated Iranians helped to provoke the Islamic revolution in 1978; we should encourage a supply of American-educated Iranians and ordinary Iranian tourists who might try another revolution.

The next U.S. administration may well face an Iran again in turmoil. If so, we will be fortunate in not having an embassy in Tehran to worry about. From a safe distance, we can watch the Iranian people, again, fight for their freedom. We can pray that the clerical *Götterdämmerung* isn't too bloody, and that the mullahs quickly retreat to their mosques and content themselves primarily with the joys of scholarly disputation.

North Korea: Beyond Appeasement

Since its inception in 1948, the Democratic People's Republic of Korea has pursued an international policy distinguished, even by the standards of our fractious era, by its breathtaking bellicosity and extreme irredentism. The quintessence of Pyongyang's foreign policy—its enthusiastically confrontational, usually ferocious, and at times plainly savage posture toward its many designated enemies abroad—has placed North Korea in more-or-less permanent conflict with what is now called "the international community." By no coincidence, Pyongyang's deliberately menacing external policies and practices have also maneuvered that government into an exceptionally hostile relationship with the United States of America.

For half a century and more, North Korea has occupied a far higher level of attention within America's international security policy than a country of its population or economic strength would ordinarily command. This is because the DPRK's leadership has regularly chosen to inhabit a high-tension, high-risk niche in international power politics—a dangerous neighborhood in which even a slight miscalculation portends catastrophe. Unfortunately, Pyongyang has been known to make just such miscalculations.

The chief instance of North Korean miscalculation, of course, came in 1950 when Pyongyang launched a surprise attack against South Korea, a blitzkrieg through which it expected to reunify the entire Korean peninsula (which had been partitioned at the end of World War II) beneath its own communist authority. To Pyongyang's surprise, however, the United States happened to come to the defense of its ally in Seoul; and the Korean War consequently escalated into a protracted multinational battle costing millions of lives, embroiling (among other parties) both Maoist China and the United Nations, and bringing the world close to another nuclear strike.

Since the 1953 ceasefire that brought the fighting to a formal halt, U.S. troops have been stationed in South Korea to deter a DPRK miscalculation that might re-ignite war in the Korean peninsula. Though the ceasefire has held for more than four and a half decades, the situation has, in military terms, remained extraordinarily tense. The so-called "De-Militarized Zone" that separates North and South Korea is actually the most militarized spot on the planet, and forces are maintained in a perpetually high state of readiness: even today American military officials expect to have no more than 24–48 hours advance warning in the event of another North Korean military offensive against the Republic of Korea in the South.[1]

By a variety of important criteria, the threats posed by Pyongyang to American interests *should have* dramatically diminished with the end of the Cold War. Indeed, with the collapse of the Soviet Bloc and Pyongyang's loss of its allies in Moscow, the danger—once very real—that a North Korean adventure might inadvertently escalate into a general nuclear war now appears to be negligible. Developments within the Korean peninsula, furthermore, have transformed Pyongyang's abiding ambition to overturn the ROK and absorb South Korea from a genuine possibility into a fantasy.

Over the past decade the ROK, once an unstable autocracy, has firmly secured its claim as a legitimate constitutional democracy. Moreover, that recently impoverished society has managed an amazing economic ascent, and today ranks as a member of the OECD, the club of affluent Western aid-dispensing countries.[2]

North Korea, by contrast, has suffered continuing political repression and severe economic decline since the end of the Soviet experiment. Before the end of the Cold War, an eminent Asia scholar described the DPRK's communist dictatorship with Korean characteristics as a "political system as close to totalitarianism as a humanly operated society could come."[3] In the 1990s, despite a worldwide wave of political liberalization, this dynastic Leninist state stubbornly resisted all pressures for a relaxation of its internal controls and if anything, grew even more illiberal. In 1998,

"Great Leader" Kim Il Sung, the state's then-four-years-dead founding figure, was officially proclaimed to be the country's "eternal
President"; Kim's reclusive son, "Dear Leader" Kim Jong Il, effectively assumed the role of all-powerful ruler, yet did not become
the country's "head of state."[4]

Political involution coincided with a drastic and apparently still
unchecked downturn in the local economy. Although reliable data
on all North Korean conditions are amazingly scarce, thanks to
Pyongyang's remarkable information control, the DPRK's hyper-
militarized economy was evidently already faltering before the end
of the Cold War, staggering under the extreme distortions caused
by official policies and practices. North Korea's economic failure
in the 1990s was so profound that a country-wide hunger crisis
erupted. In 1995, despite its officially extolled *juche* (self-reliance)
doctrine, Pyongyang issued an international humanitarian appeal
for emergency food relief. The exact dimensions of North Korea's
food crisis remain a state secret: Pyongyang has steadfastly refused
to reveal this even to the international agencies that are currently
engaged in alleviating it. But the fact that intensive international
relief operations for the DPRK are presently entering into their
sixth consecutive calendar year suggests that the country has, for
all intents and purposes, lost the capacity to feed its own population. This is an unprecedented and indeed unique instance of systemic economic failure in the modern era; nothing like this has
ever before befallen an urbanized, industrialized society during
peacetime.

Yet paradoxically, despite the disastrous performance of the
North Korean economic system, the DPRK today poses a continuing, and perhaps even an increasing, threat to the United States
and her Asian allies. Economic distress may have constrained the
conventional capabilities of the country's enormous military
machine,[5] but even as North Korea's starving subjects are forced
to look to food donations from abroad for sustenance, the regime
is racing to develop a credible arsenal of weapons of mass
destruction.

Ever since the 1993–94 nuclear drama that Pyongyang precipitated by its threat to withdraw from the Nuclear Non-Proliferation
Treaty and its refusal to allow unrestricted inspections of its nuclear
facilities by the UN International Atomic Energy Agency, the DPRK's
atomic ambitions and capabilities have commanded worldwide

attention. North Korea's decades-old nuclear weapons program, it is currently thought, may already have succeeded in producing enough separated plutonium for one or more nuclear weapons; the program is believed to be capable, when fully activated, of generating enough separated plutonium for a few new atomic weapons every few months.[6]

North Korea's nuclear program, however, is only one facet of a broadly-based quest for weapons of mass destruction. Pyongyang is thought, for example, to have amassed one of the world's largest stockpiles of chemical weapons; according to some assessments, it may already possess up to five thousand tons of these deadly agents.[7] Pyongyang has also methodically prepared to wage biological warfare. According to the Federation of American Scientists, North Korea has been engaged in biological weapon research since the early 1960s[8]; it currently possesses, in the estimate of the South Korean Defense Ministry, "at least ten different kinds of biological weapons."[9]

And Pyongyang has also been straining to perfect the long-range ballistic missiles that might deliver these weapons around the globe. In late August 1998, North Korea publicly revealed the latest advance in its missile program by launching—without advance warning—a multistage ballistic rocket over Japan. That vehicle (known as Taepo Dong I) was thought to be capable of carrying a one-ton payload as far as two thousand kilometers, thereby placing the entire territory of Japan within range of North Korean warheads. A subsequent, not-yet-tested upgrade—the Taepo Dong II missile—is thought to be capable of reaching Hawaii and Alaska.

But there is no reason to imagine that North Korea's decades-old missile development program would stop at America's shores. Once it manages to field an improved, three-stage Taepo Dong II missile, DPRK leadership should be able to threaten the American heartland—the continental states—with chemical, biological, and possibly nuclear attack.[10]

For the United States, the successes of Pyongyang's quest to acquire strategic destructive capabilities thus constitute a decidedly ominous development. Over much of the global expanse, other potentially hostile actors threaten America's interests only indirectly: through the injury they might wreak on valued but geographically distant American allies. By contrast, the DPRK's program for developing weapons of terror threatens American vital interests directly: by exposing the American homeland to constant, imminent danger of assault under circumstances entirely of Pyongyang's choosing.

From the standpoint of North Korea's leadership, the drive to develop WMDs that can strike America is logical, satisfactory, and arguably even essential. It would represent the culmination of a policy that has already succeeded in placing Pyongyang's two other prime enemies—the ROK and Japan—under seemingly permanent and inescapable North Korean military threat. It would elevate military extortion to a central dynamic within the Pyongyang-Washington relationship—and blackmail is a familiar device within the DPRK's diplomatic repertoire, one it utilizes with considerable skill and experience. Moreover, for a system whose current economic arrangements presage continuing decline—and for which alternative economic directions are officially deemed to pose incalculable political hazards—establishing a credible blackmail threat against the globe's one remaining superpower may look like an attractive option for guaranteeing state survival.

Unfortunately, neither the United States nor her allies have responded to North Korea's weapons program with a coherent, threat-reducing strategy. Instead, over the course of the 1990s Washington, Seoul and Tokyo all stumbled into a syndrome of ad hoc, reactive interactions with Pyongyang, all predicated on the idea of containing new North Korean perils by pressing Pyongyang to the negotiating table. Allied diplomats negotiated with the DPRK more intensively during the 1990s than at any time since the Korean War, and in fact constructed a succession of agreements, declarations, understandings, and "frameworks" to which North Korea assented. But because the DPRK is a government with a pre-legal and essentially situational attitude toward treaties and contracts (in Pyongyang's ethos, no commitment that might put North Korea at a disadvantage against current or potential opponents is ever treated as binding), the documents and pronouncements that Western diplomacy has struggled to fashion for Pyongyang have been disregarded or summarily reinterpreted by North Korean leadership when such behavior serves its purposes. Consequently, far from putting an end to North Korean dramas, each "crisis-solving" diplomatic foray to date has merely set the stage for the next "crisis" that Pyongyang has chosen to manufacture.

At considerable financial cost and diplomatic effort, the United

States and her Asian allies *have* managed to achieve a moratorium on the development of the DPRK's now-notorious nuclear facilities in Yongbyon and Taechon; but the Yongbyon/Taechon complex is a single component in the DPRK's far-reaching, multifaceted and mainly surreptitious weapons program. At this writing, U.S. authorities also have a verbal pledge that Pyongyang will not launch another ballistic missile while there is progress in high-level U.S.-DPRK talks about normalizing relations. But this pledge is by design highly conditional, and expressly does not suspend missile research and development or missile exports. The current approach, in short, has failed to make steady reductions in the North Korean WMD threat—much less eliminate the threat entirely.

Lacking firm foundations, the objectives and rationales of Western policies toward the DPRK have shifted somewhat erratically over the past decade. The latest theme in U.S.-ROK policy toward the North Korean threat—introduced and forcefully promoted by South Korea's current president, Kim Dae Jung—is the purported imperative of "engaging" Pyongyang, so that the regime might be transformed and moderated. But the diplomatic web that has been spun in the name of "engaging North Korea" has to date yielded precious little moderation of North Korean behavior. Instead, it has inadvertently ratified a de facto syndrome of appeasement of Pyongyang, in which Western aid and diplomatic concessions are met by renewed North Korean threats, which are followed in turn by further Western aid and concessions. Far from minimizing the dangers posed by the DPRK, the current de facto appeasement framework maximizes the DPRK's incentives to create a menace and raises the risk of another disastrous North Korean miscalculation.

South Korea's "Sunshine" Policy

Since Kim Dae Jung's February 1998 presidential inauguration, the Republic of Korea has pursued a North Korea policy characterized officially as "sunshine," or alternatively, "engagement." (The term "sunshine" alludes to one of Aesop's fables, in which a man is induced to remove his overcoat by warm sun, rather than by cold wind and rain.) In some respects, this "sunshine" policy represents a continuation of pre-existing ROK positions and initiatives toward the north. Its first principle, "We will never tolerate armed provocation of any kind," is a tenet embraced by every South Korean president from Syngman Rhee on.[11] The "sunshine" policy also builds upon the work of previous South Korean administrations, most notably that of the Roh Tae Woo government; its third principle—"we will actively push reconciliation and cooperation between the South and North"—recalls the (now lifeless) "Agreement on Reconciliation, Nonaggression, and Cooperation and Exchange between North and South" and the "Joint Declaration on the Denuclearization of the Korean Peninsula" that Seoul and Pyongyang signed back in 1991 and 1992.[12]

But the "sunshine" policy constitutes a truly new direction because at its core is not only an acceptance in principle by South Korea of the survival of the North Korean state, but also a commitment to practical measures that support the regime's existence.

The new attitude is underscored by the "sunshine" policy's second precept: "We do not have any intention to harm or absorb North Korea." Innocuous as these words might sound, they constitute a radical reversal in South Korean policy—and even a potential inconsistency with South Korea's basic laws. (Since Article 3 of the ROK Constitution states that "The territory of the Republic of Korea shall consist of the Korean peninsula and its adjacent islands,"[13] the ROK government would seem not only legally intent upon, but ultimately charged with, "absorbing" North Korea!)

Initially, President Kim justified this new stance toward the survival of the North Korean system by pointing to the enormous costs for Seoul that an immediate unification might entail for the South Korean economy.[14] Far from hastening the DPRK's collapse, "Our policy is stabilize North Korea," declared one of the president's advisers.[15] But the new government in Seoul has also contemplated measures that would legitimate the DPRK. "Peaceful co-existence presupposes an independent and sovereign North Korea," mused then–ROK Foreign Minister Hong Soon-young in early 1999, implying that South Korea might be willing to extend formal diplomatic recognition to the DPRK.[16] President Kim Dae Jung has signaled that the North Korean state should outlast its current crisis, declaring that he does not anticipate reunification during his tenure in office (which extends through early 2003).[17] If the "sunshine" policy succeeds, one senior South Korean official opined, Korea would reunify around the year 2025[18]—raising the prospect of a continuation of the DPRK's existence for another quarter-century.

Besides endorsing, and supporting, the survival of the North Korean state in general terms, the "sunshine" policy heralds other new directions for North-South relations. In his inaugural address, President Kim announced that reconciliation and cooperation with the North would be pursued "beginning with those areas which can be most easily agreed upon." In practice, this means seizing upon opportunities for interaction where Pyongyang is willing to be engaged, and deferring issues that Pyongyang finds contentious. Thus the "sunshine" policy strives, for example, to "separate business from politics" in North-South relations because Pyongyang has proved willing to conduct a limited commerce with the Republic of Korea, while remaining resolutely opposed to a substantive inter-Korean political dialogue. By the same token, although President Kim Dae Jung is surely the Korean peninsula's most prominent human rights activist (and its most famous former prisoner of conscience), he has to date carefully avoided broaching the issue of human rights in North Korea, knowing that Pyongyang would react harshly to any such questions.

All previous South Korean administrations insisted upon strict reciprocity in their give-and-take with the North Korean government. By contrast, Seoul is now willing to offer immediate political, economic and social favors to the DPRK in the hope that North Korea will offer concessions of its own at a later date. In the words of a South Korean foreign minister, the ROK expects "to receive rewards from the [N]orth sometime in the future, although [Seoul] places more weight on giving for a while."[19]

The rationale for Seoul's forbearance is the hope that it will yield a monumental breakthrough. President Kim envisions a grand international settlement with Pyongyang in which an atmosphere of enhanced trust convinces North Korea to foreswear its weapons programs and its provocations against the South in return for diplomatic recognition by the U.S. and Japan, economic normalization with Washington, and a foreign aid formula to help Pyongyang deal with its systemic troubles.[20] In Kim's view, such a settlement would permit the dismantling of the "cold war structure on the Korean peninsula," replacing the tense ceasefire between North and South with a permanent peace accord.[21] The "sunshine" policy aims to transform not only North Korea's outward behavior, but also the internal character of the North Korean system. "I believe our consistent efforts will ultimately lead North Korea toward a large flow of reform and openness," President Kim has avowed.[22] In the end, in his estimate, "engagement" policy will induce North Korea to adopt "a Chinese- or Vietnamese-style market economy, [with a] broadening of the middle class and the emergence of a multiple party system."[23] With the DPRK thus liberalized and pacified, the "sunshine" policy contends, an amicable and voluntary reunification will finally become a realistic possibility for the Korean people.

Unlike the Kim Dae Jung government, the Clinton administration has not pursued a single, consistent policy toward North Korea and the threat posed by its weapons of mass destruction. Rather, it has embraced a succession of approaches toward the DPRK problem, each with its own separate explicit objectives and implicit rationales. In the eight years of the Clinton administration, at least four distinct North Korea policies have been in force.

In March 1993—less than two months into the Clinton administration—North Korea triggered an international nuclear drama by announcing its intention to withdraw from the Nuclear Non-Proliferation Treaty. Pyongyang's move followed surprise findings in 1992 by UN International Atomic Energy Agency inspectors that the DPRK's Yongbyon nuclear facilities had generated more plutonium than the government was claiming (perhaps even enough fissile material for one or two atomic bombs), and demands by the IAEA for further inspections to determine the actual status of the DPRK nuclear program.[24] The same week Pyongyang declared it would be leaving the treaty, Kim Jong Il alerted his countrymen to "a grave situation in which war might break out at any moment" and mobilized North Korea to a "semi-state of war."[25]

The Clinton administration's first approach to Pyongyang's proliferation threat was a familiar rendition of the traditional postwar posture toward would-be proliferators. Washington insisted that North Korea meet all of its obligations under the Non-Proliferation Treaty unconditionally, as all other signatories were expected to, without preferential treatment or demand for special rewards. American officials focusing on the North Korean nuclear problem, reported the *New York Times* in late March 1993, "say their chief priority is to preserve the integrity of the inspection process that North Korea has rejected. If North Korea is seen to gain some advantage by withdrawing from the nonproliferation treaty, United States diplomats in Asia argue, other countries would be quick to follow."[26] The administration's bottom-line position was articulated most forcefully by the president himself. In November 1993, Clinton unequivocally declared that "North Korea cannot be allowed to develop a nuclear bomb. We have to be very firm about it. . . . This is a very grave issue for the United States."[27]

But North Korea showed no interest in accommodating the Clinton administration's position. On the contrary, in desultory dealings with the IAEA and in specially convened negotiating sessions with American counterparts, North Korean officials established their government's resolute unwillingness to allow the immediate and unrestricted inspections by outsiders required to determine just how far its nuclear weapons program had progressed.

Furthermore, Pyongyang loudly proclaimed that it would treat as a provocation any international efforts to put "improper" pressure upon the DPRK in order to bring it into compliance. (If, for example, the United Nations should adopt a proposed resolution for economic sanctions that the United States and her allies were considering, Pyongyang warned, this would be taken "as a declaration of war."[28]) As the inspection impasse dragged on, North Korea's threats grew more pointed and violent. Should Tokyo join the international campaign to force open North Korea's nuclear facilities, DPRK media intoned, the Japanese people would be "digging their own grave."[29] And at the Panmunjom truce site on the Korean DMZ, furious North Korean negotiators spoke of turning Seoul into "a sea of fire."[30]

Faced with Pyongyang's fierce intransigence on nuclear inspections, and troubling evidence that North Korea's reactors could soon provide sufficient additional plutonium for perhaps up to four atomic bombs, a worried Clinton administration suddenly abandoned its first approach to North Korea and settled upon another, very different, tack. Clinton officials began to talk instead of seeking "a face-saving resolution" to the North Korean nuclear impasse[31]—and seized upon a proposal for dialogue by former President Jimmy Carter, who had met with Kim Il Sung in a hastily scheduled private visit to North Korea, as the context for exploring such a deal. The outcome of the subsequent, intensive Washington-Pyongyang negotiations was an October 1994 document known as the "Agreed Framework,"[32] which may be seen as the Clinton administration's second policy toward North Korea.

The Agreed Framework is a complex and somewhat ambiguous

text, constructed to be neither a treaty nor even, in any strict sense, an "agreement."³³ The document instead lays out a vision of parallel and reciprocal actions that the United States and North Korea might undertake over an extended time horizon—a period lasting at least until the year 2003, and perhaps considerably beyond that date.

In this envisioned "framework," North Korea would freeze activity at its Yongbyon facilities, permit IAEA inspectors to verify that freeze, and remain a signatory to the Non-Proliferation Treaty. The United States would ship North Korea 500,000 tons of heavy fuel oil a year, at no cost to Pyongyang, "to offset the energy foregone due to the freeze of the DPRK's graphite-moderated reactors," and would arrange for an international consortium (later named the Korean Peninsula Energy Development Organization) to build and finance two 1,000-megawatt light-water nuclear reactors on North Korean soil. (The cost of that project was expected to total roughly $4–5 billion.) As the light-water reactor project ultimately drew toward completion, the Framework stated, North Korea would dismantle its Yongbyon facilities, dispose of the plutonium generated there "in a safe manner," and submit to inspections to resolve the remaining uncertainties about the Yongbyon nuclear program. Over the course of these activities, Washington and Pyongyang would also "move toward full normalization of political and economic relations," while the DPRK would help to implement the defunct North-South "Joint Declaration on the Denuclearization of the Korean Peninsula" and "engage in North-South dialogue."

In effect, the Agreed Framework was a departure from the established principles of nonproliferation, and an entry into a realm in which compliance with pre-existing obligations had become indistinct, unenforceable and subject to compensatory renegotiation. The Clinton administration was now implicitly reconciled to the prospect of North Korea's possessing one or more atomic weapons. And it had dropped its demand that North Korea account for its past nuclear activities in a timely manner. In this new approach, the North Korean nuclear threat would be managed by a focus on preventing the development of *additional* capabilities; prevention, in turn, would hinge upon providing or denying the regime already-promised benefits, depending on Pyongyang's behavior.

A third Clinton administration policy toward the North Korean *problematik*, which supplanted the second approach without displacing it, began to emerge in early 1996. Since this approach has never been formally acknowledged, it lacks an official title, but it might be described as "money for meetings."

Although Pyongyang had committed itself in 1991 and 1992 to sustained official and unofficial contacts between itself and South Korea, and had seemingly affirmed that commitment in the Agreed Framework of 1994, the DPRK continued to avoid anything resembling a genuine dialogue with the South Korean government. In 1994, in fact, Pyongyang summarily announced that it no longer recognized the Military Armistice Commission that had overseen the Korean ceasefire since 1953, and demanded that a "new peace mechanism" be negotiated—but only through direct talks with Washington. Seoul, the North Koreans maintained, should have no role in the proposed discussions. As Pyongyang's commentary put it, "The South Korean puppets ... have no quality and reason to interfere in the establishment of a new peace mechanism by the DPRK and the U.S."[34]

In April 1996, President Clinton and South Korean President Kim Young Sam proposed a meeting to "replac[e] the current armistice agreement with a permanent peace"; the four parties invited to these talks would be the U.S., China, the DPRK, and the Republic of Korea. North Korea—by then deep in an officially acknowledged food crisis—did not reject out of hand the idea of direct talks with South Korea, instead indicating that it would examine whether such talks were "feasible."[35] Shortly thereafter, the United States announced a donation of $6 million to the UN World Food Program for famine relief in North Korea.

Several months later, North Korea agreed to send officials to a joint U.S.-ROK briefing on the Four Party Talks proposal. Simultaneously, Washington announced another donation of $10 million to the World Food Program's North Korea operations. Later that year, when Pyongyang finally agreed to participate in an actual session of Four Party Talks, the United States donated an additional $27 million.[36]

The United States publicly insisted that there was no connection between its contributions of food and money for North Korea and North Korean attendance at Four Party meetings, averring that its donations to the Food Program were solely humanitarian. In practice, however, the quid pro quo in the "money for meeting" arrangement was obvious, and there was no doubt whatever that North Korean participation in those sessions depended upon these financial inducements.

The policy of paying by the item for specific North Korean actions not only continued, but significantly broadened over the next few years, so that by 1999 the approach was extended to include payments to Pyongyang for permitting investigation of potential new violations of its own nonproliferation promises. American intelligence had detected a massive underground construction project in progress at Kumchang-ri; its characteristics suggested to Clinton administration officials that "the North intended to build a new reactor and reprocessing center" there.[37] After heated and protracted deliberations, the United States declared it would donate an unprecedented 600,000 tons of relief food to the DPRK, which in turn consented to a U.S. team's "visit" to the Kumchang-ri facility.

Although the Clinton administration claimed that the enormous new aid commitment and the inspection visit were entirely unrelated, North Korea's foreign ministry flatly contradicted that assertion, announcing that "There was a sufficient debate on and agreement on the payment of the 'inspection fee.'"[38]

The fourth, most recent, Clinton administration approach toward North Korea is known as the "Perry Process," and was outlined in a report released in October 1999 by former Defense Secretary William J. Perry, whom President Clinton appointed the administration's "North Korea Policy Coordinator" in November 1998.[39] Perry's review of, and recommendations for, America's North Korea policy followed extensive consultations with the South Korean and Japanese governments, and a trip to Pyongyang.

The Perry Report concluded, "Much has changed in the security situation on the Korean Peninsula since the 1994 crisis" that culminated in the Agreed Framework. The "most important" changes were "developments in the DPRK's nuclear and long-range missile activities." While "the Agreed Framework of 1994 succeeded in verifiably freezing North Korean plutonium production at Yongbyon," the report continued, "the policy review team has serious concerns about possible continuing nuclear weapons-related work in the DPRK." North Korea had also been working on "ballistic missiles of increasing range, including those potentially capable of reaching the territory of the United States." Since "acquisition by the DPRK of nuclear weapons or long-range missiles, and especially a combination of the two" would threaten to "undermine the relative stability" achieved to date in Korea by deterrence, the Perry team argued that the "urgent focus of U.S. policy toward the DPRK must be to end its nuclear weapons and long-range missile-related activities."

The Perry Report admitted to "the Agreed Framework's limitations"—"such as the fact that it does not verifiably freeze all nuclear activities and does not cover ballistic missiles"—but argued that these shortcomings would be best addressed by "supplementing rather than replacing" it. It proposed a "comprehensive and integrated approach," an approach, it asserted, that "would lead to a stable security situation on the Korean Peninsula, creating conditions for a more durable and lasting peace in the long run and ending the Cold War in East Asia."

The Perry Process envisioned a grand bargain: "We would seek complete and verifiable assurances that the DPRK does not have a nuclear weapons program ... complete and verifiable cessation of testing, production and deployment of [long-range] missiles ... and the complete cessation of export sales of such missiles and the equipment and technology associated with them." In return, "the United States would normalize relations with the DPRK, relax sanctions that have long constrained trade with the DPRK [and] take other positive steps that would provide opportunities for the DPRK." Under this approach, South Korea and Japan would also, "in coordinated but parallel tracks ... improve relations with the DPRK" as the United States was doing. Although the report explicitly disavowed any intention of altering the character of the North Korean regime, the Perry Process implicitly contemplated the transformation of both North Korean behavior and the North Korean system. "[I]n a step-by-step and reciprocal fashion," the report stated, its approach would "reduce pressures on the DPRK that it perceives as threatening. The reduction of perceived threat would in turn give the DPRK regime confidence that it could peacefully coexist with [the United States] and its neighbors and pursue its own economic and social development."

(The Perry Report also alluded to a "second path" of approaches "the U.S. and its allies would have to take" in order to "assure their security and contain the threat" if Pyongyang declined the proposed bargain—but did not detail them in the unclassified version of the document.)

The Perry Report unveiled not only a new direction in North Korea policy, but a new emphasis in its diplomacy. It repeatedly stressed the importance of harmonizing Washington's policy toward

North Korea with Seoul's and Tokyo's. It warned, indeed, that *"[n]o U.S. policy toward the DPRK will succeed if the ROK and Japan do not actively support it and cooperate in its implementation"* (emphasis added). And it effusively praised President Kim Dae Jung and his "sunshine policy":

> As a leader of great authority ... the views and insights of President Kim are central to accomplishing U.S. security objectives on the Korean Peninsula.... Today's ROK policy of engagement creates conditions and opportunities for U.S. policy very different from those in 1994.

In the opinion of the South Korean government, in fact, the Perry approach was virtually identical to the "sunshine policy"—and indeed derivative from it. As South Korea's foreign minister explained, "We believe the so-called Perry report or process is based on our engagement policy toward North Korea. Therefore, we fully and firmly support the Perry Process."[40]

In late 1999 and early 2000, the Clinton administration was attempting to apply the Perry approach to its relations with Pyongyang. The first results were announced in September 1999 (about a month before the official release of the Perry Report itself). In talks with North Korean officials in Berlin, American negotiators secured a verbal pledge that the DPRK would not launch another long-range missile for the duration of pending "high-level discussions" between representatives of Washington and Pyongyang. (Pyongyang insisted, however, that development and sale of ballistic missiles remained its sovereign right.) In return, Washington immediately lifted a number of the many economic sanctions that had been imposed upon the DPRK over the decades since the outbreak of the Korean War. At this writing the "high-level discussions" are still underway, and North Korea has not fired another ballistic missile. On the other hand, according to Pentagon reports, North Korea was continuing its preparations for the launch of the Taepo Dong 2, and continued to export ballistic missile components to interested purchasers, including Iran.[41]

From Containment to Coaxing

As these episodic developments indicate, American policy toward North Korea has undergone a paradigm shift during the Clinton years. Every previous American president had dealt with the threats posed by communist North Korea through a variant of the now-classic "containment" policy that Washington originally enforced against Stalin's USSR. In his early months in office, Clinton too seemed inclined to deal with North Korean threats by confronting Pyongyang "with unalterable counter-force at every point where they show signs of encroaching upon the interests of a peaceful and stable world," as the original doctrine on the containment of the USSR had advised.[42] In July 1993, during a trip to South Korea, Clinton advocated "stronger efforts to combat proliferation of weapons of mass destruction," and sharply noted that "our goal is not to enlist discussions, but certifiable compliance" from Pyongyang.[43] "The wisdom of what our country has done for forty years [in Korea] is basically demonstrated," he argued. "We know what works. If we just stay strong and we stay resolute and we stay firm, we know that will work."[44] Such words could have been uttered by any of the president's Cold War–era predecessors.

Within months, however, American North Korea policy veered in a radically different direction epitomized by Clinton's October 1994 letter to "his excellency Kim Jong Il," where he promised to "use the full powers of my office to facilitate arrangements for the financing and construction of a light-water nuclear power reactor project within the DPRK."[45] From any earlier president, Democrat or Republican, such words would have been completely unimaginable. Now Washington was, in essence, attempting to reduce the DPRK threat by enticing the regime to act in a less menacing manner: through financial rewards, diplomatic concessions, and the promise of improved bilateral relations. Ironically, this was precisely the approach that the Perry Report derisively dismissed as "trading material compensation for security."

Between 1995 and 1999, the Clinton administration extended a total of $645 million in U.S. foreign aid to the North Korean government.[46] By some calculations, in fact, North Korea had emerged as the largest recipient of American economic assistance in East Asia.[47] And the United States was actively involved in facilitating further billions of dollars of prospective resource transfers to Pyongyang from Seoul, Tokyo, and the international community.

For the United States, such an approach to a country to which diplomatic relations had never been extended, with which Washington was still technically in a state of war, and against which

American troops were being deployed to defend U.S. allies, is utterly unprecedented.

Although Washington's and Seoul's approaches toward North Korea today happen to be unusually well enunciated and well coordinated, the policies the two governments are championing in careful consultation with one another are nonetheless self-evidently problematic.

The current U.S. approach to the DPRK is inconsistent and contradictory in execution. Despite its ostensible insistence upon a "businesslike" approach to inter-Korean trade, for example, the "sunshine policy's" flagship North-South commercial deal, the Hyundai conglomerate's six-year contract for cruise tours to North Korea's Kumgang Mountain area, is *structured* to generate only losses for the South Korean side, even as it guarantees nearly a billion dollars in subsidies for the North Korean state.[48] But more serious by far than such tactical blunders is the fact that the "engagement" approach does not actually attempt to "engage" the actual regime that currently lies north of the DMZ, but has rather been designed for interaction with a romanticized vision of what the DPRK should be.

North Korea remains mysterious to the outside world in many respects, thanks in no small part to Pyongyang's own assiduous and abiding campaign of strategic deception; yet it is also true that the regime's record of words and deeds lays out, in considerable detail, the particular logic that animates this state. Rather than face that logic squarely, and deal with its implications, current U.S.-ROK North Korea policy is being formulated to deal with a "DPRK" whose outlook, objectives and priorities bear only glancing correspondence to the DPRK in Pyongyang—that is to say, the one that possesses weapons of mass destruction and is striving to train those weapons upon the United States.

North Korean authorities, to begin, have repeatedly denounced and rejected the Kim Dae Jung government's overtures for reconciliation and détente. Pyongyang appears to have studied the "sunshine" or "engagement" policy closely, and registers opposition to it precisely in terms of its proclaimed "good intentions to pursue peaceful and cooperative relations." In the estimate of the DPRK foreign ministry, their "sunshine policy" is a variant of the "peaceful transition strategy" of the United States, an intrigue to induce the North to reform and an "opening" under the cloak of "reconciliation," and thus a coherent attempt to achieve "unification by absorbing the North" into the South's "free democratic system."[49]

DPRK leadership, in fact, maintains that the new approach has actually *increased* tensions in the Korean Peninsula: "The Great Leader Kim Jong Il has pointed out: Since the present [Kim Dae Jung] government took power in South Korea, it is not reconciliation but confrontation, and it is not peace, but the danger of war, that has deepened in North-South relations."[50] Far from promoting peace and unification, Pyongyang holds, "Such 'sunshine policy' will only result in a fratricidal war or in the disgraceful permanent division [of the peninsula]."[51]

Pyongyang's shrill and hostile reaction to Seoul's well-meaning overtures may seem puzzling to liberalized Western diplomats, but it is entirely explicable if one keeps the DPRK's own fundamental precepts in mind. In DPRK doctrine, the Republic of Korea is a wholly illegitimate entity, with no right to exist as an independent state. Despite South Korea's great economic success, its evolution into an open democracy, and the inauguration of former dissident Kim Dae Jung as president, North Korea still axiomatically regards the ROK as a monstrous outrage that cannot be tolerated or accepted.

Consider, for example, this depiction of contemporary South Korea, printed in North Korea's daily party newspaper in January 2000:

> It is a shame to the Korean people as well as to humankind that in this world there exists such a veritable hell as the South Korean society.... It is a hideous fascist society where people are exposed to armed crackdown and terrorism, a terror-ridden society where fellow countrymen are dying out. This is what the "democratic politics" of the present rulers has brought to South Korea.... The South Korean people can never get rid of the present sufferings as long as South Korea remains a colony of the U.S. and the corrupt politics is allowed to reign.[52]

For Pyongyang's ruling circles, it would thus seem, nothing short of the liquidation of the South Korean system and the unconditional extension of DPRK authority over the South can rescue the South Koreans from their "present sufferings." Correspondingly, even when the DPRK does consent to meet with South Korean officials in discussions, it emphasizes that "South Korean authorities should not misunderstand dialogue as our recognition of their independent existence."[53]

Given the internal logic of the North Korean system, hostility between the North and South is natural—even necessary for Pyongyang. From its very beginnings, the quest for unification of the Korean peninsula on its own terms—i.e., under an "independent socialist state"—has been integral to the DPRK's very raison d'être. Normalizing relations with Seoul, and recognizing the right of the ROK to exist, would be tantamount to abandoning the claim to unification on Pyongyang's own terms; doing so would naturally beg the question of the remaining rationale for DPRK rule. That question, suffice it to say, could be deeply subversive of North Korean authority. This thorny ideological problem may help to explain why North Korean leadership, to the continued consternation of Seoul and Washington, has steadfastly avoided substantive negotiations with Seoul, and instead contrived a series of military provocations against a government that earnestly proposes to end the "Cold War structure on the Korean Peninsula."

(At this writing, the DPRK and the ROK have just issued a surprise announcement that South Korean President Kim Dae Jung and DPRK "Dear Leader" Kim Jong Il will meet in Pyongyang for a two-day summit in June 2000. Whether this summit—which would be the first ever between the top authorities of divided Korea—will actually take place remains to be seen. Even if the scheduled meetings do transpire, it seems unlikely that they would suddenly uproot half a century of firmly embedded North Korean policy toward the South.)

Washington's North Korea policy is now predicated on the assumption that it is in Pyongyang's own interest to liberalize and "reform." President Clinton has stated this explicitly: "If China can begin to open up and Vietnam can begin to open up and they can have very good results from doing so, then it's predictable that North Korea would get the same kind of good results if they would take the same path."[54] North Korean authorities themselves, however, take a diametrically opposite view of their interests. As they have explained in great detail and on many occasions, the DPRK's rulers regard economic liberalization as a potentially mortal threat to what they term "our own style of socialism." In September 1998—just days after Kim Jong Il had officially been elevated to the DPRK's "top state post"—North Korea issued this categorical verdict on "economic reform," "economic opening," and global "economic integration":

> It is a foolish daydream to try to revive the economy by intro-
> ducing foreign capital, not relying on one's own strength. If one
> wants the prosperity of the national economy, he should thor-
> oughly reject the idea of dependence on outside forces, the idea
> that he cannot live without foreign capital. . . . Ours is an inde-
> pendent economic structure equipped with all the economic
> sectors in good harmony and with its own strong heavy indus-
> try at the core. It is incomparably better than the export-oriented
> economic structure dependent on other countries. . . . We must
> heighten vigilance against the imperialists' moves to induce us
> to "reform" and "opening to the outside world." "Reform" and
> "opening" on their lips are a honey-coated poison. Clear is our
> stand toward "reform" and "opening." We have nothing to
> "reform" and "open." By "reform" and "opening" the imperial-
> ists mean to revive capitalism. The best way of blocking the
> wind of "reform" and "opening" of the imperialists is to defend
> the socialist principle in all sectors of economy. . . . Even though
> anyone calls us "conservatives," we will never abandon the prin-
> ciple, but will set ourselves against all the attempts to induce
> us to join an "integrated" world.[55]

Pyongyang's antipathy to economic liberalization is grounded not just in ideology but in entirely practical considerations. As might be expected, North Korea's rulers have carefully analyzed the downfall of the Soviet and Eastern European communist sys-tems. In their estimate, "economic reform" and "economic open-ing" played direct roles in the collapse of Soviet Bloc socialism. Kim Jong Il has stated so categorically: "One-step concessions and retreat from the socialist principle ha[ve] resulted in ten and a hun-dred step concessions and retreat and, finally, invited grave consequences of ruining the [Soviet Bloc's] working class parties themselves."[56]

Moreover, in the judgment of DPRK authorities, it was simple commercial contact with the capitalist world that undermined Soviet Bloc socialism by corrupting it from within—through what Pyongyang terms "ideological and cultural infiltration." Through "economic exchanges"—including "technical cooperation, joint ventures, and joint management"—capitalist countries automatically launch "an invasion without the sound of gunfire" in socialist lands, "spread[ing] their bourgeois reactionary ideology and rotten bourgeois culture and lifestyle."[57] Such "infiltration," the DPRK government warns, constitutes nothing less than "the enemies' maneuver of seeking our internal collapse."[58] Consequently, "[t]he entire society should vigorously wage the struggle to stop the imperialists' ideological and cultural infiltration"; the DPRK's security depends upon "smashing the imperialists' 'globalization' maneuver."[59]

Given the North Korean leadership's assessment of the risk that economic liberalization poses to their system, and their view of the inherently subversive character of transactions with the world market, the proposition that outside "engagement policies" might convince Pyongyang to embark upon a path of economic reform or trade promotion looks at best somewhat inattentive.

To date, North Korea has purposely foresworn Vietnamese- or Chinese-style economic experimentation precisely because DPRK leadership believes that such changes would expose their own system to catastrophic danger. Indeed, Pyongyang is so resolutely opposed to economic reforms—even to limited, tactical, temporary reforms—that the regime has willingly accepted their grim alternatives: protracted economic decline, and now, severe mass hunger.

Out of direst exigency, the DPRK sometimes deals with the "capitalism" it decries—witness the Hyundai tourism deal. But the North Korean government polices against "capitalist tendencies" at home with amazing vigor and unapologetic fervor. (After curtailing the operation of some provisional farmers' markets in 1999, for example, Pyongyang angrily denied it had shut down "free markets," protesting that " 'free markets' . . . have never existed in the DPRK. . . . Accordingly, . . . [i]t is nonsense to assert that the DPRK 'closed free markets.' ")[60]

North Korea's Approach to State Survival

If the DPRK categorically rejects both reconciliation with Seoul and domestic economic experimentation, how does it propose to cope with its mounting systemic woes? To judge by Pyongyang's statements and actions, North Korean leaders are pinning their hopes for state survival upon a policy of international military extortion: utilizing weapons of mass destruction to generate sufficient blackmail payments and overseas tribute to preclude potentially system-destroying economic reforms.

At the same September 1998 gathering in which Kim Jong Il was formally appointed to the DPRK's "top state position," the North Korean government also unveiled a new objective: to become a "prosperous and powerful state" [*Kangsong Taeguk*]. The meaning of that slogan was spelled out the following month in Pyongyang's *Minju Choson,* which declared that "defense capabilities are a military guarantee for national political independence and the self-reliant economy."[61] Subsequently, North Korea embraced what it now terms a "military-first policy."

"The most correct way to safeguard the fate of socialism in today's world," the DPRK's New Year's Day 2000 editorial stated, "is to place importance on national defense."[62] Placing top priority on the military, North Korean leadership maintains, will enable the regime "to resolutely foil ideological and cultural infiltration, [to] further cement a socialist ideological base, and [to] safeguard fundamental interests of our revolution";[63] more specifically, it will permit Pyongyang to "build a powerful social state in our way, *not by reform or opening up*"(emphasis added).[64]

For a starving nation, of course, spending heavily to "develop ... defense industry, unaided, and [to] increase the fighting capabilities of its armed forces in every way"[65]—as the "military first" policy prescribes—can only entail severe, immediate hardship. North Korean leadership acknowledges as much—but insists that such things as long-range rockets are actually the DPRK's key to ending hunger and achieving prosperity. Kim Jong Il himself reportedly argued as much:

> *Enemies say that we spent some hundred million dollars in launching a satellite. And that is true. . . . [W]ell aware that, compared with others, our people were not eating or living well, I approved of allotting funds to the [launch] to safeguard the country . . . and to build a rich and strong fatherland.*[66]

For in the view of North Korea's current leadership, *"the nation can become prosperous only when the gun barrel is strong"* (emphasis added).[67] The praxis for this theory is indicated by Pyongyang's now-familiar technique of extracting steady streams of concessional payments from foreign governments under the threat of North Korea's weapons of mass destruction.

Proponents of this policy in Pyongyang can point to the half million tons a year of free heavy fuel oil the United States is currently providing, and the multibillion-dollar light-water reactor project that Washington is facilitating, under the Agreed Framework. The 600,000 tons of food relief that America committed to secure a 1999 inspection of the suspect underground site at Kumchang-ri also qualify as benefits secured through this gambit. In fact, most of the international aid the DPRK currently receives can be counted as "protection money," offered to propitiate a menacing presence on the world scene.[68]

But these are not the only dividends Pyongyang intends to reap from its weapons program. In June 1998, after years of denying the fact, Pyongyang publicly declared that it was an international missile salesman, and recommended that "If the United States really wants to prevent our missile export, it should ... make a compensation for the losses to be caused by discontinued missile export."[69] Elaborating later, the DPRK's vice foreign minister stated that his government would "never" forswear its sovereign right to test and launch rockets, but it was prepared to forgo missile exports if Washington "provided a lot of money."[70] In talks with American counterparts in early 1999, North Korean officials indicated that the "compensation" they had in mind would start at $1 billion a year.[71]

Pyongyang also has its eye on Japan as another prospective source of massive "compensation." If Japan normalizes relations with North Korea, a multibillion-dollar aid package from Tokyo is likely to be in the offing (prorated and priced against the $800 million package granted to Seoul when Japan-ROK ties were established in 1965), although Pyongyang has cast the money as reparations for the crimes of Japanese colonial rule in Korea rather than as diplomacy per se:

> We don't care about whether Japan will have diplomatic ties with us or not. However, Japan, an assailant, must make clear apology and adequate compensation to the Korean people, a victim. This is the primary outstanding issue between the DPRK and Japan, whose solution brooks no further delay and which can never be turned aside.[72]

The DPRK's extortive version of diplomacy includes regular dark reminders of the destruction Pyongyang might wreak if its demands go unheeded. While issuing occasional coy disclaimers about having "neither the capability nor the will to make nuclear weapons," the DPRK also broadcasts that "we are fully prepared for any type of nuclear war. And, should the United States insist on moving toward a nuclear confrontation, we have no choice but to seek countermeasures for the move."[73] And Pyongyang has pointedly commented that

> What Clinton should be on the watch for, by all means, is the conceited and arrogant U.S. attitude that the USA is the only strong country and that there are no opponents that could compete with it. If there is a single opponent to the USA today who could throw a dreadful fire in its heart, it would be the DPRK [emphasis added].[74]

In sum, North Korean policy now appears to regard its arsenal of weapons of mass destruction as the instrument for the country's economic revival, and indeed the guarantor of its future survival. More immediately, North Korea's growing store of weapons of mass destruction obviates the need for either détente with South Korea or far-reaching changes in national economic policy.

Although the extortive value of the DPRK's weapons program stands only to increase with time, the "engagement policy" pursued by Washington and Seoul is predicated on the presumption that Pyongyang will be willing to *negotiate all this away*. Governments, to be sure, occasionally do make grave miscalculations that imperil their most vital security interests. But how the North Korean government, which now plainly rests its hopes for the future on building up its WMD program, is to be convinced to disarm voluntarily—and in return for enticements that Pyongyang happens to regard as political "poison" for its system—is a question engagement theorists in Washington and Seoul not only have failed to answer, but have seldom confronted.

What Should Be Done

Western policy is now effectively harnessed to supporting the North Korean regime (although perhaps not yet as generously as Pyongyang intends). But propping up the DPRK has not altered that government's explicit priorities or its strategic objectives. Instead, it has simply empowered Pyongyang to pursue its pre-existing goals. And since these goals are plainly inimical to the security of the United States and her Asian allies (and fundamentally in conflict as well with the national interests of her other big neighbors, Beijing and Moscow), "engagement policy" perversely uses Western power and resources to preserve, and indeed magnify, North Korea's threat to the West.

A redirection of U.S. and Western policy toward threat reduction in North Korea should be informed by three simple but important assumptions:

- First, the North Korean weapons of mass destruction problem is the DPRK regime itself.
- Second, the DPRK is by all appearances an unappeasable state, and should be treated as such in the absence of compelling new evidence to the contrary.
- Third, the longer the DPRK government as we know it holds power, the greater the strategic threats it will pose to American and allied interests—and the more costly Korea's eventual reunification.

Proponents of current "engagement" policies might criticize these assumptions as confrontational. But in fact they are precisely the opposite: for their objective is to *prevent* a conflict with Pyongyang; and they are distinctly more likely to be successful at this than current "engagement" theories, which have encouraged the North Korean regime to assume that its current intransigence and bellicosity are the keys to its future survival.[75]

What would this alternate approach look like in practice? We can describe it by outlining some immediate and longer-term issues that it would forcefully address:

Enhanced Deterrence

Although foreign observers have sometimes characterized it as irrational, North Korea's leadership is in fact both careful and calculating. This is precisely why deterrence has held since the 1953 Korean War ceasefire: for all these years, Pyongyang's rulers have calculated that military adventure would result in calamity for their system and themselves.

Deterrence can continue to prevail so long as North Korea's rulers face countervailing military force that they recognize to be credible. But changing circumstances mean that the challenge for the United States and its Asian allies to maintain their deterrent force is also evolving.

In the Korean Peninsula today, enhancing deterrence will require continuing military modernization in South Korea. "Counterbattery radar" to silence North Korean artillery tubes along the DMZ and improved civil defenses against biological and chemical threats, among other innovations, will reduce the risk that Pyongyang will ever try to create a "sea of fire" in the South.

North Korea's weapons of mass destruction program necessitates deterrent measures beyond the boundaries of the Korean Peninsula as well. The North Korean ballistic threat is by no means the only reason for developing and deploying an effective system of national missile defense for the United States, but it is surely a compelling one. The United States should also assist her Asian allies in erecting their own theater missile defense systems if they are interested in doing so.

Alliance Management
Coordinating North Korea policy with the ROK, Japan and other allies is imperative, and while consensus is highly desirable, it should not require pre-emptively discarding initiatives that Washington fears may prove difficult for her partners. The United States and her Asian allies share a deep common interest in reducing the North Korean threat; U.S. "alliance management" can help to elucidate the collective and individual tasks that should be undertaken as part of this effort.

Although China and Russia are not American allies, cooperating with them on North Korean threat reduction is also valuable. And the scope for cooperation is broad: for while Washington's interests may diverge from Moscow's or Beijing's on a wide variety of issues, all three powers share a commanding interest in promoting prosperity—and averting destabilizing crises—in Northeast Asia. Managing cooperation in this area with China and the Russian Federation, consequently, is not so much a matter of convincing others to embrace an American viewpoint as of encouraging them to think clearly about their own interests, and to act accordingly.[76]

Any successful approach to reducing the North Korean threat, in sum, presupposes a focused, active and steady American diplomacy in Northeast Asia.

Dialogue, Not Negotiations

Pyongyang is eager to enter into further negotiations with the United States for obvious reasons, each of its "negotiations" to date having resulted in new rewards from the West.

To the United States and her Asian allies, on the other hand, negotiating new agreements with North Korea should look distinctly less attractive. After all, North Korea has already entered into a number of treaties and agreements whose letter and spirit it flagrantly violates today. The DPRK openly defies its obligations under the Nuclear Non-Proliferation Treaty. It completely ignores its promises to Seoul under the "Agreement on Reconciliation, Nonaggression, and Cooperation and Exchange between North and South." It has likewise contravened every pledge given under the "Joint Declaration on the Denuclearization of the Korean Peninsula."

Until such time as Pyongyang establishes a record of adhering to its *existing* security commitments, it is pointless to seek new security agreements with the DPRK.

This is not to gainsay communication between Pyongyang and Washington, or between the DPRK and South Korea or Japan. Quite the opposite: the contending sides clearly have a great deal to discuss. Such interactions, furthermore, may help to prevent needless misunderstandings, and to reduce the risk of dangerous miscalculations. But until North Korea can demonstrate that it places value on pursuing a "binding agreement," dialogue rather than negotiations should be the order of the day.

Ending Tribute To Pyongyang

Subsidizing the current North Korean state runs squarely and manifestly against America's interests. The United States must therefore determine that it will not acquiesce in new transfers of its own taxpayer resources to the DPRK, and should work closely with her allies to see that they likewise deny Pyongyang access to their national treasuries. (By extension, this also means that North Korea should not be permitted to draw funds from "International Financial Institutions" such as the Asian Development Bank, the International Monetary Fund or the World Bank.) Halting new subsidies to the DPRK will weaken the sinews of the North Korean government, and impel Pyongyang to confront the implications of its own misguided economic arrangements.

Humanizing Humanitarian Relief Operations in the DPRK
Western values dictate a compassionate response to the plight of the blameless victims of North Korea's ongoing hunger crisis. To date, Western policy has not grappled very successfully with the dilemma of how to feed these people without instead nourishing the North Korean state. Pyongyang has insisted upon highly centralized, highly circumscribed food aid programs; Western relief agencies have in the main complied with that demand. Yet some well-known charitable organizations, such as Oxfam and Medicins Sans Frontieres (Doctors Without Borders, the French medical group that won the 1998 Nobel Peace Prize), have closed their operations because of the North Korean government's unacceptable restrictions on their ministrations. And in December 1999, many of the United Nations and private voluntary groups still working in North Korea signed a joint statement condemning the "difficult operating conditions that limit and constrain implementation, accountability, verification and access to the most vulnerable."[77]

The United States and its Western allies must leave no doubt about their commitment to the principles of impartiality and non-interference—the two bedrock precepts of humanitarian relief. In North Korea today, those principles are under assault by the country's government.

Truly humanitarian hunger relief is much more likely to be accomplished by a great multiplicity of small charitable organizations assessing need and operating without interference than by, in effect, cutting massive checks to the DPRK's own Public Distribution Service (PDS). If the North Korean government refuses to permit outsiders to help rescue, without fear or favor, the most vulnerable elements in the continuing food emergency over which it is presiding, it must realize that its decision will have grave consequences.

Human Rights And Refugees
Under the pressures of their "engagement" policies, the United States and its Western allies have downplayed the issue of "human rights" in North Korea. This is both a tactical and a moral error.

It exposes Washington and other governments to the accusation that their ostensible commitment to human rights is only contingent and opportunistic. And it neglects the critical, casual connection between the DPRK's eagerness to brandish weapons of mass destruction abroad and its abominable treatment of its subjects at home.

The United States should not hesitate to call attention to, and shame, the North Korean government for its many cruel and inhumane practices, not the least of these being the destructive policies that have willfully created an easily avertable hunger crisis in their own land. But Western governments must also act on their convictions, and there is ample opportunity to do so today.

At the moment, many North Koreans—some reports say tens or even hundreds of thousands—have crossed into China in a desperate hunt for food.[78] Under the South Korean constitution, these people are ROK citizens. The most important tangible step that can be taken today for North Korean human rights is to rescue these refugees and permit them to resettle in the South—and to reaffirm that any Koreans who escape the tyranny of the North will be welcomed by their brothers there.

Coping with the Agreed Framework[79]
Dealing with the indefinite complications arising from the Agreed Framework that Washington and Pyongyang have already entered into may be one of the most nettlesome challenges to a new North Korea policy.

As already noted, the Agreed Framework is not an agreement: in formal terms, it is simply a sort of road map. Yet the ambiguous nature of the document may expose America and her allies to the worst of two diplomatic worlds by obliging the U.S. to behave as if it were bound by treaty while permitting Pyongyang to choose when and whether it would honor its corresponding obligations.

Western diplomats must honestly recognize the Agreed Framework for what it is. For one thing (representations to the contrary notwithstanding), it does not "solve the North Korean nuclear problem." Quite the contrary, it merely postpones the resolution of that issue, by allowing both sides to settle the matter later on. Nor does the North Korean nuclear "problem" derive from the technical specifications of the DPRK's Soviet-style reactors, but rather from the nature and intentions of the North Korean regime. Until those intentions change, that problem will continue as long as the North Korean state holds power. And providing the current North Korean government with *additional* nuclear reactors—as the Framework process is now poised to do—is hardly the obvious way to reduce the North Korean nuclear threat.

If Western governments believe they have some small chance of influencing that state through the Agreed Framework, they should assess such progress—or the lack of it—carefully and unflinchingly. But to allow that document to compromise a strategy for North Korean threat reduction, or to substitute for one, would be a grave mistake.

Longer Term Objectives

Pressing as the immediate imperatives of reducing the North Korean threat are, they should not distract policy-makers from the great tasks that lie further ahead. By all indications, the DPRK is a failing, and ultimately unsustainable, state intent upon extending its lease on life by manufacturing and exporting strategic insecurity. The longer the DPRK as we know it manages to survive, the greater its peril to the international community will likely be. In the final analysis, prolonging the tenure of this regime will not—indeed, cannot—serve the interests of the United States and her allies. On the contrary, if Western policy-makers face the situation squarely, they will recognize that the DPRK government stands as the single biggest impediment to the assurance of peace and prosperity in the entire Northeast Asian region, today and in the foreseeable future. Therefore, Western policy should not treat the end of the DPRK as an unimaginable or unmanageable event. Instead, it should prepare for, and indeed welcome, the advent of a post-DPRK Asia.

The potential promise of such a future is consequential for Koreans and non-Koreans alike. Without the DPRK, the Korean people could at least be reunited, to enjoy all the benefits of limited government and democratic rule. Without the DPRK, the North Korean nuclear and missile threats essentially disappear and military tensions in Northeast Asia will dramatically diminish. Without the DPRK, the entire Korean population could participate in the arrangements that have elicited rapid material advance for South Korea; and a wealthier, more productive Korean Peninsula would help enrich Korea's neighbors as well.

Naturally, the end of the DPRK would, at first, mean heavy responsibilities for the free peoples of Northeast Asia—and portentous choices for American policy-makers. Rehabilitating the immiserated, isolated North Korean populace after more than half a century of "*juche* governance" will surely be an arduous, long-term proposition. The economic reconstruction of the northern half of the Korean peninsula will likewise be a monumental task, one requiring perhaps decades of effort and necessitating the attraction of massive amounts of private foreign investment. Designing a successful security structure for a free and united Korea, furthermore, is a challenge that will require no less vision, or diplomatic finesse, from American statesmen than the great drama that brought the division of Germany to an end.[80]

All of these imposing challenges can and will be met more successfully by careful, considered and coordinated preparation between the United States and her Asian allies. Policy-makers in Washington, Seoul, Tokyo and elsewhere should continually bear in mind that the end of the DPRK will mean the end of the Cold War in Northeast Asia—and that will ultimately be a cause for celebration.

III.

Allies and Military Assets

Europe and NATO: Saving the Alliance

In April 1999, just as NATO was preparing to celebrate its fiftieth anniversary, the *Economist* observed that the alliance was "on the brink of real trouble." There should have been every reason to celebrate: NATO had survived the general existential trauma caused by the collapse of the Soviet empire a decade earlier. It had successfully expanded. The Russians appeared to be content, contrary to the gloom-and-doom scenarios of the anti-expansion camp in Washington. The alliance was ready to embrace its new Strategic Concept.

But the war in Kosovo in the spring of 1999 suddenly presented a formidable challenge—and a serious threat—to NATO and the transatlantic relationship. At one point during the conflict, things were going so badly that nervous Clinton administration officials were conceding that a debacle in Kosovo could quickly result in the emasculation of NATO and a diminishment of American standing in Europe. Kosovo was a compelling reminder of just how tenuous America's standing had become, and how fragile the new NATO is.

In the end, NATO prevailed. But the way in which the Kosovo operation was conducted raised important questions about the reliability and seriousness of the world's only superpower. As a result, fresh doubts also emerged about the willingness of the Europeans to work within the U.S.-led alliance in the future. In late summer, Henry Kissinger was asking whether Kosovo "mark[ed] the end of NATO, at least as we have known it." In fact, only strong and principled American leadership, with proper balance and vision, will reverse the disturbing trends of the last decade, of which the Kosovo episode is but one example.

The New NATO

When East German authorities opened the Berlin Wall on November 9, 1989, the political security landscape of Europe was transformed in a single stroke. It quickly became clear that if the Western alliance was to survive, it would have to adapt to new strategic realities. NATO's original mission—to keep the Americans in, the Russians out, and the Germans down, as the alliance's first secretary general, Lord Ismay, had once put it—was in need of dramatic revision.

The velocity of the changes confronting the alliance was staggering. In less than a year following the breach of the Wall in Berlin, Germany was peacefully and democratically united. The entire East Bloc collapsed. In 1991, the Soviet Union itself dissolved.

It was no surprise that voices across the political spectrum in the early 1990s, from the isolationist right to the neutralist left in the United States, would argue that it was time for NATO to retire. In fact, even before the momentous events in Berlin, there were those who anticipated the alliance's demise. "NATO may be an idea whose time has passed," suggested, for example, Ronald Steel of the University of Southern California in *Foreign Policy*. Similarly, writing in *Foreign Affairs* prior to the Wall's collapse, Richard K. Betts of the Brookings Institution puzzled over NATO's "mid-life crisis," wondering aloud whether the alliance was already, perhaps, "stumbling toward impotence."

The debate over NATO's future quickly became a serious and difficult one. "We should have to pay to keep U.S. troops in Germany, and for what?" asked Les Aspin, then chairman of the House Armed Services Committee, in 1992. A year later, the author of containment, George Kennan, wrote that "the time for the stationing of American forces on European soil has passed, and . . . the ones now stationed there should be withdrawn."

NATO advocates finally prevailed, and they did so at a pivotal moment in alliance history. For U.S. foreign policy, the alliance remained, even in the changed conditions of the post–Cold War era, central to Western cohesion and unity—and accordingly indispensable to American interests. The United States, together with its allies, decided that NATO should indeed remain the primary institutional link for political and security cooperation between America and Europe.

This decision was quickly vindicated in the early 1990s, as war in the Balkans pushed streams of refugees onto the territory of America's allies and threatened to destabilize southeastern Europe. In Bosnia, where the conflict reached a head, the European Union (EU), the Organization on Security and Cooperation in Europe (OSCE), and the United Nations all failed to end the aggression sponsored by Slobodan Milosevic's post-communist regime in Serbia. In the end, NATO remained the only Western organization capable of credible and effective intervention. Even many of its most hardened critics felt compelled to turn to NATO for relief.

Bosnia was not the only validation of NATO's post–Cold War existence. It became similarly clear that NATO could continue to serve, as it had in Western Europe after World War II, as a force for stability and an instrument for reconciliation in the new Europe. The very promise of NATO membership, for example, proved a powerful incentive for neighbors to settle border disputes, governments and political parties to resolve minority issues, and rival states to sign treaties of cooperation. It provided incentives for economic reform and political democratization. It was in this spirit that NATO not only decided to remain intact but also to admit Poland, Hungary and the Czech Republic into the fold at the Washington Summit of April 1999, when even further enlargement was envisioned.

But celebration at the summit was accompanied by pressing questions. What were the new threats? With which weapons and in what circumstances would the new NATO operate? Would a new division of labor emerge between Americans and Europeans? Was a UN Security Council mandate essential for NATO action?

A new Strategic Concept unveiled at the Washington Summit sought to address these issues, but serious fissures remained beneath the surface. The conflict in Kosovo did little to clarify the debate. On the contrary. And America's behavior toward the Balkans in the years preceding was hardly inspiring, either. It was in the Balkans that the new NATO faced its first test.

American Weakness in the Balkans

When the United States fails to lead, it causes confusion in the Atlantic alliance and damages America's standing in the world. The truth of this axiom was proved in the Balkans, where the failure and inconsistency of American leadership exacted a heavy toll on U.S. credibility and on the alliance as a whole. As Yugoslavia began to dissolve in the early 1990s, Washington policy-makers quickly established a habit of misreading events, overestimating the capability of our allies, and underestimating the importance of American leadership in providing security and stability to the region.

In 1990 and 1991, the Bush administration insisted on clinging to the increasingly unrealistic view that Yugoslavia ought to remain intact. In doing so it failed to grasp basic trends in the region, just as it had done when the Soviet Union began to break apart. The administration may also have unwittingly encouraged Belgrade's leadership to believe that the West would not object if internal efforts were made to keep Yugoslavia together by force. When it finally became apparent that coerced unity would be overwhelmingly rejected and resisted by the country's constituent republics, the Bush administration still insisted that America would not intervene. As Secretary of State James Baker memorably summed it up, America simply had "no dog in that fight."

As America and its European allies sat passively, Serbian armed forces attacked Slovenia and Croatia in 1991. The Balkan conflict soon spread, as Milosevic predictably turned his sights on the newly independent and internationally recognized state of Bosnia-Herzegovina. In the face of unrestrained Serbian aggression, the Bush administration, again in concert with the European Community and by now the United Nations, waited patiently for the slaughter to play itself out. As the U.S. dithered, the UN made toothless diplomatic efforts to resolve the crisis. But the West simply had no effective response to bloodshed in Bosnia and the Balkans.

There were momentary spasms of American assertiveness. Secretary of State Lawrence Eagleburger sent Milosevic an ultimatum, for example, warning that "in the event of a conflict in Kosovo caused by Serbian action, the U.S. will be prepared to employ military force against Serbians in Kosovo and Serbia proper." The threat was a strange one. Why did the Bush administration choose to appease Serb aggression against Bosnia, a state recognized by the United States and accepted as a member of the United Nations, but at the same time express a willingness to intervene militarily in Kosovo? After all, Kosovo remained, by all legal definitions, part of the federal Yugoslav state. The Bush administration argued that America's strategic interest would become engaged only when the conflict began to threaten the stability of the region. But it was hard to figure why war in Kosovo would raise this question, while wars in Slovenia, Croatia, and Bosnia did not.

In 1992, candidate Bill Clinton decided to exploit the Bush administration's weakness and vacillation. Clinton called for "real leadership" to end the tragedy in the former Yugoslavia and insisted that the U.S. would finally act if he became president. Once in office, though, Clinton dropped his tough rhetoric in the blink of an eye. In fact, the president deliberately pushed foreign affairs aside and chose to focus almost exclusively on domestic issues. His first secretary of state, Warren Christopher, shocked international partners at a meeting of the Trilateral Commission when he announced that the superpower's new foreign policy would now have three priorities: the economy, the economy, and the economy. As for Bosnia, Christopher argued that the conflict was nothing more than "a humanitarian crisis a long way from home, in the middle of another continent."

Not that the Clinton administration did not have its own fits of assertiveness. In the spring of 1993, Clinton decided, for instance, in favor of arming the Bosnian Muslims so that they could defend themselves against Serb attacks. When the European allies opposed this proposal, the president sent his secretary of state to Europe to marshal support for the plan. But the trip was so ill-prepared, and the standing of the president and his top foreign policy aide so low, that Christopher was humiliatingly rebuffed on a tour of major European capitols.

Of course, Bosnia was a European conflict and the Europeans themselves were failing miserably to deal with it. They had brushed aside all the early signals about conflict in southeastern Europe. (In April 1991, three European Community foreign ministers visited Yugoslavia and voiced their optimism that the country would succeed in peacefully solving its problems.) But European leaders' decision to bury their heads in the sand would have mattered less if America had exercised leadership. Every alliance has its horse and its rider, Bismarck once observed. Under Clinton, however, the NATO alliance lost its whip hand and turned into an unwieldy committee where lowest-common-denominator politics became the order of the day.

Even the Europeans, always happy to see American influence decline, seemed also to recognize the problem. German officials told reporters that they were "flabbergasted" by what they saw in the twists and turns of U.S. policy toward Bosnia. The London *Sunday Times* wrote of "baffled" ministers and outright "European despair over Bill Clinton," who had "withdrawn America into its shell." Wrote the *Financial Times*, "From his inaugural speech onwards, the [president's] focus was on his social and economic agenda at home; references to the wider world were brief, unspecific and emphasized the constraints on American leadership."

Clinton's reply was feeble. "The United Nations controls what happens in Bosnia," he commented vacuously at one point, as it became clear that America itself would don the mantle of multilateralism, one of Europe's own favorite methods for avoiding responsibility.

Appeasement of Serbian dictator Milosevic began on the watch of the Bush administration. But President Clinton made temporizing and the coddling of Milosevic into an art form. That is, until 1995, when there was a shift of outlook in Washington—though it would be hard to argue that Clinton had suddenly become a strong leader on the issue.

By the mid-1990s, French President Jacques Chirac was arguing for a tougher stance against Serbia. The U.S. Congress had passed a resolution supporting the provision of arms to the Bosnian government. The UN had failed to provide any measure of leadership or modicum of security for the victims of aggression. The international community's shameless inability to protect safe havens and the news of the massacre in Srebrenica in July 1995 in particular caused embarrassment to the administration. It was in this context, then, that Clinton finally leaned toward a tougher line and decided to convince NATO to conduct a bombing campaign. After twelve days of NATO air attacks in late summer, coupled with the stunning success of Croatian ground forces in the Krajina, Milosevic came to the negotiating table.

Negotiations for a peace agreement in Bosnia took place in Dayton, Ohio, and the so-called Dayton Accords were soon heralded as a great success for the Clinton administration. Indeed, Dayton was successful in bringing war in Bosnia to an end. At the same time, though, Dayton's serious flaws and Clinton's ill-considered compromises with Milosevic planted the seeds for the area's next conflict.

There was no question that the settlement reached at Dayton rewarded Serb aggression. Nor was there any doubt that Dayton had also legitimated Milosevic and his blood-soaked rule by designating the Serb dictator as a key peacemaker in the region and an indispensable negotiating partner of the West. In a sense, both the Kosovars and Milosevic may have learned from Dayton to harden their positions and prepare for the next war.

Kosovo

The West had already known for some time about Serbian objectives in Kosovo. Milosevic had begun his remarkable rise to power in the late 1980s by cloaking himself in the mantle of Serbian nationalism and by directing much of his harshest rhetoric toward Kosovo, a region that figures prominently in the Serbian mythology of unfulfilled conquest and occupation. A 1986 memorandum issued by the Serbian Academy of Sciences and Arts argued that the Serbs of Kosovo were the most politically persecuted people of Yugoslavia. For his part, Milosevic began to close newspapers, crack down on dissidents, and force local leaders from power. Ibrahim Rugova, a leader of the province's ethnic Albanian population, argued already in 1993 that complete and systematic ethnic cleansing of the Kosovars was "still Milosevic's ultimate objective."

By February 1998, there was no dispute that ethnic cleansing was indeed underway in Kosovo. A brief respite was provided the following October by a deal negotiated by Richard Holbrooke, President Clinton's envoy, who had been the chief U.S. negotiator and mastermind of the Dayton Accords. Milosevic's appetite was far from satiated, however. Throughout the winter, Serb-sponsored violence in Kosovo increased, as did Western ultimatums and threats of force. The temporizing, timidity and empty threats that emanated from Washington made many, including our closest allies, wonder about American purpose and resolve. Milosevic did not seem to take them seriously.

Finally, on March 24, 1999, allied planes began their bombing campaign to end Serb atrocities in the Yugoslav province of Kosovo. President Clinton spoke at the time of two primary goals: "to protect thousands of innocent people in Kosovo from a mounting military offensive," and "to prevent a wider war" in the region. In the end, after weeks of war, Milosevic permitted international peacekeepers under NATO command to enter Kosovo so as to restore order and to protect the civilian population. President Clinton spoke of a victory for American leadership via NATO.

It was the first time NATO had ever gone to war. The alliance held together and NATO was able in the end to claim victory. But the path to this victory in Kosovo had been filled with dangerous assumptions, damaging miscalculations, and contentious behind-the-scenes recriminations. NATO may have won operationally, but questions emerged about the wisdom of American leadership and the future of the alliance.

The facts speak for themselves. When the bombing began, there were 90,000 refugees from Kosovo. When NATO concluded its patient, high-altitude, low-risk air campaign, there were well over one million homeless Kosovars. In response to NATO air strikes, Milosevic had not given up in a matter of days, as the president and his advisers had expected. On the contrary, the Serbian dictator exploited the fact that the president categorically ruled out ground troops from the outset, and seized the opportunity to accelerate the Serb campaign of murder, torture, and rape. For ten weeks Milosevic was able to accomplish what the president claimed that the campaign would prevent: the intimidation, displacement, and slaughter of hundreds of thousands of Kosovars.

What's more, because NATO had initially ruled out the use of ground troops, the very prospect that the president argued that NATO intervention would eliminate—the possibility of a wider war that would destabilize neighboring countries—quickly became a real possibility. Within the first few weeks of fighting, both Macedonia and Albania found themselves on the verge of collapse as Milosevic's forces pushed column after column of refugees across their respective borders. If the Kosovo action had been designed primarily as a humanitarian intervention, as the president claimed, it involved a serious miscalculation; for the campaign in fact inadvertently unleashed a humanitarian nightmare with clear and dangerous strategic implications.

The Kosovo war came to an end through a deal, not a defeat. The Kosovo Liberation Army (KLA) had finally begun to have some success in flushing Serb forces out from cover and making them more vulnerable to NATO air attacks. The Russians, who grew increasingly impatient with the Serbs, had begun to pressure Milosevic for an end to the murderous rampage. NATO's bombing campaign inside Serbia proper—an effort that intensified in the later stages of the conflict—was beginning to take its toll. And Milosevic decided to stand back, leaving NATO with its claims of victory, while his forces could recover and regroup. He may well have been influenced by belated allied plans to consider introducing ground forces into the campaign.

The Balkans had experienced four wars in a decade in Slovenia, Croatia, Bosnia, and Kosovo. And when the last bomb had been dropped in Kosovo, the regime of Slobodan Milosevic, the primary source of the terror and instability, remained in power in Belgrade. There was good news: important institutions like the Serbian Orthodox Church had finally begun to call for Milosevic's resignation. The bad news was that many oppositionists, including the Church itself, refused to renounce the malign nationalism that was at the root of Serbia's political and economic aggression and its international isolation.

Milosevic's latest war of ethnic cleansing finally convinced the Clinton administration that the Serb dictator was no longer the indispensable negotiating partner essential to securing peace in the region. "Balkan graveyards," the president finally admitted, "are filled with President Milosevic's broken promises." At the same time, though, Clinton appeared disinclined to do anything, apart from the passive gesture of withholding aid, which he hoped would hasten the demise of the Milosevic regime. Perhaps the prospect of a forward-leaning strategy was too expensive. The U.S. alone, though, had already spent $15 billion and involved more than 20,000 American troops in the Balkans *prior* to the intervention in Kosovo. By fall of 1999, the Senate would push the administration to sign a $100 million package assembled to weaken Serbia's dictatorial rule and assist the democratic opposition. A step in the right direction, but an exceedingly modest one.

After "victory" in Kosovo, then, the United States and its European partners were left to wonder: Would Milosevic—or another like-minded regime, perhaps comparable to Saddam Hussein in Iraq—reconstitute power and return to create another crisis, perhaps this time in Montenegro? And there were other residual problems. The conduct of the war had raised fundamental questions about the reliability of American leadership as well as the willingness of the Europeans to work within NATO in the future. Such questions were being raised not for the first time. But the times were changing in important ways, and the questions were more serious than they had ever been.

NATO and the European Union

The end of the Cold War has introduced change in the transatlantic relationship in a number of ways. The Soviet Union is gone and West Europeans feel less dependent on the United States. The generation of the Marshall Plan and the Berlin Air Lift has begun to step down. A new generation is coming to power across the continent: a generation, regardless of political stripe, that is no longer as reflexively pro-American as German Chancellor Helmut Kohl's generation. Meanwhile, Europeans have also been pushing forward over the last decade with unprecedented energy and enthusiasm to develop their own independent institutions. In many instances, they have been doing so with minimal American consultation and participation.

The American foreign policy establishment welcomed the emergence of a unipolar world at the end of the Cold War. Many Americans also tend to see NATO as a complement to America's global power and wider international responsibilities: a group of allies ready to promote and defend common Western interests and values both within and beyond the borders of Europe.

An increasing number of Europeans, however, seem to feel distinctly uncomfortable with a new international arrangement organized around one remaining superpower and one major concentration of political, military, and economic might. Not surprisingly, one of the motives behind Europe's adoption of a single currency was to create a new monetary union—and eventually a new political union—that would constitute a counterweight to American power and hegemony. In a November 1999 speech in Paris, for example, President Chirac argued against the dangerous American "unilateralism" and in favor of a European Union that would "escape this serious risk" by "endowing itself with the instruments of a true power."

Of course, Europe's campaign for unity has a long and complex history. Unification had been the idea of princes, poets, and statesmen for centuries. French foreign minister Briand had proposed a United States of Europe in the 1920s. Since 1969, the European Community has discussed and pursued a single currency as a precursor for political unification in Western Europe.

Since the end of the Cold War there have been other motives behind Europe's unification project as well. For some, the euro was Western Europe's response to globalization. For others, especially of the Kohl generation, deeper integration through monetary and political union would once and for all lock in cooperation and lock out the demons of malign nationalism and lethal fragmentation that had haunted the continent earlier in the century.

But not all the motives were so constructive, benign, or in keeping with Europe's Atlantic vocation. While the French do so most explicitly, others too pursue anti-hegemonic, and at times anti-American, objectives. Former German Chancellor Helmut Schmidt has argued, for instance, that the introduction of the euro means that the United States can "no longer call all the shots" in the world. Other German commentators have applauded the fact that, in their view, a more cohesive and unified Europe will no longer be obliged to second U.S. policies around the globe.

President Chirac is neither the first nor the only politician in France to complain openly about American power. French foreign minister Herbert Vedrine similarly argues for structures that will rein in the world's "hyperpower." According to Vedrine, in fact, "the entire foreign policy of France is aimed at making the world of tomorrow composed of several poles, not just a single one." In this view, a stronger EU, more economically and politically unified, will help fit the bill. Similarly, a stronger UN also means a greater opportunity to block U.S. influence and restrict America's room for maneuver. To enhance the power of the UN, as *Le Monde* puts it, is to organize a system of international relations that is "not the private property of the United States."

U.S. Policy and the Problem of Hegemony

If weak and inconsistent American leadership, particularly as demonstrated in the Balkans over the last decade, has helped foster the Western European view that the U.S. cannot be relied upon, American bullying—not to be confused with leadership—has not helped matters either. When Madeleine Albright talks about America being the "indispensable nation," it may be gratifying for her; but such language grates unnecessarily on the nerves of our allies and reduces their enthusiasm to stand by us in a crisis.

When Richard Holbrooke runs roughshod over the allies at Dayton, deliberately stealing the diplomatic show and self-indulgently sidelining the Europeans as spectators, consequences are felt later. One problem with the negotiations at Rambouillet in spring 1999, for example, had nothing to do with Kosovars and Serbs. There were difficulties between the U.S. and its allies because, in the words of one senior NATO official, "the Europeans were still furious with Dick over Dayton."

But leadership begins at the top. And President Clinton must bear responsibility for the tone that is set in his foreign policy. Clinton was initially cool on NATO expansion. His friend Strobe Talbott, then–Secretary of Defense Les Aspin, then–U.S. Ambassador to Russia Thomas Pickering, and Jenonne Walker, the National Security Council's senior director of European Affairs, all looked askance at enlargement. In the end Clinton was swayed, in part by expansion proponents within his administration, in part by expansion's popularity within domestic ethnic populations, and in part by early German leadership on the issue.

But once the president had embraced NATO expansion, he and his foreign policy team again exhibited the habit of unproductively excluding the Europeans from important decisions and communications. Cables between European allies at the time of the expansion debate, in particular between the French and the Germans, complained bitterly about American domination and control of a process they, more than the U.S., had set in motion.

Prickliness about American leadership is likely to increase in the changed conditions of the post–Cold War world. Of course, governments across Western Europe supported the NATO intervention in Kosovo. In fact, alliance cohesion was remarkable under the considerable strains of that campaign. The Italians and Greeks remained on board throughout. The French were team players. In Germany, a Social Democratic chancellor and a Green foreign minister were steadfast—so much so, in fact, that everyone talked of the war as a watershed for the German left. But behind the scenes there were grave doubts about American leadership, and growing concern about future Western European dependency on the U.S.

In some circles, outright anti-Americanism is on the rise. The Kosovo conflict stirred up forces of traditional and extreme anti-Americanism in France to levels not seen since Vietnam, according to one leading French writer, Pascal Bruckner. German intellectuals alluded to America's steamrolling of "European" interests and spoke of America fighting a war in Kosovo far from home and at the expense of others.

Der Spiegel argued that the ten weeks of bombing in Kosovo showed the limits "of American hegemony in Europe." As a result, there was fresh impetus for Europe's own defense initiative. Maybe it would be this development, suggested the German weekly, and not the single currency as had been hoped, that would lead finally to Europe's "emancipation" from the United States. Dominique Moisi of the Paris-based think tank *Institut Français des Relations Internationales* (IFRI) mused that "perhaps Milosevic will one day be remembered as an unwilling and perverse founding father of Europe."

Will the European Union's main energies be devoted to achieving independence from the United States? Is the European Union's primary raison d'être to become an economic and political bloc that will seek to function as a counterweight to the U.S?

European Foreign and Defense Policy

In the Dutch city of Maastricht in December 1991, EU governments initialed the Treaty on European Union. Apart from plans for a single currency, the Maastricht Treaty established two other goals: a common justice and internal policy, and a Common Foreign and Security Policy (CFSP). The old European Community is being transformed. Whether a federal state eventually emerges, the EU is steadily becoming an elaborate and advanced system of supranational governance.

Steps toward Europe's CFSP proceeded at a snail's pace until Kosovo gave the project a vigorous push forward. In the spring of 1999, NATO's Secretary General Javier Solana was selected by European leaders to become the EU's high representative for foreign policy. Western European leaders had long hoped that selecting a "Mr. CFSP" would give the EU a boost in visibility and credibility as an actor within the transatlantic community and on the wider world stage.

America shouldered the burden of military action in Kosovo. The U.S. did so not because the Europeans lacked the will to intervene, but primarily in this instance because the Europeans lacked the technical and infrastructural means to share the responsibility.

Since Kosovo, there has been increased discussion in Europe of a Common Foreign and Security Policy (CFSP) and a European Security and Defense Identity (ESDI).

In late 1999, West European leaders began to push European Security and Defense Identity in earnest, culminating in an agreement in late December to create an all-European expeditionary force of 60,000 soldiers that could carry out decisions made by the EU. German defense minister Rudolf Scharping has complained about Europe having "too many institutions and too little substance." He's right, of course. Germany has been in the lead in arguing, for example, that the West European Union—an organization of ten European nations that belong to NATO—should be merged with the European Union. Scharping has also taken a lead in arguing on behalf of increased defense spending. Both he and German foreign minister Joschka Fischer have complained about Europe's near total dependence on the U.S. for air transport to move troops, for satellite communications and intelligence, and for high-tech weaponry, including precision-guided munitions.

Consolidation of national defense industries and more efficient use of existing resources will help the European members of NATO, of course. It remains unclear, though, whether allied governments will really be prepared to embark on the expensive and time consuming campaign that would be necessary to allow the Europeans to catch up. "It's all about money," says Javier Solana, the EU's spokesman on foreign policy issues.

In Germany, for example, forecasts from the German finance ministry project declines in defense spending between now and 2003. Not only does Europe spend less on defense in general than the United States, it also spends less on the procurement of new equipment ($33 billion in 1998, for example, compared to $45 billion spent by the U.S.). According to prevailing trends, the military-technological gap will widen. A recent study by the Rand Corporation observes that the U.S. outspends its Europeans allies in research and development by two to one. And while U.S. armed forces have begun to adapt to the requirements of the new security era, European members of NATO retain today, in effect, "a somewhat smaller version of the forces" they possessed a decade ago at the end of the Cold War, according to the Rand authors.

But if Europe chooses to spend more on defense, what are the EU's political goals? Traditionally it had always been the French who were most interested in developing European foreign and defense initiatives, which have traditionally been viewed by Paris as opportunities to sideline the Americans. For the French, then, CFSP and ESDI have been primarily political projects aimed at strengthening the European Union and weakening NATO and American dominance.

The United Kingdom may have taken a step toward the French position, perhaps unwittingly, when it agreed in the fall of 1998 to work to strengthen EU defense cooperation both inside and outside of NATO. Prior to this, the British had always insisted that intensified cooperation in defense matters among the Europeans be undertaken within the Atlantic alliance. Not surprisingly, the French have continued to push this new line of development, with German support and collaboration. In fact, Europeans have become increasingly united in the view that the EU should "make its voice heard in the world" and "play its full role on the world stage."

Will a stronger European Union mean a stronger partner for the United States and more burden-sharing in the future? NATO's 1991 Strategic Concept states that "the European members of the Alliance will assume a greater degree of the responsibility for the defense of Europe." And in this same spirit, NATO made decisions in Brussels in 1994 and Berlin in 1996, where, among others things, member states agreed that in the future the EU could have access to NATO assets. This might, so went the reasoning, facilitate military actions by the Europeans in instances where the U.S. felt that its own interests were insufficiently engaged to intervene.

The logic is seductive. Senator Kay Bailey Hutchison (R-Tex.) of the Armed Services Committee applauds such developments; she and like-minded thinkers argue for a new division of labor in the alliance. The Europeans would tend to problems in their own backyard with the U.S. as backup, while America looks after Western security around the globe with the Europeans as junior partner. But such proposals assume too neat a division of vital interests, just as they assume purely benign motives for Europe's desire to develop a new identity.

Europeans want to do more, and should. The mutual resentment borne of extreme dependency is healthy for neither side. The U.S. should also consider carefully, though, the benefits it enjoys as the leader of the alliance. If the Europeans are willing to spend their way to parity, is the U.S. ready to see its advantage as leader disappear? Is it in the American interest to reduce its responsibilities at the expense of leverage and influence with allies? In a rush to reduce the American role in post-war Kosovo, the United States also quickly diminished its capacity to steer issues and affect outcomes.

Despite the unifying Soviet threat during the Cold War, America and Europe proved time and again to be divided in culture, in temperament, and frequently in geostrategic outlook. Transatlantic frictions in a number of areas are now only bound to increase, as American and the European Union sort out a new relationship and terms for cooperation. The U.S. can refrain from the clumsy and heavy-handed diplomacy so easily associated by Europeans with American "hegemony." It can more carefully consider unilateral initiatives—a constant bone of contention with the Europeans.

At the same time, the United States should also begin to voice openly its skepticism about federalist approaches to European cooperation. There is no reason, as some Europeans themselves have recognized, to assume automatically that a unified federal Europe will be a strong and effective transatlantic partner. In fact, the Europeans should be reminded that attempts to build structures aimed at "countering U.S. hegemony" are likely to encourage the unilateralist behavior they say they fear and want to counter.

How will Europe's political culture develop? Will the future be defined more by transatlantic partnership or by rivalry? Under President Charles de Gaulle, France moved to nuclear independence and distanced itself from the alliance, in the name of protecting French sovereignty and autonomy. Will the Europe of the post–Cold War world turn similarly Gaullist? American foreign policy should take every precaution to ensure that it does not.

NATO Enlargement and the Atlantic Idea

The Clinton administration's response to dangerous and divisive developments within NATO has been tentative at best. The administration has repeatedly failed to recognize that European integration has changed in character, and that this change is likely to have profound consequences for American foreign policy.

The United States has always supported European integration. President Kennedy famously suggested that European unity would become a "second pillar" of the Atlantic community. The Bush administration gave a nod to deepening integration in the early 1990s. The Clinton administration has followed suit, but with some provisos. For example, it has stressed that European defense cooperation ought to avoid what has become known as the "three Ds": duplication of efforts or institutions; decoupling from NATO; and discrimination in EU efforts against non-EU alliance members such as Turkey and Norway.

Such a passive, selective, and largely reactive posture is, however, insufficient to deal with the pressures now building in the U.S.-Europe relationship. The United States should consider carefully the disadvantage it incurs by continuing to wait for new European initiatives, instead of itself taking initiative to promote and defend the Atlantic idea.

First, the United States needs to defend vigorously the integrity of NATO and the central role of American leadership. At times, the U.S. will have to approach alliance politics with finesse and a soft touch. At others times, it will be important to recognize when allies have a distinct contribution to make and permit them to lead. (The Germans, for example, played a helpful and important part in getting the Russians to take a more constructive role toward Serbia during the Kosovo crisis.) But the centrality of the alliance for the transatlantic partnership must remain paramount and be constantly reaffirmed.

Second, the U.S. should encourage the Europeans to share greater responsibility for Atlantic security, *within* the NATO framework. Efforts to create a separate European identity that is defined in opposition to the United States should be challenged and discouraged at every opportunity. This is a formula for stoking the fires of American isolationism and unilateralism—the very forces Europeans say they deplore.

Third, the U.S. should invite Europeans to join Washington in the creation of new Atlantic institutions that could be developed with the same verve as some Europeans have applied to promoting the European project over the past decade. These could include a transatlantic free-trade area and new Atlantic political institutions where Americans and Europeans meet regularly at the highest levels to discuss methods of deepening political cooperation on a range of strategically important issues. Such institutions would complement NATO, strengthen the Atlantic link, and help energize the Atlantic idea that may otherwise atrophy as new disputes between the U.S. and its allies become the order of the day.

Finally, the U.S. should insist that NATO's "Open Door" policy be affirmed and that expansion continue. The process of enlargement is critical to the life of the new NATO, and should, as former national security adviser Zbigniew Brzezinski has suggested, become part of NATO's Strategic Concept itself.

When NATO was created half a century ago, British foreign secretary Ernest Bevin understood that it was more than a military alliance. He suggested that a successful alliance would also organize, mobilize, and encapsulate "the ethical and spiritual forces of Western civilization." Czech President Václav Havel has tried to make the same point today, arguing that the alliance should be seen as "a guarantor of Euro-American civilization and thus as a pillar of global security."

If the Atlantic community is to have a future, then NATO and the Atlantic idea must be given new momentum. Americans and Europeans must reach an agreement that something called the West still exists, that it needs strong and common institutions, and that it is worthy of a serious and vigorous defense. This will require, above all, new leadership from Washington that is even-handed and is exercised in the service of shared transatlantic principles. Only this course will succeed in dampening European calls for "emancipation" from the U.S. and in countering America's isolationist impulses.

Asian Allies:
True Strategic Partners

I n its dealings with Asia over the past eight years, the Clinton administration has managed to combine all the worst features of its general approach to foreign policy: an inability to specify and then adhere to a clear conception of American interests, a lack of sustained focus, an inattention to the realities of power politics, an undue emphasis on commercial considerations to the detriment of national security concerns, an exaggerated faith in the peace-inducing properties of trade and multilateral institutions, and a weakness for loose, empty, and potentially dangerous talk.

These qualities were on display in the fall of 1997 when the administration announced its intention to work towards the construction of a "strategic partnership" with China. Designed to placate Beijing and to promote an illusion of amity and progress in Sino-American relations, this declaration did nothing to diminish the deep, underlying differences that continued to separate the two countries. On the contrary, in a little over a year the U.S.-China relationship had begun to spiral down toward its lowest point since the Tiananmen Square massacre of 1989. But the proclamation of partnership was not entirely without effect. In combination with Washington's subsequent responses to the deepening Asian financial crisis (especially its harsh public criticism of Japan's economic policies), it helped to arouse uncertainty and anxiety in the minds of America's traditional regional friends and democratic allies.

In its obsessive pursuit of better relations with China, the Clinton administration has repeatedly done damage to this country's ties to its true "strategic partners." The next president will face few tasks more pressing than the need to broaden and deepen America's long-standing Asian alliances. As the next century begins, U.S. strategists will also need to consider the possibility of forging new links with other countries in the region. Which states are the most plausible candidates for such connections and, more broadly, what should be the pattern of U.S. strategic relationships in Asia in the first decades of the twenty-first century?

Objectives

Alliances are not, or should not be, ends in themselves; they are means for the attainment of larger strategic objectives. For the better part of the twentieth century the fundamental aim of American strategy, and hence the primary purpose of its alliances, has been to prevent the domination of either half of Eurasia (or, worse yet, both halves together) by a hostile power or coalition of powers. Fear of German hegemony in Europe is what ultimately provoked American entry into the First World War. Fear of German hegemony in Europe and Japanese hegemony in Asia is what drew the United States into World War II. And the desire to prevent Sino-Soviet (or merely Soviet) hegemony over all of Eurasia is what induced the United States to maintain large standing forces, and enter into decades-long alliances and quasi-alliances, in both Europe and Asia.

Today, and for the foreseeable future, there seems little likelihood of a single, aggressive power arising to upset the tranquility of Europe. The Soviet empire is gone; in its place sit a much weakened Russia, a group of newly independent republics and, in Central Europe, a cluster of fledgling democracies with deepening ties to the West. Germany is once again unified, though for the first time under deeply rooted democratic rule.

In Asia, since the end of the nineteenth century, Japan and Russia have been the two main pretenders to regional dominance. After more than forty years as a loyal, if sometimes reticent American ally, Japan is in many respects an even less plausible candidate for regional hegemon in Asia than Germany is in Europe. The Japanese government's ability to harness the nation's considerable economic and technological potential for military purposes is constrained by complex legal and political restrictions, and the country's culture is at least as hostile as Germany's to anything that smacks of militarism or imperialism. Japan is not embedded in the same kind of regional institutional structure as Germany, but is hemmed in nonetheless by the lingering suspicion and animosity of many of its neighbors. Because Japan faces more obvious potential threats than Germany, it is easier to imagine how some or all of these conditions might change in the years ahead. But in the absence of a fundamental break with the United States (and even with one), another Japanese bid for Asian dominance is probably not in the cards.

The efforts of Russia (and later the Soviet Union) to exert a preponderant influence in Asia have historically been complicated by geography. Russia's easternmost outposts must endure harsh and inhospitable conditions for much of the year and are a very long way, by land, air, or sea, from the main centers of Russian power. The Soviet Union was able to offset these weaknesses, to a degree, through massive investments in transportation and communication infrastructure, and by using ideological appeals and offers of military and economic assistance to cultivate local clients.

Today's Russia has all the traditional liabilities of the Soviet Union and none of its advantages. Having discarded its universal ideology, and with a greatly weakened military and a moribund economy, Russia lacks the means with which to project power into Asia. On the contrary, there are real questions about Moscow's ability in the long run to keep a grip on its eastern provinces. Russia's position in Asia is, if anything, even weaker than its position in Europe; it is as weak as at any time since Japan sank the czar's fleet at the Tsushima Strait in 1905. Recovery is not impossible, but neither is it imminent.

The collapse of the Soviet Union leaves China as the only country that could conceivably be capable, over the next several decades, of establishing itself as the preponderant power in Asia. It follows that the fundamental aim of American strategy in Asia must be not merely, as recent official statements would have it, to help dampen unnamed sources of "instability" in the region or, conversely, simply to promote "stability" for its own sake, but rather to prevent Chinese hegemony. The primary purpose of America's regional alliances, in turn, must be to assist in attaining this objective.

The Question of China

What reasons are there for thinking that China might, in fact, make a bid for regional dominance? Although in the modern world size does not translate automatically into useable power, the magnitude of China's population and landmass increases its plausibility as a potential regional hegemon. China comprises 68 percent of East Asia's territory, not including India or Russia, and 65 percent of its population. "The only other region in the world where the balance of power is so dominated by a single state," writes Gerald Segal, "is North America."[1]

By some estimates, China's total economic output may already be approaching Japan's, and if it continues to grow at a rapid rate, it could exceed that of the United States by the middle decades of the next century. Because of its enormous population, China would still be a relatively poor country, but it would nevertheless have more resources than it does today to devote to its foreign policy goals, while at the same time raising the living standard of its people. Because power is, in part, a matter of perception, a China whose economy was the largest in Asia, and maybe in the world, would be more likely to inspire awe, and perhaps fear, in its neighbors.

It is worth noting that *every* modern great power has gone through a period of rapid internal growth combined with increased external assertiveness. As Samuel Huntington notes,

> *Every other major power, Britain and France, Germany and Japan, the United States and the Soviet Union, has engaged in outward expansion, assertion, and imperialism coincidental with or immediately following the years in which it went through rapid industrialization and economic growth. No reason exists to think that the acquisition of economic and military power will not have comparable effects in China.*[2]

Fast-rising powers tend to be disruptive of existing international order, in large part because they are reluctant to accept the institutional constraints, border divisions, and hierarchies of political prestige established when they were relatively weak. Emerging powers often seek to change, and sometimes to overthrow, the status quo, and to establish new arrangements that more accurately reflect their new conception of themselves and of their preferred role in the world. Thus, in the second half of the nineteenth century and the first years of the twentieth, imperial Germany risked war to gain its "place in the sun." A century earlier, the United States, having achieved independence, declared its intention to extrude the European powers from the Western Hemisphere. At the time of the promulgation of the Monroe Doctrine, most Americans simply took it for granted that their country should be dominant in "its" region.

In addition, several factors unique to China may tend to reinforce this basic correlation between growth and assertiveness. There is, first of all, Chinese history. One hundred years of humiliation at the hands of European imperialists may have left the Chinese people with a lasting sense of vulnerability, sensitivity, and resentment towards outside oppressors; it has certainly left the Chinese government with a long list of as-yet-unresolved territorial claims against many of its immediate neighbors. In this century, the experience of conquest and brutal exploitation by Japan, as well as a near war with the Soviet Union, and a war and a proxy war against the United States fought on their Northeast and Southeast Asian doorsteps, have imparted to Chinese strategists a sense of the dangers of weakness, and a heightened awareness of the possibility of military threats arising in their own neighborhood.

Delving more deeply, some analysts have argued that the two thousand years in which China did, in fact, dominate much of East Asia have left a lasting legacy. Based on their country's past experience, many Chinese may regard a Sinocentric regional system as being in the natural order of things. Other scholars dismiss the notion that a "Middle Kingdom culture," if it exists, exerts any real influence on contemporary decision-makers.[3] Given the apparent importance of historical references and analogies in Chinese strategic debate, however, it would be surprising if the image of a glorious past did not play some part in efforts to conceive of China's future.

History aside, the dynamics of early twenty-first-century Chinese domestic politics may contribute toward external assertiveness. Although the possibility of fundamental change cannot be ruled out, China will probably continue to be ruled by an authoritarian regime for which appeals to nationalism, and evidence of increasing prosperity, have replaced ideology as the main sources of legitimacy. An aggressive foreign policy may be one way for the rulers of such a regime to rally support and tighten their grip on power. Such a course would seem especially likely if economic growth slows, as many analysts believe it will in the years immediately ahead, or in the context of a succession struggle. Analysts who take a generally relaxed view of China's intentions still worry that "political instability may encourage policymakers to prefer hard-line positions on nationalistic issues, including territorial disputes, Taiwan ... and policy toward the United States."[4]

Even, or perhaps especially, if China is on the road to increasing political openness and eventual democratization, there may still be good reasons to worry about her external behavior. One statistical study of the past two hundred years suggests that it is precisely when they are in the process of making a transition from autocratic to more popular rule that states are most likely to pursue policies that bring them into conflict with their neighbors. In such societies political institutions are typically weak, political participation is rapidly increasing, and old, established interests feel threatened. Under these conditions, ambitious politicians will often seek to rally supporters behind programs that combine growth in military power with external assertiveness.[5]

Chinese analysts and policy-makers are notably reticent about their own projections of the future. Drawing on an extensive survey of recent publications, Michael Pillsbury concludes that, at least in the open source literature, "there is no discussion of alternative scenarios about the rise of China as a great power. Analysts repeat only platitudes that China will never be a superpower, never seek hegemony, and will always be a force for peace and stability."[6] Nevertheless, Pillsbury finds that many Chinese experts believe that, over the next twenty years, China will begin to approach the United States in terms of some measure of "comprehensive national power." These analysts expect that China's relative power will rise while that of the United States declines. As the distribution of international power shifts, the world will become more multipolar and also increasingly organized along regional lines. The United States will cease to be the sole global superpower, its alliances will wither, and it will decline to the status of one among several regional powers.[7]

Recent congressionally mandated reports and statements by U.S. intelligence officials are surprisingly blunt and uniform in their assessment of Chinese intentions. Central Intelligence Agency director George Tenent testified in early 1998 that China's current leadership has "a clear goal—the transformation of their country into East Asia's major power and a leading world economy on par with the United States by the middle of the 21st century."[8] In its 1998 report on "Future Military Capabilities and Strategy of the People's Republic of China," the Defense Department reached similar conclusions: "China's primary national goal is to become a strong, unified, and wealthy nation that is respected as a great power in the world and as the preeminent power in Asia." The report noted further that "the Chinese realize . . . that attaining recognition as the preeminent political power in Asia will require the weakening of U.S. political influence in the region."[9]

It may be that if China grows more open economically and politically, its desire to control events around its periphery will grow less intense at the same time as the United States becomes more willing to accept it as the dominant regional power. Until the People's Republic changes, however, Americans are likely to remain uneasy about the prospect of Chinese preponderance in Asia. And with good reason. Chinese hegemony would mean, at the very least, the snuffing out of Taiwan's fledgling democracy, and it could have serious consequences for the prospects of democracy and democratization elsewhere in the region. If Asia were dominated politically and economically by China, the United States might find its access to markets, investment opportunities, technology, and natural resources constricted or (especially in the event of a Sino-American crisis or confrontation) denied. According to some estimates, by 2020 six of the top eight economies in the world will be Asian and their combined output will be roughly 60 percent larger than that of the United States and the European Union combined.[10] Many of the world's leading centers of technological development will also be located in Asia. A hostile China able to mobilize even a portion of these resources for its own purposes would be able eventually to mount a potent military challenge to the United States.

Designing a China Policy

If American decision-makers were confident of how China would behave in the future, or if they knew with certainty how U.S. behavior could shape the evolution of Chinese policy, their problems would be greatly simplified. If China were in some sense clearly "destined" to become either a peaceful, nonexpansionist democracy, or an aggressive, hostile great power, then the implications for the United States would be clear. In the first instance a relaxed, tolerant policy of unrestricted engagement would be appropriate; in the second, a determined posture of pre-emptive containment.

China appears to be poised ambivalently between these two paths, and to complicate matters further, the U.S. is aware that its own policy may influence the outcome—perhaps in wholly unintended ways. If the United States does everything possible to engage China and avoid confrontations, no matter the provocation, it could conceivably succeed in easing China onto the path toward domestic liberalization and international conciliation. On the other hand, such an American posture could also help to prolong the life of the current regime and, if mistaken for weakness, might even increase the odds of miscalculation and conflict. Similarly, a pure policy of containment might weaken China's communist rulers or at least dissuade them from pursuing overtly aggressive behavior; but it could also have precisely the opposite effects. It is worth remembering finally that, despite its undoubted importance, what the United States does or fails to do is hardly the only factor that will shape China's domestic development or the evolution of its foreign policy. As a general rule, our ability to control events is typically much smaller than we imagine it to be. When dealing with a country as large, old, complex, and potentially powerful (but also potentially unstable) as China, this is even more the case than usual.

Many Western experts have warned that the United States can "turn China into an enemy" by treating it like one. This bit of strategic folk wisdom contains a kernel of truth, but it is less profound, and less helpful as a guide to policy, than it is sometimes made to seem. As has already been suggested, China may become an enemy, even if the United States treats it like a friend. Nor is it clear in the present situation exactly which U.S. actions would be regarded as provocative or what their full effects might be. Chinese officials regularly warn of dire consequences if the United States and its allies proceed in certain ways. Some of this rhetoric may in fact give a clear indication of China's intended response, but some of it is merely deterrent bluff. In any case, there will inevitably be some steps that the United States needs to take to bolster its own strategic position in Asia, even at the risk of arousing the ire of the present Chinese leadership. If the United States makes preserving cordial relations with China (or even maintaining "stability") the premier aim of its Asia policy, it will have effectively given Beijing a veto over everything it does in the region.

The dangers of acting in an overly provocative fashion have received a great deal of attention in recent years from American decision-makers. But there is another danger as well: If the United States appears unduly passive or detached, if it fails to respond adequately to Chinese initiatives, or appears excessively sensitive and responsive to criticism from Beijing, it may set in motion forces that could serve in the long run to undermine its geopolitical position. Unlike China, the United States is not an Asian power by virtue of geography, but rather as the result of a deliberate exercise of political determination. And so—although their urgency and plausibility may ebb and flow—there will always be questions about the willingness and ability of the United States to remain engaged in Asia. China, by contrast, is not going anywhere, and everyone in the region knows it. This fact could be a major *advantage* to the United States, because a distant great power is likely to appear less threatening to weaker states, and more desirable as a strategic partner, than one that it is close by. But this difference could also be turned into a significant liability for the United States by Chinese strategists intent on displacing it. They might try to fuel doubts about American reliability and staying power, perhaps by staging tests of resolve from which they expect Washington to back down, or by developing military capabilities that strain the American will and ability to respond, or, more subtly, by luring the U.S. into expressions of amity and deference that seem to suggest acknowledgment of China's growing strength. In responding to such stratagems, the United States will have to act in ways intended to convince its current and potential allies, as well as the Chinese themselves, of its seriousness and steadiness of purpose.

For the moment, American strategists must aim to strike a balance between doing what they can to minimize the likelihood of an overt Chinese bid for Asian dominance and, at the same time, preparing adequately to deal with such a challenge if it comes. This dual objective should shape every aspect of American policy in Asia including the overall diplomatic stance; policies on trade, technology transfer, and export control; decisions about weapons system development, force posture and possible arms control agreements; and the approach to regional alliances.

Alliances and Alignments

Discussions of American strategy in Asia tend to devolve quickly into detailed analyses of particular bilateral relationships or, at most, of the interactions among a small number of states in one or another sub-region (usually Northeast Asia). If the question is how best to deal with China, however, the scope of the discussion must be widened considerably to include the entire eastern half of the Eurasian landmass and its oceanic periphery. This, after all, is the realm that Chinese decision-makers contemplate as they look outward in all directions from Beijing. For purposes of strategic analysis, "Asia" ought therefore to be defined as consisting of five interconnected sub-regions arrayed around China: Northeast Asia (including Russia, Japan, Korea, and Taiwan), a Southeast Asian maritime zone (including the Philippines, Indonesia, Malaysia, Singapore, Brunei, Australia, and New Zealand), continental Southeast Asia (including Vietnam, Thailand, Cambodia, Laos, and Myanmar), South Asia (including India, Pakistan, Bangladesh and Sri Lanka), and Central Asia (to include at least Mongolia, Kazakhstan, Kyrgyzstan, and Tajikistan, the first tier of countries directly contiguous to China). In the larger context of its evolving relations with China, what kinds of connections, if any, should the United States seek with these states?

In answering this question it is useful to begin by rating countries according to three criteria: ideological affinity with the United States—the degree to which they are stable, functioning liberal democracies; strategic value—the extent to which a given state can contribute in a positive way to the American goal of preventing hostile domination of Eurasia or, conversely, its potential importance to a hostile power bent on regional preponderance; and risk—the likelihood that, by becoming more closely aligned with a third party, the United States may increase the chances that it will be drawn into open competition or direct confrontation with China.

Core Allies: Japan, Australia, and the Republic of Korea
America's status as an Asian power rests on its strong position in Northeast Asia and, to a somewhat lesser extent, maritime Southeast Asia. Anchoring the U.S. role in each sub-region are its relationships with the major advanced industrial democracies of the Western Pacific: Japan and the Republic of Korea to the north,

Australia to the south. These are, by virtue of the character of their domestic political regimes, America's natural "strategic partners;" they happen also to be among the strongest and most important states in East Asia, and they are countries with whom the United States has long enjoyed close political and military ties. The United States should not allow itself to be deterred by Chinese protests from strengthening its existing bilateral links with each of these three countries, and it should also attempt over time to promote closer strategic cooperation among them.

Japan: Because of its economic, technological, and military potential, Japan is clearly the most important American ally in Asia, and maintaining the U.S.-Japan alliance is therefore an absolute strategic necessity. Any substantial departure from the present close relationship would almost certainly have harmful consequences for the United States. If Japan were to adopt a position of neutrality in the face of rising Chinese power, it would become much more difficult for the U.S. to prevent China's eventual dominance across all of Asia. Overt Japanese realignment toward China would do even more damage, more quickly. On the other hand, the pursuit by Japan of a much more independent and assertive posture toward China (perhaps including the acquisition of nuclear weapons and a break from the present alliance with the United States) would raise the risks of a regional conflict into which the U.S. might eventually be drawn.

Over the course of the past decade, a growing awareness of possible threats from North Korea and, in the long run, from China have helped to make the Japanese people more nervous, more "security-minded," and potentially more inclined toward strategic assertiveness and perhaps even aggressive hypernationalism. One goal of American policy-makers over the next several years must be to present Japan's leaders with opportunities to channel these sentiments in directions that will strengthen the alliance rather than weakening it. The ultimate aim of these efforts should be to move the U.S.-Japan relationship closer (indeed, as close as Japanese domestic politics will permit) to being a true alliance between roughly equal partners.[11] Ideally, the present, awkward arrangements for partial, conditional cooperation should be replaced with more robust mechanisms for genuine joint military planning, training, intelligence sharing, research, and weapons procurement. In short, the United States should seek a strategic relationship with

Japan more like that which it has built over the past half-century with Germany.

The advantages of such an approach are manifold: a more efficient use of resources in peacetime competition and, if need be, in war; less danger of divergence, disagreement, and alliance failure in a crisis: and a reduced risk that Japan, feeling that its security concerns were not being adequately addressed, might choose to strike out on its own. The main objections to such a course are that it would provoke Chinese animosity, and that by stirring anti-Japanese anxieties elsewhere in Asia, it could ease China's efforts to gain regional influence.

Command and consultative arrangements that actually bind Japan and the United States more closely to one another—not simply increase Japan's capacity for independently projecting military power—ought to reassure friends and allies. The Chinese have long objected, in principle, to the maintenance of a U.S.-Japan alliance, but they have also accepted it, in practice, because they recognize that the alternative would probably be less conducive to their interests. To the extent that the Chinese are genuinely concerned about Japanese strategic autonomy (as opposed to fearing closer cooperation between the two powers that, together, might be able to oppose their emergence as a regional hegemon), they should welcome changes that actually reduce the likelihood of independent Japanese action.[12]

Under the prevailing conditions of uncertainty, there are obviously some limits to what the United States should encourage Japan to do. Urging it to acquire an independent nuclear force, for instance, may go beyond these limits, while urging it to cooperate in the development of a theater ballistic missile defense system would not. At the same time, the United States should not allow China to dictate the terms of its relationship with Japan, and should not allow itself to appear to side with China in blocking the emergence of Japan as a more "normal" country. Chinese decision-makers should realize also that American views on what kind of military posture Japan should have will depend in part on China's actions.

Australia: The case for a closer U.S. strategic relationship with Australia is more straightforward. The two countries enjoy a high degree of ideological and cultural affinity. Because of their long history of cooperation, and because of Australia's comparatively remote geographical location and generally cautious and defensive foreign policy, there is little danger that a closer U.S.-Australian partnership will appear as a dramatic, provocative departure, or that it will increase the risk of unwanted American involvement in future crises or confrontations.

Australia's value as a strategic partner has increased since the end of the Cold War and will probably continue to grow in the years ahead. Australia is close enough to the South China Sea and the Indian Ocean that its cooperation could prove critical to American efforts at projecting and sustaining air and naval power into these vital areas. If the U.S. loses access to bases and facilities elsewhere in Southeast Asia, Australia will become even more important than it is today. Even the development of entirely new or substantially improved means for projecting American military power into the Western Pacific (such as hypersonic transcontinental bombers or offshore submersible missile-launching "fortresses") are unlikely to eliminate entirely the need for local access. At the same time, Australia is sufficiently far away that it will remain relatively difficult for a continental Eurasian power to strike at it with ballistic missiles, cruise missiles or other forces. Finally, because of its location, economic ties, historical experience, and lower geopolitical profile, it may be easier for Australia than for the United States to build bridges to other states in its region.

Korea: Although it will almost certainly persist in its present form for as long as the Korean peninsula remains divided, there are real questions about what will happen to the U.S.-ROK alliance if and when reunification occurs. If a unified Korea continues to develop along lines that the Republic of Korea has been following in recent years—towards sturdy, deeply institutionalized, liberal democracy—then a strong basis for affinity with the United States should continue to exist. It is possible, however, that unification could be followed by shifts in Korean domestic politics, including the growth of a strain of anti-foreign nationalism, that could make close relations much more difficult to maintain.

If Sino-American relations have become more contentious and competitive in the meantime, the United States will have an especially strong interest in preserving ties to a reunified Korea—both to benefit from the resources and capabilities that Korea could eventually contribute toward counterbalancing China's rising power, and to deny those same resources to China. On the other hand, a neutralized Korea, or one that leaned toward China, could cause serious problems for the United States and, even more, for Japan. The emergence of a Korean-Japanese rivalry could divert Japanese energy and attention and strain the U.S.-Japan alliance. The United States should therefore begin now to do what it can to reduce the likelihood that unification will be followed by a deterioration in relations between its two main Northeast Asian allies. One way of doing this would be to encourage trilateral security cooperation and begin to lay the groundwork for a genuine regional alliance of some kind.[13]

As it has for the past half-century, the present U.S.-ROK alliance carries obvious and real dangers of embroiling the United States in another Korean war. In the future, U.S. efforts to maintain close ties to a unified Korea may also carry an increased risk of Sino-American confrontation. China might intervene in order to prop up a collapsing North Korean regime, or to establish a buffer zone along their shared border. Even if it acquiesced in reunification, China might object to the northward movement of ROK or U.S. forces. Because the United States would have little desire to defend a militarized land frontier with China, however, there might be some basis for a mutually acceptable resolution to this issue.

Bilateral Defense Relationships: Singapore, Philippines, Thailand
The United States now maintains bilateral defense relationships of various types with a number of countries in Southeast Asia. In some cases these connections were established only after the Cold War; others extend further back in time, although even these have undergone significant modifications during the past decade. Since 1990, the government of Singapore has permitted U.S. forces to make use of air and naval facilities on its territory. American military bases in the Philippines were closed down in 1991–92, and U.S. ship visits and joint military exercises were effectively suspended at the end of 1996, but the Philippine government has recently taken steps to permit renewed defense cooperation. The United States has a formal security commitment to Thailand that traces its origins to the Manila Pact of 1954, and it also engages in various forms of relatively low-level cooperation with the Thai armed forces. Since the early 1990s, however, Thailand has also taken a number of steps that seemed designed to distance it from the United States and align it somewhat more closely with China.[14]

For the moment it certainly makes sense for the United States to try to cultivate good relations with as many Southeast Asian states as possible. Military contacts, in addition to routine diplomatic and economic ties, can serve as tokens of American interest and commitment and may help to ease anxieties about impending U.S. withdrawal, thereby dampening any tendency on the part of smaller, weaker states to jump on what they might otherwise perceive to be a Chinese "bandwagon." Access to "places," if not to "bases," can also help the United States to maintain its peacetime military presence in the region. It cannot be assumed, however, that host governments would permit continued access in the event of a genuine crisis or conflict. The vulnerability of many fixed regional facilities will also increase as China's ability to project military power continues to grow.[15]

If China is truly intent on exerting a dominant influence throughout continental Southeast Asia, it may be difficult in the long run for the United States to prevent it from doing so. China's proximity and history of local preponderance, its growing economic importance, and the fact that most of the regimes in the region are closer to it in domestic political terms than they are to the United States, all suggest that continental Southeast Asia could become increasingly a sphere of primary Chinese influence.[16]

Fortunately, the maritime reaches of Southeast Asia are likely to be more resistant to Chinese domination, more receptive to a countervailing American presence, and more important to the larger Asian strategic balance. Here lie a group of states that have achieved high levels of economic growth and technological development and, albeit to varying degrees, have also succeeded in making progress in recent years toward building stable democratic governments. Several have experience in fending off Chinese attempts at subversion or coercion; all are sensitive to the threat of foreign domination, regardless of its source. Unless the threats to their security and independence become much more acute, these countries are unlikely to want to enter into formal alliance relationships with extra-regional powers, but they will have a strong interest in seeing that the United States remains visibly engaged in their neighborhood.[17]

For its part, the United States will want to ensure that China is not able to gain effective control of the vital sea lines of communication that run through the South China Sea, or of the energy resources that may lie beneath it. The limitations of China's current naval capabilities mean that neither objective is yet within easy reach. Still, Chinese preponderance in maritime Southeast Asia could have far-reaching implications for the security of Taiwan, Korea, and Japan. First steps toward achieving this goal might include efforts by China to exploit differences among the maritime states in order to expand its own influence, coercive diplomacy directed at one or another of the weaker or more isolated Southeast Asian states, and attempts to undermine the bilateral relationships that now permit U.S. forces relatively easy access to the region.

Possible Future Partners (a): India, Indonesia, Russia, Vietnam
The emergence of a much more powerful and assertive China will provide a strong inducement for the formation of counterbalancing coalitions. In the face of a common threat to their independence and security, states with no prior experience of cooperation, and even those with a history of mistrust, and with profound differences in outlook and ideology, can sometimes find themselves drawn together by their shared strategic interests. Just as the rise of German and Japanese power brought the United States and the Soviet Union into alignment in the 1940s, and the subsequent growth of Soviet power brought the United States together with China in the 1970s, so the rise of China could lead to the formation of new alignments that today appear implausible.

Asia contains at least four comparatively large and/or potentially powerful states, one or several of which could eventually become major strategic partners of the United States. From the American perspective, each has a distinct combination of assets and liabilities.

India: Because of its sheer size, ambition, and relatively high present level of technological sophistication, India is a leading candidate for eventual status as a great power on par with China. It is also a functioning democracy, albeit one that faces serious internal challenges to its continuing stability. India has long-standing differences with China, and its leaders have recently begun to express increasing concern over China's capabilities and intentions.

Over the next several decades, it is therefore quite conceivable that the United States and India could be drawn together by a shared desire to counter Chinese power. In different ways and to varying degrees, both countries will feel themselves threatened by increases in Chinese power. Chinese ballistic and cruise missiles capable of striking across the Himalayas at India could also be used to hit America's forward military bases and its allies in the Western Pacific. A PLA Navy capable of projecting significant power into the Bay of Bengal and the Indian Ocean, or interfering with the flow of shipping through the South China Sea, would pose a threat both to India and to America's energy-hungry allies in Northeast Asia. By appearing to menace all of them, an expansion in China's power could thus help to promote a convergence of strategic interests among India, Japan, and several of the ASEAN countries, as well as between India and the United States. And conversely, cooperation among these powers, by forcing it to divide its resources and strategic energies, would greatly complicate China's efforts to establish regional hegemony.

There could be at least three significant obstacles to Indian participation in a balancing coalition. An inability to achieve real economic reforms may prevent India from fulfilling its potential. As in the past, domestic divisions could leave India's leaders preoccupied with their internal problems, and incapable of developing and sustaining either a coherent strategic vision, or a first-class modern military. Finally, whatever their apparent commonality of interests regarding China, India and the United States may yet be kept apart by lingering mutual mistrust and misunderstanding, or by genuine divergences over other issues. In the near term, the critical question facing the United States will be how to square its continuing commitment to the principle of nonproliferation, and its consequent disapproval of New Delhi's 1998 decision to conduct nuclear tests, with its growing need to improve relations with India.

Indonesia: If it is able to negotiate the transition from autocratic rule to democracy without disintegrating or descending into civil war, Indonesia could begin to emerge over the next several decades as an increasingly attractive strategic partner for the United States. A unified, democratic, market-oriented Indonesia with a sizable population and significant energy resources could be a major force for stability in maritime Southeast Asia. Such a state would also presumably share with the United States, Japan, and perhaps India a desire to prevent China from becoming the dominant power in the region.

On the other hand, persistent Indonesian weakness would remove a potentially significant counterweight from the balance of power.

A catastrophic collapse would also preoccupy and distract Indonesia's neighbors (including Australia, which might have to deal with large outflows of refugees). Differences over how best to respond to turmoil in Indonesia could further divide and weaken ASEAN and provide new opportunities for China to increase its influence. In the longer run, persistent instability and ethnic or religiously motivated violence in Indonesia, and perhaps elsewhere in Southeast Asia, could serve as a pretext for an expanded Chinese regional presence and role. The United States clearly has a powerful interest in seeing Indonesia recover from its present difficulties as quickly as possible; China does not.

Russia: Prior to 1991, China faced a large, unified neighbor on its northern and western frontiers. The collapse of the Soviet Union left a cluster of comparatively small and weak successor states in Central Asia, and a greatly enfeebled Russia to the north. China stands to gain if these circumstances continue. A militarily weakened Russia is far less likely to pose any kind of direct challenge to China. Russia's desperate economic straits have also caused it to throw geopolitical caution to the winds and have rendered it eager to sell military hardware and strategically sensitive information and technology to a country that it once regarded as its mortal enemy. Over time, China may also be able to take advantage of Moscow's weakness to gain preferential access, or even de facto control, over the resources and territory of Siberia and the Russian Far East.

The United States has many reasons to want to see Russia evolve into a stable liberal democracy. If Russia takes this path it will become less inclined to pose a renewed threat to its neighbors to the west; it will also probably be more inclined, and perhaps better able, to set limits in its relationship with a powerful, authoritarian China. A functional, democratic Russia might also be capable, over time, of building meaningful strategic ties to the United States. Unfortunately, the prospects for a Russian recovery along these lines do not appear at this point to be very bright. It seems much more likely that Russia will continue to founder for some time to come, and that China will continue to enjoy the considerable benefits of a secure northern flank.

Vietnam: Vietnam has two attributes that commend it for serious consideration as a strategic partner: first, its location makes it a potential platform for the projection of military power into the South China Sea; and second, it has a long history of resistance to Chinese encroachments on its sovereignty. On the other side of the ledger, however, the fact that Vietnam is still governed by a rigid communist regime severely limits the prospects for close, sustained cooperation with the United States. Moreover, Vietnam's very proximity to China, and its pugnacious past, make it a risky country with which to be closely aligned.

There is a real danger that China might use force pre-emptively to break up a burgeoning relationship between Vietnam and any outside power, and to demonstrate the inability of outsiders to protect their partners in continental Southeast Asia. There is also the possibility that, if it believed it had the backing of the United States or some other major power, Vietnam might act in a provocative fashion toward China. Either way, the prospect of having to defend Vietnam against China would not be an appealing one, nor, given Vietnam's location and comparatively modest strategic value, would such an enterprise be a very effective use of American resources.

Chinese domination of Vietnam would remove a potential irritant and increase China's ability to project power to the south and east. For the time being, therefore, the United States has an interest in keeping Vietnam "in play," responding to its economic and diplomatic overtures where possible and, in general, encouraging it to pursue policies that will help it to retain the maximum feasible degree of independence from China. At this point, the risks inherent in overt strategic cooperation, to say nothing of actual American security guarantees, would exceed the potential benefits. In the event of greatly increased Chinese pressure, however, or a worsening of tensions elsewhere in Asia, the United States and its other security partners in the region would need to consider taking further steps to bolster Vietnam's ability to defend itself.

Possible Future Partners (b): The Central Asian Republics
The reopening of Central Asia presents China with both risks and opportunities. On the one hand, there is a danger that the newly independent states on China's western frontier may provide encouragement, support and refuge to separatist groups operating within its borders. On the other, there is the promise that oil and natural

gas flowing from or through these states to China could help it to
meet its rapidly growing energy needs, thereby reducing dependence
on supplies arriving via more vulnerable oversea routes from the
Persian Gulf. Since the early 1990s, China has sought to address
both of these possibilities by expanding its economic ties with Central Asia. In the process, the Chinese hope to increase their energy
security, enhance their influence in the Central Asian republics,
and, by promoting economic growth there, reduce the appeal of
Islamist movements that might cause trouble on their own territory.[18]

As with continental Southeast Asia, there is no reason for the
United States to want to see Central Asia incorporated easily into
a Chinese zone of control. Effective dominance of the areas along
its western flank might alleviate some of China's security anxieties,
but would not transform it into a placid, satisfied power. A policy
of trying to appease China by permitting it to dominate its "natural" sphere of influence would therefore be misguided. On balance,
a China that had secured its interior land frontier would be freer
to shift resources toward the Pacific rim, where the bulk of America's interests lie.

In Central Asia, as in continental Southeast Asia, the American
ability to fend off a determined Chinese bid for dominance will be
limited, while the risks of excessive entanglement will be considerable. Putting aside the question of the likely character and stability of the governments of the Central Asian republics, their
remoteness makes them extremely difficult for any outside power
to defend. Airdropping a few U.S. Army paratroopers into Kazakhstan in peacetime is one thing; sending large units to help the Kaza-
khs preserve their territorial integrity against Chinese (or Russian) incursions would be another matter altogether.

Once again, we need to distinguish between the present period
of muted competition and a subsequent phase of more open
Eurasian rivalry that may follow. In the near term, the United States
should do what it can to promote the emergence of democratic
governments and capable, civilian-controlled militaries, and to
encourage the Central Asian republics to maintain diverse economic, diplomatic, and (especially for purposes of exporting energy)
logistical links to the outside world. A continued Russian role in
the region is desirable, if only to avoid an undue expansion of Chinese influence.

In the longer run, the United States may have to face the issue of how it should respond to appeals for assistance from Central Asian governments or factions that claim to be resisting Chinese efforts at subversion, coercion, or conquest. Especially if China were unwise or desperate enough to send forces directly onto a neighbor's territory, such situations could bear some resemblance to the conflict in Afghanistan; in collaboration with other interested parties, the United States might find itself providing support to indigenous resistance movements.

Taiwan

What should be the nature of the American relationship with Taiwan? As a first step toward answering this question, it is important to try to separate the moral, emotional, and legalistic dimensions of the issue from its purely strategic aspect.

There can be no doubt that the forcible or coerced absorption of Taiwan by the mainland would be a geopolitical catastrophe for the United States. Aside from the human tragedy, such an event would give the clearest possible signal of Chinese ascendance, and of American decline, in Asia. There is also little reason to doubt the conventional wisdom regarding the likely implications of a near-term Taiwanese declaration of independence and/or the announcement of a formal American defense commitment to the island. The Chinese would certainly react with fury to these developments, probably with some use of military force, and perhaps with the initiation of large-scale hostilities against Taiwan and, conceivably, against U.S. forces in the Western Pacific.

Present American policy is based on the view that, if it can only be suppressed long enough, the Taiwan question will eventually be resolved by the passage of time. At some point in the not-too-distant future, the PRC may become more democratic and less menacing, and Taiwan will be allowed to drift off on its own or will rejoin the mainland voluntarily. But suppose instead that the mainland continues to be ruled by something resembling its present regime and the Taiwan issue continues to fester and, on occasion, flare up. As happened in 1995–96, displays of Chinese aggressiveness toward Taiwan can have a powerful impact on the perceptions of other states in Asia, rendering them far more leery of China and more amenable to cooperation with one another and with the United States. The United States needs to focus more intently on doing what is necessary to deter China from attacking Taiwan. But it should also stand ready to take advantage of the larger strategic opportunities that may be presented by Chinese bullying or brutality.

Conclusion

Preventing the domination of eastern Eurasia by a hostile power requires that the United States do what it can to keep such a power from ever emerging, while preparing to deal with one if and when it does. For the better part of the past decade, U.S. decision-makers have concentrated heavily on attaining the first objective, primarily by trying to promote China's economic development and hoping that this will lead eventually to a political transformation; the second objective has received only sporadic and inadequate attention. In its eagerness to promote "partnership" and "engagement," the administration has avoided making significant demands of China, overlooked its problematic behavior in East Asia and elsewhere, and made concessions to Beijing so that China's leaders will see us and the world we lead as friendly and open to them. At the same time, and for similar reasons, the White House has also shown a disturbing tendency to downplay our alliances in the region, as for example in the summer of 1998, when President Clinton bypassed Tokyo and Seoul while traveling to and from Beijing. Whatever the intent behind such actions, it is all too easy for a rising power like China to interpret them as signaling timidity and weakness. Not surprisingly, instead of moderating China's ambitions, the Clinton policy of "constructive engagement" appears to have fueled them.

American strategists must begin now to deepen key alliances and existing nonalliance defense relationships, especially in Northeast Asia and maritime Southeast Asia, to widen the scope for strategic cooperation among the region's advanced industrial democracies, and to explore the possibilities for new links to other states, such as India, with whom the United States may increasingly have convergent interests. Renewing and expanding our ties across Asia is a necessary step to correcting the Sinocentric policies of recent years. Not only will such steps help prepare for the possible emergence of a more openly hostile and confrontational China, they ought, at the same time, to help lessen the likelihood of such a tragic turn of events. The pursuit of engagement from a position of weakness will inevitably degenerate into appeasement. Engagement from strength is the best available formula for keeping the peace and for advancing America's interests, in Asia and around the world.

Israel and
the "Peace Process"

The usual accounts of American policy toward the Arab/Israel
conflict in the 1990s stress the discontinuities in both
Jerusalem and Washington. In Israel, the story goes, the Likud government of Yitzhak Shamir gave way to a Labor government dedicated to peace. Under Yitzhak Rabin and, after his assassination,
under Shimon Peres, Israel sought an accommodation with the
Palestinians. In the United States, meanwhile, unfriendliness toward
Israel under the Bush/Baker leadership gave way to the warm
friendship of the Clinton administration, which even many American Jews still regard as "the best friend Israel ever had in Washington." But unfortunately, the Clinton efforts on behalf of the
"peace process" were frustrated when, from 1996 to 1999, the Likud
came back to power under Benjamin Netanyahu and changed
Israel's policies back to the obstructionism of Shamir.

Such is the conventional account, as routinely reported in the
pages of the *New York Times* and the *Washington Post*. But the real
story of the Middle East peace process in the 1990s is really one
of deep—and deeply disturbing—continuities. On the American
side, both the Bush and Clinton administrations have pursued a
consistent strategy aimed at pushing Isreal into a "land for peace"
deal with Yasser Arafat's Palestinian Liberation Organization that
would inevitably result in a Palestinian state. Under both President Bush and President Clinton, the chief American strategist and
Middle East negotiator has been Dennis Ross. And the theory
underlying Ross's approach has been as unvarying as his influence
in the State Department and at the White House: that Palestinian

radicalism was based in legitimate grievances and could not be vanquished until those grievances were satisfied by Palestinian statehood. Once that justifiable longing for statehood was met, the radicals would be displaced and a moderate, democratic polity (Jordan without a king?) could be built. The suggestion that Palestinian irredentism would only be nourished by these successes was dismissed as obstructionism by the Clinton administration as it had been by Bush.

On the Palestinian side, Yasser Arafat's PLO, now transformed into the Palestinian Authority and soon to be the government of Palestine, has remained faithful to its patented mixture of peaceful rhetoric for audiences abroad and an ever-present threat (and occasional practice) of terrorism in Israel. Given the success of this rifle-and-rhetoric mix, the Palestinian fidelity to a policy based on it is hardly surprising.

And on the Israeli side, once Prime Minister Rabin agreed to a land-for-peace deal with the PLO, Israeli policy—under Rabin, Peres, Netanyahu, and now Barak—has varied only in short-range tactics, not in broad strategy. Netanyahu accepted and implemented the Oslo Accords and sold them to Israel's right wing or "national camp," something a Labor government could never have achieved. As the Israeli election campaign of 1999 demonstrated, the consensus within that country on security issues is now extremely broad, in essence uniting the old Labor and Likud coalitions in support of the Oslo territorial concessions that the 1990s have brought.

If the 1990s have been characterized by the common commitment of the United States, Israel and the Arabs to the Oslo approach, however, the future will test all sides of this strategic triangle. The devil is in the details, and as core issues emerge about the future of Jerusalem, the return of refugees, and the rights of the new Palestinian state, compromise between the Israeli and Palestinian positions will become far harder. Moreover, the American pattern of indulging rather than challenging Palestinian misconduct will become far more dangerous. The United States will find it far more difficult to play honest broker, peace monitor, and chief ally of Israel all at once.

The next acts in this drama, moreover, will be played out against a changing security situation in the region, where Cold War alliance patterns are giving way to new divisions between radical states and an increasingly warm Israeli-Turkish military alliance. And they will be played out during a time when succession problems are about to strike several Arab states. King Hussein in Jordan and King Hassan in Morocco have already been succeeded by young sons (Abdullah and Mohamed, respectively) whose staying power is questionable. Egypt's President Mubarak is seventy-one, has ruled for eighteen years, and has no obvious successor. Syria's Hafiz al-Asad is two years younger, but there are persistent reports of his poor health. His son Bashar, who was trained as an ophthalmologist, may not have the set of skills necessary to survive long after his father's departure from the scene, and it is noteworthy that Asad has yet to name a successor. His death after twenty-nine years in power would spark a potentially bloody power struggle as the Alawite ruling elite seeks to protect itself from predictable reprisals. In Saudi Arabia, King Fahd is seventy-seven and ill, and Crown Prince Abdullah is seventy-five. The probable next-in-line, Prince Sultan, is also over seventy. The kingdom may have to replace its ruler several times in the coming decade, which will only exacerbate fierce succession struggles and may put the royal family's future at risk.

American interests require what was once called an "agonizing reappraisal" of our policy in the region. Those interests do not lie in strengthening Palestinians at the expense of Israelis, abandoning our overall policy of supporting the expansion of democracy and human rights, or subordinating all other political and security goals to the "success" of the Arab-Israel "peace process." At the very least, the comfortable assumptions of the 1990s, upon which the American and Israeli search for a "comprehensive" agreement between Israel and the Arab states have been based, may not long hold in a world where increasingly unstable Arab nations could lurch to more radical Islamic fundamentalism. Over the past decade, successive American administrations have defined U.S. interests in the Middle East as the achievement of a final resolution of the Arab-Israeli dispute. The next administration, however, will be required to make a clear distinction between the search for a Middle East "peace" and the search for genuine security for the United States and its allies.

The Origins and Limits of Oslo

In broad outline, Israeli policy in the 1990s involved expanding its peace treaty with Egypt to include the Jordanians and the

Palestinians, and beginning under the Barak government in 1999 to focus on arrangements with Syria and Lebanon. What made these changes possible was U.S. victory in the Cold War and the Gulf War, rather than any "peace process." The Soviet collapse ended Soviet support for client states like Syria, for the PLO, and for Arab radicalism in general. Immediately after the demise of the Soviet Union came the American victory in the Gulf War, which vastly increased American prestige in the region. For the PLO leadership, the lessons were clear: new relations with the United States and a new policy toward its ally, Israel, were necessary, for neither country was likely to disappear from the region.

The sense of enhanced American power was not only felt in PLO headquarters, however; it was also evident in the White House and the State Department, at least in those quarters that viewed Israeli/Palestinian relations as the central American interest in the entire region. Progress toward an Arab/Israeli settlement, which would necessarily be based on some sort of land-for-peace agreement, became the central Bush administration policy for the region. Recalcitrance by the Shamir government, which distrusted the PLO and argued that control of land was a better basis for security than Palestinian promises, aroused greater and greater hostility from the Bush/Baker/Ross team in Washington. The Israeli government's policy of expanding settlements in the West Bank was the basis (or excuse) for the bitter dispute of 1991 and 1992, when the U.S. government refused certain loan guarantees to Israel and stepped up its rhetoric about obstructionism. There was no corresponding increase in pressure on Arafat, and a distinct chill set in on American/Israel relations.

But this Israeli "old think" became part of Cold War history itself when the Likud government fell in 1992 and Yitzhak Rabin came into power. Rabin began secret negotiations with the PLO in Madrid in October 1991, which led, after further secret talks and after a new American government had been elected in November 1992, to the Oslo Accords. In October 1993, under Oslo I, Israel gave the PLO control of Jericho and Gaza; and in September 1995, under Oslo II, the PLO gained control over all the major cities of the West Bank and the vast bulk of the Palestinian population.

What was Rabin's calculation? Did he really put his faith in a transformed Arafat, now dedicated to peace and abandoning all his previous goals? Norman Podhoretz has offered a better analysis:

It had to do with his stress on the overriding importance of Israel's strategic relationship with the U.S. Rabin persuaded himself, I would guess, that unless he endorsed Oslo and went to the White House lawn, he would jeopardize that relationship, and that this would prove more dangerous to Israel than a Palestinian state ruled by Arafat.[1]

For Rabin, the Palestinians were not an "existential" threat to Israel; the new missiles being built by Iran, Iraq and other "pariah" states were ultimately more serious problems. But Washington was pushing hard for a settlement with the Palestinians, and Washington was an irreplaceable ally, so Oslo was worth the candle.

With the Oslo Accords came, at least briefly, a sort of honeymoon period in the triangular relationship between Israel, the Palestinian leadership, and the United States. Israel's international isolation seemed to fade away as that nation expanded diplomatic relations with Arab nations, attended major regional economic conferences, and saw the United Nations repeal its "Zionism is racism" resolution. Meanwhile, the PLO became master of increasing territory and population, basked in the approval it gained in the Clinton administration, and became awash in cash as international aid grew steadily. Irritating demands that the PLO improve its respect for human rights or accounting procedures for its financial windfall were rarely heard, and Arafat's own prestige and power grew steadily. The handshake on the White House lawn was a high-water mark. The assassination of Prime Minister Rabin in 1995 seemed to deepen all parties' commitment to Oslo, and Shimon Peres, Israel's new leader, was if anything more enthusiastic about the peace process than his predecessor had been.

The honeymoon lasted longer than most between antagonists on the international scene, reaching at least from late 1993 to mid-1996, when the Netanyahu government was elected. Why the era of good feeling ended is a controversial question. The popular wisdom among American and Palestinian officials, and among American journalists, lays the blame at Netanyahu's door: Netanyahu was not committed to the peace process or to its then-current manifestation in the Oslo Accords, so the argument went. Untrusting and untrustworthy, a saboteur of peace, he dragged his feet, needlessly and dangerously slowing down the peace process and increasing Palestinian frustration to the boiling point. All would have gone well without him—and will now, with him gone and Labor back in power.

This version is coherent and comforting to those obsessed with the Oslo Accords; in fact, what was striking about Netanyahu was his fidelity to Oslo. Whatever his private doubts (and 1996 campaign rhetoric), he came to believe that he could not escape the commitments his predecessors had made, and he was in some ways better able than they to meet those commitments. His government's spokesman, David Bar Illan, put the point sharply soon after Netanyahu's defeat:

> *Few leaders have been more consistent than Netanyahu. Unlike his martyred predecessor, Yitzhak Rabin—who was elected by vowing never to recognize the PLO, never to negotiate with Yasser Arafat, and never to offer to relinquish the Golan, but reneged on all three—Netanyahu stuck to his election promises with exemplary firmness. He scrupulously adhered to the Oslo accords, but insisted that the Palestinians reciprocate by fulfilling their commitment to combat terrorism. . . . The dramatic decline in Palestinian terrorism in the past three years is at least partly due to this insistence on reciprocity. . . . Netanyahu also created a revolution in the thinking of Israel's "national camp." He was the first right-wing leader who made most of his followers accept the partitioning of the Land of Israel. His agreements with the Palestinians, unlike those signed by the Labor government, enjoyed overwhelming support both in the Knesset and with the public. It is now fashionably forgotten that the peace process collapsed in 1996, under Shimon Peres, following the worst two and a half years of terrorism ever to plague the state. All talks with the Palestinians were suspended and the withdrawal from Hebron canceled. It was Netanyahu who rescued and revived the peace process.[2]*

There is no question that Netanyahu slowed the process down, arguing that calendars were not as important as real compliance, but delays *per se* were not the heart of the problem. At one level, growing difficulty was inevitable no matter who governed in Jerusalem, for each step "forward" in the peace process was harder, bringing Israelis and Palestinians closer to matters that were, if not irreconcilable, then at least unreconciled. If it was agreed that the Palestinian Authority would rule in Hebron, for example, it was not agreed how many Israeli settlements, and how many Israelis, would remain on the West Bank.

But in the 1990s this was not yet central. The key was whether the peace process was at bottom a slow Israeli abandonment of both territory and what had once been unchallenged positions and principles, before the inevitability of Palestinian statehood and ever-growing Palestinian power—or was instead a negotiated exchange of peace for limited territorial and political compromise. To Israelis, or at least to Netanyahu, the peace process had to be the latter. It was Netanyahu's stated policy to insist on reciprocity: on Palestinian compliance with promises extracted from them in the elaborate, detailed documents that were signed under American tutelage and often drafted by American hands. From Netanyahu's perspective, the peace process was subverted when the Palestinian Authority disregarded promises it had made, and it was up to the Americans to help ensure that the PA hewed to the straight and narrow.

To Arafat and his colleagues, however, the peace process was part of the broad sweep of history—and recent history has certainly taught them that on truly fundamental issues it is Israel that gives in. Just as the Israelis once refused to recognize the PLO or the Palestinian people, just as they once refused to give up land in the West Bank, so the current "red lines" will one day disappear, if only Palestinians hang tough. Moreover, tactical promises forced on the Palestinian leadership—about ending terrorism, disarming the population, changing the rhetoric employed in reference to the Jewish state, promoting democracy and protecting human rights— were not part of a solemn diplomatic pledge, but mere words, to be enforced to a greater or lesser degree as outside pressure required.

Arafat was, in practice, true to this understanding of the peace process, while Netanyahu was unable to sustain his own declared policy. Although he told the Knesset in October 1996 that he would demand "security and reciprocity," he soon found the pressure too great to bear. This was most apparent in his agreement to withdraw, in accordance with Oslo, from Hebron, which he ordered Israeli troops to do in January of 1997. The background was memorable. Continuing Israeli settlement activity had been called an "obstacle to peace" by President Clinton. In September 1995, after Netanyahu opened to tourists a new part of a tunnel under the

Temple Mount, there were bloody riots in which fifteen Israelis were killed. Israel, not the Palestinian Authority, was blamed for this violence even though official PA rhetoric helped incite it and the PA police did not act to prevent it. At an emergency summit in October 1995, again the Americans avoided any placing of blame on the PA. By 1996, then, it was clear to the Israelis both that the Palestinians were continuing to use violence in violation of Oslo, and that the Americans were refusing to challenge them on this tactic.

The bargain underlying Oslo was coming apart—yet Israel was expected to continue its withdrawals. The *Jerusalem Post* put it well:

> *The problem with the formula of compliance-for-territory is that compliance is easily reversible, while territorial concessions are not. But this is precisely the problem with the Palestinian approach to the agreement: security cooperation has been treated as a bargaining chip, rather than as an unshakeable pillar of the agreement.*[3]

In the face of this conduct by the PA, and the tacit American acceptance of it, Netanyahu nevertheless went ahead with the Hebron withdrawal. If he had once announced a policy of strict reciprocity, he had now abandoned it—perhaps in the same calculation attributed to Rabin, that the alliance with the United States could not be risked no matter what the sacrifice. In the Hebron case, he received in return for the withdrawal an American "Note for the Record" repeating that the Palestinian Authority must, for example, combat terrorism, confiscate illegal firearms, limit the number of police, and prevent hostile propaganda. Later, in October 1998, the PA repeated these promises yet again in the Wye River Accords, another negotiation that the American team (now Clinton/Berger/Ross in place of the original Bush/Baker/Ross) engineered to force the pace of the then-stalled peace process. Here the PA promised, for example, to prohibit "all forms of incitement to violence" and adhere to "internationally recognized norms of human rights." It was *deja vu* all over again.

And in official American eyes, any problems that arose were still the product of Netanyahu's foot-dragging. In April 1999, just before the Israeli elections, Secretary of State Albright told the American Jewish Committee that

On the Palestinian side, we have seen serious efforts to prevent terrorist strikes, to renounce the Palestinian Covenant, and to avoid a unilateral declaration of statehood. On the Israeli side, implementation has stalled, and, unfortunately, unilateral settlement activity has persisted. This is a source of real concern to us, because of its destructive impact on the ability to pursue peace.

Here were clear, concrete, and public claims that Israel was not complying with Oslo and Wye in letter or spirit; but there were no similar challenges to the Palestinians. In its place remained the remarkable assumption—or cynical claim—that the PA was a reliable peace partner.

This was a dangerous policy, because it is always dangerous to ignore reality. For while Oslo and Wye were being signed and implemented and the PA was gaining recognition, land, people, and power, the entity it was becoming was a reality that American policy ignored.

To begin with the terms of the agreements, it was evident the PA had not abandoned violence as a tool, had not ended incitement of violence, had not eliminated terrorists, had not confiscated illegal weapons, had not kept its men under arms down to agreed levels. Instead, the PA was developing, with American and Western financial support, into yet another Arab dictatorship where arms rather than elections decided who held power. The letter President Clinton sent Arafat after the latter agreed to hold off on a declaration of statehood in May 1999 (lest it prevent Labor from unseating Netanyahu, a key American goal) committed the United States to supporting "a free people in their own land." A European Union statement on Palestinian statehood in 1999 argued that "the creation of a democratic, viable, and peaceful sovereign Palestinian state ... would be the best guarantee of Israel's security." But neither the Americans nor the Europeans actually seemed to care about the true political structure of Arafat's new land.

During the Israeli occupation (from 1967 to 1994), for example, nongovernmental organizations and civil society had flowered, from the Palestine Human Rights Information Center and the Palestinian Center for Peace and Democracy, to rural medical clinics and the Security for the Care of the Handicapped. By 1995, it was estimated that there were seven hundred NGOs in the West

Bank and Gaza. But the PA "aborted and reversed the process of social democratization even before it had a chance to take hold," and the NGOs were systematically crushed while their Western financial support disappeared.[4] Similarly, while there were compliments about the new and independent Palestinian Legislative Council, there was no support for that body when Arafat ignored and humiliated it. A typical case came in 1997, when the Legislative Council issued a report complaining of corruption by Arafat's ministers and demanding that two of them resign. Arafat juggled his cabinet, but by replacing the more independent actors and pointedly keeping those whom the Legislative Council had found to be stealing money.

Such actions had no consequences for Arafat, as Western donors kept the money flowing. Indeed, the Palestinian Authority received roughly $550 million from donors in 1997, in addition to the $800 million in tax revenues transferred by Israel. When it was later discovered that 40 percent of this money, more than $300 million, was missing, Western governments responded by raising donations to $750 million for 1998 and nearly the same in 1999 and 2000. That there was massive corruption, that Arafat used these funds to buy loyalty, that there was a total lack of transparency, were matters never addressed by the United States government or any other major donor, despite what it said about the prospects for Palestinian democracy. It should have come as no surprise when, in November 1999, seven signers of a statement accusing the Arafat government of "tyranny and corruption" were immediately arrested.

As in other Arab lands, the incipient Palestinian state was overwhelming the society it ruled. The Human Rights Watch *World Report 1999* said the PA

> *failed to institutionalize important safeguards against human rights abuses that included patterns of arbitrary detention without charge or trial, torture and ill-treatment during interrogation, grossly unfair trials, and persecution of its critics.... Palestinian security forces arbitrarily arrested and detained individuals for long periods without charge.... In cases where the High Court did order a detainee released, the security services sometimes refused to act on the order.... Trials often lacked minimal due process guarantees, and judges who complained about*

judicial abuses sometimes faced retaliation.... The State Security Courts and military courts lacked almost all due process rights.... Security forces were repeatedly implicated in torture and corruption.

Nor was such criticism coming only from Western sources. At a Palestinian conference held at Bir Zeit University in the West Bank in June 1999, for example, the lack of democracy and the widespread corruption in the PA were central themes. One leading delegate decried "permitting Arafat to maintain his autocracy," and the director of the Independent Authority for Human Rights said "our institutions are nothing more than decor, power is in the hands of one man and there is no law and order."[5]

But far from joining in the Palestinian criticism of such abuses, the West—despite its rhetoric about a "free people" and human rights—continued to subsidize them. Human rights was, in fact, not a subject that the U.S. or other governments raised with Arafat and the PA in the expectation that serious progress would be made or that future diplomacy would turn on the matter.

Nor was there any serious American reaction to continuing incitement of violence and hatred, including anti-Semitism. Hillary Clinton's embrace of Suha Arafat in November 1999, after Palestinian leader Yasser Arafat's wife charged the Israelis with using poison gas against Palestinian children, aroused considerable comment. But in fact such statements are far from unusual in the PA's Arabic-language communications. The following statement by Naser Ahmad, an official at the Palestinian Authority's Political Guidance Directorate, for instance, appeared in the Palestinian Authority daily, *Al-Hayat Al-Jadida*, on November 7, 1998.

Corruption is a Jewish trait worldwide. So much so that one can seldom find corruption that was not masterminded by Jews or that Jews are not responsible for. They are well known for their intense love of money and its accumulation. The way in which they get hold of that money does not interest them in the least. On the contrary—they would use the most basic despicable ways, to realize their aim, so long as those who might be affected were non-Jews. A Jew would cross any line if it were in his interest.

Such rhetoric by high-ranking PA officials aroused no notice in Washington or any other Western capital, and of course the lesson for the PA was once again that its promises, made at Oslo, Wye, or anywhere else, were nowhere taken seriously.

Worse yet, the PA's commitment to the entire peace process has been brought into doubt by its flirting (in 1999) with UN General Assembly 181, the partition resolution of 1947, as a basis for a peace settlement in place of Security Council Resolutions 242 and 338, which were the basis for Camp David and Oslo. Resolutions 242 and 338 assumed that whatever the fate of the lands Israel conquered in the 1967 war, the territory she held prior to that date was beyond challenge. But Resolution 181 established Jerusalem as a *"corpus separatum"* to be administered by the UN and thus challenged Israeli sovereignty even in West Jerusalem. By reverting to the proposed partition borders of 1947, the PA suggests that those that existed in 1967 were illegitimate.

Yet even this departure from the basic premise of Israeli/Palestinian peace negotiations met with no denunciations in Washington. (The European Union agreed that no part of Jerusalem could rightfully be regarded as Israeli and revived the *corpus separatum* language in an official March 1999 message to the Israeli Foreign Ministry.) On the contrary, American official rhetoric ignores inconvenient facts. When President Clinton addressed Palestinian leaders in December 1998, he told them that

> *Your leaders came to an agreement at Wye because a majority of people on both sides have already said, now is the time to change.... More and more, Palestinians have begun to see that they have done more to realize their aspirations in five years of making peace than in forty-five years of making war. They are beginning to see that Israel's mortal enemies are, in fact, their mortal enemies, too.*

There is, unfortunately, no evidence for this conclusion about Palestinian public or official opinion. Fouad Ajami, a more reliable informant about the Middle East, has suggested that the contrary is true:

> *There has been no discernible change in the Arab attitudes toward Israel. The great refusal persists ... in that "Arab street" of ordinary men and women, among the intellectuals and the*

*writers, and in the professional syndicates. The force of this
refusal can be seen in the press of governments and of the oppositionists, among the secularists and the Islamists alike, countries that have concluded diplomatic agreements with Israel
and those that haven't.*[6]

American policy, then, has largely overlooked inconvenient facts
about Palestinian opinion and conduct, Palestinian violations of
the peace accords, and the nature of the state Arafat is building.
As a Palestinian state moves closer to reality, its own commitment
to the peace process remains in doubt, but Western (including
American) willingness to hold Arafat and the PA to its commitments is weak. Such a policy is bound to increase Palestinian
appetites rather than to inhibit Palestinian aggression.

As if to ensure this outcome, the Clinton administration
adamantly refused to move the U.S. Embassy from Tel Aviv to
Jerusalem in 1999 on dual grounds: "preserving the prospects for
a comprehensive, just, and lasting peace between Israel and its
neighbors and safeguarding the personnel and missions representing the United States abroad from terrorist threats." The latter explanation simply bows to terrorists' threats, in violation of
all stated American policy toward terrorism. The former suggests
that the U.S. cannot prejudice final status negotiations by acknowledging Jerusalem now as Israel's capital, as this matter will be on
the negotiating table. Yet the U.S. has supported Palestinian statehood although this will be on the table as well, while Israel's ability to designate Jerusalem as its capital cannot possibly be a matter for negotiations between it and the Palestinian Authority. Here
again the American position, while presented as mere "balance"
or "moderation," constitutes a threat to the peace process, because
it tantalizes Palestinians with the prospect of forcing the Jews to
abandon Jerusalem—and doing so with Western support.

This is particularly dangerous as Israel and the PA move ahead
in their talks and reach issues such as the "right of return" for
Palestinian refugees or the status of East Jerusalem. These are
matters on which it is difficult, today, to see any compromise acceptable both to Arafat and to Barak. It may be that Arafat, as the Israeli
journalist Ehud Ya'ari put it, "sees his historic mission not as solving the Palestinian problem but as establishing the Palestinian
state."[7] This might permit him to accept certain temporary "fixes"

for intractable problems such as Jerusalem or the refugees, but those same fixes are likely to be acceptable to the Israelis only if they are set in concrete as absolutely final. Thus optimism about a final settlement is difficult to sustain.

A Policy Based on Interests, not Illusions

A sound American policy in the Mideast must avoid the naive optimism that has marked the Bush-Clinton years and also avoid pressures on Israel based on the notion that more "flexibility" on its part would bring permanent peace. We should abandon as well the double standard that assumes Palestine is incapable of democratic self-rule and winks at repression or corruption in the Palestinian Authority. Many of the issues Israelis will see as critical when "final status" talks are reached are, in fact, critical to U.S. policy in the region and require the United States to defend its interests and allies. Limitations on Palestinian weaponry, prohibition of a Palestinian air force, and refusal to permit Palestinian military alliances with other states, to take three examples, should be American as much as they are Israeli security issues. The policy of playing down and thus condoning massive Palestinian violations must be abandoned before Israelis come to think that the peace process is stacked against them and a threat to their national security—or, worse yet, before it culminates in the creation of a sovereign, repressive, and aggressive Palestine aligned with the region's radical states.

For what, after all, are American interests in the Palestine/Israel dispute? Forgetting for a moment our commitment to and compatibility with Israeli democracy, surely the bottom line is to avoid the creation of another radical Arab state that would weaken Jordan and Israel and perhaps Egypt while it draws close to Syria, Iraq, Libya, or Iran. The risks to Israel from a land-for-peace deal that does not deliver peace are quite clear. But Washington has focused far too little on the nature of the state it is helping to establish in the heart of the Middle East. The United States has two paramount interests in the region today: keeping peace between the Arabs and Israelis, and toppling Saddam Hussein. The American goal now should not be to help create a Palestinian state, but to ensure that if and when such a state appears, it will be on the American side of those two issues.

As I noted at the beginning of this essay, it was the American victory in the Cold War and then the Gulf War, above all, that created today's Middle East political situation. Because of these exercises of American policy, it is now possible to envision a Middle East where a weakened Syria turns away from Iran and enters into an agreement that stabilizes Israel's entire northern border; where Saddam Hussein's regime has been replaced; and where the main strategic force in the region is a Turkish-Israeli alliance. But such an outcome is impossible unless it becomes the object of determined American effort.

The Barak government began to reduce the Israeli presence in Lebanon soon after coming to office, and as of this writing still appears to desire quick action on the Syria/Lebanon diplomatic front. This would fulfill a Barak campaign promise to be out of Lebanon in about a year. Whether Israel can actually reach a decent settlement with Syria that permits withdrawal from the Golan remains an open question.

Hafiz al-Asad had the chance to reach such an agreement with Yitzhak Rabin and pulled back. Can it be that, for domestic political reasons, he can't risk such a move? Would a state of peace undercut the minority Alawite claim to power and the justification for maintaining a police state? Would it destroy Syria's whole foreign policy stance by transforming its image from that of a militant front-line state to just another poor Arab neighbor of Israel? What concessions would the Israelis demand in the agreement, and could Asad agree to make them?

Then there is the American angle: Would the agreement require an American presence, much like the Sinai force that still, twenty years later, sits between Israelis and Egyptians in the Sinai Desert? Certainly the presence of the United States cannot be a substitute for real agreements between the Syrians and Israelis on Lebanon and on other key issues between them—from the crucial matter of water, to the many military issues that they must discuss, such as early warnings and demilitarized zones. At best a U.S. presence can help implement, but cannot replace, a satisfactory bilateral arrangement between Israel and Syria. Prime Minister Barak's statements that American troops will not be needed as part of a settlement with Syria suggest that he shares this conclusion.

Israel's policy toward Lebanon remains obscure. Is it to minimize the Syrian presence, or bind the Syrians to controlling

Hizbollah guerrillas there? Acquiescence in continuing Syrian domination would be a foolish error, giving hostages over to fate by
leaving in Asad's hands the means to inflame the Israel/Lebanon
border at will and at the same time dooming Lebanon to years
more of oppression, thievery, and strife. Given the weakness of the
Syrian military, which has not been modernized in a decade as a
result of financial problems, Lebanon remains Asad's only real
means of pressuring Israel. It should therefore be Israeli and U.S.
policy to take those means out of his hands. Any settlement with
Syria that leaves the status quo in Lebanon is doing too little for
Israel's security, while a comprehensive agreement with Syria that
includes respect for Lebanese self-rule would truly secure the last
of Israel's insecure borders.

The United States and Israel have for too long accepted the Syrian destruction of Lebanese society as inevitable, and the U.S. has
not used its influence to end this terrible period in Lebanese history. To see American secretaries of state pay court in Damascus,
or to see Israeli war planes punishing Lebanon for decisions made
by Asad, is to see influence wasted. An alternative approach was
taken by Turkey when it became fed up with Syrian support for
PKK terrorism: the Turks threatened war, and Asad immediately
expelled the PKK leader Ocalan (now in Turkish custody). While
the analogy is inexact, it suggests that part of any deal with Syria,
even one that includes Israeli withdrawal from Lebanon, should
be an ultimatum to Syria about support for Hizbollah and terror
against Israel.

Whatever the first steps in Israeli-Syrian negotiations, American
policy should promote a steady withdrawal of Syrian and Syrian-
backed forces and growing respect for Lebanese sovereignty. If
regional *realpolitik* casts Lebanon in the role of buffer between
Israel and Syria, it does not require that that country be forever
dominated by Syria and her terrorist allies. The ultimate goal, the
re-creation of a sovereign and pro-Western Lebanon, would be a
major step forward in the search for peace and stability in the
region. Even if this goal is unattainable while Asad remains alive,
it should be unequivocally asserted as an American interest and
made part of American calculations in dealing with Syria.

The broader context in which Israel and its neighbors play out
their negotiating strategies offers both danger and great promise.
The most promising factor is the new, or to be more precise, newly

enhanced, Turkish-Israeli military alliance. This new development began in February 1996 with the establishment of the first formal link between Israel and any Muslim country, a joint military training agreement. A free trade accord followed the next month, one of thirteen soon signed. In February 1997, the chief of staff of the Turkish Army visited Israel, and in April of that year Israel's foreign minister went to Turkey and the Turkish defense minister went to Jerusalem. By June, joint naval and air maneuvers had begun in the Mediterranean, and events since then—including Israel's immediate humanitarian response to the Turkish earthquake in the summer of 1999—have only deepened the relationship.

It is quite obvious that promoting that relationship is now a key U.S. interest in the Middle East, for it constitutes the main building block of pro-Western forces and the main resistance to the military and ideological push from radical Arab states and Iran. The United States should foster increasing political and economic relations between the two countries as well as their military cooperation. Given continuing European Union rejection of Turkey, and Turkey's own political uncertainties in the wake of the 1999 earthquake, that nation deserves greatly increasing American attention and a greater call on U.S. diplomatic and economic resources.

If Israel's negotiations with the PA and Syria are the focus of our attention today, in the long run the main threat to U.S. interests in the region comes from the acquisition of weapons of mass destruction and missile delivery systems by Iraq and Iran. To this threat there are two remedies: regime change in Iraq, and the building of missile defenses. As to the former, Saddam Hussein's fall would favorably affect the entire Middle East political and military situation. Unfortunately, under the Clinton administration the containment of Iraq is failing. There is no effective inspection regime at all now in place, and it is therefore fair to assume that Iraq is once again replacing its stocks of chemical weapons and of missiles and continuing with its nuclear program. The United States rather than Iraq appears to be growing diplomatically isolated, and Saddam to be growing bolder. One need not rehearse in detail the American errors that contributed to these developments, including our apparent undercutting of the UNSCOM inspection teams when they existed, to acknowledge that the gravity of this situation is increasing.

Maintaining Western support for the containment of Iraq, with an effective inspection system and the continuing use of air power to punish violations, seems increasingly unlikely. This makes the alternative of replacing the current regime, endorsed by the U.S. Congress, an even more urgent goal. Achieving this outcome will require an immense commitment of time, ingenuity, and resources, but it is obvious that the prize is worth the effort. An increasingly powerful Iraq under Saddam is a danger to every American interest in the region and beyond, not only because of the actions it would undertake, but because a rehabilitated Saddam is eloquent testimony to our inability to persevere in an effective policy.

While Iran and Iraq, as well as other nations near and far such as Libya and North Korea, are building weapons of mass destruction, it is folly for the United States not to give top priority to building missile defenses. This topic remains mired in partisan wrangling in the Congress and in jesuitical debates over the ABM treaty, but its growing importance to American security and foreign policy cannot be denied. Whatever the role of missile defense in American global strategy, in Middle East policy it is central. The government of Israel has recognized this, and an entire generation of military thinkers has suggested that the real threat to Israeli security comes today—and especially tomorrow—not from the "inner ring" of threats (Palestinian terrorism, war with neighbors like Syria or Egypt) but from the "outer ring" where rogue states are developing missiles.

In the Middle East as elsewhere, missile defenses can provide protection both from actual missile attack and from the political blackmail that a state armed with missiles can use in its foreign policy. That blackmail is likely to be effective when employed by states that, like Iraq, have shown themselves willing to use chemical weapons (against Iran) and launch missile strikes against enemies (in the Gulf War)—unless those enemies are able to defend themselves. It is a simple fact that possession of missile delivery systems and a combination of conventional, chemical and biological, and nuclear weapons by Iraq, Iran, and others vastly increases the vulnerability of Israel and of American forces in the region. While this threat would be greatly diminished with the demise of the current Iraqi regime, it would not be eliminated. It must be met with a workable missile defense system, if our ability to protect and advance our interests in the Middle East is not to be compromised.

ooooo

As the advances in the "peace process" since the Cold War and Gulf War have demonstrated, progress on individual issues depends less on the brilliance of our negotiators than on the overall balance of forces in the region. None of the players in the Middle East—not even Qadafi, it seems—is irrational, and all are constantly measuring our ability and will to promote American policies and interests. And both will and ability are going to need significant enhancement in the coming years. As noted above, building missile defense system, nurturing the Israeli/Turkish defense alliance, and ending Saddam's regime in Iraq would obviously strengthen our position and the prospects for a durable peace. But all of these developments require clearer vision and greater resolve. To overlook and therefore acquiesce in Palestinian violations of agreements already signed, to wait humbly for audiences with Hafiz al-Asad, or to permit Saddam to escape the constraints under which he was living, reflect an unwillingness to use American power fully.

The next decade will present enormous opportunities to advance American interests in the Middle East, but not for the most part through painstaking negotiations of documents. Here, as elsewhere, the principal means of asserting our national interests will be boldly asserting our support of our friends and opposing with equal boldness our enemies. Here, as elsewhere, much depends on judgments others make about our ability to see our interests clearly and our resolve to protect them. Here, as elsewhere, our military strength and willingness to use it will remain a key factor in our ability to promote peace.

In the years ahead, we must move from accommodating ourselves as best we can to "inevitable" historical processes, to asserting American goals. It is not inevitable that the new Palestinian state be yet another radical, despotic entity, but avoiding that outcome will require realism and perseverance. Not so many years ago, it would have been considered outrageous to assume that Lebanon, that pro-American outpost, would fall under permanent Syrian domination. In fact, few outcomes in the region—good ones and bad—are inevitable, any more than the Suez Crisis of 1956 and President Eisenhower's reaction to it or the Iraqi invasion of

Kuwait and President Bush's decision to reverse it were inevitable. The coming years will bring new crises and challenges whose outcome will depend in large part on our ability and willingness to act. That much, at least, is not changing in the Middle East.

The Decline of America's Armed Forces

The end of the Cold War and the collapse of the Soviet Union inaugurated a period of unprecedented international peace and security—that much everyone knows. But students of history also know something a bit more sobering: that the current epoch of relative peace is but an interlude between the end of the Cold War and the beginning of the next major conflict. How long this time of peace lasts and what degree of security can be preserved for the world's democratic powers are questions that only the United States has the power to answer. Unfortunately, since the collapse of the Soviet Union and the American victory in the Gulf War, the United States has failed to meet the challenge of maintaining a military capable of preserving international peace and stability now and in the future. As a consequence, we may someday look back on a fleeting post–Cold War era of peace that was an opportunity missed.

The simple fact is that today's U.S. armed forces are smaller, less well prepared for combat, and operating older equipment than those of a decade ago. The United States spends about half as much on defense, as a percentage of gross domestic product, as it did during the mid-1980s, and less than half the Cold War average of 7.5 percent. Indeed, U.S. defense spending as a proportion of national wealth has fallen to levels not seen since before Pearl Harbor. Meanwhile, this smaller force is working harder than ever to keep up with an increasing pace of operations around the world— a pace, according to the Joint Chiefs of Staff, that has increased threefold over the past decade.

The unsurprising result of this growing gap between America's military commitments and the resources allocated to defense has been a corrosion of the health of the armed services and a reduction of combat effectiveness to a state comparable to the infamous "hollow" army of the late 1970s. Last year, the Army rated two of its divisions unfit for combat. Top Army officials reported significant and risky declines in readiness across the board. And the Army is not alone. The Air Force chief of staff, General Michael Ryan, has reported "an overall 14 percent degradation in the operational readiness of our major operational units" since 1996. By the end of this year, the average Air Force aircraft will be twenty years old; by 2015, even allowing for the introduction of new fighters, the average age of the fleet will be thirty years old. The story is the same in the Navy and Marine Corps. The chief of naval operations has reported that the Navy has inadequate ship-building resources to maintain a force of even three hundred ships—down from the nearly six-hundred-ship Navy of the 1980s. Manpower shortages are so severe that forward-deployed naval forces, the carrier battle groups that are the core of the Navy's overseas mission, now put to sea with significantly reduced crews. When the *Lincoln* carrier battle group fired Tomahawk cruise missiles at terrorist camps in Afghanistan and at suspected chemical weapons facilities in Sudan, it conducted the operation with less than 90 percent of its normal manpower. As for the Marines, retired General Charles Krulak declared a state of near-crisis: "Our problems today are caused by the fact that we are, and have been, plowing scarce resources—Marines, money, material—into our old equipment and weapons systems in an attempt to keep them operational."

The gap between American commitments and defense resources is more than just a problem for our fighters, who have to work much harder and take more risks with inadequate equipment—though that ought to be reason enough for action. There is also increasing question about the U.S. military's ability to implement the nation's foreign and defense policies. Last year the chairman of the Joint Chiefs of Staff acknowledged that there is now a "high risk" involved in executing the missions called for under the national military strategy. During the allied bombing of Serbia and Serb forces in Kosovo last year, the Joint Chiefs actually declared the risk unacceptable: It was clear that if faced with a crisis in the Persian Gulf and on the Korean Peninsula—the two-major-war scenario

that has provided the basis for American defense planning throughout the post–Cold War era—the United States would not be able
to react in time to forestall defeat. This was a remarkable admission, though it went largely unnoticed by the press. What would
be the consequences for American security, and for the world, were
the United States ever to lose a war in the Persian Gulf or on the
Korean peninsula?

How did the magnificent force that won the Cold War and triumphed decisively over Iraq in 1991 come to such a sorry state?
The story of America's military decline in the 1990s has gone largely
untold. Partly it has been obscured by the peace and prosperity
Americans have enjoyed these past ten years. But the hidden story
of the past decade is worth recounting, for it provides an object
lesson on how *not* to articulate America's strategic objectives and
how *not* to prepare America's military for the demanding tasks of
the present and the needs of the future.

Origins of the Base Force

From the start of the post–Cold War era, American defense planning was shaped by the new strategic circumstances brought about
by the disappearance of a Soviet threat. During the Cold War, most
of America's conventional military effort was devoted to the task
of maintaining active armed forces at a very high level of readiness and preparing to transport them at virtually a moment's notice
to the central front in Europe. Ironically, that capability was never
employed against the Warsaw Pact through fifty years of Cold War
confrontation. Instead, it made possible the spectacular victory
against the Iraqi army in 1991. Once the Cold War ended, however, the need for such readiness and, it was felt, such large armed
forces had passed. By 1992, Pentagon planners were claiming that
they would have ten years' warning before a revived Soviet Union
could once again threaten to overrun Western Europe. The Bush
administration consequently proposed a 25 percent reduction in
America's conventional armed forces over a period of five to seven
years, and began to consider how the purpose and mission of the
U.S. armed forces had changed in the new environment.

In fact, the disappearance of the Soviet threat undermined the
rationale for the American military's force structure. The administration, led by Secretary of Defense Dick Cheney, Joint Chiefs

Chairman Colin Powell, and Undersecretary of Defense Paul Wolfowitz, worked to develop a new force structure based on the new circumstances, and with a new mission.

Cheney, Powell, and Wolfowitz rejected the notion that the end of the Cold War meant the end of threats to America's security or the end of a need to maintain adequate armed forces. They argued that the collapse of the Soviet Union did, indeed, provide America with a unique opportunity. But it was not an opportunity to disarm and bask in the new peace of some alleged "strategic pause." Rather, they argued, the United States had the chance to defend the new strategic depth it had gained with the victory in the Cold War.

The Bush administration's new force structure, which officials dubbed the "Base Force," was oriented toward the future. It was not designed to fight any particular conflict or to meet only the obvious threats of the moment. Instead, the idea of the Base Force was to provide the military might to maintain America's predominant position over the long term by shaping the international environment, deterring or thwarting aggression, and providing the global leadership that would avoid the creation of power vacuums that would-be regional hegemons might seek to fill. Critics of the Base Force frequently complained that the force structure, and the expense of maintaining it, were not justified by any of the existing threats to American security after the Cold War. But Cheney, Powell, Wolfowitz, and others insisted that the concept had been designed to deter not only immediate threats, but future threats as well.

The most important element of the Bush administration's strategy, particularly from the standpoint of determining the size and composition of the armed forces, was the need to be able to deter and defeat major regional aggressors in areas of importance to the United States. This strategic concept came to be known as the "two-MRC" standard: the armed forces had to be able to fight and win two "major regional conflicts" nearly simultaneously while retaining the ability to handle smaller conflicts elsewhere in the world.

Although often derided by critics of military spending, the two-war standard was actually based on sophisticated strategic thinking. Bush officials recognized that maintaining such a standard was the key both to global stability and to preserving American global leadership. If the United States could not respond to more than one major crisis at a time, it could soon find itself in the position of being hesitant to respond to any crisis. If, for instance, Iraq invaded Kuwait again, would the United States devote sufficient resources to rebuffing the attack if it knew that it would be leaving South Korea undefended from a North Korean invasion? Would a U.S. military without a two-MRC capacity not, in fact, be inviting such a disaster?

Maintaining less than a two-war standard would also wreak havoc with American allies. What good would an American guarantee be if our allies knew that once the U.S. military became embroiled in a crisis elsewhere, it would not be able to come to their defense should they face attack? Any strategy that seriously aimed at deterring both current and future challenges had to be based on at least a two-war capability. The Bush administration readily understood that having the ability to handle only one major conflict at a time could be incapacitating, entailing the abandonment of America's commitments and security in all other theaters while that one conflict raged.

Although defense planners could envision two simultaneous wars involving Iraq and North Korea, the Base Force was not premised on an evaluation of the threat at any given moment, but on the need to shape an uncertain future and be able to respond to those developments that were beyond control or prediction. In a post–Cold War world, the threat consists less in the rise of any particular competitor than in America's unwillingness or inability to maintain international peace by deterring future challenges.

The Base Force Comes up Short

Although the Bush administration had settled on the appropriate strategy for the post–Cold War era, it was unable to put together a force that could really meet the two-war standard. The most obvious reason for this failure was domestic politics. A genuine two-war force structure cost more than American politicians wanted to spend on the military in the early 1990s. Under pressure from Democrats in Congress, and to some extent even from Republicans, the Bush administration felt pressured to provide voters a large post–Cold War "peace dividend." Powell and his colleagues tried to ensure that these inevitable cuts at least made some military sense. But the pressure of large budget deficits led them to propose a force that was inadequate to the task they set for it. Despite the Bush administration's sound strategic thinking and good intentions, the Base Force came up short.

The Base Force consisted of 12 active and 8 reserve Army divisions (down from 18 and 10), 28 Air Force tactical fighter wings (down from 35), and 450 ships, including 12 carriers (down from 574 and 15).[1] Was this force sufficient to meet the administration's own two-war standard? During the consideration of the 1992 defense budget, the first to attempt to implement the Base Force, the Bush administration was repeatedly asked if the Base Force would be able to repeat Operation Desert Storm and still be able to conduct another major operation at the same time. In testimony before Congress, the answers were always disturbing. For instance, Admiral David Jeremiah, vice chairman of the Joint Chiefs of Staff, testified that the Base Force could accomplish a Gulf War–type operation, "but with greater risk." He elaborated: "As you draw down the numbers of forces here, you're going to have fewer forces available in Europe, for instance . . . and you would have a greater risk in our ability to reinforce in areas around the world such as Korea or some other hot spot where we would have a requirement to do so."[2]

The most telling evidence of the weakness of the Base Force, however, surfaced during General Colin Powell's testimony before the House Armed Services Committee when Representative Ike Skelton pressed him, asking if America's armed forces could conduct a successful Desert Storm operation at that moment. Powell said, "Today, yes, sir." Skelton asked if America could repel a massive North Korean conventional attack on South Korea at that moment. Powell replied, "In my judgment, yes, without question, if there was no other major contingency taking place. If there was a Desert Storm taking place at the same time, a little more difficult proposition for us, but probably yes." Powell then added, "When we go down to the Base Force, what we are losing is flexibility to handle two scenarios at the same time. We're trying to structure the Base Force to handle two at the same time, hoping that two at the same time will not occur."

Skelton pressed further, asking if in 1997, with the Base Force as Powell described it, American forces could still conduct a Desert Storm. Powell replied, "Yes." Skelton asked the same question about a North Korean invasion in 1997. Powell replied, "Yes, with great difficulty and no longer any reserves available to us to handle anything else that came along." Skelton asked, finally, about a Korean contingency and a simultaneous Desert Storm contingency in 1997. Powell answered that in such a situation, the force would be stretched to "the breaking point."[3] It was clear that the Base Force was not really able to handle two nearly simultaneous major regional conflicts and would, in fact, have to strain to handle even one.

From the outset, therefore, America's post–Cold War military posture was based on something of a myth. The Bush administration had rightly stated that it was essential to have a force that could meet the two-war standard. But the Base Force did not really provide that capability.

The Clinton Administration Build-Down

The failure of the Bush administration was nothing compared to what followed. When President Bush left office, the Base Force was gradually dismantled as the Clinton administration, in search of ever greater defense budget savings, began hollowing out America's armed forces.

The incoming Clinton administration believed Bush's cuts had been too small and was determined to wring an even larger "peace dividend" out of the already depleted defense budget. In 1992 Clinton had campaigned on a promise to cut an additional $60 billion from defense over five years. Clinton's first defense secretary, Les Aspin, set about justifying those cuts by means of a new calculation of American defense needs, the "Bottom-Up Review." In the end, it was not George Bush and Dick Cheney but Bill Clinton and Les Aspin who established the size and structure of America's post–Cold War armed forces.[4]

Les Aspin had never accepted the logic of the "capabilities-based" approach of the Regional Defense Strategy or the expense of the Base Force. He was among those who lambasted the Bush administration for failing to identify real-world foes and obvious threat scenarios as the bases of any proposed force structure and defense program. Although he claimed to offer "new thinking" about post–Cold War security, Aspin insisted on asking the same old Cold War question: where is the threat? Finding none in the vacuum created by the triumph of the West, he could not accept the idea of building a force that looked beyond immediate dangers. In deliberate contrast to the "vagueness" and lack of concrete scenarios underlying the Base Force, Aspin chose an entirely empirical approach. As he explained his thinking in early 1992, his idea was to shape the force around the need to re-fight recent wars.

> *Essentially the concept that we're playing with is trying to do this in terms of Iraq equivalents or Panama equivalents. Without the Soviet Union, the long pole in the tent is probably ... Iraq of Saddam Hussein and Desert Storm.*
>
> *So you start with a basic force concept that looks at what we needed to deal with that threat. Then we look at other parts of the world in terms of Iraq equivalence. What is North Korea? Is that a three-quarters of an Iraq? Or is that an Iraq and a half? What is Syria? What is Libya? What is Iraq post–Desert Storm? Is it one-quarter of an Iraq? Or is it half of an Iraq? Or is it an eighth of an Iraq? ...*
>
> *And you figure how many forces we needed to fight Iraq before Desert Storm, look at those kind of notions around the world, and then decide the old question how many do you want to deal with simultaneously, and try and get to a US force structure by that kind of a means.* [5]

Aspin's "Bottom-Up Review" (BUR) was founded on this mechanical, threat-based thinking and was, therefore, the antithesis of the Base Force in every way. The BUR looked only at obvious current threats and largely ignored future ones. It considered primarily how to defend America today and paid little heed to how America might prevent new threats from arising tomorrow. Above all, where the Base Force had avoided presenting specific scenarios in an attempt to maintain flexibility of thought and preparedness, the Bottom-Up Review laid open for all to see the concrete and inflexible bases of its analysis.

Thus, for the first time, a "major regional conflict" publicly received concrete definition. In such a conflict, according to Aspin's calculations, the U.S. would face an enemy with:

- 400,000–750,000 total personnel under arms
- 2,000–4,000 tanks
- 3,000–5,000 armored fighting vehicles
- 2,000–3,000 artillery pieces

- 500–1,000 combat aircraft
- 100–200 naval vessels, primarily patrol craft armed with sur-face-to-surface missiles, and up to 50 submarines
- 100–1,000 Scud-class ballistic missiles, some possibly with nuclear, chemical, or biological warheads.[6]

The forces required to meet such a foe were also described in detail:

- 4–5 Army divisions
- 4–5 Marine Expeditionary Brigades
- 10 Air Force fighter wings
- 100 Air Force heavy bombers
- 4–5 Navy aircraft carrier battle groups
- Special operations forces[7]

Specific foes—Iraq and North Korea—were penciled in to play the roles of adversary in the two putative MRCs, with the obligatory and unconvincing warnings that the selection of those two cases was only for illustrative purposes.

With these definitions and building blocks in place, the BUR proceeded to lay out four alternative force structures.

BUR FORCE STRUCTURE OPTIONS[8]

	Option 1	Option 2	Option 3	Option 4
	One MRC	One MRC with"hold" in another	Two MRCs	Two MRCs with smaller missions
Army	8 Active Divisions (AD) 6 Reserve Divisions (RD)	10 AD 6 RD	10 AD 15 Reserve Brigades[9]	10 AD 8 RD
Navy	8 Carrier Battle Groups (CBGs)	10 CBGs	11 CBGs 1 Reserve Carrier	12 CBGs
Air Force	10 Active Fighter Wings (AFW) 6 Reserve Fighter Wings (RFW)	13 AFW 7 RFW	13 AFW 7 RFW	14 AFW 10 RFW
Marine Corps	5 Active Brigades (AB) 1 Reserve Division (RD)	5 AB 1 RD	5 AB 1 RD	5 AB 1 RD

One dubious feature of these force structure options was that the difference between the "one-MRC force" and the "two-MRC force" was described as consisting of only two active Army divisions, three active Navy aircraft carriers with one reserve, and three active Air Force wings with one reserve. This was a good deal short of what the BUR itself had identified as a force necessary to fight an MRC.

Once again, the disparity may well have been the consequence of domestic politics. The Clinton administration's first budget called for cuts of over $100 billion in defense spending, much more than the $60 billion in cuts originally called for by candidate Clinton. Aspin's proposed force structure for fighting two simultaneous wars had fallen victim to the president's desire to produce a bigger "peace dividend" for American voters.

Faced with this obvious gap between his stated defense strategy and the planned force structure and budgets, Aspin attempted some sleight-of-hand. In January 1993, he floated a trial balloon: the "win-hold-win" strategy. The idea was that American airpower could blunt a North Korean offensive and hold it in place until ground forces engaged in Iraq could re-deploy to finish the job. This trial balloon, however, dropped like a brick. Critics immediately dubbed it "win-lose-lose" and "win-hold-oops."[10] Meanwhile, from May to September of 1993, the "official" Pentagon assessment of what forces were required to win two nearly simultaneous major regional conflicts was reduced from 12 active Army divisions to 10, from 12 carrier battle groups to 11, from 14 active Air Force fighter wings to 13.

Pentagon officials labored to demonstrate that the reduced force could still meet the two-war standard, arguing that "force enhancements"—modernization of equipment and the more rapid introduction of precision-guided munitions—would compensate for the reductions. It was clear, however, that Aspin's team had merely glossed over the problem: they had constructed a force that could fight only one war at a time, but they sold it as a force that could fight two. The fact was that the BUR analysis was driven not by strategic considerations but by budget pressures, which meant that force structures had been calculated to fit budget ceilings.

The Clinton administration's Bottom-Up Review established the basic outlines of the American military force structure which has persisted ever since. Where the Base Force had called for 12 active and 8 reserve Army divisions, 28 Air Force wings, and 12 carrier battle groups, the BUR's force structure consisted of 10 active Army divisions supported by 15 National Guard enhanced readiness brigades, 20 wings, of which 13 were active and 7 reserve, and 11 aircraft carriers.

Today, that remains the size and structure of the American armed forces.[11] If such a force was not capable of fighting two major regional conflicts in 1993, then it is certainly not capable of doing so today. The gap between American commitments and American defense capabilities remains. Indeed, as a subsequent defense review conducted by the Clinton administration in 1997 demonstrated, the gap has actually widened in recent years.

The Quadrennial Defense Review (QDR) provided a far more coherent strategy for America's armed forces than the simplistic threat-based analysis of the Bottom-Up Review. The QDR based its force-planning analyses not only on the two-war standard, but also on the obvious fact that "smaller-scale contingencies"—the missions to Somalia, Haiti, Rwanda, and in the Balkans, the maintenance of no-fly zones over northern and southern Iraq—were inevitably going to be a part of American foreign policy. In addition, the QDR went beyond Aspin's exclusive concentration on current threats and, following the line of thinking of the previous Bush administration, pointed to the need to "prepare now for an uncertain future" in which American forces would have to investigate new ways of fighting and new ways of organizing themselves to take advantage of a possible "revolution in military affairs."[12]

While acknowledging these new demands, the Quadrennial Defense Review in no way minimized the vital importance of being able to fight and win two wars nearly simultaneously. On the contrary, it offered the most comprehensive and convincing argument in favor of the two-war standard. "A force sized and equipped for deterring aggression in more than one theater," the QDR's authors declared, "ensures that the United States will maintain the flexibility to cope with the unpredictable and unexpected. Such a capability is the *sine qua non* of a superpower."

> *If the United States were to forego its ability to defeat aggression in more than one theater at a time, our standing as a global power, as the security partner of choice and the leader of the international community would be called into question. Indeed, some allies would undoubtedly read a one-war capability as a*

signal that the United States, if heavily engaged elsewhere, would
no longer be able to defend their interests....

A one-theater-war capacity would risk undermining both
deterrence and the credibility of U.S. security commitments in
key regions of the world. This, in turn, could cause allies and
friends to adopt more divergent defense policies and postures,
thereby weakening the web of alliances and coalitions on which
we rely to protect our interests abroad.[13]

Beyond reaffirming the importance of preserving the two-war
standard, the QDR also acknowledged that doing so was more difficult than Aspin and his planners had suggested. The QDR stressed
that a successful "halt phase"—"being able to rapidly defeat initial enemy advances short of their objectives in two theaters in
close succession, one followed immediately by another"—was a
"particularly challenging requirement." The report also noted the
danger of fighting adversaries armed with chemical or biological
weapons and the means of delivering them against airfields and
ports. Finally, the QDR admitted that making the transition from
engagement in multiple smaller contingencies to major theater
wars would be difficult. Even the effort to assemble scattered forces
to meet the timelines specified in the war plans of the theater commanders in chief would exceed U.S. lift capabilities.[14]

The shocking thing about the QDR was that although it set forth
a far more expansive set of requirements for the armed forces than
the BUR, it retained—and even slightly reduced—the BUR's budget,
force structure, and defense program. At the end of 1996, Deputy
Defense Secretary John White issued a memorandum directing
that the Quadrennial Defense Review be conducted under the
assumption that defense spending would be limited to $250 bil-
lion per year.[15] The number of overall active-duty "end-strength"
personnel, therefore, was cut from 1.42 million to 1.36 million.[16]
The Navy surface combatant fleet was reduced, as was the number of submarines and Air Force fighter wings. The QDR assumed
that these force reductions would produce significant savings, and
it relied for more savings on a further round of base closings and
increased management efficiencies. Congress, of course, rejected
the base closings, and the other savings did not appear likely either.
Once again, the Clinton administration had merely glossed over
the glaring fact that American defense strategy—indeed, the

administration's own assessment of American defense obligations—far outstripped the resources the administration and Congress were willing to spend on the military.

The Hollow Army

The effect of this gap has become all too obvious. Today's armed forces are overly strained simply in performing the "smaller scale contingency" operations of the present day. In the last two years, an increasing number of senior officers have begun to admit openly that the current force structure is not capable of fighting two nearly simultaneous conflicts. The formal FY99 posture statement released by the Joint Chiefs of Staff states that America's risk in the first such conflict is now "moderate" and in the second, "high."

But the best evidence for the incapacity of the current force structure, as well as for the continued need for a two-MRC capability, came in 1994.[17] In the first half of that year a crisis of immense proportions developed over the North Korean nuclear program. A signatory to the Non-Proliferation Treaty, Pyongyang nevertheless consistently refused to allow the International Atomic Energy Agency to make the inspections required under that treaty. The United States government found itself contemplating the use of force against North Korea. As the crisis came to a head in June 1994, Secretary of Defense William Perry and President Clinton were forced to take seriously the possibility of war on the Korean peninsula. The briefings they received from the commanders in the theater were as far away from Aspin's happy delusions about "win-hold-win" as they could be.

There was no talk in those briefings of confining U.S. action to the use of crippling airpower to stop the North Korean advance. For one thing, there was not enough airpower in the theater. For another, the generals in command in Korea did not, apparently, believe that airpower alone could do the trick. Instead, they offered three options, all of which involved the introduction of additional ground forces into South Korea at once, but all of which, in the end, were inadequate to fight a war in Korea. The Pentagon plan for fighting such a war reportedly called for an additional 400,000 reinforcements to be sent to the peninsula.[18]

Fighting a war in Korea was hard enough given the military's limited resources. What if the United States had been forced to deal with Iraq at the same time? In fact, the Korean crisis missed coinciding with an Iraq crisis by only a few months. In October 1994, four months after the resolution of the Korean crisis, Saddam Hussein moved three divisions of the Republican Guard from permanent cantonments around Baghdad to the Kuwaiti border. In contrast with previous adventures, Saddam was much slower to back down in response to American warnings. As a result, the U.S. military, which already had 20,000 soldiers in Haiti, was compelled to place on alert and begin to deploy more than 210,000 troops, of whom 194,000 were ground forces.[19]

The crises in Korea and Iraq could easily have overlapped more closely. What if these crises had been more "nearly simultaneous?" What if they had not been so easily diffused? Did the American armed forces in 1994 have the ability to fight Iraq and Korea at about the same time at an acceptable level of risk?

The answer would seem to be no. To fight a defensive war in Korea and maintain a deterrent presence in the Persian Gulf during a major crisis, while still keeping forces in Haiti, would have required more than 620,000 troops. In January 1994 there were only 540,000 soldiers in the active Army. Of course, there were 174,000 Marines and several hundred thousand more soldiers in the Army National Guard and the Army Reserve. But could all these forces simply be plugged in to fill the gaps? Would there be time to call up, train, and deploy the reserves? Would the more optimistic scenarios for defeating and deterring our two adversaries unfold as envisioned, or would Americans face the kind of unanticipated setbacks that occur so often in war?

American military planning may, in fact, be premised on a faulty assumption about our potential adversaries: that they will be content to re-fight the same kind of war that Saddam lost so miserably in 1991. More specifically, it is based on the assumption that they will, like Saddam, allow the United States the time it needs to conduct a massive buildup of forces in the theater of operations. But there is good reason to believe that any future potential adversary will not be so cooperative.

During the 1994 crisis, in fact, senior American officers in command in Korea doubted that the North Koreans would give American forces the time they needed to deploy. One American general was convinced that the North Koreans had studied the lessons of the Gulf War almost more than we did, "and they learned one thing:

you don't let the United States build up its forces and then let them go to war against you." The general believed that "the North Koreans were never going to let us do a large buildup. They would see their window of opportunity closing, and they would come." Adding to this officer's apprehension was a chilling fact not well known outside the U.S. Command: at Panmunjom in May, a North Korean colonel told a U.S. officer, "We are not going to let you do a buildup."[20]

If North Korea had launched a pre-emptive attack during a U.S. buildup, then the assumptions underlying American planning would have to have been abandoned. The best that could be said of America's forces in 1994, when they were nearly called upon to fight two major wars almost simultaneously, is that they might just have been barely adequate, and only if their enemies were accommodating. Given any sort of unexpected setback, or an intelligent foe, the crisis facing America would have been dire indeed.

The situation has only deteriorated since then. The active Army has been reduced by another 60,000 soldiers to 480,000—barely enough to cover the estimated reinforcements required for the Korean contingency alone in 1994. In 1991, the Army deployed the equivalent of six heavy divisions to the Kuwaiti theater of operations. Today there is a *total* of six and one-third heavy division equivalents in the entire active Army. The deployment of even one of those divisions, into the Balkans or into some other low-level crisis, would hinder the deployment of a Desert Storm–size heavy force. It is also clear that today's Army could not field anything like *two* Desert Storm–size forces. At best it could send to each of these two wars a heavy force that was half the strength of the one that defeated Iraq in 1991.

Of course, defenders of the current American force structure like to argue that the threats posed by Iraq and North Korea are smaller than they were ten years ago. The Iraqi army was decimated by the Gulf War, and North Korea is an economic basket case. They also insist that America's technological superiority, especially in airpower, allows us to deploy smaller, more lethal forces, and that the large forces used to defeat Iraq in 1991 need not be replicated in a similar conflict in the future. Military officials note, in addition, that America's ability to project force quickly to the scene of a crisis has improved over the past decade.

These judgments, reasonable though they may seem, cannot withstand careful scrutiny. True, our technological prowess was a considerable part of the reason for the rapid and relatively blood-less victory in the desert in 1991, but it was by no means the whole reason. The men and women wielding our high-tech weapons were part of the most highly trained and best-prepared armed forces the United States has ever had. That training and preparedness helped them to overcome most of the unanticipated problems they faced. Indeed, they solved these problems so smoothly that most observers were not aware there were problems at all. A less ready force, of the kind the United States is fielding today, would have acted more cautiously, made more mistakes, and provided Iraq with more opportunities to preserve its forces and fight to a less conclusive result.

This would have been true regardless of American technological superiority. The accidents of last year's Kosovo air campaign are testimony to the fact that even today, technology is no better than the people who control it. And the Kosovo air campaign also revealed other problems with the triumphalist view of technology and airpower. As one seasoned observer put it,

> This experience is a lesson that it is dangerous to assume that an air and missile war can be fought with the precision made possible by guided weapons. This lesson is reinforced by the fact that the U.S. faced growing constraints because it had only a limited number of advanced cruise missiles and GPS guided weapons, and allied air forces had even more restricted numbers of advanced guided weapons. Kosovo was not a major war by any means, but even it placed limitations on some aspects of U.S. and NATO munitions stocks.
>
> NATO's problems were further compounded by the weather limitations of laser-guided weapons and the weather-visibility limits of most optical sensors, and by the fact that much of the target mix involved low cost–low value military equipment with limited strategic and tactical value. It simply does not make sense to fight a low-grade war with nothing but precision weapons.[21]

If it is a mistake to imagine that a "low-grade" war can be fought only with precision weapons, it is sheer folly to imagine that the United States could depend exclusively on such weapons in a much larger and more extensive conflict, particularly if this conflict did not take place under the open skies and good weather of the desert.

This is especially true when one considers the much larger set of targets a major opponent presents, the limitations on the size of the precision-guided weapons arsenal the U.S. maintains under current budgets, and the impossibility of fighting only where the weather accommodates such systems. There may be solutions to these problems; indeed, there almost certainly are, but for now the systems we are fielding suffer from such defects.

The Kosovo campaign also undermined another pleasant delusion: that the armed forces today are much better off technologically than they were during the Gulf War. "Improvements in lethality" have frequently been cited to justify reductions in military end-strength, but in truth, there have been very few such improvements. The main weapons systems in all of the services remain not only the same types as they were during the Gulf—M1 tanks, F-14, F-15, and F-16 fighters, and so forth—but in almost all cases, they are the very same pieces of equipment that fought in the desert campaign, only now eight years older. The Air Force and the Navy, it is true, have worked hard to increase dramatically the proportion of their fixed-wing airplanes that can fire and control precision-guided munitions, but the munitions themselves, as well as the targeting systems that operate them, are fundamentally the same. There has been no major technological change in the U.S. armed forces since the Gulf War, and none is foreseen for many years to come in current defense budgets.

Finally, despite the increased faith that many strategists place in American airpower, that airpower has been depleted in recent years. Since 1994 the Air Force and the Navy have lost five wings of aircraft—310 planes in all. Last year's air campaign in Kosovo demonstrated the significant over-extension of the Air Force almost as forcefully as the crises of 1994 underlined the overextension of the armed forces as a whole. Although Operation "Allied Force" was a limited operation conducted from friendly bases under no threat of attack and facing little resistance, and although its intensity was a mere fraction of the air campaign launched against Iraq in 1991, it involved over five hundred U.S. strike aircraft at its peak and lasted over seventy days. According to some reports, the U.S. Air Force was compelled to use over 90 percent of its expeditionary assets to sustain this campaign.[22]

Apologists for what has become the military status quo have made much of the apparent weakness of our would-be foes compared to a decade ago, yet such calculations often fail to acknowledge the serious degradation of our own armed forces during that same time. True, our potential foes may not be getting much stronger, but we are definitely getting weaker. Since 1994 regular warnings of readiness problems and training shortfalls have resounded in the Pentagon. The effect of these shortfalls is cumulative. An armed force that has not been able to train adequately on a consistent basis for a period of years will not only lose its edge, but can even begin to forget what its edge once was. Soldiers and officers who have never seen excellence in a combat unit will not know what it looks like and will not know how to achieve it. This is a problem that takes time to reverse, and the longer the repair is delayed, the harder it becomes. Even gauging the extent of this problem in a peacetime force is hard. The real test comes in combat, and the measure is likely to be in errors and casualties. What is certain, however, is that the men and women in the armed forces today are not trained to anything like the standard of those who fought the Gulf War.

The present weakness of our enemies, moreover, is apparent to them as well as to us. They are not likely to attack us when they are weak. Instead, they are likely to seek to restore their strength in anticipation of a conflict with us and to wait until they have succeeded before striking. There is no reason to believe that we will rearm faster than they once we have detected their efforts. On the contrary, there is every reason to believe that they will win the rearmament race. After all, our most likely adversaries are authoritarian regimes, and such regimes have an inherent advantage when it comes to building armies. They control their media and have organs to control their people as well as their industries and their economies. They have no need to convince parsimonious legislatures to vote funds. Furthermore, being much smaller and having to focus only on one or two major threats or opportunities, they can rearm or reorganize their forces much more rapidly than the U.S., with its enormous organizational and industrial military base and its global commitments and concerns. If one of these states decides to prepare its forces to strike a blow at one of our allies, it will be able to do so, while our preparations are likely to be slow and inadequate.

A Rational Military Posture

The harsh reality is that a force capable of fighting two wars simultaneously, while also attending to other, smaller crises that may erupt, will have to be considerably larger than the one the U.S. currently fields, larger even than the Bush administration's Base Force. In fact, by all the obvious tests, the last time the United States had a force capable of meeting the two-war standard was in 1991, when the ground and air force sent to fight Desert Storm represented half of the total ground and air assets available. This left almost another half available then to fight another war should the need have arisen. Today, the picture is quite different:

	Heavy Division equivalents[23]	Light Division equivalents	Total Division equivalents
1991 assets	11	7⅔	18⅔
Desert Storm force	6⅔	2	8⅔
1999 assets	6⅓	4⅓	10⅔

So, we have little more than a Desert Storm–size total force, when two-MRC capability would require something closely approaching the conventional forces maintained to fight the Soviet Union.

We must recall that America's strategy during the Cold War was supported by three separate military pillars: our nuclear forces, our conventional forces, and NATO's forces, both nuclear and conventional. By far the most important elements of that strategy from the standpoint of deterring the Soviets were America's nuclear forces within Europe and without, and the independent nuclear forces of France and England. The ground forces of Great Britain, France, and Germany added eighteen heavy and six light divisions to America's forces in the theater, bringing the total number of immediately available divisions to almost forty-three. Such a force might conceivably have been able to halt the advance of the more than two hundred divisions in the Soviet order of battle and those of their Warsaw Pact allies, as NATO hoped. It is certain that American forces alone could not have met that threat, nor were they ever intended to.

But in the post–Cold War world, only America's conventional forces can be figured into the calculus of responding to major

regional aggressors. It is widely believed that the United States
would never use nuclear weapons against a regional foe, at least
as long as that foe refrained from using weapons of mass destruction of its own (and probably not even then). Our nuclear capabilities, therefore, so important to deterring the Soviets, have
become far less relevant with regard to regional aggressors today.
Nor can we rely upon NATO's forces to join us in meeting all the
challenges we may face, or even most of them. In the first place,
NATO's forces are not ours to command. Their significant involvement in any campaign, particularly a campaign outside of Europe,
as any MRC is likely to be, will require time to convince them to
join us and to work out the arrangements for their participation.
In the second place, all of our NATO allies have cut their armed
forces even more dramatically than the United States. The only
forces the United States can rely upon to be in existence and ready
to deter or oppose regional aggressors are its own.

Finally, the conventional armed forces maintained during the
Cold War were always merely the leading edge of America's military power. War with the Soviet Union would have been a war of
national mobilization. Hundreds of thousands, if not millions, of
Americans would have had to be drawn into the war to see it through
to the end. The provision of standing conventional forces, then, represented a calculation of what was necessary to halt or delay a Soviet
advance for long enough to allow the allied nations to mobilize
behind that shield, not an evaluation of what would be necessary
to win the war. MRCs, on the other hand, are *not* wars of national
mobilization. Whatever conventional forces are maintained in peacetime will be the only forces available to pursue such conflicts. Mobilization could result only from real military catastrophe.

For all of these reasons it should not seem so absurd that a conventional force approximately as large as that maintained during
the Cold War will be necessary to pursue a two-MRC strategy today,
even though the forces of any regional aggressors are small compared to those of the Soviet Union. Given the testimony of the
authors of the Base Force, and in light of recent history, it is clear
that the United States needs a force about the size of the armed
forces of 1991. That force would cost tens of billions of dollars
more annually than we are currently spending on defense.

Even this may not be enough, however. To be secure into the
future, America must do much beyond maintaining a two-war

capability: It must prepare to transform its armed forces to meet the challenges of a new epoch of warfare. It must restore the capability to prepare for conflicts *larger* than MRCs, and add the capability to handle smaller conflicts without harming its MRC capabilities. In plainer terms, America must be able to fight Iraq and North Korea, and *also* be able to fight genocide in the Balkans and elsewhere without compromising its ability to fight two major regional conflicts. And it must be able to contemplate war with China or Russia some considerable (but not infinite) time from now.

By far the most expensive and important of these tasks is the technological transformation of the armed forces. The congressionally mandated National Defense Panel has estimated that it would cost up to $10 billion annually for experimentation in new technologies. Yet none of the major systems currently fielded can expect to survive on a battlefield or on the high seas dominated by precision-guided munitions directed by GPS, laser designating systems, or even more advanced targeting systems. Within twenty years we will need to replace virtually every tank, every strike aircraft, every missile system, possibly even every aircraft carrier and major surface combatant, although it might conceivably be possible to salvage the naval forces with major refits instead. It seems unlikely that we will be in a position to undertake such a major transformation of our armed forces for just $10 billion annually.

To understand the magnitude of the problem, we must briefly consider how we arrived at such a level of technological sophistication in the first place. During World War II, America's major weapons systems were, on the whole, technologically inferior to those of the Germans, our foes, and even of the Soviets, our temporary allies. With the launching of Sputnik, it even seemed for a time that the Soviets would take the lead in missile and space technology. That fear, however, spurred a massive scientific and technological effort during the 1960s that bore its most important fruit militarily in the 1970s with the fielding of the current generation of military equipment: F-14s, F-15s, F-16s, F/A-18s, M1 tanks, Bradley armored personnel carriers, Apache helicopters, and so on.

One of the reasons this generation of equipment held so commanding a lead technologically over that of our adversaries was because the Soviets rapidly realized that they could not beat us at the technology game and chose a different course. Opting as they had during World War II for quantity and simplicity over quality and complexity, the Soviets built a force designed to overwhelm NATO with an enormous number of relatively cheap, relatively easy to build and maintain, technologically inferior systems. It is open to question whether that approach would have worked to defeat NATO during the 1980s. Consistently, however, that approach failed to work in the third world. Egypt, Syria, Iraq, and Jordan, applying the Soviet approach during the wars with Israel, which applied the American approach on the whole, consistently failed. Desert Storm, of course, was the ultimate validation of the American approach and refutation of the Soviet approach, at least in the third world.

The problem is that we were not the only people to realize that our approach had been validated. The Soviets concluded at the time that it was necessary to start moving toward a smaller, more professional, highly technical force and began working toward that goal. For all the immense reserves of manpower they possess, the Chinese have also recognized that only a technologically competent force can hope to face down an American threat. Iraq and North Korea, as well as Syria and other lesser powers, are all working to acquire more sophisticated weapons systems.

At the same time, none of the forces that America fought during the Cold War had been designed to fight America. The North Koreans designed their force to defeat the South, hopefully before American power could arrive in any strength—and they very nearly succeeded. The North Vietnamese and the Viet Cong, rather than attempting to field a force capable of fighting America, instead adopted a strategy that minimized our technological advantages, and they succeeded indeed. The Gulf War, the only other major test of America's armed forces, was fought only because Saddam badly miscalculated. He never intended to fight America, did not design his forces to do so, and invaded Kuwait only because he was convinced that America would not resist him.

The situation today is different. Although the next war is almost certain to begin when a regional aggressor attacks an American ally rather than with an attack against America itself, every potential American adversary will be preparing its forces to fight the U.S. military. They all are seeking out our weakness, learning the lessons of past wars against America, and seeking to maximize their advantages. The technological edge honed against a Soviet

Union that chose not to compete with us technologically, and used against powers that never intended to fight us but largely aped the Soviet approach, is likely to diminish markedly in a world in which all of our potential enemies are hard at work designing forces to attack our weaknesses and defend against our strengths. We should not imagine that an evolutionary development of systems designed to fight the Soviet Union in Europe will protect us against such foes in the future.

All of our most likely foes, for instance, are focusing on developing weapons of mass destruction and the means to deliver them in hopes of deterring our involvement in their conflicts with their neighbors. China, already a nuclear power, is working hard to develop the capability to rain nuclear warheads on the whole of the continental United States. That capability will change the strategic equation concerning Taiwan dramatically. The deterrent value of America's commitment to defend Taiwan is certain to diminish if China can present us with a credible nuclear threat. What if North Korea could present a credible nuclear threat to South Korea and Japan? What if Iraq had a credible weapon of mass destruction? In the absence of any real ability to defend against such threats, the development of such weapons systems would dramatically reduce America's ability to protect its friends and interests in critical regions.

National missile defense and theater missile defense, therefore, have taken on unparalleled importance for America's security, even in the relatively near future. Yet they both receive short shrift in current defense budgets. Developing and fielding such systems in the shortest possible time is critical to America's security. The Chinese and others are also working hard to develop systems to keep American forces from getting to the theaters of war in which they are interested. Anti-ship missiles like the Chinese Silkworm already pose a considerable threat to America's ability to enter contested waters. We can be certain that new generations of advanced surface-to-air missiles are already on the drawing boards in Peking, Moscow, and Baghdad. It may even be that SAMs capable of locking onto stealth aircraft will make their appearance in a decade or so. The systems to defeat these systems must also be developed now and fielded soon.

The task before us is an enormous and expensive one, but it is well worth the cost. Today the United States spends about 3 percent

of its gross domestic product on defense. To accomplish our strategic objectives, it might require that we spend closer to 4 percent.
That is not too much to pay for national and international security, and especially if one calculates the cost of fighting a war should
our deterrent force be inadequate.

Indeed, by far the cheaper course is to prevent conflicts before
they erupt, which is why the ability to deter potential adversaries
must be at the core of any strategy for prolonging the peace. It is
impossible to prevent the other powerful states in the world from
increasing their power or from striving for aims at odds with America's interests. It is not impossible, however, given America's strength
and enormous relative advantages, to maintain America's power
at a level high enough to make clear to such states the futility of
challenging the U.S. That should be the fundamental goal of American foreign and defense policy.

Deterrence, however, cannot be accomplished on the cheap. A
wise enemy will only be deterred by the existence of forces that
could, in fact, actually defeat him in war. It is extremely rare in
history that aggressive states have been curbed by the potential
power of peaceful states that have not troubled to maintain real
strength. The enormously greater military potential of Britain, Austria, Prussia, and Russia never daunted Napoleon; the theoretical
mobilized strength of Britain, France, and Russia did not daunt
Germany in 1914; the latent power of France and England did not
scare Hitler in 1939; the overwhelming potential advantages of
America and NATO did not deter Saddam Hussein. In each case
the aggressor convinced himself that the more powerful coalition
arrayed against him lacked the will to use the forces at its disposal
or to mobilize its much greater latent strength against him. In each
case the aggressor was proven wrong, but only after horrific and
costly wars that could have been avoided had the leading peaceful powers maintained adequate armed forces in peacetime and
demonstrated the resolve to use them to defend the peace. When,
on the other hand, the U.S. both maintained powerful peacetime
armed forces and repeatedly demonstrated the will to use them to
oppose Soviet aggression during the Cold War, the result was the
avoidance of war and the peaceful collapse of America's foe.

Deterring the Soviet Union, difficult though it may have seemed
at the time, may turn out to have been relatively easy compared
with the difficulties of maintaining a policy of deterrence today.

Today we must deter not one present foe, but any and all possible future foes. Worse still, this deterrence must be managed in an era of explosive change in the nature of war driven by changes in technology. This task is difficult, and it is no wonder that America has largely put it aside, preferring to believe that the current peaceful era will last so long that no real provision need be made for its end and no real sacrifice is required to maintain it. But history is quite clear on the awful dangers entailed in such happy self-delusion. America cannot afford to deny its responsibility to pay the price for maintaining the peace.

What is that price? It is the price of accomplishing three critical goals: 1) working actively to maintain the smooth and peaceful functioning of the current international system; 2) creating and maintaining the ability to deter aggression from China and Russia or any other state or group of states capable of posing a global challenge to the U.S. now or in the future; 3) transforming our armed forces technologically, organizationally, and doctrinally to meet the challenges of a new era in warfare. Whatever the cost of attaining those goals, it must be paid. Failure to do so will ensure that this peaceful interval will be shorter than it might have been and its end more violent and harmful to America.

Weapons Proliferation and Missile Defense: The Strategic Case

The collapse of the Soviet empire marked a fundamental shift in the international environment. With the passing of the Cold War standoff between the two superpowers, many predicted that the bipolar world would give way to a strategic free-for-all in which individual nations maneuvered for advantage in a new multipolar universe. But in fact, there was less room for states to assert themselves than there first seemed. The 1991 Gulf War demonstrated that even a regional power like Iraq could not act aggressively against American interests and principles. In the face of massive U.S. conventional military power, it mattered little that Saddam Hussein possessed the fourth largest army in the world. Desert Storm was a striking demonstration that the post-Soviet world was unipolar, not multipolar. The post–Cold War world in fact was one of *Pax Americana*.

But even as the Gulf War revealed the futility of contesting the United States by conventional means, it also suggested a way to avoid Iraq's fate: acquire ballistic missiles and weapons of mass destruction. One Scud warhead hitting a Saudi Arabian warehouse produced the largest number of American casualties during the war, while missile attacks on Israel threatened the cohesion of the American-led coalition. Moreover, there was little the U.S. military could do to stop the attacks. Thousands of coalition air sorties were diverted in a largely fruitless effort to track and attack mobile Scud missiles hiding in Iraq's western desert, while jerry-rigged Patriot air-defense batteries were given the job of destroying incoming missiles and warheads. And what if Iraq had been

268PRESENT DANGERS

able to top its missiles with nuclear-armed warheads? As a former chief of staff of the Indian Army remarked, "The Gulf War emphasized once again that nuclear weapons are the ultimate coins of power. In the final analysis, they [the coalition forces] could go in because the United States had nuclear weapons and Iraq didn't."[1] In short, the Gulf War reflected American military pre-eminence but also revealed America's Achilles heel. The U.S. had no effective answer to a hostile state equipped with mobile ballistic missiles. For states trying to check America's enormous advantage in conventional military power, ballistic missiles and weapons of mass destruction appeared to be the quickest and cheapest solution.

This new strategic imperative on the part of America's adversaries collides, of course, with the long-standing international effort to frustrate the development and control the use of weapons of mass destruction and their means of delivery by ballistic rockets. Restricting the proliferation of these weapons has been—and remains—the primary goal of the multilateral arms control arrangements put in place over the past four decades, and the core of U.S. nonproliferation policy. These agreements seek to control or prohibit the testing of nuclear weapons in the atmosphere, underwater, underground and in space; the acquisition of nuclear weapons by nations that had not tested them prior to 1968 (the date of the Nuclear Non-Proliferation Treaty); and the development of biological and chemical weapons. Other multilateral agreements have attempted to ban production of fissile material and limit the transfer of missiles and missile-related technologies for military applications.

But absent the explicit strategic guarantees and implicit restrictions on the behavior of states that evolved over the course of the Cold War, these agreements have little attraction for regimes contending with the strategic realities of today's unipolar world. Without the prospect of a Soviet nuclear umbrella to protect them, anti-American regimes from Baghdad to Tehran to Pyongyang have seen the need to acquire a deterrent capability of their own. In the post–Cold War world, India and Pakistan were no longer content to be potential nuclear-and-missile powers; both pursued ballistic missile development, and in 1998 each conducted a series of tests to make a clear statement about its nuclear capabilities. Even China appears to be rethinking its traditional posture of minimal nuclear deterrence. Assisted by successful espionage against the U.S. nuclear labs, China is developing a far more potent offensive capability of its own, while helping other states do the same in an effort to counter American power.

Despite the change in the security environment and the new strategic realities it has generated, the Clinton administration continues to make the reinforcement of the existing multilateral agreements its principal nonproliferation policy objective. To this end, the Nuclear Non-Proliferation Treaty was made permanent, the Chemical Weapons Convention was ratified, and START II completed. However, the administration's attempt to preserve the 1972 Anti-Ballistic Missile Treaty in the face of widespread missile proliferation skates precariously on thinning ice, and the Senate's rejection of the Comprehensive Test Ban Treaty in 1999 indicates that the political constituency for these kinds of multilateral agreements is losing strength. Americans are less and less interested in arms control measures that have not in fact stopped the proliferation of these weapons and actually impede our own ability to provide security for ourselves and our allies in the face of that proliferation.

The Clinton administration is fighting the proliferation of missiles and weapons of mass destruction with the tools of a bygone strategic era. It has not come to terms with the new strategic logic generating today's weapons proliferation. Although the number of states with these weapons is still relatively few, some of the countries most hostile to the United States have made very rapid progress since the end of the Cold War. The scope and pace of these developments have exceeded government expectations, and led a recent bipartisan commission, headed by former Secretary of Defense Donald Rumsfeld, to conclude that "the threat to the U.S. posed by these emerging [WMD and ballistic missile] capabilities is broader, more mature and evolving more rapidly than has been reported in estimates and reports by the [U.S.] Intelligence Community." Indeed, when it comes to the spread of ballistic missile technology, the "U.S. might have little or no warning before operational deployment" of missiles capable of threatening American territory.[2]

The Failure of U.S. Nonproliferation Policy

How did this happen? How can it be that a policy that has been so intensely pursued, for so long, and supported by such a broad consensus has failed? The short answer is that over the past decade, policy-makers have misunderstood the strategic incentives for proliferation and failed to grasp the underlying changes in technology and economics that made the spread of missile and WMD capabilities not only desirable but likely. Advocates of the administration's approach to nonproliferation often fall prey to the central fallacy of arms controllers: that the weapons themselves are the problem, not the regimes that possess them. This fallacy has been reinforced by the highly touted "successes" of nonproliferation policy, especially the voluntary renunciation of WMD and missile programs by states like Sweden or Argentina. These decisions are often portrayed as being an obedient response to "international norms" created by multinational arms control agreements. Yet, in fact, Sweden, unbeknownst to the United States, had a covert nuclear weapons program until 1975. This program was abandoned not in response to international norms but because the Swedes decided—covertly—that nuclear weapons were not relevant to their security policy. Likewise, other nations including Argentina, Brazil, Egypt, South Africa, South Korea, Switzerland, and Taiwan abandoned their WMD and missile programs, either because the weapons lacked military or diplomatic utility, or because U.S. security guarantees were more credible and less costly, or because a change in a country's form of rule (from autocratic to democratic) modified its understanding of its own security needs.

In contrast, the sole attempt to force a nation to renounce such weapons by agreement and through collective inspection regimes— the post–Gulf War effort by the United Nations to force Iraq to terminate its missile and WMD programs—has been a conspicuous failure. The UN inspection teams left Iraq in defeat, and the shaky international consensus to force Iraq to eliminate its WMD and longer-range missile capabilities has long since evaporated. According to UN weapons inspectors, Iraq will be able to reconstitute viable WMD and missile capabilities within six months once it emerges from the current sanctions regime, augmenting the remaining weapons stockpiles successfully hidden from the inspection teams.

Failing to understand the changed strategic circumstances of the post–Cold War era, the increased appeal of ballistic missiles and weapons of mass destruction among America's adversaries, and the ineffectiveness of Cold War–era arms control measures, the Clinton administration has enacted policies which have actually accelerated proliferation rather than retarding it. What follows is a catalog of what has gone wrong.

Russia First
U.S. efforts to sustain good relations with Russia following the collapse of the Soviet Union caused the administration to ignore, minimize and conceal its concerns about Russian proliferation behavior. Indeed, if there has been one overriding factor that has confounded U.S. nonproliferation efforts in Russia for the past decade, it has been the subordination of those efforts to supporting that country's flawed leadership—especially President Boris Yeltsin and Victor Chernomyrdin—as a prerequisite for building the ever-elusive "strategic partnership" with Moscow.

Administration concern for Russian interests in sustaining the mirage of their co-equal nuclear status with the United States (to preserve their Cold War–era "seat at the table") left it reluctant to renegotiate or exercise its right to withdraw from the 1972 Anti-Ballistic Missile Treaty, which limits the development and deployment of U.S. missile defense systems. To remain compliant with the ABM Treaty, theater missile systems had to be "dumbed down" in a manner that minimized their effectiveness while maximizing their cost. Similarly, the creation of a national missile defense system that assuages Russia's treaty-based concerns will cost at least $11 billion to build and deploy, and an equal amount to operate, and will be intentionally designed to handle only the most rudimentary threat: five incoming warheads. Moreover, without space- and sea-based components, the system will be vulnerable to various countermeasures (decoys, penetration aids, or submunitions) designed to confuse or overwhelm it. Thus, the administration's policies—stemming from both an oversensitivity to Russian concerns and the long-held tenet of arms controllers that effective missile defenses would be "destabilizing"—ensure that the United States will remain virtually defenseless against all but the most modest ballistic missile attacks. Unless current plans for a national missile defense are changed to add increased capabilities, the system will do little when deployed to diminish the incentive that America's adversaries have in acquiring ballistic missiles armed with weapons of mass destruction.

Rewarding Rogues

The Clinton administration has also rewarded its adversaries for their proliferation, while punishing those who otherwise enjoy normal bilateral relations with the United States. The most conspicuous example is North Korea: Not only is it now the largest recipient of U.S. foreign assistance in Asia, but it also enjoys U.S. government support in vastly expanding its nuclear energy capacity. The Clinton administration has persuaded South Korea and Japan to fund the construction of two modern nuclear reactors— despite the absence of a power grid to exploit it and despite the fact that these new "civilian" reactors will themselves produce more weapons-usable nuclear material than could be produced by the older reactor North Korea has agreed to close. And, as a further reward for not testing its newest long-range ballistic missile, the administration has promised North Korea that it will upgrade diplomatic relations and remove all sanctions on American trade with it. Conversely, after India (the world's largest democracy) and Pakistan (long a pivotal state and American ally in South Asia) conducted their nuclear tests, foreign assistance was refused and access to U.S. sources of nuclear energy assistance denied.

The perverse character of rewards and punishments meted out by the administration does not stop there. North Korea is granted privileged access to trade, technology, diplomacy, and foreign assistance simply because it is a signatory to the Nuclear Non-Proliferation Treaty, instead of being punished for violating it. North Korea has been caught virtually red-handed in breaking the NPT's proscription against diverting nuclear materials from reactors whose declared purpose is production of civilian nuclear energy to its covert nuclear weapons program. The administration's response has been to cobble together a massive program of inducements to encourage Pyongyang's future good behavior. Given the fact that North Korea's proliferation-related activities have been underway for nearly two decades, it is unlikely that the Kim regime will learn the intended lesson.

Trade Above All

Adding to these problems is the fact that the Clinton administration has virtually abandoned export controls as an instrument of nonproliferation policy. This has made it much easier for our adversaries to acquire the technology and systems to develop and deploy weapons of mass destruction and their means of delivery.

In the minds of many Clinton administration officials, the Cold War's end eliminated the rationale for export controls on dual-use technology and equipment (that is, technology which has both civilian and military applications). These controls were primarily aimed at diminishing the ability of the Soviet Union to exploit Western technology to modernize its armed forces. Evidence collected since the end of the Cold War has confirmed their effectiveness. Tightened in the early 1980s, the controls helped convince the Soviet military that it could not win in a technological competition with U.S. armed forces nor could it offset superior American technology with sheer mass. Particularly effective in limiting Soviet access to advanced technologies was the allied Coordinating Committee on Multilateral Trade Controls (COCOM). This system of allied cooperation on exports initially involved only NATO members (though it was not itself a NATO institution). Under U.S. leadership, COCOM by the 1980s had broadened to include cooperation agreements with two dozen non-NATO countries that might serve as sources for the export of COCOM-controlled technology.

Once the Soviet threat receded, however, prospects for increased high-tech trade around the world trumped whatever security rationale remained for maintaining COCOM-like controls over exports from the U.S. and our allies. In place of COCOM, the so-called Wassenaar Arrangement on Export Controls for Conventional Arms and Dual-Use Goods and Technologies (1995) was set up. But the Wassenaar Arrangement is little more than an after-sale notification system. Moreover, the assumptions underlying it and the revised system of export controls established here and abroad are not relevant to the nature of the proliferation problem we face. Current U.S. export controls focus largely on the most advanced technology and equipment; they do not cover the less sophisticated technologies and equipment that are nevertheless sufficient to bring strategically important capabilities to proliferating states. As a result of these changes, a thriving global trading regime in advanced dual-use technologies is now the norm.

In addition, the links between the various U.S. bureaucracies that oversee American exports and the U.S. intelligence community have been sharply downgraded in importance. Accordingly, those charged with stopping possible exports of proliferation-significant technologies and equipment have too little information on what our adversaries are seeking to acquire and how they are attempting to do so. In addition, the ability of export licensing authorities to examine the bona fides of an overseas "end-user" (the party receiving transferred U.S. technology) is extremely limited without significant intelligence support. China, for instance, has had virtually unrestrained access to advanced "dual-use" technology and, predictably, has diverted many advanced U.S. technologies from declared civilian end-users to military-related programs. Without greater support from the intelligence community, it will be impossible to stop such diversions and difficult to revive collaboration among our allies and other states in stemming leaks of dangerous dual-use technologies and equipment.

"The Right to Know"
On top of loosening export controls, the Clinton administration has also released what in the past was presumed to be sensitive nuclear data. Administration policies on declassification have made information about the military applications of atomic energy more widely available than ever before.

The bulk of the public information now available about nuclear weapons technology has been provided by the U.S. government as part of its effort to reduce the volume of classified information in the interest of the public's "right to know." Indeed, when confronted by a congressional report marshaling evidence of espionage targeted at American nuclear secrets, Chinese officials referred to nuclear weapons information available on several Internet websites to buttress their claims of innocence. (A further irony is that the information is often made available on Internet websites operated and maintained by organizations that have been activists for arms control and environmental causes.) Partly as a result of these disclosures, the basic scientific and technical knowledge about how to design and manufacture first- and second-generation nuclear weapons is now accessible to nations seeking to acquire these technologies. This situation is contributing to the realization of Herman Kahn's prophetic warning nearly four decades ago: "Nuclear weapons will not be inexpensive, they will be cheap."[3] And, in fact, it is precisely some of the most economically strapped nations on earth—Iran, Iraq, India, North Korea, and Pakistan—that are developing nuclear weapons capabilities most vigorously.

Mirror Imaging

A related problem in combating proliferation is the assumption made by policy-makers and analysts that other states will make the same choices we would make in developing and acquiring these military capabilities. But there is no reason to believe they will follow our own typically deliberate and technically sophisticated development. Nuclear weapons and ballistic and cruise missile technologies are now more than fifty years old, and there have always been alternative technical approaches to acquiring these capabilities. When it comes to these weapons, states don't need to reinvent the wheel.

In some cases, those seeking to acquire nuclear weapons have taken paths previously rejected by the United States. Driven by a different strategic calculus, taking advantage of technological opportunities made possible by holes in U.S. classification policy, and perhaps knowing that U.S. and Western intelligence agencies might not readily detect technological approaches that differed from their own, some states have managed to make considerable progress using alternative weapons-development strategies.

For example, scientists and engineers working on the Manhattan Project, America's secret Second World War program to develop nuclear weapons, identified and rejected several techniques for developing fissile materials, including electromagnetic isotope separation (EMIS), a technique for producing a weapons-grade uranium isotope. Rejected by the United States because it was not thought to be a cost-effective solution to the large-scale production of weapons-grade uranium, EMIS technology was not protected to the same degree as those production techniques that were actually chosen, making it more available and attractive to states requiring a method of producing a small arsenal. Because *we* did not regard EMIS as an efficient technique for obtaining weapons-grade uranium we assumed that other states would also ignore it. In the case of Saddam Hussein's Iraq, this meant that U.S. intelligence dismissed Iraq's nuclear program as being a decade away from producing a weapon because there was no evidence (or, as the intelligence community might say, no "signature" for overhead reconnaissance to pick up) that Iraq had built or was planning to build the huge gaseous diffusion facility required to enrich uranium in what *we* judged to be the most cost-effective manner.

Only after Operation Desert Storm did UN inspectors learn that Iraq was six months—not ten years—away from producing a nuclear weapon. Iraq, of course, employed a whole system of deception and denial to keep the U.S. and the West from uncovering the scale and progress of its nuclear weapons program. But its success in keeping its program under wraps was enhanced by its choice of the EMIS technique to produce weapons-grade uranium and our reluctance to take seriously the possibility that Iraq might not follow our own nuclear weapons development path.[4]

A similar saga concerns the development and production of long-range ballistic missiles. Scientists and engineers involved in the development of Nazi Germany's V-2 short-range ballistic missile were captured by the Red Army at the German test facility at Peenemunde in 1945. Taken to the Soviet Union, the Germans helped the Soviets develop a derivative of the V-2. This missile and its follow-ons was designated by NATO as the "SCUD" series of short-range ballistic missiles. In the years that followed, Scuds in several variants were widely distributed within the Warsaw Pact and to other nations allied to the Soviet Union. In time, nearly thirty nations possessed some version of the Scud missile.

One of those states, North Korea, learned to "reverse engineer" a Scud and began making missiles itself instead of relying on the USSR as a supplier. Indeed, building and selling Scuds is one of the few clear successes of North Korean industry. Income from the sale of hundreds of short-range Scud missiles to Iran during the 1980–88 war against Iraq also allowed Pyongyang to invest the capital necessary to develop missiles capable of delivering heavier payloads at increasingly greater ranges. North Korea's "No Dong" missile was financed from these sales. The No Dong, essentially a scaled-up version of a Scud, has a range of 1,300 kilometers and is capable of hitting targets in both South Korea and Japan. Although U.S. intelligence assessed its first flight test in May 1993 to be a failure and assumed further testing would be necessary before deployment, the North Koreans began serial production of the missile almost immediately. Only years after the fact did the CIA learn that the 1993 test was successful and that the missile had been deployed.

Beginning with World War II–era technology, North Korea now stands on the brink of deploying a truly intercontinental-range ballistic missile. In August 1998, Pyongyang tested the "Taepo Dong

I" missile, thus demonstrating the ability to build a vehicle with multistage separation, a capacity essential for the intercontinental delivery of military payloads. The Taepo Dong I missile is a two-stage system, basically a Scud placed on top of a No Dong. In the August 1998 flight test, a third stage was added in a failed effort to deploy a satellite into low earth orbit. But it may be that the North Koreans learned enough with this test to be confident to start building, deploying and selling an even longer-range, higher-payload missile without further testing—just as they did in the case of No Dong. At any rate, both the North Korean No Dong and Scuds are now in international commerce, largely unaffected by either export controls or multilateral arms control regimes, and are used by states like Pakistan and Iran as the basis for their own programs to develop longer-range ballistic missiles. Little in North Korea's missile program has followed the path that either the U.S. or the Soviet Union took in developing and fielding new ballistic missiles. Instead of designing each new missile essentially from scratch and testing it extensively, North Korea has relied on older, nonindigenous rocket technology, modified it as necessary to field newer and longer-range missiles, and settled for far less testing. Looking for a missile program more like our own or that of the Soviets, U.S. intelligence has been surprised by the rapidity with which North Korea has developed its family of longer-range missiles.

Russia and China

Another factor complicating post–Cold War nonproliferation policy is the breakdown in restraint in China and Russia on exporting sensitive technologies, material, subsystems, and systems. Well into the 1960s and 1970s, both China and the Soviet Union were reluctant to traffic in such sensitive commerce. After all, the spread of WMD and missile technologies and capabilities would complicate the bipolar superpower balance, devalue the "China card" which was Beijing's entré into great-power politics, and create potential "wild cards" within the two power blocs. Uncontrolled and rapid proliferation—especially to unstable regimes like North Korea or Iraq—ran counter to the interests of the great powers.

In the 1980s, however, China's strategic calculations began to change, especially when it came to checking Indian regional ambitions in South Asia. China has provided direct assistance to Pakistan's nuclear weapons program and assisted its ballistic missile program, sometimes ignoring in the process its obligations under the NPT and its commitments to the MTCR (Missile Technology Control Regime). In 1988, China supplied a medium-range ballistic missile, designated the CSS-2, to Saudi Arabia. And today, in the post–Cold War unipolar world, Beijing is spreading weapons and weapons technology to American adversaries in key regions in order to complicate the exercise of American power and reduce America's global advantage. Assisting Iran, for example, in its advanced cruise missile and chemical weapons program is no doubt an attempt to solidify relations with a major oil supplier, but it also raises U.S. costs in protecting allies and taking a leadership role in the region.

In Russia, matters of strategic calculation have been strongly influenced by economic decline. Like China, Russia is providing assistance to Iran, particularly in the development of long-range ballistic missiles and nuclear energy. Playing the China card diplomatically as well as financially, Russia is also providing extensive assistance to China's space program and fissile material production infrastructure, help that will be important if China is to exploit effectively its clandestine acquisition of modern U.S. nuclear weapon designs.

The mounting evidence of proliferation activities by Russia and China, reflecting their geopolitical interests in their relationships with Iran, Iraq, Pakistan, and India, has forced the Clinton administration to choose between its attempts to develop strategic partnerships with Moscow and Beijing and its commitment to nonproliferation. The administration has consistently resolved this conflict on the side of "partnership." In case after case, it has been reluctant to impose sanctions on either nation, even when mandated by law. Neither Russia nor China has been obliged to pay a cost—economic, political or diplomatic—for its proliferation-related activities.

Politicized Intelligence

Not surprisingly, these administration policy priorities have had a significant negative impact on the work of the intelligence community when it comes to reporting on and analyzing the proliferation of WMD and missile technologies. The now-famous 1995 National Intelligence Estimate (NIE) of the foreign missile threat to the United States focused on a time when the United States might be threatened by the "indigenous development" of an ICBM by states other than Russia and China.[5] Since none of the states seeking to acquire long-range missiles possessed the development, test and manufacturing infrastructure to produce ICBMs in the manner of the U.S. or the former Soviet Union, the American intelligence community forecast that the time required to acquire this capability indigenously was ten to fifteen years in the future. But this approach ignored the possibility that North Korea, Iran, Pakistan, India and Iraq were not developing an "indigenous" ICBM capability and, instead, were relying on existing foreign missile technology and technical assistance. In addition, the NIE ignored alternative threat scenarios, for example, launching shorter-range missiles from merchant or naval vessels off the U.S. coast. Having dismissed these possibilities as "wild cards," it was then easy for the intelligence community to conclude that the ballistic missile threat to the United States was remote, and for the administration to declare that there was no need to take "offsetting action," such as deploying missile defenses.

The politicization of the intelligence effort takes place in other ways, as well. Frustrated by the failures of U.S. policy and inaction on the part of the executive branch in this area, Congress has passed any number of bills that commit the United States to the mandatory imposition of sanctions on those responsible for the proliferation of WMD and long-range missiles. In the case of the Clinton administration, these mandated sanctions have clashed repeatedly with its desire to promote "engagement" with China and Russia. Something had to give, and very early on the intelligence community learned that this was not a White House that wanted to hear "bad news" on the proliferation front. If necessary, the administration, as the president himself admitted, was even willing to "fudge" the facts in order to avoid having to impose sanctions. Not only has this produced a situation in which the intelligence community is reluctant to pass certain intelligence reports up the chain of command—since they are seen as unwelcome by the White House—but, in response, it has also generated scores of leaks of proliferation-related intelligence by a bureaucracy offended that the administration is ignoring the information that has been collected.

The Proliferation "Hot House"

Finally, developments of the past decade have created what can only be called an "international proliferation infrastructure," with a de facto network of mutually reinforcing WMD and missile development and production capabilities among various states. This global network is simply beyond the ability of current U.S. nonproliferation policies to control: the WMD and missile genies are out of the bottle and they are not going back in.

During the Cold War and for the decade since its end, American nonproliferation policy has focused on containing the diffusion of missile and WMD technologies and hardware from the traditional, primary producing states including the United States, France, Britain, Japan, China and Russia, as well as "nondeclared" nuclear powers like Israel and other nuclear-capable states. The primary tools of these policies included a variety of multilateral agreements and a good deal of exhortation. Given the overall strategic caution that characterized the competition between the United States with its allies and the Soviet empire, these tools functioned well enough. But removed from that strategic context, they have proven to be weak restraints in today's new security environment. As a result, proliferation among a variety of nations, including nations that are profoundly hostile to the United States, its allies and its interests, will be difficult, if not impossible, to prevent. Nations like Iraq, Iran, North Korea, and Pakistan now have in place an industrial and scientific infrastructure to sustain production of weapons of mass destruction and missiles without a need for further access to the original sources of the proliferation.

Moreover, because their own missile and WMD requirements are fairly well limited to acquiring a basic arsenal capable of either deterring the U.S. from a military intervention or gaining the upper hand in possible conflict with regional adversaries, they will want to export systems and technological know-how as a means of keeping their own engineering and manufacturing infrastructure active and, if possible, profitable. North Korea has exported its No Dong missile both to Iran, where a Russian-improved version is called the "Shahab 3," and to Pakistan, where it is known as the "Ghauri." Now, Pakistan in turn is attempting to sell the Ghauri to Saudi Arabia. Such interaction permits the rapid and self-sustaining diffusion of knowledge about improvements in warhead and missile programs that multilateral agreements on nonproliferation among the world's major powers can do little, if anything, to arrest. Unless countervailing initiatives are taken to devalue strategically the investment in acquiring WMD and ballistic missiles, the basis for an enduring proliferation problem is now firmly established.

What Is To Be Done?

Although President Clinton and his administration regularly speak about the great security threat posed by the proliferation of missile technology and weapons of mass destruction, their efforts to do something about it have been nullified by contradictory policies (unsupervised trade, the declassification of state secrets, "engagement" with China and Russia) and by an unrealistic faith in arms control agreements.[6] At a time when weapons of mass destruction and the means to deliver them are more easily acquired and more highly prized than ever by America's adversaries, the administration has stubbornly followed a policy path that has left the country and the world more at risk than when it came into office eight years ago. Regional powers like Iraq and Iran are on the verge of developing a deterrent to American power and an unstable regime in North Korea is already blackmailing the United States with the possibility that it has or will acquire such a capability. Russia is making its own know-how and technology available to those with the cash to pay for it. And China, Pakistan, North Korea and Iran have formed an unholy alliance in which missile and WMD technology and expertise are shared and spread.

The essential task now for the United States, working with its allies, is not to continue trying to cajole these countries into agreements—the diplomatic equivalent of closing the barn door after the horse has gone—but in *devaluing* the investments its potential adversaries are making in these weapons and their means of delivery. Of course, there is no simple antidote for a decade of misdirected national effort at coping with the problem of proliferation. But neither is the situation hopeless. Already, Israel, faced with the inevitability of proliferation in the Middle East, has adopted a number of policies designed to deal with this strategic fact of life. There is no reason that the United States and its allies cannot, in a similar fashion, bring their considerable resources to bear on this problem and rob the rogue states of the fruits of their "proliferation on the cheap." Here is how it could happen:

Deploy national and theater missile defenses driven by threat, not by treaty. The essential first step for the United States is the construction of effective missile defenses. Without a serious investment in missile defenses, American nonproliferation policy is empty rhetoric. The ABM Treaty, signed in 1972 and geared to the stable, bipolar balance of the Cold War, is now less a guarantee of America's security than an effort to accommodate Russia's nostalgia for its Cold War–era superpower status. The treaty's architects did not foresee a world in which the Soviet Union no longer existed, in which a host of small states had nuclear and missile capabilities, and in which missile defenses could be implemented cost-effectively. But now missile defenses offer a means to undermine these states' investment in such weapons and the military and strategic advantages that follow from their possession.

However, since its first days in office, the Clinton administration has either eliminated funding for the promising missile defense technologies or unilaterally reduced their effectiveness out of concern for the ABM Treaty. The result is a self-fulfilling prophecy in which the national and theater missile defense systems now under development are not nearly as effective as they might be and, hence, are open to the charge that they are not worth the diplomatic and strategic costs involved in overturning or substantially modifying the ABM Treaty with the Russians.

Make theater missile defenses available to friendly nations that abstain from acquiring WMD and their means of delivery. This would both buttress U.S. nonproliferation policy and generally foster strategic stability. The United States enjoys a substantial lead over its allies in the development of effective theater-level missile defenses. In addition to an advanced version of the Patriot air defense system used in the Gulf War, five other U.S. and allied theater missile defense systems are in various stages of development. These systems include the sea-based Navy Theater Wide program being developed with Japanese collaboration, the Army's Theater High Altitude Defense System, the Air Force Airborne Laser System, the "Arrow" missile defense system being developed with Israel, and the multinational Medium Extended Air Defense System. Over the next decade, these efforts are likely to give the United

States and its allies technologically mature and militarily effective theater level missile defenses and the means of creating the kind of layered network of defenses necessary for fully addressing the missile threat.

By offering access to or, in some cases, even financing the acquisition of effective theater defenses to nations threatened by ballistic missiles, the United States and its allies will be achieving nonproliferation by other means. For example, recently the Republic of Korea has indicated that it would rather acquire long-range missiles than deploy missile defenses to counter North Korea's threat or use of WMD/missile delivery systems. However, because North Korea's missile forces are either mobile or installed in deep underground facilities in hard rock in mountainous terrain near the Chinese border, only South Korean missiles with nuclear warheads would be able to hold such targets at risk. Of course, South Korea is capable of developing the missile and nuclear technologies. But such a move on South Korea's part would be highly destabilizing in the region, presenting Japan, in particular, with difficult choices. Only a resolute and forthcoming U.S. policy of making effective theater missile defenses available to threatened nations like South Korea, backed by a U.S. space-based sensor network to enhance the effectiveness of the theater system, will persuade them to hold off on such a weapons program.

Deploy military capabilities to hold the WMD/missile capabilities of proliferators at risk. In addition to developing effective missile defenses, the United States and its allies should develop new military capabilities that can hold proliferation-related targets at risk. There is a need to improve dramatically on the costly and mostly fruitless effort at "Scud hunting" that marked the Gulf War. To do so requires enhancing a number of supporting capabilities, including intelligence collection and processing, advanced command-and-control systems that can support military operations against proliferation-related targets, enhanced precision-guided conventional and nuclear weapons and delivery systems, and Special Operations Forces trained to conduct, if needed, military operations against targets typically deep behind the lines.

Strengthen anti-terrorism capabilities. Ballistic missiles armed with WMD payloads are the delivery means of choice for proliferators because of the demonstrated geopolitical leverage they provide. There are of course other means of delivering such weapons,

ranging from aircraft to terrorism. For most rogue regimes, however, such means are less desirable than ballistic missiles because
they are more expensive to build and maintain and to control operationally. This may not always be the case. Indeed, improved American and allied capability against missiles may lead hostile nations
to consider anew the use of terrorism. The limitations of America's existing counterterrorist defenses are well known; counterterrorist programs have been underfunded, and the administration
of them is divided among various federal agencies and departments and between federal, state and local governments. Despite
the need for centralized management, coordination efforts are limited at present to a single National Security Council staff member,
an effort woefully short of the scope of the potential threat.

Diminish U.S. vulnerability to biological weapons. Biological
weapons are easy to produce and potentially widely destructive.
Moreover, as a result of declassification, considerable engineering
detail has been published concerning the military applications of
biological organisms. Biological weapons have an important advantage over nuclear weapons: a typical BW payload for a warhead
weighs approximately one hundred kilograms; a nuclear warhead
weighs from five to ten times as much. This makes it possible for
an intermediate-range system such as the North Korean Taepo
Dong missile to achieve intercontinental range with the much
lighter biological payload. Similarly, nations encountering difficulty in acquiring fissile material for nuclear weapons may shift
to biological payloads. However, biological weapons do not have
the immediate lethal impact of nuclear weapons. By fielding sen-
sors to detect specific types of biological organisms and stockpil-
ing vaccines and (when technically feasible) antidotes, passive
defenses are possible.

Conclusion

The proliferation of missile and WMD technology has the potential to become the greatest threat of the new millennium. Left
unchecked, it will certainly cripple the exercise of American
power—deterring us and our allies from challenging states that
threaten our interests and principles abroad out of fear of devastating attacks on our homelands or our armed forces. What is at
risk is nothing less than the current international order, an order

more favorable to the United States and its interests than any in our history, but one that rests on the credibility of American power.

The policies of the past eight years have not only been slow to address the threat posed by weapons proliferation but, arguably, have made the problem worse. Even the Clinton administration itself now admits that the threat posed by ballistic missiles is real and "growing," and will require, sooner rather than later, a national missile defense system.[7] However, having slashed funding for missile defenses, killed or debilitated promising technologies, and expended so much political capital on unverifiable and strategically out-of-date arms control measures, the administration has left the country poorly situated to arm itself against these new threats.

Nevertheless, policy alternatives, technology, and resources are available to reverse these dangerous developments. And, fortunately, a decade of surprises on the proliferation front—from Iraq's missile and nuclear program to North Korea's launch of a three-stage rocket over Japan—has generated a wider political consensus on the need for missile defenses and a more realistic assessment of our ability to deter rogue-state adversaries. But a new administration will have to make countering these threats a core strategic concern and back up its rhetoric and policies with the kind of administrative muscle that turns general precepts into effective programs.[8] Ultimately, this will require an acknowledgment that the post–Cold War era has generated a new set of incentives for our adversaries to acquire the world's most dangerous weapons. Until those governments are turned out of power or those incentives are significantly reduced by programs to devalue the utility of the weapons themselves, the problem of proliferation will only get worse.

I V.

American Leadership:
Strength and Principle

WILLIAM J. BENNETT

Morality, Character and American Foreign Policy

In recent years, an old debate has resurfaced over the role of morality and principle in American foreign policy. What should be the relationship between maintaining fidelity to our ideals on the one hand, and pursuing policies that protect our national security, the well-being of our allies, and our economic self-interest on the other? It is perhaps not entirely coincidental that this argument over the role of morality in foreign policy has emerged at a time when many Americans wonder about the moral standing of the man who has inhabited the White House for the past eight years. I would like to argue that there is, in fact, a strong connection between an American president's own moral reputation and the successful conduct of a principled American foreign policy, a connection that is fixed in our Constitution and our unique system of government, and should be fixed in the expectation of our people.

Morality and American "Nationalism"

For the United States, the relationship between morality and foreign policy should not be nearly as complex and vexing an issue as some would have us believe. While some self-proclaimed "realists" argue that the United States must pursue its "national interest" divorced from considerations of morality and must abjure the aim of advancing its liberal democratic principles around the world, and while some liberals seem to think that American intervention overseas is justified *only* if undertaken for principled, selfless reasons, our historical traditions remind us that American foreign policy has always been most successful when interest and principle converge. It is, indeed, our great fortune that historically, principle and interest have been virtually indistinguishable on the big issues that the nation has confronted. Even Hans Morgenthau, the intellectual father of American foreign policy realism, understood that for Americans, the real choice was "not between moral principles and the national interest, devoid of moral dignity, but between one set of moral principles divorced from political reality, and another set of moral principles derived from political reality."

Our Founding Fathers well recognized the essential truth about their new republic's place in the world and about the uniquely American conception of the "national interest." President Washington, concluding forty-five years of public service, offered the best answer in his elegantly composed official farewell to the nation. As a nation, Washington wrote in 1796, we must be able to "choose peace or war, as our interest, guided by our justice, shall counsel." To be able to have this choice, the first president wrote later in the same document, America must have "the command of its own fortunes." That meant it had to be secure, safe from foreign attack, able to prosper economically, and therefore, capable of looking beyond mere survival in its foreign policy. Once it achieved that level of security, Washington suggested, Americans could think and act not only in pursuit of "interest" but also in pursuit of "justice."

As Washington's words suggest, when Americans grapple with the problem of how best to promote their "national interest," they dare not neglect the unique quality of American nationhood. It has become something of a cliché to talk of American "exceptionalism," but there is no ignoring the fact that the American nation itself was founded in exceptional circumstances and on an exceptional statement of timeless principles. Put simply, the United States was the first nation ever to base its very sense of nationhood on a set of universal principles derived from natural rights, as enunciated in its Declaration of Independence. In a century when nationalism has been, and unfortunately remains, one of the great engines of destruction, it is worth reflecting a moment on the distinction between American nationalism and that of most other countries, and more specifically, on the unique quality of American "patriotism."

Over the last five centuries, as the idea of nation-states took root and grew in the West, people began to connect themselves with their surroundings. Individuals formed profound bonds with the land itself, the religion of their fellow citizens who inhabited it, their common language, shared racial identities, particular cultural characteristics, and the myths and history of the region. The sum of these links tied the individual to his country and produced what we call patriotism. In this, the nationalist form of patriotism, the nation-state is a kind of father (or mother) who gives citizens the important traits that distinguish them as a nation.

History's most destructive and corrosive form of nationalism was Germany's National Socialist—Nazi—Party. Helping to blaze the trail of this century's politicization of science, the Nazis manufactured spurious scientific analyses to show that blood linked together a group of Caucasian, non-Semitic peoples that Adolf Hitler called Aryans.

Nationalism has played a role in more recent conflicts as well. Slobodan Milosevic's successful campaign to rouse Serbian nationalism in order to seize and keep political power in the former Yugoslavia is perhaps the most prominent example. At a rally attended by an estimated one million Serbs in Kosovo in 1989 on the six hundredth anniversary of Serbia's defeat at the hands of the Turks, Milosevic shouted, "No one should dare to beat you!" Calling on the huge crowd to remember the "bravery and dignity" of their Serb ancestors, Milosevic told his listeners that "six centuries later again we are in battles and quarrels. They are not armed battles, though such things should not be excluded yet." The former communist apparatchik had no need to cite the ancient Serbian saying, "wherever a drop of Serbian blood has been shed, there lies Serbia." The crowd knew by heart the lines of the national poem they heard recited:

> Whoever is of Serb birth,
> And who does not come to Kosovo Polje [the battlefield
>   where the Serbs lost]
> To do battle against the Turks,
> Let him have neither a male
> Nor female offspring,
> Let him have no crop.

This is the language of extreme nationalism. The nation is tied by blood to the very soil. The Serb who does not act piously toward the fatherland by honoring its sacred shrine should have no children and his crops—the means of his earthly sustenance—should wither. He himself should disappear from the face of the earth leaving no trace.

The American Founders had a very different view of patriotism. They saw the American nation not as an end in itself, but rather as the embodiment of an elegant political ideal intended to protect citizens' liberties—and thus deserving of the citizens' deep and abiding loyalty.

This idea—that the proper purpose of government is to protect our basic God-given liberties—is at the very heart of the American experiment in self-government. John Jay in Federalist No. 2 describes his fellow citizens as "no less attached to union than enamored of liberty." This is a rational, pragmatic statement of means and ends. It correctly summarizes the Founding Fathers' implicit expectation that Americans would be attached to their country because it protected their rights and thus gave them the best opportunity to lead better and more fulfilled lives.

The best explicit statement about Americans and their patriotism comes from Alexis de Tocqueville, who compared the traditional forms of patriotism he had seen in Europe with the new variety found in the United States. Of the old kind he wrote,

> *This natural fondness (i.e. for one's birthplace) is united with a taste for ancient customs and a reverence for traditions of the past; those who cherish it love their country as they love the mansion of their father. It is in itself a kind of religion: it does not reason, but it acts from the impulse of faith and sentiment.*

Tocqueville found something entirely different in American patriotism:

> *But there is another species of attachment to country which is more rational than the one I have been describing. It is perhaps less generous and less ardent, but it is more fruitful and more lasting: it springs from knowledge; it is nurtured by the laws; it grows by the exercise of civil rights; and in the end, it is confounded with the personal interests of the citizen.*[1]

No sentiment besides patriotism speaks more directly or eloquently to the question of how citizens think of their country and see its purpose in the world. All states aim to survive and prosper, but their commonality ends there. The Nazis sought the triumph of what they called the "master race." The Milosevic regime seeks to expand the territory under the control of a particular group of people united by language, ethnicity, and religion. Americans believe that all men and women, by virtue of their birth, are endowed by their Creator with certain unalienable rights, which legitimate governments safeguard, and that the progress of other governments toward this ideal completes the natural order of things even as it assures our own safety.

There are other strong proofs of the principled—rather than nationalistic—character of American national existence. For example, our military and its commander in chief, the president, swear oaths, not to support a political party or a leader, nor the citizens of the country, nor even the country itself, but rather to uphold and defend the Constitution of the United States.

Consider Abraham Lincoln's first inaugural address, written, of course, before the carnage of the Civil War had begun. Addressing the southern states even as they considered secession, Lincoln said,

We must not be enemies. Though passion may have strained, it must not break our bonds of affection. The mystic chords of memory, stretching from every battlefield and patriot grave to every living heart and hearthstone all over this broad land, will yet swell the chorus of the Union, when again touched, as surely they will be, by the better angels of our nature.

As Lincoln spoke, the instinctive bonds of affection were actually quite tenuous, and they certainly proved insufficient in preventing a civil war. What was required, Lincoln suggested most notably in his address at Gettysburg, was a new sense of nationhood: one that transcended mere sentiment for one's own, be it one's family, state or particular history. The true "mystic chords of memory" were of *both* an event, the War for Independence, and the principles that gave rise to it. Accordingly, the "our fathers" of the Gettysburg Address were not the actual forefathers of the audience who stood before the president that day. Rather, they were the men who had begat the Declaration some "fore score and seven years" before. The solution to the great and awful test of American nationhood presented by the Civil War was not, in Lincoln's mind, a call to remember our common ancestry but, instead, a renewed dedication to the Declaration's principles of liberty and equality for which so many had died and upon which "a new birth of freedom" was deemed possible.

It is hardly surprising that these same principles have consistently shaped American foreign policy. Those who argue that the United States has no business trying to advance American ideals abroad, who consider it to be hubristic, the act of an arrogant empire, either don't know their country very well or have lost confidence in their nation's leadership. I suspect the latter explanation to be closer to the truth. After all, the history of American involvement abroad has been characterized by its generosity and humane acts—even toward nations it has defeated in war. The record shows that in the overwhelming number of instances America has been a liberating force from oppression. America is *not* interested in territorial conquest, subjugation of others, or world domination. Behind our attempt to advance American ideals abroad has been the belief that basic rights are unalienable, universal, God-given, and therefore all people, wherever they may be, are deserving of them. This, of course, has not meant that we could or should act everywhere. It has merely meant that we retain confidence in certain enduring principles and that we energetically advance them, where we prudently can. And we know that in nations where political stability, the rule of law, basic freedoms and economic prosperity take root, American interests are advanced.

Saddam Hussein's iron grasp on Iraq, the local aggression of Serbia, the potential aggression of North Korea, and terrorism, both freelance and state-sponsored, are the kinds of dangers that concern most Americans these days. What gives these threats a higher priority when local disputes in other places matter less? It is a combination of our self-interest in the stability of the Middle East, Europe, and East Asia, *and* our broader interest in establishing an international climate that is hospitable to the success of democratic values.

Moral action by an individual does not consist merely of expressing noble sentiments; it requires actions and judgments that are measured by a moral standard. It is the same with nations. Talk doesn't count for much; right actions do. But there is an obvious and crucial difference between individuals and nations. The former live under laws whose violation is not excused by ignorance or good intent. Among the latter, there is no law which is universally recognized or enforced. As a result, the power to judge is each nation's own: there is no final arbiter save the character of our intention and the judgment of history.

Because the political values that are at the core of the United States' existence are honorable and estimable, the judgment of history is likely to be positive. But principles alone are not enough; the test is whether we act on those principles, or whether we fall prey to indifference, selfishness, inattentiveness, or a persistent disregard of basic military and diplomatic facts. "It is a piece of idle sentimentality that the truth, merely as truth, has any inherent power denied to error, of prevailing against the dungeon and the stake." So said John Stuart Mill, one of the greatest exponents of liberty. All of which means that the citizens of democracies must be willing to support the arsenals of democracy. We must be willing to maintain our defenses in a manner consistent with our role in the world and the threats posed against us. In the end, our survival and the survival of all we believe in and care most about—the defense of Western civilization and the nurture and protection of our children—will depend on whether we are vigilant and strong and committed in purpose.

Our foreign policy has long reflected this imperative, even in moments of controversy, as when it aimed to turn back monarchic Spain's toehold in the New World in 1898 and when it struggled to bring democracy to the Old World in the wake of World War I. Our foreign policy mirrored the nation's principles as it confronted and stopped the Axis powers' search for global domination in the Second World War and as it contained and eventually triumphed over Soviet communism during the Cold War.

Morality and the American Presidency

The great triumph of American principles in this century has not of course happened on its own. Like America's experiment in self-government itself, the working out of our principles on the world stage has required good fortune, sound constitutional structures and significant acts of statesmanship. And the key institution, the critical nexus of practice and principle in the case of the United States is, and has been since the first days of the republic, the presidency. As the only unified representative of the nation, institutionally independent of the other branches of government, and commanded by the Constitution to set out the "state of the Union" and recommend measures for congressional action, presidents are the most prominent and effective force in the articulation of the nation's priorities and its role in world affairs. As Thomas Jefferson noted early on, the president is the only national officer who commands "a view of the whole ground." He is inevitably, as Woodrow Wilson remarked nearly a century after Jefferson, the nation's "political spokesman."

As the only national officer so positioned, much depends on the character of the person holding the office. Again, as Wilson notes,

> Let him once win the admiration and confidence of the country, and no other single force can withstand him. . . . If he rightly interpret the national thought and boldly insist upon it, he is irresistible; and the country never feels the zest of action so much as when its President is of such insight and caliber. . . .
> It is for this reason that it will often prefer to choose a man rather than a party. A President whom it trusts can not only lead it, but form it to his own views.

Such a definition of the presidency is not a modern development, an invention of Wilson, Franklin Roosevelt or those who came after. The first generation of American leaders possessed exactly the extraordinary personal qualities necessary for the consolidation of the new republic, although ironically the institutional system they designed was to rely on a regime of checks and separated powers to promote wise government, not on the fortuitous election of great statesmen to high office.

The nation's trust in George Washington allowed him to maintain popular support in the face of some of the most divisive and controversial issues of his day, most of which—establishing a policy of neutrality toward the warring states of Europe, signing the Jay Treaty with Great Britain, and putting down the Whiskey Rebellion—concerned security issues of great moment for the nation. Confident in Washington and the principles he adhered to, the country supported policies that they might have disputed, perhaps disastrously so, if they had been put forward by a man of lesser character.

Both his peers and his countrymen recognized the superiority of Washington's integrity, perseverance, judgment, and vision. In his biography, Henry Cabot Lodge wrote that when, in 1775, Washington became

*head of the American army, effective ridicule became impossi-
ble, for the dignity of the cause was seen in that of the leader.
The British generals soon found that they not only had a dangerous enemy to encounter, but that they were dealing with a
man whose pride in his country and whose own sense of self-
respect reduced any assumption of personal superiority on their
part to speedy contempt.*

Washington's character was the bulwark of the emergent nation,
too. Lodge continues:

*he brought dignity to the new government of the Constitution
when he was placed at its head. The confederation had excited
the just contempt of the world, and Washington as President,
by the force of his character and reputation, gave the United
States at once the respect not only of the American people, but
those of Europe as well. Men felt instinctively that no government over which he presided could fall into feebleness or dis-
repute.*[2]

Indeed, it is likely that *only* Washington's reputation for moral seriousness, constancy of purpose, and dignity could have commanded
the popular support needed to steer the new nation through the
dangers posed by contending European giants. Character—measured in foreign policy terms by sober objectives and the ability to
see them to completion in the face of withering attacks—counts.

Washington's idea of what America was, and should be, guided
his policy. He sought to *shape* public opinions, not follow them.
Finally, he was blessed with the personal sense of self-respect and
dignity that—as Henry Cabot Lodge observed—made it as hard
for his enemies to make light of the enterprise he led as it was easy
for the new nation's citizens to feel the confidence on which the
success of their government rested. In a democracy, even the most
intelligent and well-conceived policies require the public's belief
that the chief executive is capable of carrying them out. Personal
character in the conduct of *both* domestic and foreign policy matters a great deal. In many respects, and at certain critical times, it
is the essence of the American presidency.

Washington's example reminds us that the president's leadership
role is not fundamentally an egocentric invention by twenthieth-

century presidents, but is intrinsic to the constitutional scheme as laid out by the founders. It ought also to remind us of the complex and awesome task that confronts presidents in the exercise of that role. A president may be essential in setting the national agenda but, in the end, he cannot simply command results. In leading the nation, he faces and has to take into consideration: a large, socially and commercially diverse republican citizenry; a government of divided powers and responsibilities; and an ever-evolving set of domestic and international circumstances. Presidents who are dogmatic in their views are bound to fail as they run up against the realities of governance, just as presidents who lack conviction and attempt to "lead" by opinion polls will see their ad hoc efforts at policy-making overtaken by unforeseen events and new crises.

In short, what we want in presidents is strength of public character: a combination of principled vision, sound judgment about how to apply those principles in practice, and a level of conviction that is able to instruct and inspire America as a whole.

The Presidency Two Hundred Years Later

It is no less true today than it was in Washington's time that a president's character is of paramount importance in the conduct of foreign policy, both for the respect it commands at home—summoning the people to greatness while simultaneously expressing the people's desires and aspirations for their nation—and for the respect it commands abroad, from both friends and adversaries.

In our own time, President Clinton's manifest misconduct of foreign affairs underscores this point. His ends have been largely determined by an effort to intuit public opinion rather than by a sure sense of America's purpose as a force for democracy and peace in the world. His means have been a sporadic series of threats, in the service of uncertain purposes and supported by irresolute force.

President Clinton's fecklessness in articulating and pursuing foreign policy is, I believe, born of his dubious character and moral qualities. When responding to Iraq's evasion of the arms control regime it agreed to after the Gulf War, for instance, the president threatened Saddam Hussein repeatedly from 1993 through 1998. When, and only when, Iraqi noncompliance—following United States threats and repeated deployments of American military units to the Middle East—would have caused irreparable public and political embarrassment, Clinton used force. And even then he used it only sparingly, ineffectively, unwisely. In December of 1998, the United States launched an aerial bombardment that lasted less than a week. Did it topple Saddam or stop his violations? No, its only achievement was effectively to end all international arms control inspections and allow Iraq to develop, largely unfettered, nuclear, biological, and chemical weapons.

Is there anyone who doubts that there will eventually be a high cost to the United States and its allies for Clinton's weakness toward Saddam Hussein? Does anyone believe that Saddam, chastened by a weekend of bombing, has abandoned his aggressive ways and dedicated himself to peace and the welfare of his hapless subjects? When he re-emerges from his ineffectual quarantine with new and improved weapons of mass destruction, no one should forget the critical role played by our president's indecisiveness.

The same frailties characterized President Clinton's leadership in other places in the world, most notably the Balkans. For three years, repeated threats in the face of Slobodan Milosevic's baleful influence over the Bosnian war yielded nothing but concentration camps and further bloodshed against Muslim civilians. Again, only when unheeded warnings against increasingly violent attacks on unarmed innocents left the United States a choice between public embarrassment or the use of force, Clinton took action. By this time, however, some two hundred thousand people had perished.

The same pattern was repeated in Kosovo. President Clinton warned Milosevic as early as 1993 not to use force in the formerly autonomous province where ethnic Albanians constituted a 90 percent majority. He repeated the warnings as Milosevic cracked down hard on the Kosovars. Not surprisingly given the pattern of threat and inaction that had characterized U.S. policy, Milosevic felt free to ignore the United States. Finally, the Serbs' attacks on ethnic Albanians reached a point where the president felt humiliated for having failed to make good on his threats and finally had to act. The aerial bombardment campaign that followed neither protected the Kosovars from murder and pillage nor forced the author of their brutalization, Slobodan Milosevic, from power.

At the conclusion of hostilities, the NATO alliance congratulated itself. But declaring a victory is not the same as achieving one. As in Iraq and Bosnia, the president had moved only when backed into a corner, while the feebleness of his policy left the source of trouble wounded but still very much in power and capable of future mischief. In both the Balkans and in Iraq—as well as in other unfriendly states where America's actions are watched extremely closely—the question is not whether, but when and at what cost, the consequences of uncertain and weak presidential leadership will be reckoned.

We have heard much about the resurgence of isolationism in this country, and there have indeed been signs of a trend in this direction, some of it unfortunately within a Republican Party once known for its Reaganite internationalist principles. Few commentators, however, have bothered to ask whether this isolationist sentiment has been the direct result of a popular loss of confidence in the character and leadership of President Clinton. How many Republican congressmen who voted against the war in Kosovo did so because they mistrusted the dependability, the moral sturdiness, and the leadership abilities of the commander in chief? How many questioned whether Clinton could be counted on to send American soldiers to battle out of principle rather than to achieve crassly political motives? Americans were not alone in believing that the president had bombed Iraq on at least one occasion as a means of distracting attention from his scandalous behavior in the White House—a real-life rendition of the movie "Wag the Dog." Most foreign leaders saw domestic political motives in almost every foreign policy decision by this president.

There is a problem of renewed isolationism in this country. But no small part of the reason has been Clinton's feckless leadership and his debasement of the office of the presidency. If it is true that the presidency is the place where the nation's interests and its moral sensibilities are uniquely joined and made manifest, then the United States has, indeed, been suffering from a want of character in the White House.

A Foreign Policy of Principled Internationalism

It is precisely because we cannot afford a turn to isolationism that we cannot afford presidents who do not command the respect of Americans or make them feel certain that the conduct of foreign affairs is based on steady vision and purpose. The years ahead require Americans to make some hard decisions. We are currently spending just 3 percent of our gross domestic product on defense—

in contrast with 6 to 9 percent during most of the Cold War. Maintaining our position of global leadership will not break America's bank, but it will require a larger commitment of resources. We will need a president who can summon Americans to meet their great destiny as a people, who can appeal to their unique sense of idealistic patriotism and inspire them to engage in present sacrifice, when necessary, to promote future security.

What ails us at home is in no small measure due to the growing conviction that what defines Americans is their particular ethnic, racial, sexual and religious identities, and not the deep truths expressed in the Declaration of Independence. When the United States engages the world based on an explicit appeal to universal truths—and the peoples of the world, in turn, judge the legitimacy of their own governments on how well they measure up to those principles—it reminds us of who we are as a people, what we cherish, and why those cherished beliefs are not only our heritage, but the world's at large. As Lincoln noted, the principles expressed by the Declaration gave liberty "not alone to the people of this country, but home to the world for all future time." One need only recall the students of Tiananmen Square and the statue of the Goddess of Liberty to see this fact in vivid display. American internationalism helps strengthen our national self-definition. Rather than a distraction, as the New Isolationists would have it, American global leadership based on American principles *reinforces* our commitment to common, ancient, honorable ideals and reminds us who we are.

There is no shortage of challenges before us. With the weapons of mass destruction Saddam Hussein seeks to build, Iraq bids for supreme leadership of the Arab world. His belligerence aims not only to control a vital supply of oil, but to crush and destroy Israel, our ally and the region's sole democracy. Our immediate and far-reaching interests are threatened equally.

In North Korea, an unstable tyrannical regime cloaked in secrecy and paranoia and capable of starving its own people to arm itself mixes a brew of nuclear programs and ballistic missiles whose range is increasing before our eyes. Our interest in protecting American soil is engaged at the same time as we are bound by honor and treaty to look to the dangers faced by our increasingly democratic allies, South Korea and Japan.

And Colombia has become an unabashed narco-state that—absent firm, dramatic action—will consolidate and extend the success of the Latin American drug producers. This is an extraordinary threat; indeed, the drug trade has replaced communism as the greatest threat to democracy and democratic institutions in this hemisphere. And most of the financial support for this threat comes from the United States, via the huge amount of drugs consumed in this country.

But nowhere in the world are the moral issues of foreign policy clearer than in America's relations with the People's Republic of China, a state ruled by a brutal one-party communist dictatorship that sees the future as a reflection of China's ancient and influential role throughout Asia. The PRC possesses the world's largest population and enjoys—since discarding the crippling inefficiency of Soviet-style economics—an increasingly productive economy. Thus China's rulers have the means to build a large and powerful military. Every indication demonstrates that this is their intent.

American technology, such as powerful computers, with critical defense applications to which the Chinese are given access, they purchase. Other products of American ingenuity, such as advanced nuclear technology, they steal. They build and sell increasingly advanced ballistic missile technology to other hostile states such as North Korea and Iran. China's rulers have stated their intention to become a foremost military power, and they have increased the frequency and belligerence of their rhetoric against the Republic of China on Taiwan so as to raise the most serious questions about a conflict across the Strait of Taiwan.

Both in word and deed they have made it clear that they intend to contest the United States' position as the world's sole great power. There is no disputing that at this moment the United States is preeminent in almost every important category: economics, technology, military might and much else. But the task of America's political leaders is to maintain the long view and anticipate how events will eventually unfold. Once having done that, the goal is to formulate, and then implement, an intelligent, comprehensive strategy that takes these things into account.

A challenge from a nation like China that regards freedom as a threat and persistently and deliberately violates its own citizens' rights, presents us with the real possibility of another serious, prolonged confrontation with a well-armed and dangerous state—except that China would have far greater financial resources to trouble us than the Soviets ever dreamt of. Moreover, the region of the world that China seeks to dominate—the Asian nations living under her giant shadow—hold a productive capacity with extraordinary economic consequences that far exceed the commercial impact of the Warsaw Pact on the United States or its allies during the Cold War.

If it is true that American foreign policy should take far-seeing steps to help ensure peace and stability, the U.S. national interest, and the spread of American ideals, then nothing could be more foolish than to aid—directly or otherwise—China in its quest to offset American military pre-eminence in Asia. Nor should we delude ourselves into thinking that business-as-usual is a policy that will make China more liberal within and more accommodating without. Our policy toward China must be firmly rooted in facts—stubborn, empirical, unassailable facts—about the nature of their regime. To paraphrase Franklin Roosevelt, only a foolish optimist ignores dark realities. Among many of the foreign policy elite these days, there is too much foolish optimism. This is especially true among the so-called "realists" who refuse to see the current Chinese regime for what it is and, in the name of engagement, advocate policies that actually fuel rather than deter Beijing's most dangerous ambitions. We must see China for what it is, and replace a policy of de facto appeasement with steely resolve. In the end, of course, we hope for the day when the brutal, repressive Chinese regime is replaced by rulers who act more justly toward their own people and are more reasonable in their regional and global ambitions. Such a change will not only advance rights for the Chinese people, but also America's strategic interests.

As the United States was built on a solid moral framework of respect for the self-interest of individuals in their lives, liberties, and property, so our foreign policy can rest securely and justly on the nation's self-interest in its own preservation. Or as Thomas Jefferson put it in his second inaugural address, "We are firmly convinced, and act on that conviction, that with nations, as with individuals, our interests soundly calculated, will ever be inseparable from our moral duties." This includes not only the immediate defense of American citizens and soil, but also the protection of our allies and those commercial interests that touch the nation's vitality, and the widening of the circle of democratic nations upon which a safer world depends.

Failure to discharge these responsibilities simultaneously weakens both the United States and the cause of liberty in the world.

The disappearance of Soviet communism does not relieve America of this burden. We should take very seriously the strong desires of the peoples east of the old Iron Curtain—who seek to join the free alliances and institutions of the West—as well as the fate of the Taiwanese, who have built a fledgling democracy that is now under the threat of communist China's ambition. Indeed, for a nation based on principle such as ours, the questions of morality and foreign policy are not restricted to whether particular actions fit the standard, but whether, in the failure to act, we have failed to protect ourselves, and thus mankind's general interest in freedom.

So long as we stay true to the principles of America's founding, our self-interest as a great power will be inextricably linked to mankind's universal interest in life, liberty, and the pursuit of happiness. The American founders clearly understood the unique character of the nation and what it could mean to the world. Two hundred years later Ronald Reagan was able to apply their wisdom to the great challenge posed by the Soviet Union. Displaying the qualities of presidential leadership so essential to the effective governance of our democracy, Reagan accomplished what many thought impossible: relegating communism to the ashbin of history. He did so by inspiring Americans with confidence that their ideals and their interests converged in this great effort, that their security and their prosperity could be preserved only if they stood for something in a world threatened by evil. At a critical moment in our nation's history, Reagan was the embodiment of Americans' noblest aspirations. He was an American nationalist, which is to say he believed in America's destiny to be a force for good in the world.

George Washington's commitment to a foreign policy of "interest, guided by justice" remains the simplest and best description of our lot in the world. At the present time, the danger to ourselves and to our principles does not come from acting forcefully on their behalf; it comes instead from diffidence, lack of confidence, fear, and an unwillingness to rise to the great challenges of our time. That posture will not only put us in harm's way; it is antithetical to the meaning of America.

Today, America sits at the summit. Our military strength is the envy of every nation on earth, and our accomplishments as a world power would elicit awe and admiration from every nation that has gone before us. America has "the command of its own fortunes." It would be tragic indeed if we did not use this extraordinary historical moment to promote the ideals at the heart of our national enterprise and, by so doing, take the steps that will ensure stability and the steady growth of freedom throughout the world.

Statesmanship in the New Century

E ven though more than a decade has passed since the Berlin Wall came down, we still have no better name for the world in which we live than the "post–Cold War era." Although many have aspired to play the role of the next George Kennan by defining American strategy for this new era that does not yet have a name, no one has so far succeeded. But one thing seems clear: we can't succeed at the task of defining a new strategy if we ignore the historical record of the basis on which the old strategy was developed and defended, how it was implemented over a long period of time despite various obstacles and criticisms, and why it was eventually victorious.

However, given the rate at which some participants in the foreign policy process are "correcting the record" concerning their own views during the Cold War, it may not be too long before someone disputes Kennan's authorship of the original containment strategy. For it seems that we have all become Cold Warriors now.

A good example is provided by Bill Bradley who, in his first presidential campaign speech on foreign policy, declared that "for fifty years after the end of World War II and until the fall of the Berlin Wall in 1989, we were sure about one thing: We knew where we stood on foreign policy." Today, the former senator from New Jersey went on to lament, we face a more difficult challenge: "When it comes to foreign affairs, things are not so clear. The world's a more complicated place and it's no longer divided like it once was into good and evil, clear enemies, obvious friends. The choices are no longer so stark, and stark choices are always the easy ones."

This nostalgia for the supposedly easier choices of the Cold War is not confined to Bradley. From time to time President Clinton has also complained that the decisions he confronts in foreign policy are so much more difficult, because the world is so much more complex than it was during the Cold War. While today's world is certainly complicated, it is astonishing to hear the Cold War described as a time when the choices were clear and easy. On the contrary, at many points during the Cold War, the country was deeply divided over serious foreign policy issues—most bitterly with respect to the war in Vietnam, but also over issues dealing with arms control, nuclear weapons and ballistic missile defense; the deployment of U.S. troops in Europe and Korea; resistance to communism in Central America; and almost every year's defense budget. And in the academy, it was for a time fashionable to claim that the Cold War, far from being a fundamental clash of good and evil, was the result of American overreaching, which supposedly triggered the fears of a weak and defensive Soviet Union.

The assertion that the Cold War was universally understood at the time to be a fight between "good and evil" in which our choices were clear is particularly astonishing coming from the leaders of a Democratic Party that, during the 1970s and 1980s, ceased to be the party of Harry Truman or "Scoop" Jackson—who were dismissed with that liberal term of abuse "Cold Warriors"—and became instead the party that nominated George McGovern and called on America to "come home." This party's congressional leadership supported the Mansfield Amendment to halve the number of U.S. troops in Europe, and its 1976 presidential candidate, Jimmy Carter, promised to remove them altogether from Korea. Many of its leaders advocated a "nuclear freeze" at the very time the Reagan administration, in response to forward moves by Moscow, was trying to convince NATO to proceed with the deployment of intermediate-range nuclear forces. Far from believing that the Cold War was about as clear a struggle between good and evil as one is likely to experience in the real world, its leaders attacked President Reagan as a warmonger for his declaration that the Soviet Union was an "evil empire."

The residue of this skepticism concerning the use of American power in the world was still strong enough at the end of the Cold War that the Senate, voting largely along partisan lines, supported President Bush by only a small majority on the question of going to war to evict Saddam Hussein's forces from Kuwait. Although then-Senator Bradley now describes "Iraq, 1991" as one of those occasions on which "the national interest [was] clear," at the time he joined the great majority of congressional Democrats in voting against the president. And certainly for then-Governor Clinton, the issue wasn't at all clear. In a characteristically hedged statement he said, "I guess I would have voted for the majority if it was a close vote. But I agree with the arguments the minority made."

All this forgetfulness might be merely a matter for amusement were it not that it helps obscure the importance of a half-century of America's world experience. If the Cold War is remembered as a period of easy choices with no relevance to the more complicated times in which we live, we will ignore the lessons that our hard-earned experience could teach us. As difficult as it will always be to foresee all the future effects of our actions, it will be that much more difficult if we do not understand where we are and how we got here. Indeed, this historical amnesia also affects more recent policy debates, including one that occurred at the very beginning of the "post–Cold War" period.

How We Learned to Stop Worrying and Love the *Pax Americana*

In 1992, a draft memo prepared by my office at the Pentagon, proposing a post–Cold War defense strategy, was leaked to the press and touched off a major controversy. That draft—like the Regional Defense Strategy subsequently issued by Secretary of Defense Dick Cheney—suggested that a "dominant consideration" in U.S. defense strategy should be "to prevent any hostile power from dominating a region whose resources would, under consolidated control, be sufficient to generate global power." Those regions were specified as including Western Europe, East Asia, the territory of the former Soviet Union and Southwest Asia.

The *New York Times*, having published the leak, editorialized vehemently against it. Senator Edward Kennedy said that the Pentagon plans "appear to be aimed primarily at finding new ways to justify Cold War levels of military spending." Senator Robert Byrd commented that "We love being the sole remaining superpower in the world and we want so much to remain that way that we are willing to put at risk the basic health of our economy and well-being of our people to do so." Senator Joseph Biden ridiculed the proposed strategy as "literally a *Pax Americana* ... It won't work. You can be the world superpower and still be unable to maintain peace throughout the world."

These critics never said which hostile superpower they would be willing to see dominate one of those areas. They were critical of the suggestion that NATO might extend security guarantees to the new democracies of Central Europe. Instead of relying on U.S. leadership, they seemed to believe that the United Nations could provide security in the post–Cold War world. The *New York Times* editorialized, "With its focus on this concept of benevolent domination by one power, the Pentagon document articulates the clearest rejection to date of collective internationalism, the strategy that emerged from World War II when the five victorious powers sought to form a United Nations that could mediate disputes and police outbreaks of violence."

Strangely, just seven years later many of these same critics, without having visibly changed their minds, nevertheless seem very comfortable with a *Pax Americana*. They support—on occasion, even clamor for—American military intervention in places like Haiti, Rwanda and East Timor, far beyond anything required by basic principles of the Regional Defense Strategy. Moreover, they apparently believe that all of this can be accomplished, and our commitments to our European and Asian allies maintained, with a greatly reduced defense burden.

Today, this strategy is criticized not by those who reacted so vociferously to the *New York Times* leak of 1992, but by the isolationist right of Patrick Buchanan who complains that "containment, a defensive strategy, had given way to a breathtakingly ambitious offensive strategy—to 'establish and protect a new order.'"[1] Buchanan—who seems willing to let almost any hostile superpower dominate Europe or Asia if the alternative is risking major war—laments the fact that the 1992 Pentagon strategy seems to have been "passively accepted by the American people." By 1998, he correctly notes, "the administration—with Biden and Kennedy's support—had indeed extended NATO to Poland, Hungary, and the Czech Republic and had offered membership to the Baltic States."[2]

But apart from Buchanan, there is currently a remarkable degree of agreement on a number of central points of foreign policy, even if it involves, and may to some degree depend on, forgetfulness about the divisions of the past. No one is proposing to withdraw troops from Korea; the stationing of U.S. troops in Europe is not a divisive issue; and the view that NATO is obsolete now that the Cold War is over has no political force. American forces under President Clinton's command have been bombing Iraq with some regularity for months now, but that action occasions not a whimper of opposition in Congress and barely a mention in the press.

One would like to think that this new consensus reflects a recognition that the United States cannot afford to allow a hostile power to dominate Europe or Asia or the Persian Gulf; that the safest, and in the long run the cheapest, way to prevent such a development is to preserve the U.S.-led alliances that have been so successful—to paraphrase Lord Ismay in more diplomatic language—at keeping the Americans engaged, the allies reassured and the aggressors deterred; and that the best way to avoid another world war is not by being willing to cede Europe or Asia to hostile domination, but by making it clear in advance that we will oppose it and thereby prevent any such effort. Unfortunately, today's consensus reflects as much the complacency bred by our current predominance as agreement on how to shape the future to prevent another world war, or even concern about the possibility of such an event.

This consensus exists partly because the congressional Democrats, who in the past were most inclined to oppose an activist national security policy, have followed the lead of a Democratic president. But it is also because the very absence of threat, which is said to make it harder to know where we stand on foreign policy, actually makes it much easier to take stands almost anywhere. The extension of NATO membership to the new democracies of Poland, Hungary and the Czech Republic was a valuable strengthening of the U.S. commitment to European security and of NATO's commitment to stability in Central Europe. But it is also true that it was a step taken with relatively little debate, no doubt precisely because there was very little perceived risk involved.

It is only now, when the costs of confronting Iraq seem relatively low, that everyone has become a "hawk"—and happy to forget the courage required on the part of President Bush to lead American troops into a war against a not-yet-defeated and seemingly formidable Iraq. The most amazing indication of this general sense of safety is that President Clinton has been able to lead U.S. armed forces in operations involving tens of thousands of troops in Haiti,

Bosnia, Kosovo and Iraq—and to conduct military strikes against Afghanistan and Sudan—with virtually no American casualties.

But the absence of threat, which makes it so easy to achieve consensus on once-difficult issues, also makes it possible to believe that the whole problem of national security has gone away or been transformed into a kind of international social work. Thus, a presidential campaign can be run under the slogan, "It's the economy, stupid," and the vice president can argue that the environment and AIDS are foremost national security issues. What is wrong with those statements is not that AIDS and the environment are not serious problems, but rather the implication that security is no longer something we need to worry about. The world has changed dramatically with the end of the Cold War, but it has not been turned upside down.

Nation Shall Not Lift up Sword against Nation?

In a world where American primacy seems so overwhelming, it is hard to imagine how a threat of the magnitude of that posed by Napoleon, Kaiser Wilhelm, Hitler, Tojo or Stalin could ever come about. Perhaps, we are entitled to hope, we have reached the stage where the Biblical prophecy will come true, at least for ourselves. But if we look at the last century we can find abundant evidence that twenty years—a mere moment in the life of nations—can bring about enormous changes in world affairs. And if that was true several generations ago, how much truer is it today when the tempo of change has increased so dramatically. Preventing another world war is certainly not the only task of American foreign policy. With any luck, we will never even know if it was a necessary task. But if it does prove necessary and we fail, there would be no more significant failure with which this generation could burden the next, no failure that would more thoroughly undermine any other successes—economic or environmental or scientific—that we might achieve.

In the record of past attempts to avert war, the Munich Agreement of 1938 quickly became a reference point for the remainder of the last century; even if the lesson has been somewhat overused, it should not be forgotten in this century. Addressing the British people by radio two days before his departure for Munich for the fateful meeting with Hitler that sealed the fate of Czechoslovakia,

Prime Minister Neville Chamberlain made the case for appeasement in stark terms:

> *How horrible, fantastic, incredible it is that we should be digging trenches and trying on gas masks here because of a quarrel in a far-away country between people of whom we know nothing.... I am myself a man of peace to the very depths of my soul.... But if I were convinced that any nation had made up its mind to dominate the world by fear of its force, I should feel that it must be resisted.... but war is a fearful thing, and we must be very clear, before we embark on it, that it is really the great issues that are at stake, and that the call to risk everything in their defense, when all the consequences are weighed, is irresistible.*[3]

As it turned out, of course, the "great issues" *were* at stake, and Chamberlain's failure to come to the aid of those far-away Czechs about whom the British people knew "nothing" meant that Britain would soon face a much more terrible war on more disadvantageous terms. Few decisions by a democratic leader have proven so clearly to be wrong or have had such dire consequences.

As a result, the lesson of the Munich Agreement was seared into the consciousness of the western democracies and their leaders. It contributed to the resolve of President Truman to resist communist aggression in such "far-away" places as Korea, Iran, Turkey, Greece and Berlin, and of President Kennedy to resist Soviet pressure in Berlin and Cuba. But it was also with Munich in mind that British Prime Minister Anthony Eden and French Prime Minister Mendes France decided to oppose with force Nasser's takeover of the Suez Canal, and, with even worse consequences, that Presidents Kennedy and Johnson decided that Vietnam was a similar case of aggression that had to be opposed by force.

With the end of the Cold War, the United States and its allies are again confronted with a series of wars in far-away places, and many, echoing Chamberlain, say we have no business intervening in conflicts among people we do not understand, where "we have no dog in the fight." We hear echoes of Chamberlain's argument that "However much we may sympathize with a small nation confronted by a big and powerful neighbor, we cannot in all circumstances undertake to involve [ourselves] in war simply on her account." Of course, the fact that the arguments have a similar ring doesn't mean that those who sound like Chamberlain today are necessarily wrong, any more than those who argue for intervening in messy civil wars or ethnic conflicts for moral purposes are necessarily repeating the mistakes of Vietnam.

It has been said that "history has more imagination than all the scenario writers in the Pentagon"—or perhaps even in Hollywood. Hence it is no surprise that history doesn't provide us with simple lessons or rules to tell us how to act in particular situations; it can, however, alert us to some of the alternatives we should consider. Perhaps because the rule of law plays such an important role in our domestic life, or perhaps because of sheer impatience with a complexity that resists our will, Americans often look for "doctrines" or legal criteria to dictate foreign policy action. Americans often demand a kind of consistency or fairness in foreign policy: Why did the United States act to stop crimes against humanity in Kosovo but not in Rwanda? Why do we favor self-determination for East Timor and Croatia but not for Chechnya or Tibet? But foreign policy is not about consistency; if it were, it would be much easier. It is rather about discrimination, the application of judgment and the balancing of competing but valid claims—and all this in circumstances that inevitably vary in significant ways.

Shaping the Future in the Midst of Uncertainty

The ultimate test of foreign policy is how successfully it shapes the future. If the United States were a small country whose actions had little impact on the surrounding world, it might indulge the notion that the principal goal of foreign policy should be economic or commercial gain. And even for the United States, there is a considerable sphere of action where it may be appropriate for economic considerations to dominate, because the other consequences are relatively minor. But the United States is not Switzerland (nor, for that matter, is it the United States of George Washington's or John Quincy Adams's time), which can afford to isolate itself from a world over which it has little control and focus simply on how to make money and enjoy its life in peace. With so great a capacity to influence events comes a requirement to figure out how best to use that capacity to shape the future.

Unfortunately, knowing the effects of our actions on the subsequent course of events is an uncertain business even after the fact.

It is rare to have a case where the consequences of an action are so calamitous as with Chamberlain at Munich, or where we can see them so clearly. Despite the widely held view that the Vietnam War was a costly and unmitigated defeat for the United States, no less a figure than Singapore's Senior Minister Lee Kuan Yew has argued that the American commitment was critical for buying time for the other Southeast Asian countries—and that that is the reason why the famed "dominoes" did not fall after Indochina did. That may be true, but history at best shows us only the costs and consequences of the actions taken, not those of any alternative courses.

Still, it does not take much imagination to consider what would likely have happened had England and her allies successfully resisted Hitler in the Rhineland or at Munich. Germany might then have been "contained." But in that case we would have been treated, would we not, to learned discourses about how the resulting "cold war" with Germany was the unnecessary product of unwarranted Western suspicion and hostility toward a country that was legitimately supporting the right of self-determination of nationals living beyond its borders, and chafing under the harsh and unequal impositions of the Versailles Treaty. Or, to take a more recent example, we will never know what might have happened if Saddam Hussein's occupation of Kuwait had not been reversed: Would he, as seems entirely probable, have brought the governments of the Arabian peninsula under his control and, with the wealth that provided, built up his arsenal of conventional and nuclear weapons in preparation for a much bigger war with Iran or Israel? If so, then what President Bush achieved was much more than just the liberation of Kuwait; but that achievement will never be as clear as Chamberlain's failure.

When the consequences of any course of action are so uncertain, even in hindsight, how much more difficult is it to weigh different courses of action in advance. It is little wonder that "futurologists" often have a kind of shady reputation. Who in their right mind would defy Yogi Berra's famous advice that "it's a mistake to try to make predictions, especially about the future"? Who predicted in 1920 that a prostrate Germany, in the space of twenty years, would become the master of Europe? Who predicted the rise of fascism and communism as two world-consuming ideologies that would bring with them so much tragedy? As George Orwell wrote in 1942, "One effect of the ghastly history of the last twenty years has been to make a great deal of ancient literature seem much more modern.... Tamerlane and Genghis Khan seem credible figures now, and Machiavelli seems a serious thinker, as they didn't in 1910. We have got out of a backwater and back into history."

Of course, the period between the two world wars was uniquely turbulent and Hitler himself was uniquely monstrous. But it was hardly the only time that our ability to envision the future proved inadequate. In 1945, very few people foresaw the coming confrontation called the Cold War, much less that in five short years the United States—which had just assembled the most powerful armed force the world had ever seen—would be almost driven off the Korean Peninsula by the army of a third- or fourth-rate power; or that the next twenty years would bring a terrifying competition in nuclear-armed ballistic missiles, at the end of which the United States would humble the Soviet Union in the Cuban Missile Crisis—and, at almost the same time, begin a war with an army of ill-equipped guerillas who would inflict a humiliating defeat upon it.

Even the supposedly stable and predictable Cold War saw massive swings between confidence and fear concerning the West's prospects. It witnessed dramatic changes in the development of nuclear and thermonuclear weapons, intercontinental ballistic missiles and nuclear submarines, and conventional weapons with the extreme accuracy that transformed them into true strategic weapons. It also demonstrated that guerillas and terrorists could expose vulnerabilities that even a superpower could not counter. Yet no matter what the uncertainties, the soundness of foreign policy decisions depends on how well they anticipate the future and also influence it. The power of George Kennan's argument—the argument that shaped American policy for decades—came precisely from the prescience with which he understood the dynamics of Soviet foreign policy and the internal contradictions that would, ultimately, fatally weaken the Soviet Union.

The Shape of the Post–Cold War World

The key social-economic trend of the post–Cold War world is often characterized as "globalization," and that world's system of international politics is often described as "unipolar." These two terms may be merely different descriptions of the same phenomenon, since globalization, which refers primarily to the increasing inter-connectedness of the world economy, occurs within the context of the global dominance of American economic and political ideas, accompanied by the spread of American mass culture.

In fact, however, the diffusion of American technology and culture and American ideas about efficient economic organization can lead to the diffusion of power. If the liberal democracy–free market model is successful in more and more parts of the world, then those countries will develop greater economic power and the U.S. share of global economic activity can only go down in percentage terms. Many have argued that this will lead to more, not less, multipolarity, leading to a major change in the international system.

Moreover, if today's world is indeed "unipolar," it is not so much because the United States—in that much-overworked phrase, "the sole remaining superpower"—can dominate others in the way that Rome, for example, dominated its world for centuries. It stems more from the fact that all of the economically powerful countries in the world are America's allies. The United States is the leader and the dominant member of that alliance, but it is an alliance of democratic countries, not a collection of satellites responding without question to a superpower's will.

America's current preponderance and the strength of its alliance structure render the possibility of a hostile competitor threatening the United States and its allies—as they were threatened three times in the last century—remote for the time being. Even if a major conflict were to emerge in the foreseeable future, it seems unlikely that it would take an ideological form. One of the most obvious features of the world after the collapse of Soviet communism is the loss of belief in left-wing utopias, not only in the former Soviet Union but throughout the world—including, perhaps most significantly, in China where the Communist Party nevertheless still exercises single-party control.

This development is not simply a result of the Soviet system's failure, but also in significant—perhaps even equal—measure a product of the perceived success of democratic market economies in Western Europe and parts of East Asia. As a bastard form of religion, seeking salvation in this world rather than the next, communism was particularly vulnerable to demonstrations of worldly success or failure. And, just as the seeming failures of Western societies in the 1920s and 1930s contributed to an enormous growth of communism, their successes at the end of this century, contrasted with the failures of the Soviet Union, contributed to the latter's collapse.

It would be wrong, however, to describe this apparent end of the ideological competition between communism and capitalism as the end of ideology itself, as some of the rosier prophets of globalism are inclined to do. There is no evidence yet that human beings care only for their material well-being and that there are no greater causes that they live for—and may be willing to die and kill for. Nevertheless, unlike during the post–World War I period, there are no visible philosophical contenders, at least in the West, with the idea of liberal democracy. Even in Russia, where the Communist Party continues to have some residual appeal, that appeal is not ideological and certainly has no world-revolutionary spirit. It is only in the Muslim world that a revolutionary notion of societal organization has philosophical roots, and that notion, at least for now, is very much on the defensive in Iran, its own home base. From today's vantage point, it seems that it would take a collapse of the global economy on the order of the Great Depression to revive ideological politics in the developed world.

But although most of the major struggles of the twentieth century have had an ideological basis, the absence of ideological competition does not guarantee peace. Some may claim that the current absence of major-power conflict is the result of globalization, or economic interdependence, or the supposedly pacific character of democracies. But it would be a mistake to ignore the possibility that it may be equally the product of the alliances that were constructed because of the Cold War but which continue, long afterward, to provide security to the most powerful countries of the world in a way that does not threaten the security of anyone else. And it would be a mistake to assume that the emergence of new powers in the world, particularly China, will automatically take a more peaceful course than the emergence of other great powers in the past.

Some Lessons of the Last (Cold) War

The refusal by one side to remember the deep divisions and sharp debates over policy that took place during the Cold War is part of the effort to deny that there are any lessons to be learned from the

Cold War experience. After all, if the Cold War is over, what could be less useful or relevant than Cold War attitudes?

From the other side, correspondingly, comes the conviction that since the policies that won the Cold War clearly worked, every effort should be made to keep them in place in order to repeat that success. But while there are important lessons to be learned from the Cold War—lessons that still have pertinence today—it would be a mistake to apply them without recognizing the very different circumstances now prevailing. Let us consider a few of the more important lessons of the Cold War and then try to apply them to the case of China—in the opinion of many, the most serious policy issue facing us in the immediate future.

At the beginning of the Reagan administration, when Congress refused to confirm its first nominee for the position of Assistant Secretary of State for Human Rights, some saw it as an opportunity to do away entirely with the State Department's Office of Human Rights. Fortunately, then–Deputy Secretary of State William Clark, a personal friend of the president, successfully led an effort to preserve the office, and human rights and the promotion of democracy became major features of Reagan administration foreign policy. There can be little doubt that this aspect of policy contributed in an important way to our triumph in the Cold War. Perhaps more surprising to Reagan's numerous critics, his administration also witnessed and supported an enormous advance of democracy in countries on "our" side of the Cold War, not only in Latin America but in some surprising places in Asia such as South Korea, Taiwan and the Philippines.

Nothing could be less realistic than the version of "realism" that dismisses human rights as an important tool of American foreign policy. There were no doubt policies put forward in the name of human rights that damaged or could have damaged other U.S. interests, but often these policies were bad for human rights and democracy as well—for example, the notion that undermining the Shah's regime would be a great advance for the Iranian people, or the belief that weakening South Korea's ability to defend itself from the North was necessary in order to advance human rights. What is more impressive is how often promoting democracy has actually advanced other American interests.

That this was so in the struggle with the Soviet Union is so obvious that it would hardly seem necessary to argue the case, although the validity and prudence of Reagan's talk of the "evil empire" was certainly disputed at the time. Democratic change is not only a way to weaken our enemies, it is also a way to strengthen our friends. This fact first impressed itself strongly on me in dealing with the Philippines in the mid-1980s, during the last years of the Marcos regime. As the United States put pressure on Marcos to reform, we asked ourselves the reasonable question whether doing so would simply pave the way to a regime that would in retrospect make Marcos look good, as the Ayatollahs in Iran had done for the Shah. In fact, though, it was Marcos who was in the process of paving the way to victory of a particularly vicious communist insurgency; moreover, there was available a true democratic alternative in the Philippines. Although political change might jeopardize American military bases in the Philippines, it was more important to have a healthy ally without American bases than a sick ally with them.

History has amply vindicated that judgment. Similarly, the transition to democracy in South Korea has not only been good for the Korean people but has strengthened U.S.-Korean relations enormously. As one contemplates the enormous problems of Indonesia today, one can only wish that the transition to a more representative government there had begun ten years earlier.

At the same time, one should be wary of a policy that devotes equal effort to promoting democracy everywhere, regardless of the particular circumstances. Aside from the question of the importance of a country for U.S. interests, we cannot ignore the uncomfortable fact that economic and social conditions may better prepare some countries for democracy than others. The fact that President Aristide received 70 percent of the vote in Haiti did not by itself make him a democrat and did not guarantee that he could deal prudently with that country's extreme inequalities. In such circumstances, it is no surprise that the use of the American military to build a democracy there has been an expensive failure. Oddly, we seem to have forgotten what Vietnam should have taught us about the limitations of the military as an instrument of "nation-building."

Promoting democracy requires attention to specific circumstances and to the limitations of U.S. leverage. Both because of what the United States is, and because of what is possible, we cannot engage either in promoting democracy or in nation-building as an exercise of will. We must proceed by interaction and indirection, not imposition. In this respect, post–World War II experiences with Germany and Japan offer misleading guides to what is possible now, even in a period of American primacy. What was possible following total victory and prolonged occupation—in societies that were economically advanced but, at the same time, had profoundly lost faith in their own institutions—does not offer a model that applies in other circumstances.

One of the important lessons of the Cold War is that some regimes are more open to change than others, and that there is indeed a difference between authoritarian and totalitarian governments. Fundamental change in the Soviet Union was not possible until the system had loosened up considerably and had become convinced that it was losing the Cold War competition. Our ally South Korea was a very different matter, even though severe human rights criticisms could be leveled at the Chun Do Won regime. Reagan's willingness to receive Chun as his first foreign visitor at the White House was criticized by human rights groups, but it secured the reprieve of Kim Dae Jung's death sentence and his release from prison. Reagan's own visit to Korea two years later was also criticized, but it secured Chun's pledge to honor the Korean Constitution and step down at the end of his term of office, not something that could otherwise have been taken for granted.

But even with regimes that are open to change there are limits to U.S. leverage, and if we try to accomplish too much with too little we may achieve nothing at all. Despite Marcos's great dependence on the United States, the notion popular among members of Congress that he would step down simply if President Reagan asked him to do so was nonsense. Our leverage over Marcos centered on his hope that by permitting some movement toward democracy he could preserve the relationship with the United States. Had we pronounced ourselves in total opposition to his regime, his only course of action would have been to clamp down ruthlessly. Marcos only became willing to listen to advice to step down when his own people had made his position untenable.

Deterrence Works
It is surprising, after not only the Cold War experience but also the earlier history of this century, that we still hear echoes of "Why die for Berlin?" or "Why die for Danzig?" The purpose of extending

security guarantees, such as the ones recently extended to NATO's newest members, is not to fight wars on their behalf but precisely to avoid having to do so. And it is impressive how often American clarity during the Cold War worked, and how often ambiguity led to trouble. This doesn't mean that deterrence always works and that we can always be comfortable that showing resolve will be enough to ensure that our resolve will not be tested. But neither should we entertain the illusion that the mere refusal to extend guarantees will always enable us to avoid war; vital interests do not become less vital merely by our failure to articulate them beforehand.

In fact, what is being weighed in all such cases are the chances that deterrence may not work and the consequences that would then follow, against the consequences of acquiescing in an attack and the chances that it would then extend beyond the issue at hand. Chamberlain not only sacrificed Czechoslovakia at Munich, but brought on the wider war that he was trying to avoid, and under far worse circumstances. Acheson's declaration that Korea was outside our defense perimeter not only invited a North Korean attack, but could not even keep the United States out of war when the attack did come. American declarations in 1990 that we took no position on the disputed border between Iraq and Kuwait may have encouraged Saddam Hussein to think that he could attack with impunity.

In this connection, one might observe a persistent source of mis-understanding between democracies, which look constantly for pragmatic solutions to resolve concrete problems in isolation, and more ruthless leaders, whose real goal is to change the existing power relationship and who misinterpret a democracy's evident desire to resolve a dispute peacefully as a sign of weakness. Henry Kissinger has observed that in 1959, Prime Minister Harold MacMillan's "exploration" of "pragmatic" concessions that might resolve the Berlin crisis was seen by Khrushchev "as another confirmation of a favorable tilt in the balance of forces and the augury of even better things to come."[4] Subsequent American efforts were seen in the same light. It was only with the frustration of his final attempt to raise the ante on Berlin by placing missiles in Cuba that Khrushchev was finally forced to stop testing the West; as a result, for a decade the Soviets declined to engage further in such testing.

Coalitions Count

Perhaps no Cold War lesson can teach us more than the remarkable record of the United States in building successful coalitions. This can teach about the importance of leadership and what it consists of: demonstrating that your friends will be protected and taken care of, that your enemies will be punished and that those who refuse to support you will regret not having done so. It illustrates the difference between coalitions that are united by a common purpose and collections of countries that are searching for a least common denominator and the easiest way out of a problem. And it shows that the "enemy of my friend" does *not* have to be my enemy also: whether we are dealing with Egypt and Israel, Israel and Saudi Arabia, Greece and Turkey, Russia and Ukraine or China and Taiwan, the United States has demonstrated a remarkable "Bismarckian" capacity to work effectively with both parties to a conflict. In a world in which, for many countries concerned about their security, the U.S. will be the only game in town, this ability will be challenged to the utmost.

The Importance of Principle

There is much else to be learned from the experience of the Cold War: that it is conflicts that cause arms competitions, not "arms races" that cause conflicts; that it is far better to equip others to fight for their country than to send Americans to fight for them and that refusing to arm our friends, whether in Bosnia or Cambodia or Iraq, is a strategic as well as a moral mistake; and that force, when used, should be used decisively. "Signaling" with military force should not be done without a careful calculation of what might come next.

As important as any other lesson, however, is that in international relations as in personal ones, leaders can't always be tactical. Principles count. This is a practical as well as a moral point, because principle is a powerful force in politics and particularly in democratic politics. Any criteria for the conduct of foreign policy have to be applied to specific cases, and that requires judgments about the facts. Even at Munich, as Churchill acknowledged, the facts weren't as clear as they proved to be with hindsight. However, as Churchill wrote, there is *one helpful guide, namely, for a nation to keep its word and to act in accordance with its treaty obligations to allies.... An exaggerated code of honour leading to the performance of utterly vain and unreasonable deeds could not be defended, however fine it might look. [At Munich], however, the moment came when honour pointed the path of duty, and when also the right judgment of the facts at that time would have reinforced its dictates.*

Applying the Principles: The Case of China

While we can never base policy on a single projection of the future, we can say with moderate confidence that if China manages to continue anything like the high economic growth rates that it has sustained now for two decades, managing its emergence as a major power in East Asia and the world is likely to be the biggest challenge to maintaining a peaceful world through the first part of this century.

China may be emerging as a major power, but it has not yet become one. It would be a mistake either to exaggerate China's present strength or to underestimate its future potential. Persuading an emerging power to accept the status quo except in so far as it can be changed peacefully has always been a challenge historically, and the failure to do so with Germany and Japan in the last century had catastrophic consequences.

Almost surely, China will neither become an ideological threat like the old Soviet Union, nor try to conduct the ideological crusades and campaigns of subversion that it did in the 1950s and 1960s. Not only is the ideological fervor gone in China, but also the ideology has no appeal internationally, least of all perhaps to "overseas" Chinese. It is sometimes suggested that China might become the representative of the grievances of the developing world, but that suggestion also lacks plausibility.

Yet China does have historical grievances, much more legitimate than those voiced a century ago by Germany or Japan, concerning its treatment by the Western powers in the nineteenth century and by Japan in the twentieth. And the Chinese leadership has shown a tendency to manipulate this sense of grievance. The oft-cited fact that historically, Chinese emperors were more inclined to extract tribute from vassal states than to engage in overt conquest is not as comforting as it is sometimes said to be, since the real contest is likely to be over who exerts the most influence over maritime East Asia and by what means. Both history and the present debate in China suggest significant dissatisfaction with U.S. predominance in the Western Pacific—with the fact that the countries around the Pacific Rim are America's allies—and in the Persian Gulf. Whether China will come to see that the continuation of a peaceful status quo in the Western Pacific best serves its own interests, or instead seek to impose its will by threats and intimidation, will become an increasingly important question as China's strength grows.

Despite the challenges that China's increasing strength will pose to the United States and its allies, it would be a mistake to treat China like the Soviet Union in the Cold War, restricting trade in order deliberately to weaken it or using trade as human rights leverage. A China weakened by such policies might take longer to become a military competitor, but what we might gain in that respect would be canceled out in enmity.

The most important reason, however, for treating China differently from the old Soviet Union is that an evolution is taking place in China bearing some resemblance to the earlier development of the Asian "tigers," including Korea and Taiwan, which today stand as rebuttals to the argument that democracy is incompatible with Asian values. Unlike the Soviet Union or the China of Mao Zedong, today's China is no longer a completely closed society where the party and government dominate everything; there is a substantial private sector whose scope and sphere are growing. It is in the U.S. interest—and that of Taiwan and Hong Kong—to encourage that growth, which is dependent on trade with the West. That is the most important reason for continuing normal trade relations with China, encouraging Chinese membership in the WTO and compliance with its structure. (It is not, however, an argument for subsidizing Chinese bureaucracies or military industries with World Bank loans or export credits.)

The U.S. interest in supporting democratic trends in China is more than just "international social work." Although our capacity to influence China is limited, the U.S. has a fundamental strategic interest in encouraging greater openness there. Even though democracies are not as irenic as the extreme proponents of "democratic peace" like to argue—consider the Mexican War as just one example—in the case of China there are reasons to think that a more democratic China will also be more accepting of a peaceful status quo in the Western Pacific. Democracy in China will not automatically resolve all the points of potential competition with the U.S.—nor did it in Japan. Nevertheless, a China that governs its own people by force is more likely to try to impose its will on its neighbors, while conversely, a China that is democratic is more likely to respect the choice of its neighbors. And its neighbors, including the United States, are more likely to trust it and accept its growing influence.

There are other reasons as well why democratic change in China has strategic as well as humanitarian significance. The Chinese Communist Party formally claims the right to govern more than a billion people on the basis of Marxism-Leninism, a doctrine that has little more legitimacy in China today than the "divine right" of kings had in England in the early nineteenth century. Yet the British had already developed a substantial alternative basis for the legitimacy of government, whereas China's leaders seem afraid to do so. That leaves them only with economic growth and nationalism as claims for legitimacy. A government whose legitimacy rested on valid claims to be "representative" would have less need to make dangerous appeals to nationalism. Finally, and not insignificantly, a democratic China would have a far better chance of coming to terms with Taiwan peacefully; until then, Taiwan's own success at democracy is a disturbing example for Beijing's rulers. I have even been told by a Chinese Communist Party member that what "terrifies those old men in Beijing" is the demonstration by Taiwan that Chinese *can* manage democracy successfully.

Is Taiwan an obstacle in U.S.-China relations or might it actually be an opportunity? For the last twenty-five years, U.S.-PRC differences over Taiwan have been successfully managed within a framework that has two essential premises: 1) that the issue must be addressed peacefully, i.e., no PRC use of force; and 2) that the issue must be resolved by agreement of both parties, i.e., no unilateral declaration of independence by Taiwan. This is called the "one China" policy as a shorthand, although the policy rests on a fundamental ambiguity concerning its very name: both sides have different views of what "one China" means and the U.S. has never advanced a view of its own—although President Clinton's adoption of the PRC's "Three No's" formulation during his visit to

Shanghai in 1998 was seen as a substantial tilt toward the PRC's view. "One China" was supposed to be open to any interpretation the two sides could agree on.

Although today's circumstances are vastly different from when the Shanghai Communiqué was signed in 1972, the "one China" policy remains the best framework for handling a difficult and sensitive issue. It is a framework that preserves freedom and democracy and a prosperous market economy on Taiwan, even though it denies Taiwan the formal independence that many of its people desire. At the same time, by avoiding a direct affront to PRC sovereignty, it helps to avoid military conflict. However, it will be more difficult to sustain this framework in the post–Cold War period because of the enormous changes that have occurred on both sides of the Taiwan Strait.

The most important of these changes has been the development of a genuine democracy on Taiwan, which twenty years ago was still ruled by a brutal dictatorship, one that sent an assassin to California to murder one of its critics. The change does, however, complicate Taiwan's dealings with the mainland. The government in Taiwan must now answer to its people, the great majority of whom are native Taiwanese with no attachment to the mainland. In the post–Cold War period, when Macedonia, Kyrgyzia and East Timor have acquired independence, it has become even harder to explain why a prosperous democracy of more than twenty million people should not.

On the PRC side, fear that this pro-independence sentiment might lead to a de jure assertion of independence by Taiwan has apparently strengthened the view in some quarters that the issue of reunification must be pressed more rapidly. It may also be that Jiang Zemin, like some other world leaders, has a personal-legacy complex and believes that, following the recovery of Hong Kong and Macau, he can somehow complete reunification in his lifetime. Nor can one discount the possible influence of the kind of strategic thinking that sees Taiwan as the "crucial point in the first chain of islands," the key to realizing Admiral Liu Hua-qing's assertion that "the Chinese navy should exert effective control of the seas within the first island chain," defined as comprising the Aleutians, the Kuriles, Japan (including the Ryukyus), Taiwan, the Philippines, and most of Indonesia. As expressed in a 1995 article in a journal called *The Navy*,

If [China] wants to prosper, it has to advance into the Pacific in which lies China's future. Taiwan, facing the Pacific in the east, is the only unobstructed exit for China to move into the ocean. If this gateway is opened for China, then it becomes much easier for China to maneuver in the West Pacific.[5]

The stiffening of the PRC's approach to Taiwan is probably also a result of the end of the Cold War. China no longer needs the United States to balance a threatening neighbor and can instead contemplate the prospect of its own growing power. In addition, it appears that China's assertiveness may be encouraged by a U.S. tendency to overestimate its strategic importance, a tendency which goes back to the Cold War and the notion that China was a "trump card" to be played by the U.S. in its dealings with the Soviet Union. George Shultz, who described his own attitude as "a marked departure from the so-called China-card policy," observed at the time he became secretary of state,

When the geostrategic importance of China became the conceptual prism through which Sino-American relations were viewed, it was almost inevitable that American policymakers became overly solicitous of Chinese interests, concerns, and sensitivities.... On the basis of my own experience, I knew it would be a mistake to place too much emphasis on a relationship for its own sake. A good relationship should emerge from the ability to solve substantive problems of interest to both countries.[6]

"You owe us a debt," Deng Xiaoping said to Kissinger in one negotiating session in 1974, apparently on Mao's instructions, referring to the American use of the "China card" in its dealings with Moscow. Yet in this case, as in so many others, the Chinese managed to convince the U.S.—or to help the U.S. convince itself—that it needed the relationship more than they did, when the situation was more nearly the reverse. It is a mystery why the United States needed China's help to reach two Strategic Arms Limitation Agreements that conceded large advantages to the Soviet Union. It is much more obvious what China gained from having a relationship with a nuclear superpower during a period when the Soviet Union was threatening preventive war against China and massively building up its military forces in the Far East.

Most amazingly of all, it was the Americans who sought a hasty conclusion of the normalization negotiations in late 1978. If either side needed normalization in a hurry it was China, which was preparing to invade Vietnam, a country that had just signed a Treaty of Friendship and Cooperation with the Soviet Union. But as happened so often, before and later, the U.S. acted as though it needed the relationship more than China did. The results of that kind of negotiation are easy to predict. In this case, an opportunity to achieve clarity on the crucial issue of arms sales to Taiwan was lost. Instead, the United States agreed to a moratorium on arms sales to Taiwan during the first year after normalization, mumbling an explanation that afterwards, "the sale of selected, defensive arms ... would continue in a way that did not endanger the prospects for peace in the region," while taking "note of China's continuing opposition to arms sales."

This lack of clarity on a central issue led directly to the crisis that culminated in the 1982 Communiqué on arms sales, itself a classic of ambiguity. Once again, the American side was driven by fear that it might "lose" China—and the Reagan administration feared that it would take the blame. Reagan at least resisted the pressure to agree to a commitment to end arms sales to Taiwan. But the 1982 Communiqué rests on conflicting understandings by the two sides: President Reagan was convinced by his experts that the Chinese characters used to express their "fundamental peaceful policy" toward Taiwan represented a new commitment to a peaceful approach, and he based his willingness to reduce arms sales on that idea. The differing views of the two sides on this issue may eventually cause a serious disagreement, but we have managed to live with the ambiguity for almost twenty years. We can probably continue to do so as long as the Americans preserve their original understanding, which made it possible—albeit with difficulty—to reconcile the Communiqué with the Taiwan Relations Act.

Clarity is not always a virtue; often, ambiguity is a practical way to get an agreement that both sides can live with. The very term "one China" is ambiguous, and the United States should leave any attempts at clarification to the parties themselves. By adopting the PRC's "Three No's" when he was in Shanghai in 1998, President Clinton foreclosed some possible avenues of agreement. More dangerously, he undermined the confidence of the Taiwanese and appeared to go back on one of the six assurances given to them at the time of the 1982 Communiqué, i.e., that the U.S. would not change its position on who has sovereignty on Taiwan. Taiwanese anxiety was further heightened by the appearance that the United States was responding to PRC pressure for movement on the Taiwan issue, as reflected in Assistant Secretary of State Stanley Roth's talk about an agreement on "interim measures," or NSC China specialist Kenneth Lieberthal's proposal for a fifty-year interim agreement on reunification. Although the Clinton Administration was unhappy with Lee Teng-hui's statement that PRC-Taiwan relations should be based on a kind of "special state-to-state" relationship, it is hard to see how a democratic leader of Taiwan could have failed to assert in some way Taiwan's equal status in negotiations with Beijing, in the face of efforts to impose a subordinate status on it. In fact, looking back over the last eight years, it is remarkable how much President Lee has done to create a situation in which some 70 percent of Taiwanese polled express a preference for the status quo over de jure independence and how effectively he has competed with the pro-independence Democratic Progressive Party (DPP), forcing them to modify their own position on the issue.

Despite the laudable American instinct to try to find a solution to every problem, there are some that do not yield to American activism. The more we seem to be pressing Taiwan to negotiate with China, the more fearful Taiwan becomes and the more we encourage the PRC to keep up the pressure. The United States needs to encourage maximum patience on this issue, where the status quo is quite satisfactory and where any serious movement, if it comes at all, can only come if the PRC offers serious inducements to Taiwan, not pressure. The record suggests strongly that the PRC and Taiwan—not unlike Arabs and Israelis—deal best with one another when they are convinced that they have to do so directly, rather than by getting the U.S. to carry their water. Certainly those were the conditions that led to the surprising agreement that made them both members of the Asian Development Bank in 1985.

Although the PRC sometimes expresses the view that pressure is needed to get Taiwan to negotiate, the record suggests that it does better when Taiwan feels secure in its reliance on us. Despite warnings from the "experts" that several strong U.S.

demonstrations of support for Taiwan's security in the past—the Taiwan Relations Act of 1979, Reagan's 1982 refusal to agree to terminate arms sales, the Indigenous Defense Fighter project in 1985, the sale of F-16's in 1992—would produce a severe downturn in the PRC-Taiwan relationship, in fact each of these events was followed by a period of warming relations. What causes problems is when we send mixed signals, as with the administration's shifting position on the question of a visa for the visit of Lee Teng-hui to Cornell in 1985, which indicated to both sides that U.S. policy will change under pressure.

While ambiguity on the definition of "one China" is desirable and ambiguity on the subject of arms sales is probably necessary, there are two areas where greater clarity is needed. These involve questions about U.S. intentions, rather than disagreements among the parties. The first concerns the U.S. attitude toward the use of force to resolve the Taiwan issue, the second our attitude toward Taiwanese independence. There seem to have been far too many occasions in the past when U.S. officials have failed to take exception to Chinese statements that the Taiwan question must ultimately be settled by force, or the milder one that Taiwan will only negotiate under military pressure. Ambiguity on this point is sometimes alleged to be desirable, so that China will think that we would resist the use of force even if Taiwan declared independence, while Taiwan would fear that we might not, thereby discouraging independence sentiment. But we seem to be achieving more nearly the opposite. A senior Clinton defense official reportedly told the Chinese that our response to their use of force against Taiwan would "depend on the circumstances," while at the same time some in Taiwan may believe that they would have the sympathy of the Congress no matter what they did. Both sides are under potentially misleading impressions. It is time for some clarity on these two points.

Any use of force by China would be dangerous and counterproductive. It is good to see that Deputy Assistant Secretary of State Susan Shirk, at least, has said "the use of force would be catastrophic for China as well as for Taiwan, and of course disastrous for U.S.-China relations.... So even in such an eventuality [Taiwan independence] we would urge China not to use force." In fact, it would be a strategic as well as a moral mistake for the United States to let China have its way with Taiwan by force. No matter how much other countries in the region might criticize Taiwan for having contributed to the crisis, and no matter how much they might try to distance themselves from helping us, they would also view it as a test of America's strategic will. We might prefer our tests to come in places that are politically less ambiguous, like Korea, or geographically closer, like Cuba. But we do not get to choose where we will be tested. Berlin was not favorable ground, but if the West had failed, that would not have mitigated the consequences. In any case, there is no way the United States could reliably assure China that we would stand aside from an attack on Taiwan under any circumstances, and it is a great mistake to encourage them to test whether we would.

At the same time, while making it clear to Taiwan that the U.S. will not abandon them or force them to negotiate under pressure, we should also make it clear that we expect reasonable behavior in return, including no unilateral declaration of independence. There are many ways to oppose such a move should it happen, but condoning a Chinese use of force should not be one of them. This may be a hard position to defend in American political discourse, but it is nonetheless necessary. And it is a more viable strategy than playing on Taiwan's insecurity to try to get it to be reasonable.

There are those who wish that the Chinese civil war had ended with a more complete Communist victory, so that we wouldn't have to deal with the Taiwan "obstacle." One of my predecessors as assistant secretary of state for the Far East is reported once to have wished in jest that a tidal wave might literally wash the problem away. But this view is as unrealistic as it is morally blind. Consider, by comparison, that after World War II, Eisenhower and many others in the West saw Berlin as an anomaly left over from the way the war ended, an obstacle in East-West relations that was best gotten out of the way. Years of restless attempts to find a solution to the problem of Berlin produced crisis after crisis. It was only after it was finally made clear that Berlin was non-negotiable that it ceased to be a constant bone of contention. Similarly, we will only have peace in Asia when the promising democracy of Taiwan is accepted as a fact of life. Then, perhaps, it can finally be seen as an opportunity more than a problem. Then, too, the friends of Taiwan should be able to see why it is genuinely better for Taiwan to be a part of China—a part that points the way to the kind of government that the great Chinese people deserve.

Avoiding a Major (Hot or Cold) War

Our discussion of China illustrates the most fundamental national security issue that we face: what policies should we follow now to minimize the likelihood that we will be forced to engage in another major (hot or cold) war in the future and, if such a conflict cannot be averted, to best position ourselves to wage it. The threat is probably remote; but if we heed the lessons of the past century concerning how rapidly the international situation can change, we should recognize that it isn't nonexistent.

In general, a threat of this magnitude will require both a major power that seeks to upset the international status quo, and troubled waters in which it can fish. Hence our policies should aim at reducing the likelihood that these prerequisites will exist. Ideally, the spectrum of such policies would include the following:

First: Strengthen the liberal democratic–free market consensus, including the global free-trade regime, with the goal of making the status quo attractive to all comers (to the extent possible). This involves building on the successes of the past decades, which have been so dramatic. These successes—as well as the collapse of communism—have destroyed the credibility of the pre-1980s "formula" for progress, which centered on statism, protectionist economic doctrines and a willingness to sacrifice democracy and human rights on the altar of "efficiency."

Second: Maintain and strengthen the alliance structure of the liberal democratic states, including NATO and the bilateral alliances the U.S. has in other parts of the world. Demonstrating that problems are better solved within that alliance structure than independently reduces any incentive that its members might have to pursue policies that could bring them into conflict with each other. Strengthening the international norms in favor of democracy and human rights would demonstrate that this alliance structure rests not only on the practical necessities of power relationships but, more fundamentally, on a shared moral vision of human life in the twenty-first century.

Third: Deal effectively with rogue states and minor disturbers of the international order. This not only protects the rest of the world from their depredations, but deprives a future great-power challenger of potential allies. A country determined to mount a major attack on the status quo would find in a country like Iraq a willing ally and a source of leverage against the U.S. and its allies. The Clinton administration's tendency to temporize rather than go for the jugular, although understandable in many circumstances, has had the effect of piling up future problems.

Fourth: Maintain the U.S. leadership role, including its military pre-eminence. This is a necessary underpinning of the global democratic consensus: while we should strive for allied cooperation and participation in shouldering the burdens, we must remember that somebody has to raise the flag if others are to rally around it, as the Gulf War coalition rallied around President Bush's determination to undo the Iraqi conquest of Kuwait. Maintaining U.S. military pre-eminence may seem like an easy task, given the relative size of the U.S. defense budget compared with those of other nations. Nevertheless, the burdens placed on the U.S. armed forces are also significantly larger than those placed on the armed forces of any other nation. We must both support the military's capabilities in meeting current responsiblities *and* ensure that the U.S. continues to lead with respect to new weapon systems based on rapidly evolving technologies. We cannot expect to do this on the cheap.

The Necessity for Statesmanship

We have examined a set of general principles that the United States should follow to secure our future well-being; these principles are both practical and moral in nature. Unfortunately, general principles, while important, cannot be applied in a rigid or automatic way; specific circumstances and dangers are always forcing policy makers to weigh competing interests and objectives.

Once we understand this, we must descend from the realm of general principles to the making of specific decisions. It is at this point that we encounter the necessity for statesmanship, whose core is melding the necessities of the moment with our strategic objectives and moral ideals. Thus, foreign policy decisions cannot be subject to the kind of "rule of law" that we want for our domestic political process. The downside is that this can cause difficulties in securing public understanding; it often seems too much like "trimming" or insincerity.

Observers of democracy from Tocqueville onward have identified the short-term perspective of the public as an obstacle to statesmanship; many policies may take time to bear fruit, and public willingness to pursue a line of policy in a steadfast manner may be lacking. This traditional criticism was to some extent answered in the course of the Cold War, when the democracies were able, although with considerable controversy, to maintain a generally consistent line of policy until it finally succeeded in a manner that was foreseen in general terms, but which nonetheless came as a surprise at the time. This success was based, it is true, on the existence of a clear threat; duplicating it in support of securing ourselves against the unclear possibility of a future threat will be perhaps more difficult.

Thus, while the core of American foreign policy is in some sense the universalization of American principles, this is not a Kantian notion in which ultimately only the purity of one's intentions counts. Rather, policies must be effective in the world. The chief prosecutor of the international war crimes tribunal for Yugoslavia could say of Slobodan Milosevic in connection with that body's indictment of him, "I don't know what he will do, I know what he must do." But no U.S. president can justify a policy that fails to achieve its intended results by pointing to the purity and rectitude of his intentions.

Statesmanship requires, therefore, not only a moral vision, but a willingness and ability to take a hard-headed and clear-eyed view of the world. The presence of the former cannot compensate for the absence of the latter. For example, President Clinton's devotion to the principles of ethnic diversity and tolerance, which underlay his Kosovo policy, has to be balanced by a more accurate understanding of the difficulties involved in achieving it. The difficulties in which the NATO forces find themselves in Kosovo in early 2000 are a reminder that a deeper understanding of the issue and of the underlying realities of the situation is necessary.

This is not to argue that statesmanship is not difficult to achieve in any case, or that there are not, in our current situation, additional obstacles. The widely-recognized "CNN effect," the fact that foreign policy decisions must now be made in the glare of intensive and instantaneous publicity, certainly makes statesmanship harder.

Nevertheless, statesmanship must seek to overcome these obstacles and refuse to give in to self-pity. And these obstacles *can* be overcome, or at least mitigated. At an unusually favorable time in

terms of our national security situation, Clinton campaigned successfully for the office of president on the slogan "It's the economy,
stupid." Not too surprisingly, his administration has not really
addressed the issue of statesmanship. The next administration will
have to.

Strength and Will:
A Historical Perspective

T he dominant view of American foreign and security policy
today rests on the assumption that the United States faces no
serious threat at present and will face none in the foreseeable
future. The Soviet Union has collapsed, and there is no equivalent
to a Nazi Germany or an imperial Japan on the horizon. Because
there is no "peer competitor," the U.S. can enjoy the benefits of the
"peace dividend," sharply reducing its defense spending, which
will result in a windfall for domestic programs, tax cuts, deficit
reduction and other delightful benefits. Even after enormous cuts
in the defense budget, the argument is made, the U.S. still spends
more on military power than all the other nations combined, is
ahead of the others in military technology and is bound to remain
ahead for a long time.

To be sure, the advocates of this view concede, there are some
unpleasant people out there—the North Koreans, Saddam Hussein, the Communist Chinese—but they can be tamed by patience,
restraint, and the magic of trade and participation in the global
economy; and in any case, none of them represents a serious military challenge to America. Defense experts wedded to this view
speak of a "strategic pause" which permits the U.S. to cut its forces
sharply now and spend its money better by preparing for the world
of the future. Meanwhile, they say, there is no great danger in our
reduced force structure.

This is a natural perspective for a nation like our own, a liberal,
democratic, commercial republic, satisfied with the state of the
world, and defended by two great oceans, as well as our relative

military superiority. We are reluctant to maintain strong military forces, especially ground forces. We prefer to believe in and rely upon the wonders of technology, the prospect of some technological "magic bullet" that will make considerable conventional forces, and the expense and casualties they may entail, unnecessary. Confronted with the responsibility to preserve the peace in our own and the world's interest, we put our faith in international organizations, in the "end of history" brought by the "inevitable" spread of democracy and the inescapably irenic consequences of a global economy and the communications revolution.

These are like the delusions of states throughout history that have reached a secure position and have decided to take a rest. They glory in their temporary superiority and imagine it will become permanent with little or no effort on their part. But, as one historian points out, "wealth and power, or economic strength and military strength, are always relative; ... the international balances can *never* be still, and it is a folly of statesmanship to assume that they ever could be."[1]

In fact, there is no "strategic pause." In international relations and military affairs, change can come with lightning speed. In 1930 no power seemed willing or able to disrupt the peace. Germany was effectively disarmed and Japan seemed to pose no threat. But then, in 1931, Japan conquered Manchuria and defied the League of Nations and the world to do anything about it. Two years later, Hitler came to power, tore up the Versailles Treaty and began rapid rearmament. In 1935 Italy attacked Ethiopia; in 1936 Hitler resurrected German power by occupying the Rhineland. Only a few years after the "strategic pause" that provided a rationale for Britain's defense policy in the 1920s and early 1930s, the world had become a very dangerous place, which Britain's armed forces were no longer in any condition to manage. When the "strategic pause" turned out to be an illusion, the British faced increasingly serious dangers to their interests and security. Soon their allies had been conquered, their homeland was under attack, and they stood alone on the verge of defeat and conquest.

Our current "strategic pause" is so beguiling that we forget that dissatisfied states around the world are working hard to increase their military power and to nullify American advantages. We forget too that the appearance of a "peer competitor" is not a prerequisite for war. North Korea was nothing like one in the 1950s,

North Vietnam was not in the 1960s and 1970s, nor was Iraq in 1990; yet each of these states, with only regional ambitions, nevertheless involved America in a costly war. In terms of global powers neither Germany nor Japan, not to speak of Italy, was a "peer competitor" to the British Empire or to the United States, yet together they brought about the most terrible war in history and came close to winning it.

Winston Churchill rightly called the Second World War "the unnecessary war." It was only one among many that could have been prevented by responsible behavior on the part of those nations with the greatest reasons to preserve peace and the means to do so. Deterring such wars requires the will to create and maintain a sufficient military force and the will to use that force when necessary. The behavior of great powers, even in small crises, gives important signals that are carefully read by dissatisfied and hostile states. When they read strength and a strong will, they tend to retreat and subside. When they read weakness and timidity, they take risks. Understanding of and generosity toward the desires of dissatisfied nations, great and small, can be sound policy in a context of strength and demonstrated courage and commitment. But when such gestures are seen as evidence of weakness and fear, the results may be terrible for both sides.

The chief problems facing American foreign policy today, as they have since the end of the Cold War, are how to maintain and strengthen a situation in the world that is unusually conducive to peace and to the goals and values of the United States, its allies and friends. This condition is not the result of historical happenstance; it was achieved mostly by a readiness on the part of the West to acquire and sustain predominant military force and the demonstrated willingness and capacity to use it when necessary. The collapse of the Soviet Union removed the main reason for an unprecedented commitment and sacrifice in peacetime on which the preservation of peace rested. Since then the U.S. has sharply reduced its military power, and its reactions to world events have raised serious questions about its readiness to continue in the role of chief keeper of the peace.

Because of its extraordinary economic and military strength and the breadth of its influence, the U.S. may be uniquely placed in modern history to enjoy such an opportunity, but its relative position is not dissimilar to that of Great Britain in the nineteenth and the first half of the twentieth century. Both states had the advantage of separation by water from the great Eurasian land mass and all its troubles. Before the era of strategic air warfare, and later of missiles, both states enjoyed an unmatched sense of security from attack and invasion, and from the burden of maintaining a large standing army, so long as they were protected by an adequate navy. Their geographic circumstances also encouraged a sense that political and military isolation from the turmoil of the rest of the world was desirable and possible. "Normal" conditions were those without alliances with foreign nations and the commitments they imposed.

Both states, however, were highly commercial, depended on trade and were eager to expand their commerce with the rest of the world. Inevitably, this brought them into contact, sometimes into conflict, with each other and with the nations of Europe and Asia. On such occasions they were often compelled to abandon their isolation, make military alliances, increase naval and military expenditures and accept the burdens imposed by war. When the threat passed, Great Britain then and the United States today did not decide that their "normal" policy was inadequate to preserve the peace, their interests and their security, but rather, they regarded the recent war as an aberration; so they sharply reduced their defense expenditures, especially for ground forces, abandoned alliances and returned to their preferred policy.

Throughout the eighteenth and nineteenth centuries the U.S. was protected from European conflicts by the size of the Atlantic Ocean but also by the British fleet, which did not wish its European competitors to gain a foothold in the Western Hemisphere. The Americans, therefore, did not need to face the consequences of their policies until a mighty threat challenged British power in the twentieth century. The British, however, discovered the dangers of their traditional approach as early as 1702.

ooooo

In the latter part of the seventeenth century the rise of French power and ambition under Louis XIV threatened to overthrow the European balance of power on which Britain's interests and safety rested. In 1689, King Louis gave financial and military support to James II, the English king just driven from power, with the intention of restoring him to the throne and imposing the Catholic faith on the English. Louis's policy of persecuting Protestants also threatened the religious allegiance of the British people and aroused their fear that French domination of the continent would threaten not only their security but also their deepest values. In 1692 Louis prepared for an invasion of the British Isles, which a naval defeat in the Channel prevented.

The English joined a great European coalition against France, spending great sums of money and sending a considerable army to the continent. In 1697 they compelled Louis to make peace, to recognize the protestant William III as king of England and to restore almost all the territory he had gained by force. Neither peace, however, nor safety was assured. France had not been defeated, only worn down. The power of Louis and his great wealth were intact, checked only by the vigilance, unity and commitment of his opponents. Safety depended on British persistence and determination. At the conclusion of peace, England had 87,000 soldiers. King William calculated that a peacetime army of 30,000 would be needed for security. Wrote Winston Churchill, "To deal with Louis XIV as an equal—the only key to safety—it was imperative that he be strong." The parliament voted funds for the ridiculously low number of seven thousand men. Writing in 1933, during a similar period of irresponsibility and folly, Churchill described their thinking as follows:

> The wars were over; their repressions were at an end. They rejoiced in peace and clamoured for freedom. The dangers were past; why should they ever return? Groaning under taxation, impatient of every restraint, the Commons plunged into a career of economy, disarmament, and constitutional assertiveness which was speedily followed by the greatest of the wars England had ever waged and the heaviest expenditures she had ever borne.

From the perspective of two centuries' time and armed with bitter experience he made a general observation:

> This phase has often recurred in our history. In fact, it has been an invariable rule that England, so steadfast in war, so indominable in peril, should at the moment when the dire pressures are relaxed and victory has been won cast away its fruits. Having made every sacrifice, having performed prodigies of strength

and valour, our countrymen under every franchise or party have
always fallen upon the ground in weakness and futility when
a very little more perseverance would have made them supreme,
or at least secure.[2]

In 1700 the king of Spain died, confronting Louis with the decision whether to honor the treaty that would have divided the Spanish empire's possessions among the powers or accept the
opportunity to put his nephew on the throne, bring Spain's wealth
and power under French influence and guarantee the great war
that must involve England. Among the several considerations that
influenced his decision, the reckless and short-sighted irresponsibility of the English Parliament must have been weighty. England
had clearly demonstrated its military power in the previous war,
and the prospect of its involvement again ought to have served as
a powerful deterrent to Louis's ambitions. The action of Parliament, however, raised the most serious question about England's
will to do what was necessary and encouraged him to take the risk.
Louis supported the testament and his nephew's ascension to the
Spanish throne; England entered the war, which lasted until 1713,
costing unprecedented sums of money and a great number of
casualties.

Britain survived that war and one no less great against a France
led by Napoleon. Victory in 1815 permitted Britain to avoid continental warfare almost entirely for a century during which time
it grew to be the richest nation with the greatest empire in the
world. Britain's military reputation acquired in war and its mighty
navy permitted the luxury of reducing its army to what amounted
to an imperial constabulary. The situation changed with the emergence of a new German empire that emerged as Europe's leading
power after the Franco-Prussian War and as a threat to Britain at
the turn of the twentieth century.

Germany's Kaiser Wilhelm II was determined to raise his new
and powerful nation to a rank at least equal to the world's leading
power, Great Britain. In addition, Germany's goals came to include
the domination—economic, political and military—of Europe from
the English Channel to the Russian frontier, with further penetration planned deep into the Middle East. For that purpose he
undertook a program to build a great battleship navy, "a sharp
knife, held gleaming and ready only inches away from the jugular

vein of Germany's most likely enemy,"[3] whose obvious target was Britain's Royal Navy. At the very least, his goal was to make Britain stand aside while he pursued a "World Policy" of colonial expansion and a continental one of achieving a *Mitteleuropa* under German control. There is some evidence to suggest that for the navy he had an even more ambitious goal of surpassing the British fleet in both size and quality so as to be able to defeat it at sea, which would leave the British Isles open to conquest. Even if the lesser goal alone were achieved, Germany's control of the continent could do terrible harm to Britain's economy and so strengthen Germany as to enable it to build the great conquering fleet later on.

At the turn of the century, before such grand aims became apparent, the British failed to come to an amicable agreement with the Germans. They became so alarmed that they launched an expensive and unwelcome naval race to maintain their superiority at sea and abandoned their cherished stance of "splendid isolation" and long-standing peaceful competition with their colonial rivals France and Russia. In an unprecedented reversal of policy in only five years, they made an alliance with Japan and agreements with France and Russia to form the "Triple Entente," which grew from a set of colonial accords to an informal but visible check on German ambitions.

The naval race preserved Britain's advantage at sea, which saved the British from defeat and invasion when the war broke out in 1914. Even so, Britain refused to take the even more unwelcome and also costly steps that alone could deter the Germans from using their military power to defeat France and Russia on land and gain control of the continent. The British refused to enter into binding military alliances with France and Russia or to acquire a large army with reliable and numerous reserves, requiring the introduction of compulsory military service, unprecedented in peacetime. The Germans caused and took advantage of crises with the aim of breaking the Triple Entente their policy had created. On each occasion Lord Grey, Britain's foreign secretary, stood with his country's new friends to resist German threats. He even instructed his military leaders to engage in secret conversations with their French counterparts to prepare against a German attack. But he firmly resisted all proposals for a true military alliance, urging restraint on his friends no less than on his enemies. He and other British leaders spoke fondly of maintaining a policy of "the free hand," one that committed Britain to no one. The British wanted to protect their friends without provoking the Germans, but the deliberate ambiguity of their policy was a delusion. Increasingly it became obvious that the danger to British interests and security could come only from the Germans and that efforts to dissuade them from their goals through negotiation and diplomacy were vain.

Deterrence was the only hope of avoiding a conflict, but the British refused to pay the price: forging military alliances backed by the kind of formidable army that could render German military plans hopeless.

For a decade before the war, the only German strategy was to launch an attack in the west through Belgium into France to win a quick victory before Russia could be fully ready to fight. Germany and its only remaining major ally, Austria-Hungary, were weaker than their potential opponents in numbers and resources, and knew they would lose a long war. Their only chance was to defeat France quickly and then Russia. They hoped that Britain would hold to its favored policy of avoiding sending an army to fight on the continent, permitting Germany to gain control of Europe and then confront the British from a position of unprecedented strength. They expected a British expeditionary force of 100,000 men, which they thought would probably land at Antwerp, where, according to General Schlieffen, "They will be shut up ... together with the Belgians."[4] So the Germans thought it safe to ignore Britain's army. Without alliances backed by a large and ready army, successful deterrence was unlikely.

As international tensions between the Central Powers, Germany and Austria, and the Entente grew, the Germans' alarm grew with it. On the one hand, they recognized their reliance on their only powerful ally and were determined to protect Austria's interests in the Balkans, even if it meant a clash with Russia. On the other, they recognized the enormous potential power of the Entente and were terrified by the prospect of a future war against an increasingly powerful Russia supported by France and Britain. When the Austrians decided to attack Serbia in 1914, which almost certainly meant war against Russia and France, the Germans urged their allies forward. What made their action "a leap in the dark" was the possibility of British intervention. What made them take the chance was the hope that Britain would stand aloof.

How could the Germans have clung to such a hope in light of Britain's treaty commitment to defend Belgian neutrality that went back to 1839; its association with France and Russia; its obvious naval cooperation and suspected military conversations with the French; and statements made by British statesmen at various times that their country would fight if the Germans attacked France? The answer was that Britain's commitment and national will remained in doubt. Lord Grey, still less the British Cabinet, never fully accepted the implications of their own policy. Having abandoned "splendid isolation," they clung, nevertheless, to the notion of the "free hand." To the end, they firmly denied that they had a binding obligation to France and saw themselves as free to act or not. Almost to the last, Grey refused to abandon the hope that he could work with Germany to defuse whatever crisis might arise, to the great alarm of his French and Russian associates. Up to the last pre-war days, Grey was discussing with the Germans what it would take to keep Britain neutral. The majority of the cabinet regarded it as possible not to come to the aid of the French; and some thought that Britain need not go to war if Belgium was invaded. Even after they accepted the idea that war was inevitable, many thought Britain should not send an army to the continent. Not only could Britain's friends and enemies not be sure what the British would do until the last minute, the British themselves did not know.

But amidst all this confusion and ambiguity, the greatest evidence for Britain's lack of will was its failure to raise an army to check the German danger. Grey's belief that he could "pursue a European policy without keeping up a great army" was, as one scholar has put it, "the greatest of all British illusions."[5] It is not surprising that the Germans were willing to take the great risk that brought on the war.

Yet the consequences of vacillation and unpreparedness were not the lessons the British learned from the First World War. Scarred by the terrible number of casualties and weakened by the enormous economic costs of the war, their political and intellectual leaders convinced themselves that the disaster was the result of too much, not too little, involvement in international affairs, and too great a reliance on traditional ways of preserving the national interest. They blamed armaments and arms races, alliance systems, the willingness to send an army to the continent, and the reliance on political and military power generally.

In August 1919, the victorious government of Great Britain adopted the policy that the armed services were to make their plans for the future on the assumption that there would be no major war or need for any expeditionary force for ten years.[6] The ten-year rule, originally intended to apply only to the next year's estimates, became the guideline for defense estimates for 1921 and remained in force until finally abandoned with the rise of Hitler in 1932.[7] Less important than the rigid view of international relations for a decade was the cast of mind that underlay the ten-year rule. The British government and its military advisers simply chose not to consider the real possibility of a war in the future. The British cut defense spending by more than half for 1920 and by more than half again over the next two years. In 1922 the Geddes Committee, formed to recommend sharp cuts in all government expenditures, urged that a sum of money be made available for defense, "leaving the services to work things out as best they could."[8] The forces to defend the empire and the nation would, therefore, be determined not by what the international situation actually required but by what money the government chose to make available. In the 1920s all parties took the same approach. "Arms were discussed solely in terms of what they cost, not of what they were needed for."[9] The final figure was less than a quarter of the sum for 1919, where it stayed over the next decade, by which time the Japanese had conquered Manchuria, Mussolini was ready to attack Ethiopia, and Hitler's Germany was launched on a program of rapid rearmament, only a year away from demilitarizing the Rhineland.

The British acted as they did even though victory and the mandate system had vastly increased their responsibilities all over the globe. In July 1920 a General Staff assessment of the "Military Liabilities of the Empire" reported that "our liabilities are so vast, and at the same time so indeterminate, that to assess them must be largely a matter of conjecture."[10] In October 1922 Prime Minister Bonar Law declared that "We cannot act alone as the policeman of the world ... the financial and social condition of the country makes that impossible."[11]

Britain's political parties, Conservatives, Liberals and Labour, looked to economic prosperity as the chief national goal and also as the solution to the problem of war. They believed that the restoration of economic well-being would mollify resentments and bring peace. This pointed to assistance for the German economy, to recognizing German economic predominance in *Mitteleuropa,* to providing credit to help Germany obtain raw materials, and to bringing it back into the international trading system. They hoped for a new international economic situation that would bring prosperity to Britain and also could bring an end to war.

They also put great faith in the establishment of a new world of international agreements and organizations, disarmament and goodwill. They meant to behave as generous winners, seeking to preserve the peace not through the old means of military superiority and balance of power diplomacy but through understanding and efforts to ease the discontents of dissatisfied nations by appeasing their irritations. In 1921 even so tough a warrior as Winston Churchill said, "The aim is to get an appeasement of the fearful hatreds and antagonisms which exist in Europe and to enable the world to settle down. I have no other object in view."[12]

If it had been backed by the military superiority Britain and France enjoyed in 1919, and by acceptance of a unique responsibility to preserve the peace and the newly established international order, such a plan might have been effective. But there was no such commitment. Almost at once, the British began their stunningly rapid disarmament, a decision that radically altered the international situation. It sharply curtailed the range of choices truly available to Britain in the next two decades and opened new opportunities to those who wished to overthrow the international order. The British might later contemplate strong responses to the challenges they faced, but the most effective possibilities provided by deterrence or pre-emptive military action were not available.

This is not to say that disarmament seemed an unreasonable course in 1919. The German, Austrian, and Russian empires were gone. France and the U.S. were British allies, and a war against either of these powers was inconceivable. Italy was an ally and, in any case, no realistic threat. In the Far East, Japan too was an ally. Winston Churchill, as chancellor of the Exchequer in the 1920's, replied to the navy's fears of Japan, "Why should there be a war with Japan? I do not believe there is the slightest chance of it in our lifetime."

But the German Weimar Republic, disarmed and democratic as it was, deeply resented the peace imposed on it at Versailles and engaged in secret and illegal rearmament to undo its terms. Its population and industrial strength were far greater than those of

France, and the disparity was growing. As it rid itself of the burden of war reparations and disarmament limitations, and as its economy grew with the aid of expanded trade supported by American loans, it would surely seek to recover lost territories and restore its dominant position on the continent, even without the demonic leadership of Adolf Hitler. To avoid another calamity, Britain would need firmly to support French security, on which its own depended, and that of Poland, Czechoslovakia, and Austria. But when the French sought a firm military alliance, the British refused even to hold military conversations lest such talks appear to provoke German resentment.

Another small problem emerged on the other side of the globe. Since 1902 Japan had been Britain's ally, but in 1922, pressed by the United States, the British let the alliance lapse. The Japanese were angered and insulted by the British decision. From then on, the British had no choice but to regard Japan as a potential enemy that represented a threat to its interests in Asia and the Pacific. The Japanese were emerging as a powerful industrial and military power, a "restless and aggressive power, full of energy, and somewhat like the Germans in mentality," as Britain's foreign minister Lord Curzon put it in 1921.[13]

The lapse of the Japanese alliance increased the need for a strong navy, but the letter of the Washington naval agreements of 1921 and, even more, the spirit of disarmament that underlay them, led the British to reduce their naval power. Plans for a large Far Eastern Fleet were abandoned, and the fleet in general shrank, and with it the industrial and skilled labor base needed for future rearmament. Each year the existing ships grew more obsolete. Even the base at Singapore, on whose construction any chance of British influence in East Asia rested, suffered from neglect and delay. The absence of forces and a base adequate to protect British interests in the Far East would have important consequences. Not only would it bring the swift collapse of the British Empire in that region when war came, but the knowledge of their weakness and the fear of unchecked Japanese power would, at crucial moments, paralyze Britain's capacity to react to dangers closer to home.

For any who wished to see, however, there was ample evidence of the danger Japan posed to the status quo in East Asia and to the considerable British interests there. In 1894–95 it fought a war against China which, against general expectations, it won, gaining control of Taiwan, influence in Korea, a foothold in Manchuria, and the same kind of privileges in the exploitation of China as the Western powers. The Japanese victory in the war with Russia in 1904–5 came as a shock to the Western world, and brought Japan confidence, respect and recognition. In 1910 the Japanese annexed Korea and the Russians formally recognized a Japanese sphere of influence in Manchuria.

The First World War permitted Japan to seize German holdings on the Chinese coast and the Marshall, Marianas, Palua and Caroline islands in the Pacific, and the Paris Peace Conference allowed the Japanese to keep them as mandates under the League of Nations. The Washington Naval Conference, where an objective observer might say the Japanese did very well, only inflamed Japanese nationalists. They regarded its terms as a betrayal and those who agreed to Japanese naval inferiority as traitors. Behind the external correctness and relative liberalism of the Japanese regime in the 1920s lurked a dangerous, aggressive nationalism that was deeply anti-Western.

Disregarding advice from the military, British leaders denied that there was any problem with Japan. At the Imperial Conference of 1923 the foreign secretary, Lord Curzon, said, "I do not think that, although the Japanese Alliance has terminated, there is any weakening in the ties that unite us." To be sure, there was nothing to stop Japanese expansion into China, but he believed that the Japanese were no longer interested in an aggressive policy. Lord Salisbury reported that "there is not a cloud, so far as I know between us and Japan, not a cloud in sight."[14] Early in 1925 the new foreign secretary, Austen Chamberlain, expressed much the same view. He acknowledged that Japan was "an uneasy and rather restless power whose action is not easy to predicate" but thought that war in the Far East was very remote, requiring unlikely international developments of which there was no sign.

The Committee of Imperial Defense made the decision that there was no danger of such a war for ten years. As late as 1931 a Foreign Office minute on an alarming report from the British ambassador in Tokyo took an optimistic view: "I see every prospect of Japan evolving some kind of a party government such as ours. There is no doubt whatever that the naval and military authorities are rapidly losing the enormous influence they had formerly in internal politics, while the Cabinet are more and more taking over control of higher policy." That piece of wishful seeing was written just three weeks before the Kwantung army, in defiance of the Japanese Cabinet, launched the Manchurian campaign.

Unable or unwilling to face the real challenge to their position in the Far East and its place in their overall strategic situation, British leaders simply refused to confront the truth. To do so would mean a turn away from the comfortable and optimistic assumption that all would be well. It would require expenditures for rearmament that might otherwise be used for social programs or tax cuts, and it would demand a policy of confrontation that might lead to fighting. For any such policy the British lacked the will.

ooooo

The threats posed by a resurgent Germany, an ambitious Japan and an ambitious, if not very strong, Italy under its bumptious dictator Benito Mussolini, could be seen as remote and even fanciful in the 1920s, when the memory of British will and military power had not yet faded, when relatively liberal regimes still ruled in Germany and Japan and when a general economic prosperity softened resentments and discontents. The unanticipated Great Depression that ended the decade also put an end to the calm.

In 1933 Adolf Hitler and his Nazi party came to power in Germany, withdrew from disarmament negotiations and the League of Nations, made clear his intentions to destroy what remained of the Versailles Treaty as a start to restoring and expanding German power, and undertook a major rearmament program to achieve his ends. Even as unprepared as they were, the British, not to mention the French, easily had the military power to insist on preserving the conditions on which their security rested. But they had long since lost the will to use it. Hitler's great talent was to understand and take advantage of that fact. Until the outbreak of the war in 1939 he repeatedly dared the victorious powers to stop his violations of the treaty and his attacks on international order and the balance of power, secure in the knowledge that they lacked the will to resist.

Soon, even Mussolini, tin pot dictator of a second-class power, felt safe in making such a challenge. In 1935 he launched a war against Ethiopia that was condemned by the League of Nations as a clear act of aggression and a violation of the Charter deserving of economic and military sanctions. Hitler expected Britain to stop

Mussolini. When the Italians asked him for a loan of ships for their expedition, he told the minister carrying the message,

> *Let the Italians have a hundred ships! We'll go back, undamaged. They will go through the Suez Canal, but they will never go further. The British navy's battleship* Repulse *will be waiting there and signaling: "Which way are you going?" "South," the Italians will reply. "Oh no you're not," the* Repulse *will reply. "You're going north!" and north they will go.*

To his personal adjutant he said,

> *If I had a choice between the Italians and the English, then I would take the English. Mussolini is closer to me, but I know the English from the last war. I know they are hard fellows. If Mussolini thinks he can chase away the English fleet from the Mediterranean with his own, he is very much mistaken.*[15]

But the English stood aside, and Mussolini took Ethiopia. Foreign Minister Anthony Eden defended his government's policy in the House of Commons by saying, "you cannot close the Suez Canal with paper boats."[16] But Hitler and Mussolini knew that the British ships were of steel and fully capable of stopping the Italian fleet. Britain's Admiral Cunningham said, "Had we stopped the passage of Italian transports through the Suez Canal, and the import of fuel oil into Italy, the whole subsequent history of the world might have been altered."[17] But British leaders in 1935 lacked the will to use their overwhelmingly superior navy, even against so negligible an opponent as Italy.

The lesson was not lost on Hitler. On March 7, 1936, in the middle of Britain's crisis of will, the Germans marched into the demilitarized Rhineland, violating the Versailles Treaty, which they had been compelled to sign, and the Locarno Pact to which they had agreed voluntarily. This move provided Hitler with a key part of the economic and industrial muscle needed to prepare and to wage a war in the West, and also freed the Germans to build fortifications on their western front that could be held with relatively few troops. French and British inaction, moreover, encouraged Belgium to move to neutrality, which left a critical gap at the end of the Maginot Line, further increasing France's defensive mentality and putting even the defensive strategy in greater doubt. It helped persuade Mussolini to conclude the "Rome-Berlin Axis" that further complicated France's strategic problems. It also entailed withdrawal of Italian protection from Austria, a prerequisite for Hitler's annexation. After March 1936, "there could be no doubt that, with the disappearance of the demilitarized Rhineland, Europe had lost her last guarantee against German aggression."[18] Having permitted the coup, the French could not prevent the fortification of the Rhineland nor defend their allies in Central Europe.

British leaders were aware of the Rhineland's significance but were unwilling either to use or even to threaten to use force to prevent Hitler's action. One Foreign Office official found in the diplomats "a feeling of profound relief . . . that there could be no question of endorsing any foreign policy at all since arms were palpably lacking."[19] The lack of will was not limited to civilian leaders. Disarmament and the failure to resist Japanese aggression in Manchuria in 1931 and Italian aggression in Ethiopia in 1935 had infected Britain's military leadership with the same fearfulness and hesitation. Only months before Hitler's coup the Committee on Defense Requirements had begged the ministers to "avoid the simultaneous and 'suicidal' hostility of Japan, Germany and any power on the main line of communication between the two." Military leaders had worried that a conflict with Italy over Ethiopia might bring on an attack by Japan. Now they feared that a clash with Hitler might cause Mussolini to attack Egypt and also bring about an attack on Britain's Asian interests north of Singapore, which were "at the mercy of the Japanese."[20]

These fears were unjustified. French and British power were more than adequate to drive Hitler out of the Rhineland and reassert their position of leadership. German rearmament had barely begun, and "Germany had literally no forces available for war. . . . Hitler assured his protesting generals that he would withdraw his token force at the first sight of French action: but he was unshakably confident."[21] Hitler himself later said that "A retreat on our part would have spelled collapse. . . . The forty-eight hours after the march into the Rhineland were the most nerve-wracking in my life. If the French had then marched into the Rhineland we would have had to withdraw with our tails between our legs, for the military resources at our disposal would have been wholly inadequate for even a moderate resistance."[22] But the German dictator had something more valuable than a strong army: a knowledge that his opponents lacked the will to fight.

This knowledge enabled Hitler to press forward swiftly with his plans for conquest. In 1938 he occupied Austria, violating another clause in the Versailles Treaty and enabling him to surround Czechoslovakia, his next victim, on three sides. Britain's permanent undersecretary at the Foreign Office blamed his predecessor for making a great fuss about Austria "when we can't do anything about it,"[23] and said, a month before the *Anschluss*, "Personally, I almost wish that Hitler would swallow Austria and get it over." A month later he wrote, "Thank goodness Austria's out of the way.... After all, it wasn't our business."[24]

Hitler's pressure on Czechoslovakia led to the dismemberment of that country with the blessing and cooperation of France and Britain. Even as European security crumbled, the nations who benefited from it refused to resist. For the leaders of great powers, especially in democratic countries, however, the space for retreat is not infinite. To save face the French insisted on a guarantee of the Czech state that remained, and Chamberlain was compelled to agree. In such ways does the failure of the will to fight sometimes lead to extraordinary foolishness, for he committed Britain to the dismemberment of Czechoslovakia and a continental commitment, not to a France that could be defended, but to a small Central European country whose defenses he was about to give away. When a nation's failure of will, moreover, has hardened into a standing policy, it also can lead to extraordinary moral obtuseness. When British newspapers doubted the government's true commitment to its new guarantee and warned against the "betrayal of Czechoslovakia," the permanent undersecretary in the Foreign Office wrote in his diary that the contemplated action was "inevitable, and must be faced.... *How* much courage is needed to be a coward!"[25]

When Hitler broke his agreement and took the rest of Czechoslovakia in March 1939, the British government still refused to resist. But now there was outrage in and outside the cabinet and parliament. The British people would no longer put up with appeasement and weakness but demanded a new policy of resistance and strength. As often happens in great powers with democratic governments at such times, the new resolve came from a sense of shame and anger over principles betrayed rather than from a need to protect British interests. Typically, fearing the charge of inaction in this atmosphere, Chamberlain over-reacted. Rumors of a German plan to attack Rumania, as well as fears that Hitler was about to attack Poland, led the British to guarantee Poland against aggression and then to extend the same guarantee to Rumania and Greece. The British had no access to Poland and no means of defending it. The only effective help they and the French could give the Poles would have been an invasion of Germany from the west, but for that there was no will and no plan.

Even though the British were at last rearming, mere words following two decades of disarmament and retreat would not avail. Hitler never took his opponents' warnings seriously. As he laid plans for the attack on Poland he discounted the danger from the leaders of Britain and France. "I saw them at Munich," he said; "they are little worms." The war that broke out in September and lasted more than five years rained down destruction on Britain from the air and came close to ending in disaster and defeat. In a mere twenty years the British had gone from dominance, security and peace to suffering, danger and war, not because of any material inferiority but because of a failure of will not merely to maintain military power but also to see reality and to act accordingly. It was, as Churchill called it, "the unnecessary war." As another distinguished scholar has put it, "even Hitler took a little time before he realized that Europe had no policeman in its international streets ... and that the British Government's view of their role varied between that of a town planner and that of a traffic warden."[26]

In both world wars Britain encountered an opponent with the potential power and resources to dominate Europe and to challenge the security even of its home territory—a "peer competitor," if an asymmetric one, to use today's terminology. But even ambitious lesser powers, when the greater powers they challenge lack the will to defend their interests, can do terrible harm and create serious danger when not deterred by resolution backed by military strength.

ooooo

Another classic illustration is the Pacific War between Japan and the U.S. that began with a Japanese attack on Pearl Harbor on December 7, 1941. Japan is a small island nation with a population a fraction that of the U.S. and few natural resources. Its swift industrialization and the growth of its military and naval forces brought it military success and great ambitions. At no time, however, did serious Japanese people consider a role outside Asia greater than that of what we would call today a major regional power. But even those ambitions brought Japan into conflict with American interests and ideals.

During the 1920s Japan prospered and seemed to some observers to be pursuing a path of modernization that was leading it towards a liberal regime like that of Britain and the U.S. Any such hopes were dashed when the great depression ended Japanese prosperity, undermined government by political parties, and increased the influence of the armed forces, especially the army. One consequence was the Japanese conquest of Manchuria in 1931. This was the first major violation of the League of Nations Charter and, therefore, of the whole concept of peace through "collective security." Britain, as the chief bulwark of the League and the power with the greatest interests in the Far East, would be expected to take the lead in any resistance to this aggression. The British recognized the danger but were aware of their incapacity. In February 1932 Sir Robert Vansittart, permament undersecretary at the Foreign Office, recognized the danger from Japan, which "may well spread to the Middle East," but felt that Britain alone could do nothing to check it and would be "done for in the Far East" and "must eventually swallow any and every humiliation" there unless the United States were prepared to use force.[27] The past and future Prime Minister Stanley Baldwin had no confidence in that possibility. "If you enforce an economic boycott," he said, "you will have war declared by Japan and she will seize Singapore and Hong Kong and we cannot, as we are placed, stop her. You will get nothing out of Washington but words, big words, but only words."[28]

He was right. During the Manchurian affair the Americans' response was limited to a note issued by Secretary of State Stimson that his government would recognize no agreement between China and Japan that violated American treaty rights or impaired Chinese sovereignty or gained territory by means that violated the Kellogg-Briand Pact. This was a perfect example of America's ambiguous posture toward Japanese ambitions and aggression in the 1930s. On the one hand, it had interests and strong opinions about affairs in East Asia and felt that these should be respected. On the other, it was unwilling to back them with force, in considerable part, because it lacked the military and naval forces needed.

During the 1930s the U.S. continued to complain of Japan's behavior while holding to a position of disarmament and neutrality. The conquest of Manchuria was a shock, a violation of the international system on which peace was thought to rest and a threat to U.S. interests in East Asia. Yet American businessmen wanted good relations with Japan, which was America's third-largest customer. Secretary of State Henry Stimson was deeply concerned by the Japanese action but believed that the U.S., "by avoiding provocative statements and quietly mobilizing world opinion, could strengthen moderate leaders in Tokyo" to control their more violent colleagues.[29] In 1932 the Japanese navy became involved in a fight with Chinese forces in Shanghai, angering and frightening the Western countries with interests there. Stimson thought of sending the American fleet from Manila to Shanghai as a show of strength to intimidate the Japanese. When this was rejected he talked of an economic boycott. This, too, was thought too provocative, so Stimson confined himself to warnings and denunciations. But these had no good effect. Soon Manchuria became the puppet state of Manchkuo under Japanese control. "All the words and gestures directed at Japan seemed to have no effect on that nation's policy."[30]

In the mid-1930s the Japanese continued their expansion in China. Rumors flew that they were fortifying the Pacific islands under their mandate. The U.S. made no effort to investigate the reports or to fortify its Pacific islands. America's new Secretary of State Cordell Hull "reasoned that American interests in East Asia did not justify the use of force and that, in any event, the United States lacked the necessary naval power for offensive action in the Western Pacific."[31] The Americans were unwilling to accept the weakening of their position in the Far East or to permit the Japanese to advance without protest. But protest was all President Franklin Roosevelt was willing to contemplate. He rejected demands for building up the navy and insisted on efforts to achieve arms limitation agreements. When Japan withdrew from the resulting naval conference at London in 1935 and continued to build its navy, Roosevelt still refused to accelerate American shipbuilding.

Japan's fleet, to be used in the Pacific only, continued to close the gap with the American fleet, with its responsibilities in two oceans and around the world. American naval officers considered Japan to be expansionist and the greatest threat to American interests. They thought that if the U.S. continued to hold to its

Asian interests, especially to the defense of Chinese integrity, a war with Japan was all but certain. But their only plan to deal with such a war was using Hawaii and the Philippines as bases, to sail to the Western Pacific, defeat the Japanese navy and force a surrender by blockade, and they knew that the U.S. Navy was too small to achieve that goal. The Army, aware of America's military weakness, wanted to withdraw from the Philippines and the Western Pacific entirely. But civilian leaders would neither strengthen the armed forces nor reduce their responsibilities.

In Japan the depression had emboldened the aggressive elements in the army and navy, and in 1937, under a new and aggressive prime minister, the war in China intensified and brought a major Japanese offensive. The new regime and the army acted in the belief that the U.S. lacked the will to intervene, that "the United States would not go beyond diplomatic protests and that, whatever the content of its notes, it would grudgingly acquiesce in Japan's control of China."[32] They appeared to be right. The U.S. turned down repeated British suggestions for joint action and tried to follow a moderate course. Although the president would not invoke the neutrality act for fear of hurting China's war effort, the Americans forbade the shipment of weapons and materials of war in government vessels, which had the same effect.

But Japan's bold and blatantly aggressive new policy began to change attitudes in the U.S. Some government officials began to press for stronger action, and public opinion began to swing in the same direction. The State Department felt the need to make a public condemnation of Japan's actions, and President Roosevelt's famous Quarantine Speech in October 1937, which denounced "world lawlessness," implicitly included Japan among the lawbreakers. Still, the Americans refused to go beyond words. Even when the Japanese sank the American gunboat *Panay* in December 1937, the U.S. did not retaliate.

As the Japanese assault on China continued, American opinion turned increasingly hostile and put pressure on the government for action, especially for economic sanctions. Businessmen, who had argued for unfettered trade with Japan as a force for liberalization and moderation, continued to resist, despite evidence that a flourishing commerce had not produced that effect. The government, however, found it necessary to impose some economic sanctions, even though some officials warned that it might provoke a war for which the U.S. was not prepared. Roosevelt was not impressed, sharing the widespread confidence that Japan, as a second-rate power, would not dare fight the U.S.

Germany's victories in Europe, and especially the fall of France in 1940, increased Japanese ambitions and their doubts that the U.S. had the will to fight. In September their troops occupied northern Indochina. The new foreign minister Matsuoka Yosuke, who had spent nine years in America, "contended that bold diplomacy would intimidate the American government and force its gradual acquiescence in Japan's new empire."[33]

Only after the fall of France did Roosevelt call for a two-ocean navy, far too late to deter Japanese ambitions. Several members of his cabinet were convinced that previous passivity and timidity had encouraged the Japanese aggression, but the only available active and "tough" measures to achieve deterrence were economic sanctions and embargoes. Popular opinion had swung powerfully against the Japanese. When Roosevelt forbade the sending of scrap iron to Japan, 96 percent of Americans polled approved. The overwhelming majority of business leaders, however, said they wanted to appease Japan or to do nothing. By 1939 the relative weakness of the Navy persuaded its leaders to retreat from their traditional forward-thinking posture in favor of a defensive one that relied on economic blockade. The chief of naval operations opposed even an oil embargo, but opinion in and outside the government made inaction impossible.

The economic sanctions imposed by the U.S. only increased the Japanese's anger and desperation without convincing them of American ability and will to fight a war in the immediate future. At the same time, many Japanese in the army, navy and government became convinced that the U.S. would always stand in the way of their aims in China and Southeast Asia. As the pressure compelled Roosevelt to tighten the economic noose on the Japanese, their leaders felt pressure to launch a pre-emptive war while they could still hope to win it. The great naval program begun in 1937 gave them a lead of three years over the Americans. In autumn 1941 they were the equal of the American, British and Dutch naval forces, but they saw that their relative position would begin to decline in 1942.

There was a window of opportunity that would soon slam shut. Admiral Yamamoto, a Harvard graduate who knew America, warned against the size and industrial power of the U.S. The finance and foreign ministers also argued against immediate war, but for different reasons: they believed that the U.S. would not attack Japan even after three years, when the empire was relatively weak. The Japanese chief of staff, Admiral Nagano, however, thought otherwise: "Don't rely on what won't come.... In three years enemy defenses in the south will be strong and the number of enemy warships will also increase." The finance minister asked: "Well, then, when can we go to war and win?" Nagano answered, "Now! The time for war will not come later!"[34] The decision was made. The Japanese expected that German victories in Europe, "combined with staggering defeats Japan would inflict on the United States in the early phases of the Pacific war, would destroy America's will to fight and lead to a negotiated peace."[35]

The situation confronting the Japanese bore some resemblance to that facing the Germans in 1914. They did not launch the war in a mood of optimism but one of desperation. Their ambitions had produced a crisis in which only one side could be satisfied. If the Japanese were willing to abandon their greatest ambitions they could have peace, but their sense of honor and pride forbade such a retreat, even in the face of superior power. As Admiral Nagano said, in a tone similar to the Germans', "If there is a war, the country may be ruined. Nevertheless, a nation which does not fight in this plight has lost its spirit and is already a doomed country. Only if we fight to the last soldier will it be possible to find a way out of this fatal situation."[36]

The weakness of Britain and the U.S. had done much to create that situation. It was the kind of inadvertent trap that such countries often set for ambitious challengers to the international order and for themselves. Unwilling to face reality and to pay the price for defending their interests and values, they deny the dangers and minimize their concerns. For a time they escape from the burdens and challenges of a realistic policy, but ultimately find that their weakness has encouraged a serious threat they are no longer free to ignore. When it is too late for deterrence and for the aggressive opponent to retreat with honor, countries that have let their power deteriorate become alarmed, attempt inadequate appeasement, rearm in haste. So it was that the U.S. stumbled into a war against Japan in December 1941.

ooooo

And this brings us back to the "strategic pause" of today. It must be understood, of course, within its context. The Cold War of 1945 to 1990 was an unusual historical experience. The threat of the Soviet Union was inescapable to those who would not avert their eyes, and the memory of the isolationism and irresponsibility that had produced World War II was fresh. The U.S. and its allies accepted the challenge and costs of this often invisible conflict— vast expenditures and compulsory military service in peacetime; more remarkable still, a continuing military alliance with the nerve-wracking mission of containment and being constantly ready for a military conflict that everyone hoped would not come. In spite of occasional lapses of will, the U.S. and its allies met their responsibilities for almost a half-century, preserving security, interests and the general peace until their opponent was exhausted and collapsed. It was one of the great achievements in the history of international relations and a model for what is needed to preserve the peace in a world where stability is under constant challenge.

The key to success in the Cold War was the will of the United States, which emerged from the Second World War as the richest and strongest nation in the world. Yet the Americans' decision to accept the burden of the conflict that grew out of the prior victory was by no means inevitable. Even after the experience in being drawn into the last war unprepared, the U.S. reverted to traditional behavior in 1945 and imprudently reduced their armed forces. Although the Truman Doctrine, the Marshall Plan and the NATO alliance committed America to defend Western Europe against Soviet communism, its will to wage Cold War was by no means certain. In 1950, when the Korean War broke out, the U.S. appeared both unable and unwilling to defend its South Korean ally. Swift and enormously deep reductions in the size and quality of the army right after World War II had decreased it in just a few years from some ten million to about 552,000, half of them on occupation duty overseas serving as clerks and policeman, the other half in the U.S. performing various administrative tasks. General Omar Bradley, who inherited this army in 1948, described it as one that "could not fight its way out of a paper bag."[37] There were diplomatic problems as well. Early in 1950, for instance, the American secretary of state gave a speech that mentioned a number of states in the Far East that the U.S. would fight to defend, but excluded South Korea from the list. The combination of America's evident military weakness and its apparent lack of will together encouraged North Korea to launch an attack and its Soviet sponsor to permit and support it. The ensuing war almost ended in swift defeat and disaster for the South Korean and American forces. It lasted for years, and cost a fortune in money and American lives before ending in a stalemate that kept an American army in Korea for more than four decades.

The Korean War was an object lesson American politicians and military leaders took seriously. It led to a major military buildup and a new determination and commitment that sustained the policy of peace through strength and deterrence that eventually brought success. But the end of the Cold War and the collapse of the obvious enemy have presented a new challenge. One would have thought that the lessons of this century, both of failure and success, would have made plain the necessity of maintaining a military force adequate to deter aggression long before any state was capable of undertaking it. Even before the U.S. began to dismantle the military power that had been crucial in bringing down the Wall, however, questions arose about its will. In July 1990 Saddam Hussein, military dictator of Iraq, launched a diplomatic assault on Kuwait, outlining a variety of "grievances," and began to mass large numbers of troops and tanks along its border.

The United States responded by stating that it would support "the sovereignty and integrity of the Gulf states" and by insisting "that disputes be settled peacefully and not by threats and intimidations,"[38] but it regarded Iraq's efforts as aimed at intimidation rather than war. When Ambassador April Glaspie continued the conciliatory policy, Saddam treated her to some tough talk: "'If you use pressure we will deploy pressure and force. We cannot come all the way to you in the United States but individual Arabs may reach you.' To emphasize his point, he observed that the Americans lacked Iraq's readiness to lose 10,000 men in a day's combat."[39] She remained conciliatory, assuring Saddam that she had direct instructions from the president to try to improve relations with Iraq. Although she repeated the American view that disputes must be settled peacefully, she also stated that the United States had no opinion on the border dispute between Iraq and Kuwait. "The natural interpretation for Saddam to put on this, especially in the light of his opening harangue, was that the United States was still offering him a hand of friendship while urging him to be good."[40]

The weakness of American policy that encouraged Saddam to move against Kuwait has been characterized as an "ambiguous policy combining threats with appeasement."[41] The threats came chiefly from Congress and the appeasement from the administration. Asked by a congressman what would happen if the Iraqis crossed into Kuwait, a State Department official replied that the United States would be very concerned but that it had no treaty obligations to use force. In any case, Congress, he added, would not have supported anything but economic sanctions. Saddam had good reason to believe that the United States would not get in his way. From his ambassador in Washington he heard there were "few risks of an American reaction in case of an intervention in Kuwait."[42] As in Korea, the U.S. had once again set the kind of trap that too frequently leads it into unnecessary wars.

There is good reason, too, to believe that the violence, loss of life, and threat to the stability of Europe when Yugoslavia disintegrated could have been avoided by timely intervention on the part of the United States and its allies. Given the power of American military forces, so recently demonstrated in the Gulf War, there would probably have been no need to use it if the U.S. and NATO had made it clear that violence would not be tolerated. Instead, they both attempted to avoid the responsibility of intervention, thus permitting and encouraging the horrors and disruptions that followed. When, at last, they resorted to intervention, it required the serious use of arms and the deployment of a considerable force for years. All this happened *after* the Bosnian horrors had taken place, and now, even after the war in Kosovo, the end of the difficulties and of American involvement are far from evident.

These examples show that the denial of American interest and attempts to avoid involvement, especially the threat or use of military force, can have a result opposite to what is desired. Instead of preventing the expenditure of resources and the risk of American lives, they often create conditions that cause greater expenditure and risk. The twentieth century has repeatedly shown that for a great power, and especially for the world's leading power, there is no escape from the responsibility its position imposes. Recent history has also demonstrated that the cost of these burdens is small compared with the costs of failure to bear them forthrightly; and in dealing with the issue of its power, a country like the U.S. is really dealing with its values and its security.

About the Authors

Robert Kagan is a director of the Project for the New American Century as well as a senior associate at the Carnegie Endowment for International Peace. He is the author of *A Twilight Struggle: American Power and Nicaragua,* and served as a State Department official in the Reagan administration. Mr. Kagan is a contributing editor at the *Weekly Standard* and a monthly columnist at the *Washington Post.*

William Kristol, chairman of the Project for the New American Century, is editor and publisher of the *Weekly Standard.* Mr. Kristol served as Chief of Staff to Vice President Dan Quayle during the Bush administration and to Secretary of Education William Bennett under President Reagan. He taught politics at the University of Pennsylvania and Harvard's Kennedy School of Government.

ooooo

Elliott Abrams, president of the Ethics and Public Policy Center, also serves on the U.S. Commission on International Religious Freedom. He has served as Assistant Secretary of State for Inter-American Affairs, for Human Rights and Humanitarian Affairs, and for International Organization Affairs. He has published several books including *Faith or Fear* and *Security and Sacrifice.*

William J. Bennett is co-director of Empower America. He has served as director of the Office of National Drug Control Policy under President Bush, and as Secretary of Education and chairman of the National Endowment for the Humanities under

President Reagan. Bill Bennett co-chairs, with former Democratic Governor Mario Cuomo, the Partnership for a Drug-Free America. He is the author of several best-selling books.

James W. Ceasar is professor of government and foreign affairs at the University of Virginia. Professor Ceaser is the author of several books on America and American politics, including *Presidential Selection: Theory and Development, Reforming the Reforms, Liberal Democracy and Political Science,* and *Reconstructing America: The Symbol of America in Modern Thought.*

Nicholas Eberstadt holds the Henry Wendt Chair in Political Economy at the American Enterprise Institute. He is also a member of the Harvard University Center for Population and Development Studies. Mr. Eberstadt has published extensively on international issues in both scholarly and popular journals, and is the author of several books including *The End of North Korea.*

Aaron L. Friedberg is professor of politics and international affairs and director of the Research Program in International Security at Princeton University. He is the author of *The Weary Titan: Britain and the Experience of Relative Decline, 1895–1905* and *In the Shadow of the "Garrison State": America's Anti-Statism and Its Cold War Grand Strategy.* Dr. Friedberg has served as a consultant to the National Security Council and the Departments of Defense and Energy.

Jeffrey Gedmin is executive director of the New Atlantic Initiative and a resident scholar at the American Enterprise Institute. His areas of specialization include Germany and Central and Eastern Europe. In addition to publishing several books on foreign affairs, he has published articles in *National Review,* the *New Republic,* the *Wall Street Journal, Wilson Quarterly,* the *Financial Times,* the *Washington Post,* and the *Los Angeles Times.*

Reuel Marc Gerecht is a former Middle Eastern specialist in the Directorate of Operations of the Central Intelligence Agency. He is the author (under the pseudonym of Edward Shirley) of *Know Thine Enemy: A Spy's Journey into Revolutionary Iran.* Mr. Gerecht has written for the *Atlantic Monthly, Foreign Affairs,* the *New Republic,* the *Weekly Standard,* the *New York Times,* and the *Wall Street Journal,* among other publications.

Donald Kagan is Hillhouse Professor of classics and history at Yale University. His books include *The Great Dialogue: A History* *of Greek Political Thought from Homer to Polybius,* a four-volume history of the Peloponnesian War, *Pericles and the Birth of the Athenian Democracy, On the Origins of War and the Preservation of Peace,* and *While America Sleeps,* with Frederick W. Kagan.

Frederick W. Kagan is assistant professor of military history at the U.S. Military Academy, West Point, NY. He has published on current American military policy, as well as on Russian military history. His works include *While America Sleeps,* with Donald Kagan, and *The Military Reforms of Nicholas I: The Origins of the Modern Russian Army.*

Ross H. Munro is director of Asian Studies at the Center for Security Studies in Washington, D.C. He is the co-author of *The Coming Conflict with China.* Mr. Munro was a *Time* magazine correspondent in Asia and bureau chief in Hong Kong, Bangkok, and New Delhi. Previously he was Beijing bureau chief for the Toronto *Globe and Mail.*

Richard N. Perle is a resident fellow at the American Enterprise Institute. He was the Assistant Secretary of Defense for International Security Policy and the chairman of the North Atlantic Treaty Organization High Level Defense Group from 1981 to 1987. Mr. Perle is the co-director of the AEI Commission on Future Defenses. He is the editor of *Reshaping Western Security* and the author of *Hard Line,* a political novel.

Peter W. Rodman is director of National Security Programs at The Nixon Center. He is the author of a history of the Cold War in the Third World, *More Precious than Peace,* and a series of annual Nixon Center strategic assessments, the most recent of which is *Uneasy Giant: The Challenges to American Predominance.* He has served as a Deputy Assistant to the President for National Security Affairs and as director of the State Department's policy planning staff.

William Schneider is an adjunct fellow at the Hudson Institute. He has served as the Undersecretary of State for Security Assistance and chairman of the President's General Advisory Committee on Arms Control and Disarmament. Dr. Schneider was a member of the Commission to Assess the Ballistic Missile Threat to the United States and the Commission to Assess the Organization of the Federal Government to Combat the Proliferation of Weapons of Mass Destruction.

Paul Wolfowitz is the dean of the Paul H. Nitze School of Advanced International Studies at The Johns Hopkins University. He has served as Undersecretary of Defense for Policy, Ambassador to Indonesia, Assistant Secretary of State for East Asian and Pacific affairs, and director of policy planning at the State Department. He is the author of numerous articles on foreign policy and defense issues.

Notes

Introduction: National Interest and Global Responsibility

1. "A Normal Country in a Normal Time," *The National Interest*, fall 1990: 40–44.
2. Quoted in John Lewis Gaddis, *The United States and the Origins of the Cold War* (New York: Columbia University Press, 1972), 11.
3. Quoted in David Fromkin, *In the Time of the Americans* (New York: Alfred A. Knopf, 1995), 435.
4. Quoted in Walter LaFeber, *The American Age* (New York: Norton & Co., 1989), 380.
5. John Lewis Gaddis, *We Now Know: Rethinking Cold War History* (Oxford: Clarendon Press, 1997), 12.
6. "Address before a Joint Session of the Congress, April 16, 1945," in *Public Papers of the Presidents of the United States: Harry Truman, 1945* (Washington, D.C.: U.S. Government Printing Office, 1961), 6.
7. "Address on Foreign Policy at the Navy Day Celebration in New York City, October 27, 1945," in *Public Papers: Harry Truman, 1945*, 432–33.
8. Henry Kissinger, *Diplomacy* (New York: Simon & Schuster, 1994), 833.
9. Kay Baily Hutchison, "The Case for Strategic Sense," *New York Times*, September 13, 1999.
10. "The Stability of a Unipolar World," *International Security*, summer 1999: 5–41.
11. Josef Joffe, "How America Does It," *Foreign Affairs*, September/October 1997: 13–27.
12. Quoted in Frank Ninkovich, "Theodore Roosevelt: Civilization as Ideology," *Diplomatic History* 10, no. 3 (summer 1986): 225–26.

13. Theodore Roosevelt, paper delivered at the American Sociological Congress, Washington, D.C., 28–31 December 1914, in *The Writings of Theodore Roosevelt*, ed. William Harbaugh, (Indianapolis, 1967), 357, quoted in Ninkovich, "Theodore Roosevelt," 233.
14. Reinhold Neibuhr, *The Irony of American History* (New York: Scribner, 1962), 7.
15. George Kennan, "The Sources of Soviet Conduct," *Foreign Affairs* 25 (July 1947), reprinted in *Containment: Documents on American Policy and Strategy, 1945–1950*, ed. Thomas H. Etzold and John Lewis Gaddis (New York: Columbia University Press, 1978), 84–90.

China: The Challenge of a Rising Power

1. See Richard Bernstein and Ross H. Munro, "The New China Lobby," chap. 4 in *The Coming Conflict with China* (New York: Knopf, 1997).
2. For a sophisticated analysis of China's military buildup and how China has initiated "a focused strategic modernization program" aimed to a significant degree at neutralizing U.S. military power in Asia, see Mark A. Stokes, *China's Strategic Modernization: Implications for the United States* (Washington, D.C.: Strategic Studies Institute, September 1999). For an earlier account of China's post–Cold War military buildup and its defense budget, see Bernstein and Munro, *The Coming Conflict with China*, 51–81. See also Michael Pillsbury, *China Debates the Future Security Environment* (Washington, D.C.: National Defense University Press, 2000).
3. Willy Wo-lap Lam, "The Barriers That Still Remain," *South China Morning Post*, 17 November 1999.
4. The letter has not been released, but both U.S. officials and Chinese academics privately confirm that it stated the "Three No's": declaring Washington's opposition to Taiwan's independence, to its membership in international organizations requiring statehood, and to any form of one-China, one-Taiwan policy. This was a major concession by Clinton, and the Chinese successfully pressured him to state it publicly in Shanghai in 1998.

Russia: The Challenge of a Failing Power

1. Deputy Secretary of State Strobe Talbott, "America and Russia in a Changing World," address at the celebration of the 50th anniversary of the Harriman Institute at Columbia University, New York City, 29 October 1996. See also Deputy Secretary Talbott's address at a conference on "Russia at the End of the 20th Century," School of

Humanities and Sciences, Stanford University, Palo Alto, California, 6 November 1998.

2. Avi Shama, "Notes from Russia's Underground: Russia's Economy Booms," *Wall Street Journal*, 24 December 1997, 10.

3. See, e.g., Murray Feshbach, "A Different Definition of National Security: Environmental and Health Issues in Russia and Its Impact on the West," paper prepared for the First Symposium in the 40th CERES Anniversary Series, "Russia in the 1990s and Beyond," 11 September 1998; Murray Feshbach, "What a Tangled Web We Weave: Child Health in Russia and Its Future," paper for Science Applications International Corporation, Inc., July 1998.

4. See sources in Ariel Cohen, "What Russia Must Do to Recover from Its Economic Crisis," *Heritage Foundation Backgrounder*, no. 1296 (18 June 1999).

5. For the best analyses see Dimitri K. Simes, "The New Oligarchy," chap. 7 in *After the Collapse: Russia Seeks Its Place as a Great Power* (New York: Simon & Schuster, 1999); and Fritz W. Ermarth, "Seeing Russia Plain," *The National Interest*, no. 55 (spring 1999).

6. "Sergei Kiriyenko on the Russian Economic Crisis," *East European Constitutional Review* 8, nos. 1–2 (winter/spring 1999), excerpting an address by Kiriyenko at the New York University School of Law on 30 November 1998.

7. Simes, *After the Collapse*, 138.

8. E.g., President Bill Clinton, "Strategic Alliance with Russian Reform," address to the American Society of Newspaper Editors, Annapolis, MD, 1 April 1993.

9. U.S. Department of State, Office of Research, "Russians' Mistrust of the U.S. at New High," Opinion Analysis #M-30-00, 14 March 2000.

10. Simes, *After the Collapse*, 141–147, 189–191; John Lloyd, "The Russian Devolution," *New York Times Magazine*, 15 August 1999, 35–40, 52; Robert G. Kaiser, "Pumping Up the Problem: Has Investing in the Yeltsin Machine Put America's Relationship with Russia at Risk?" *Washington Post*, 15 August 1999, B1.

11. See Chubais's confession in his interview in *Kommersant Daily*, 8 September 1998 (referring to the 1998 episode), and the IMF confirmation of the 1996 episode in Stephen Fidler, "Russian Central Bank 'Lied to IMF,'" *Financial Times*, 30 July 1999, 2.

12. E. Wayne Merry, "Reinventing Russia: Al Gore's Misguided Quest," *Wall Street Journal*, 8 September 1999, A26; Lloyd, "The Russian Devolution," 52.

13. See the September 1999 hearings on Russian money laundering and corruption before the U.S. House of Representatives, Committee on Banking and Financial Services.

14. President Boris Yeltsin, address to the collegium of the Ministry of Foreign Affairs, Moscow, 12 May 1998, reported by ITAR-TASS and Interfax, in FBIS-SOV-98-132, 12 May 1998.

15. The change was not just a question of personalities. It was hard to detect significant differences of perception between Primakov and Yeltsin—or between either of them and Igor Ivanov, who succeeded Primakov as foreign minister in September 1998, or between Yeltsin and Putin, or indeed among most members of the Russian foreign policy elite. The new foreign policy reflects a new national consensus, strongly supported by the Russian public.

16. Minister of Foreign Affairs Yevgenii Primakov, statement to the 51st session of the United Nations General Assembly, 24 September 1996, Embassy of the Russian Federation Press Release #27 (25 September 1996), 4.

17. Yeltsin, address at the Ministry of Foreign Affairs, 12 May 1998.

18. Vladimir Putin, "Russia at the Turn of the New Millennium," statement, 28 December 1999, at <http://www.government.gov.ru/>.

19. Interview with Kiriyenko by Yevgenii Artemov in *Izvestiya* (online), 23 March 2000.

20. For Primakov's text, see Foreign Minister and Academician Yevgenii Primakov, "Russia in World Politics: A Lecture in Honor of Chancellor Gorchakov," *International Affairs* (Moscow) 44, no. 3 (summer 1998): 7–12.

21. Joint Russian-Chinese communiqué of Premier Li Peng's visit to Moscow, 28 December 1996, in FBIS-SOV-96-251, 28 December 1996.

22. Joint Russian-Chinese communiqué of President Yeltsin's visit to Beijing, 25 April 1996, in FBIS-CHI-96-081, 25 April 1996, 15.

23. Quoted in M. Dmitriyev, "China's Western Impromptu?" *Zavtra*, May 1996, in FBIS-SOV-96-125-S, 27 June 1996, 5. In later joint statements, the rhetoric is somewhat toned down; assurances are given that the Sino-Russian partnership is "not directed at any third party." But the stress is on their "increased consensus on international issues and strengthened coordination." E.g., Joint Chinese-Russian communiqué of Premier Li Peng's visit to Moscow, 19 February 1998, in *China Daily*, 20 February 1998, 4; and the Xinhua report on Yeltsin's meeting with Jiang in Bishkek on 25 August 1999, in FBIS-CHI-1999-0825, 25 August 1999.

24. Joint Russian-Chinese communiqué of President Yeltsin's visit to Beijing, 10 December 1999, in FBIS-CHI-1999-1210, 10 December 1999.

25. Li Jingjie, "China and Russia," in *Damage Control or Crisis? Russia and the Outside World*, ed. Robert D. Blackwill and Sergei A. Karaganov, CSIA Studies in International Security, no. 5 (Washington: Brassey's, 1994), 247.

26. A. Kotelkin, former head of Russia's main arms exporter, Rosvooruzhe-nie, quoted by Alexander Lukin, "Russia's Image of China and Russian-Chinese Relations," *East Asia* 17, no. 1 (spring 1999): 32.

27. *Krasnaya Zvezda*, 2 July 2 1996, in FBIS-SOV-96-129, 3 July 1996, 34. See also Pavel Felgengauer, "Taiwan Crisis and Russian-Chinese Ties," *Nezavisimaya Gazeta*, in *Current Digest of the Post-Soviet Press* 48, no. 11 (10 April 1996): 11.

28. Primakov quoted by Xinhua, 18 November 1996, in FBIS-CHI-96-224, 18 November 1996.

29. For this information and for a comprehensive examination of the Russian-Chinese military relationship, a good source is Stephen Blank, *The Dynamic of Russian Weapon Sales to China* (Carlisle Barracks, PA: U.S. Army War College Strategic Studies Institute, 4 March 1997). See also Stephen Blank, "Which Way for Sino-Russian Relations?" *Orbis*, summer 1998.

30. Charles W. Freeman, Jr., quoted in Jim Mann, "China Emerges as Clinton's Knottiest Foreign Problem," *Los Angeles Times*, 9 September 1996, A3.

31. The demographic issue is discussed in Vladimir Abarinov, "Benefits of Alliance With China are Doubtful: It Will Bring Moscow Nothing but New Complications," *Segodnya*, 13 March 1996, 5, in FBIS-SOV-96-070-S, 10 April 1996, 6. See also Ariel Cohen, "A New Paradigm for U.S.-Russia Relations: Facing the Post-Cold War Reality," *Heritage Foundation Backgrounder* no. 1105 (6 March 1997): 6.

32. Deputy Foreign Minister Aleksandr Panov briefing of parliamentari-ans, quoted by ITAR-TASS, 7 June 1996, in FBIS-SOV-96-112, 19 June 1996, 28. See also Ambassador to China Igor Rogachev, interview in *Trud*, 4 January 1996, in FBIS-SOV-96-004, 5 January 1996, 17–18.

33. See sources collected in U.S. Senate Committee on Governmental Affairs, *The Proliferation Primer: Majority Report of the Subcommittee on International Security, Proliferation, and Federal Services* (January 1998), 20.

34. Bill Gertz, "Russia Sells Missiles to Iran," *Washington Times*, 16 April 1997, A2.

35. The text of the Russian-Iranian Nuclear Cooperation Accord of 8 January 1995, as released by the Natural Resources Defense Council, is published in Michael Eisenstadt, *Iranian Military Power: Capabilities and Intentions*, Policy Papers no. 42 (Washington, D.C.: Washington Institute for Near East Policy, 1996), Appendix III, 106–107.

36. Aleksei Malashenko, "Russia and Iran: Relations Remain Solid," *Jamestown Prism* II, no. 11, pt. 2 (31 May 1996).

37. IRNA report of Velayati-Primakov news conference on 22 December 1996, in FBIS-NES-96-248, 23 December 1996.

38. See the backgrounder in *al-Hayat* with an unnamed "senior Russian official" in late May 1995, quoted in Stephen Grummon, "Russian Policy toward Iran: Preparing for Halifax and Beyond," *Policywatch*, no. 152 (Washington, D.C.: Washington Institute for Near East Policy, 6 June 1995).

39. Velayati-Primakov news conference, 22 December 1996.

40. E.g., Yevgenii Primakov, "Russia Does Not Oppose Islam," *Nezavisimaya Gazeta*, 18 August 1996.

41. See, e.g., Robert O. Freedman, "Yeltsin's Russia and Rafsanjani's Iran: A Tactical Alliance," *Middle East Insight*, July–August 1995; Stephen J. Blank, "Russia's Return to Mideast Diplomacy," *Orbis*, Fall 1996.

42. IRNA report, 8 March 1995, in FBIS-NES-95-045, 8 March 1995, 51, cited in Blank, "Russia's Return to Mideast Diplomacy," 530.

43. Quoted in Freedman, "Yeltsin's Russia and Rafsanjani's Iran," 92.

44. See Robert O. Freedman, "Russia's Middle East Ambitions," *Middle East Quarterly*, September 1998: 35–36.

45. *Nezavisimaya Gazeta* 28 November 1997, in *Current Digest of the Post-Soviet Press* 49, no. 48 (1997): 11, quoted in Freedman, "Russia's Middle East Ambitions."

46. Radio Free Europe/Radio Liberty, *Iraq Report* 2, no. 16 (30 April 1999).

47. UPI dispatch, "Russia Denies Accusation of Iraq Sale," 15 February 1999.

48. Primakov, "Russia in World Politics," 11.

49. Foreign Minister Igor Ivanov, "Russia in a Changing World," *Nezavisimaya Gazeta*, 25 June 1999, 1, 6, in Official Kremlin International News Broadcast, Federal Information Systems Corporation.

50. Russian Defense Minister Igor Rodionov's remarks to a CIS conference, 25 December 1996, quoted by Interfax, in FBIS-SOV-96-249, 25 December 1996. Rodionov was reprimanded for these statements, however, by the presidential office and the foreign ministry.

51. Joint Statement of President Bush and President Yeltsin on a Global Protection System, Washington, 17 June 1992; testimony of Stephen J. Hadley before the U.S. Senate Committee on Foreign Relations, 13 May 1999.

52. See Richard Nixon, Statement on the Occasion of the Twentieth Anniversary of the ABM Treaty, 30 September 1992; Henry A. Kissinger, letter to Senate Armed Services Committee Chairman Strom Thurmond, 3 August 1995; Kissinger, letter to House National Security Committee Chairman Floyd Spence, 16 October 1995; and Kissinger, "The Next President's First Obligation," *Washington Post*, 9 February 2000.

53. See, e.g., Joint Statement between the United States and the Russian Federation concerning Strategic Offensive and Defensive Arms and Further Strengthening of Stability, Cologne, 20 June 1999.

54. MIRV stands for Multiple Independently Targeted Reentry Vehicle technology.

Iraq: Saddam Unbound

1. August 11, 1999. The letter read, in part: "As the principal proponents of last year's Iraq Liberation Act, we are writing to express our dismay over the continued drift in U.S. policy toward Iraq. . . . Since the beginning of this year . . . we have noted signs of a reduced priority in U.S. policy toward Iraq. The last six months have been notable more for what has not happened rather than for what has been achieved. . . . International inspections no longer constrain Saddam's weapons of mass destruction programs. . . . The administration is not giving the Iraqi opposition the political support it needs to seriously challenge Saddam. . . . The administration is not giving the Iraqi opposition the material support it needs to seriously challenge Saddam. . . . The administration is not willing to deliver Assistance to the opposition inside Iraq. . . . The administration is not willing to give appropriate security assurances to anti-Saddam Iraqis, including the Kurds and Shi'a." It was signed by Senators Trent Lott, Joseph Lieberman, Jesse Helms, Robert Kerrey, Richard Shelby, and Sam Brownback as well as Representatives Benjamin Gilman and Howard Berman.
2. The Iraq Liberation Act can be found on-line as "House Liberation Act of 1998," HR 4655 in the Congressional Record of the 105th Congress, Second Session, at <http://thomas.loc.gov>.
3. Still others may write theses on how easily Congress can be gulled into accepting even the most transparently disingenuous administration policy.
4. Warren Christopher had last served in the Carter administration whose failure in the Gulf was a significant factor in its defeat. Madeleine Albright, Tony Lake, Sandy Berger, William Perry, William Cohen, John Deutsch, George Tenent—none of these officials would have been invited to a conference on Iraq before they assumed responsibility for directing American policy with respect to the Gulf.
5. See Patrick Clawson, "A Look at Sanctioning Iraq: The Numbers Don't Lie—Saddam Does," *Washington Post*, 27 February 2000, B3.
6. The CIA made a similar error of judgment in its long-held belief that it could collaborate with Cubans close to Castro. In every case they proved to be working for Castro, not against him.
7. At the date of this writing the UN Security Council approved a "compromise candidate, Hans Blix, to head the UN inspection team in Iraq. Even the *New York Times* found the choice to be "disappointing." The fact that Iraq's approval (obtained through the French and

Russians) was necessary to achieve a "compromise" candidate almost certainly makes Mr. Blix a compromised inspector.

8. Currently, air strikes against Saddam are sporadic, defensive, and disorganized. In fact, they are localized reactions to challenges by the Iraqi military. Saddam chooses the time and place, and they are designed to serve his purpose at a cost he feels he can bear. Under these circumstances, they do little to advance our national objectives.

9. See Jim Hoagland, "Virtual Policy," *Washington Post*, 7 March 1999, B7; and Hoagland, "Playing with the Angels," *Washington Post*, 18 December 1998, A29.

North Korea: Beyond Appeasement

1. And quite possibly even less than this: in 1997, General John H. Tilelli, the head of the U.S.-ROK Combined Forces Command (CFC), stated that "any sign of war [in the Korean Peninsula] can be detected [only] 12 to 24 hours ahead of time." *Chungang Ilbo* (Seoul), 6 September 1997, 3, translated in U.S. Foreign Broadcast Information Service (hereafter FBIS) as "South Korea: Article Views Tilelli's Comments on Early Attack Detection," FBIS-EAS-97-249, 9 September 1999 (electronic version).

2. The ROK formally applied for membership in the Organization for Economic Cooperation and Development in late 1994, and acceded to the OECD in late 1996.

3. Robert A. Scalapino, *The Politics of Development: Perspectives on Twentieth Century Asia* (Cambridge, MA: Harvard University Press, 1989), 67.

4. Kim Jong Il's top governmental post is Chairman of the DPRK National Defense Commission (NDC). According to the September 1998 DPRK Constitution, however, the NDC is merely "the highest *military* leading organ of State power" (emphasis added). The question of who actually serves as head of state for North Korea—or whether this extraordinarily centralized system even *has* a head of state—is now constitutionally ambiguous.

5. Not all specialists, however, conclude that North Korea's ongoing economic crisis has as yet eroded its *overall* military capabilities against the South. See, for example, Bruce William Bennett, "The Dynamics of the North Korean Threat: Is the Erosion of North Korean Military Capabilities Real or Imagined?" *International Journal of Korean Studies* 3, no. 1 (1999): 1–34.

6. Many reports on the suspect DPRK atomic program have been published over the past decade. For one recent nongovernmental assessment of the status of the North Korean nuclear weapons program,

see the Federation of Atomic Scientists' report "Nuclear Weapons Program," available electronically at <http://www.fas.org/nuke/guide/ dprk/index.html>, accessed 10 January 2000.

7. *Yonhap* News Agency (Seoul), 4 November 1999, reprinted as "DPRK Said to Have over 5,000 Tons of Chemical Weapons," FBIS-EAS-1999-1104, 4 November 1999 (electronic version). The item reports on a release by the Washington-based Center for Defense Information.

8. Federation of American Scientists, "Biological Weapons Program," available electronically at <http://www.fas.org/nuke/guide/dprk/bw>, accessed 13 January 2000.

9. *Korea Times* (Internet version), 12 October 1999, reprinted as "More on 19990 [*sic*]–2000 Defense White Paper," FBIS-EAS-1999-1012, 12 October 1999 (electronic version).

10. On Taepo Dong I, see Joseph S. Bermudez Jr., "A History of Ballistic Missile Development in the DPRK," *Center for Nonproliferation Studies Occasional Papers*, no. 2 (1999), available electronically at <http://cns.miis.edu/pubs/opapers/op2/index.htm>, accessed 20 February 2000. On prospects for DPRK ballistic missile development, see the unclassified version of the "Rumsfeld Report": "Report of the Commission to Assess the Ballistic Missile Threat to the United States," 15 July 1998, available electronically at <http://www.fas.org/irp/threat/ missle/rumsfeld/index.html>, accessed 10 January 2000.

11. From Kim Dae Jung's inaugural address, 25 February 1998; available electronically from the ROK Ministry of Unification at <http:// unikorea.go.kr/cgi-eg/eb.cgi?31C31/C318.htm>, accessed 24 January 2000.

12. Formal texts of both documents are available electronically at the ROK Ministry of Unification website: for the former, <http://unikorea. go.kr/cgi-eg/eb.cgi?41D41/D4130.htm>; for text of the latter, <http://unikorea.go.kr/cgi-eg/eb.cgi?41D41/D4129.htm>; both accessed 24 January 2000.

13. ROK Constitution available electronically at <http://www.uni-wuerzburg.de/law/ks00000_.html>, accessed 24 January 2000.

14. AAP Newsfeed, "Asia: Unified Korea at Least a Decade Away—Kim Dae Jun [*sic*]," 24 February 1998. Some of President Kim's advisers went even further: one of them was quoted in the *Economist* as saying that a North Korean collapse would be "a complete disaster" for the South. "Rumblings from Across the Razor Wire," *Economist*, 9 May 1998, 41.

15. John Burton, "Hard-Liners Casting Doubt on Seoul's Overtures to North," *Financial Times*, 31 July 1998, 4.

16. Roger Dean du Mars, "South Korea Hints at Recognizing North Korea as a Sovereign State," *Korea Herald*, 9 March 1999 (Internet version).

17. *Korea Times* (Internet version), 10 February 1999, reprinted as "Kim Tae-chung Not Expecting Reunification during His Term," FBIS-EAS-1999-0210, 10 February 1999 (electronic version).

18. *Yonhap*, 3 January 2000, reprinted as "ROK ForMin Says Korean Unification to Come around 2025," FBIS-EAS-2000-0103, 3 January 2000 (electronic version).

19. *Yonhap*, 28 April 1999, reprinted as "Foreign Minister Explains Engagement Policy," FBIS-EAS-1999-0428, 28 April 1999 (electronic version).

20. KBS-1 Television (Seoul), 24 February 1999, transcribed as "Kim Answers Questions at News Conference," FBIS-CHI-1999-0224, 24 February 1999 (electronic version).

21. *Korea Times* (Internet version), 4 January 1999, reprinted as "President Outlines Policies to End 'Cold War Legacy,'" FBIS-EAS-99-004, 4 January 1999 (electronic version).

22. *Chungang Ilbo*, 21 September 1998, translated as "Daily Interviews President Kim Tae Chung," FBIS-EAS-98-265, 22 September 1998 (electronic version).

23. *Korea Times* (Internet version), 19 February 1999, reprinted as "Kim Tae-chung Wants DPRK to Adopt Chinese Economic Model," FBIS-EAS-1999-0219, 19 February 1999 (electronic version).

24. For more details on the North Korean nuclear drama of 1993–94, consult Don Oberdorfer, *The Two Koreas: A Contemporary History* (Reading, MA: 1997), chap. 11–14, and Chuck Downs, *Over the Line: North Korea's Negotiating Strategy* (Washington, D.C.: AEI Press, 1999), chap. 9.

25. Korean Central Broadcasting Station (Pyongyang), 8 March 1993, translated as "North Korea; Kim Chong-il Declares 'Semi-State Of War,'" *BBC Summary of World Broadcasts*, FE/1962/B, 9 March 1993.

26. David E. Sanger, "Neighbors Differ on How to Chasten North Korea," *New York Times*, 31 March 1993, A9.

27. Doyle McManus, "Clinton Warns N. Korea Not to Build A-Bomb," *Los Angeles Times*, 8 November 1993, A1.

28. Agence France Presse, "Pyongyang Denounces U.N. Security Council Measure," 12 May 1993.

29. James Adams, "North Koreans Threaten Japan in Nuclear Row," *The Times* (London), 27 March 1994.

30. Norman Kempster, "U.S. to Urge Sanctions for N. Korea," *Los Angeles Times*, 20 March 1994, A1.

31. Douglas Jehl, "U.S. is Pressing for Sanctions for North Korea," *New York Times*, 11 June 1994, A7.

32. "Agreed Framework Between the United States of America and the Democratic People's Republic of Korea," Geneva, 21 October 1994, text available electronically at <http://kedo.org/Agreements/agreed-framework.htm>, accessed 1 February 2000.

33. Personal conversation with Ambassador Robert L. Gallucci, October 1998.

34. Korea Central News Agency (KCNA), 10 January 1996, reprinted as "North Urges Peace Mechanism with USA, South Should Not 'Interfere,'" *BBC Summary of World Broadcasts*, FE/D2506/D, 11 January 1996.

35. *Chungang Ilbo*, 19 April 1996, 2, translated as "ROK Daily Analyzes DPRK's True Intention over Four-Party Talks," FBIS-EAS-96-077, 19 April 1996.

36. This sequence of meetings and U.S. food contributions is documented in Marcus Noland, Sherman Robinson and Tao Wang, "Famine in North Korea: Causes and Cures," *Institute for International Economics Working Papers* (Washington, D.C.), no. 99-2 (1999), Table 4.

37. David E. Sanger, "North Korea Site an A-Bomb Plant, U.S. Agencies Say," *New York Times*, 17 August 1998, A1.

38. KCNA (Pyongyang), "4th DPRK-U.S. Underground Facility Negotiations," 18 March 1999, available electronically through *People's Korea* website at <http://www.korea-np.co.jp/item/1999/9903/990318.htm>, accessed 5 January 2000.

39. William J. Perry, *Review of United States Policy toward North Korea: Findings and Recommendations* (Washington, D.C.: United States Department of State, Office of the North Korea Policy Coordinator, 12 October 1999, unclassified). The unclassified version of the "Perry Report" is also available electronically at the State Department website: <http://www.state.gov/www/regions/eap/991012_northkorea_rpt.html>, accessed 20 January 2000.

40. "Seoul Firmly Backs 'Perry Process,'" *Korea Times*, 7 February 2000.

41. Bill Gertz, "N. Korea Sells Iran Missile Engines," *Washington Times*, 9 February 2000, A1, A8.

42. "X" (George F. Kennan), "Sources of Soviet Conduct," *Foreign Affairs*, July 1947, reprinted in *The Soviet Union: A Foreign Affairs Reader*, ed. Philip E. Mosley (New York: Praeger Paperbacks, 1963), citation at 183–84.

43. *Yonhap* (Seoul), 12 March 1993, reprinted as "Clinton Addresses South Korean National Assembly on Regional Security," *BBC Summary of World Broadcasts*, Special Supplement, FE/1739/C1, 13 March 1993.

44. U.S. Newswire, "Remarks by President Clinton in Question and Answer Session at Camp Bonifas, Korea, July 11," 12 July 1993.

45. Kyodo News Service (Tokyo).

46. U.S. House of Representatives North Korea Advisory Group, "Report to the Speaker," (Washington, D.C.: Government Printing Office, November 1999), ix.

47. Peter Brookes, "The Four Party Talks: A Perspective," *PacNet Newsletter*, no. 12 (20 March 1998), available electronically at <http://www.csis.org/pacfor/1298.htm>, accessed 9 February 2000.

48. The Kumgangsan venture commits Hyundai group to a minimum of $942 million in payments to the DPRK over the course of the six-year contract. Independent South Korean assessments have concluded that Hyundai will lose at least $750 million on the project. But these assessments may prove optimistic: in the first eleven months of operation, the Hyundai cruise tours reportedly lost $258 million. For more details, see Ki-Jung Kim and Deok Ryong Yoon, "Beyond Mt. Kumgang: Social and Economic Implications," in *Kim Dae-jung Government and Sunshine Policy: Promises and Challenges*, ed. Chung-in Moon and David I. Steinberg, (Seoul: Yonsei University Press, 1999), 105–134, esp.112–116; and *Yonhap* (Seoul), 17 December 1999, reprinted as "Naval Clash 'Biggest Headline' in DPRK-ROK Relations," FBIS-EAS-1999-1217, 17 December 1999 (electronic version).

49. "A Statement by the Spokesman for the Ministry of Foreign Affairs, Democratic People's Republic of Korea, Pyongyang, August 17, 1999," accessed through the *People's Korea* website <http://www.korea-np.co.jp/pk>, 1 September 1999.

50. Pyongyang Radio August 22, 1998, cited in "Kim Jong-il Lashes Seoul's North Policy," *Korea Herald* (internet version), 24 August 1998, available electronically at <http://www.koreaherald.co.kr>, accessed 1 February 2000.

51. KCNA (Pyongyang), "S. Korean Authorities' 'Sunshine Policy' Flawed," 6 November 1999, available electronically at *People's Korea* website <http://www.korea-np.co.jp/pk>, accessed 10 November 1999.

52. KCNA (Pyongyang), "Roding Sinmun on True Nature of S. Korean Society," 31 January 2000, available electronically at *People's Korea* website <http://www.korea-np.co.jp/pk>, accessed 1 February 2000.

53. Korean Central Broadcast Network (Pyongyang), 29 September 1998, translated by FBIS as "Radio Denounces ROK Policy on DPRK." This translation, apparently never published in FBIS's daily reports, was transmitted to me by Randolph Fleitman of the U.S. Embassy in Seoul.

54. "Press Conference by President Clinton and President Kim of South Korea, June 9, 1998," available electronically through Nautilus Institute website <http://www.nautlius.org>, accessed 2 January 2000.

55. *Nodong Sinmun* and *Kulloja* joint editorial, 17 September 1998, translated by FBIS as "Nodong Sinmun-Kulloja 17 Sep. Joint Article," (SK1809132898). I am indebted to Mr. Randolph Fleitman for bringing it to my attention.

56. *People's Korea*, 15 February 1992, cited in Hy-Sang Lee, "Economic Factors In Reunification," in *Korea and the World: Beyond the Cold War*, ed. Young Hwan Kihl (Boulder, CO: Westview Press, 1994), 205.

57. *Nodong Sinmun,* 24 May 1997, 6, translated as "North Korea: Daily Warns against Ideological 'Infiltration,'" FBIS, *East Asia Daily Report,* 26 June 1997.
58. "Let's Make This Year a Turning Point in Building a Powerful Nation," joint editorial in *Nodong Sinmun, Choson Inmingun,* and *Chongnyon Jonwi,* 1 January 1999. I rely here on the translation of the text as broadcast: "Radio Carries New Year's Joint Editorial" (SK0101132499).
59. "Let Us Glorify This Year, the 55th Founding Anniversary of the Party, as a Proud Year of Victory Amid the Flame of Great Upsurges of Ch'ollima," joint editorial issued by *Nodong Sinmun, Choson Inmingun,* and *Chongnyon Jonwi,* 1 January 2000. Again, I draw upon an FBIS translation here, and thank Major Stephen J. Gransback in Seoul for passing this on.
60. "KCNA on Japan's False Propaganda," KCNA, 8 September 1999, available electronically through *People's Korea* website <http://www.korea-np.co.kr>, accessed 1 November 1999.
61. *Minju Choson,* 24 October 1998, cited in Pak Hon-ok, "North Korea's Effort to Become a Military Power and Kim Chong-il's Choice," *Pukhan* (Seoul), December 1998, translated in FBIS as "North Korea: DPRK Pursuit of Military Power Examined," 24 December 1998.
62. "Let Us Glorify This Year, the 55th Founding Anniversary."
63. Central Broadcasting System (Pyongyang), 5 December 1999, translated as "North Korea Radio Praises Leadership of Kim Chong-il," *BBC Monitoring: Asia Pacific,* 15 December 1999 (electronic version).
64. Korean Central Broadcasting Network (Pyongyang), 24 April 1999, translated by FBIS as "KCI on Satellite Funding" (SK3004003199).
65. "Independence, Self-sustenance and Self-reliance Termed Way Out," KCNA (Pyongyang), 8 January 2000, available electronically at *People's Korea* website <http://www.korea-np.co.jp>, accessed January 10, 2000.
66. "KCI on Satellite Funding."
67. *Minju Choson,* 24 October 1998.
68. Some would object that the emergency relief aid flowing to the DPRK is different—prompted by humanitarian concerns. There may be some merit in that argument. On the other hand, it is true that the international relief program is now entering its sixth calendar year, in contravention of the stricture that such efforts be *temporary.* International relief workers have also endured restrictions that would not be tolerated in other places. The special treatment North Korea has been accorded is surely related to the security threat its government so successfully poses.
69. KCNA (Pyongyang), 16 June 1998, reprinted as "News Agency Defends Missile Exports as Forced by U.S. Policy," *BBC Summary of World Broadcasts,* FE/D3255/D, 17 June 1998.

70. *Korea Times* (Internet version), 8 August 1999, reprinted as "DPRK 'Never' to Give up Right to Launch Missile," FBIS-EAS-1999-0808, 8 August 1999 (electronic version); *Yonhap* (Seoul), 7 August 1999, reprinted as "DPRK Willing to Halt Export of Missiles If Given Money," FBIS-EAS-1999-0807, 7 August 1999 (electronic version).

71. "U.S. Ends Talks in N. Korea; North Resists Halt to Missile Exports," *Washington Post*, 1 April 1999, A16.

72. KCNA (Pyongyang), February 14, 2000, reprinted as "North Says Abduction Issue is Japanese Plot to Evade 'Liquidation of Past,'" *BBC Summary of World Broadcasts*, FE/D3765/S1, 16 February 2000.

73. *Nodong Sinmun*, 3 November 1999, cited in *Chungang Ilbo* (Internet version), 3 November 1999; translated as "DPRK Holds U.S. Accountable for Nuclear Threat," FBIS-EAS-1999-1104, 3 November 1999.

74. Korean Central Broadcasting Service (Pyongyang), 21 February 1999, translated as "Radio Says North Korea a Strong Military Nation, Competitor to USA," *BBC Monitoring: Asia Pacific*, 5 March 1999 (electronic version).

75. A "containment" policy, incidentally, is designed to contain a *regime threat*, not to seal off an already captive people. In point of fact, vastly increased exposure of the North Korean populace to foreign faces, places, ideas, and practices is consonant with, and indeed invited by, the concept of "containment."

76. This argument is laid out in greater detail in Nicholas Eberstadt, *The End of North Korea* (Washington, D.C.: AEI Press, 1999), 134–135.

77. Shogo Kawakita, "U.N. Agencies, NGOs Deplore N. Korea's 'Aid Blocking,'" Dow Jones Economic Newswire, 4 January 2000.

78. See John Pomfret, "N. Korea Refugees Insecure in China," *Washington Post*, 19 February 2000; and "NK Defectors Form Human Rights Group," *Digital Chosun Ilbo: English Edition*, 27 December 1999, for estimates ranging from 30,000–50,000 to 100,000–200,000.

79. This section draws upon *The End of North Korea*, 135–136.

80. For background on America's diplomatic initiatives, strategy and tactics in the German unification, consult Philip Zelikow and Condoleezza Rice, *Germany United and Europe Transformed: A Study in Statecraft* (Cambridge, MA: Harvard University Press, 1995).

Asian Allies: True Strategic Partners

1. Gerald Segal, "East Asia and the 'Constrainment' of China," *International Security* 20, no. 4 (spring 1996): 108–109.

2. Samuel P. Huntington, *The Clash of Civilizations and the Remaking of World Order* (New York: Touchstone, 1996), 229.

3. Andrew J. Nathan and Robert S. Ross, *The Great Wall and the Empty Fortress* (New York: Norton, 1997), 228.

4. Nathan and Ross, *The Great Wall and the Empty Fortress*, 321.
5. Edward D. Mansfield and Jack Snyder, "Democratization and the Danger of War," *International Security* 20, no. 1 (summer 1995): 5–38.
6. Michael Pillsbury, "China's Assessment of the Future Security Environment" (typescript, n.d.), ix.
7. *Ibid.*, 27–75.
8. Statement to a Hearing Before the Senate Select Intelligence Committee, *Current and Projected National Security Threats to the United States*, 105th Congress, 2nd session (Washington, D.C.: U.S. Government Printing Office, 1998), 23.
9. See Department of Defense, "Future Military Capabilities and Strategy of the People's Republic of China," Report to Congress Pursuant to Section 1226 of the FY98 National Defense Authorization Act (Washington, D.C.: Department of Defense, 9 July 1998).
10. See Michael W. Doyle, "Forward to the Past? Balances of Power, Past and Future," in *Recasting International Relations Paradigms: Statism, Pluralism and Globalism*, ed. Eun Ho Lee and Woosang Kim (Seoul: Korean Association of International Studies, 1997), 129.
11. Crucial to that end would be a change in the prevailing interpretation of Japan's Constitution, and perhaps ultimately a change in the Constitution itself, to permit Japan to participate in "collective self-defense." See the discussion in Mike M. Mochizuki, "American and Japanese Strategic Debates: The Need for a New Synthesis," in *Toward a True Alliance: Restructuring U.S.-Japan Security Relations*, ed. Mochizuki, (Washington, D.C.: Brookings Institution, 1997), 43–82. See also the essays in Michael J. Green and Patrick M. Cronin, eds., *The U.S.-Japan Alliance: Past, Present, and Future* (New York: Council on Foreign Relations, 1999).
12. For useful analyses of Chinese reactions to recent changes in the U.S.-Japan alliance see Banning Garrett and Bonnie Glaser, "Chinese Apprehensions about Revitalization of the U.S.-Japan Alliance," *Asian Survey* 37, no. 4 (April 1977): 383–402; and Thomas J. Christensen, "China, the U.S.-Japan Alliance, and the Security Dilemma in East Asia," *International Security* 23, no. 4 (spring 1999): 49–80.
13. For a carefully worded proposal for development along these lines, see Jonathan D. Pollack, Young Koo Cha, et al., *A New Alliance for the Next Century: The Future of U.S.-Korean Security Cooperation* (Santa Monica: The RAND Corporation, 1995). Regarding recent improvements in Japan-ROK relations, see Akira Ogawa Jr., "The Miracle of 1998 and Beyond: ROK-Japan Security Cooperation," *Korean Journal of Defense Analysis* X, no. 2 (winter 1998): 21–50.
14. In 1995 the Thai government refused a U.S. request for permission to station supply ships in the Gulf of Thailand. In February 1999, China and Thailand signed an agreement to "strengthen security coop-

eration and expand economic and technical cooperation." The text of the agreement is contained in "Joint Statement Issued with China on Cooperation," Xinhua News Agency, Beijing, in English 0924 GMT, 5 February 1999, *BBC Summary of World Broadcasts,* 8 February 1999). See also Ben Barber, "New Pact with Thais Troubles U.S. Allies," *Washington Times,* 23 February 1999, A1.

15. See Paul Bracken, *Fire in the East* (New York: Harper Collins, 1999).

16. For useful summaries of the post–Cold War expansion of China's influence to its south and west, see Russ H. Munro, "China's Waxing Spheres of Influence," *Orbis,* fall 1994, 585–605; Gary Klintworth, "China: South of the Border," *Asia-Pacific Defense Reporter,* June/July 1999, 6–8; and Nathan and Ross, *The Great Wall and the Empty Fortress,* 100–22.

17. For a review of attitudes in a number of Southeast Asian countries, see Allen S. Whiting, "ASEAN Eyes China: The Security Dimension," *Asian Survey* 37, no. 4 (April 1997): 299–322. See also Rosemary Foot, "China in the ASEAN Regional Forum: Organizational Processes and Domestic Modes of Thought," *Asian Survey* 38, no. 5 (May 1998): 425–440.

18. See Munro, "China's Waxing Spheres of Influence," 598–605. The fullest account of China's recent energy ventures in Central Asia, and their possible strategic motivations and implications, is contained in Munro, *Chinese Energy Strategy* (Strategic Assessment Center, Science Applications International Corporation, July 1999).

Israel and the "Peace Process"

1. Norman Podhoretz, "Israel and the United States: A Complex History," *Commentary,* May 1998.

2. David Bar Illan, "Why Bibi Fell," *National Review,* 14 June 1999.

3. Editorial, *Jerusalem Post,* 1 April 1998.

4. Mehran Kamrava, "What Stands between the Palestinians and Democracy?" *Middle East Quarterly,* June 1999, 7.

5. Quoted in *Middle East Media and Research Institute Special Dispatch* no. 37, 30 June 1999.

6. Quoted in Podhoretz, "Israel and the United States: A Complex History."

7. Ehud Ya'ari, "The Impossibility of a Final Deal," *Jerusalem Report,* 13 September 1999, 40.

The Decline of America's Armed Forces

1. Lorna S. Jaffe, *The Development of the Base Force, 1989–1992* (U.S. Department of Defense, Joint History Office, Office of the Chairman of the Joint Chiefs of Staff, July 1993).
2. Testimony of Vice Chairman of the Joint Chiefs of Staff Admiral David Jeremiah before the House Armed Services Committee, 12 March 1991.
3. Testimony of the Chairman of the Joint Chiefs of Staff General Colin Powell before the House Armed Services Committee, 6 February 1992.
4. For a more detailed discussion of this issue, see Donald Kagan and Frederick W. Kagan, *While America Sleeps* (New York: St. Martin's Press, 2000), chap. 12 & 13.
5. Les Aspin, "Understanding the New Security Environment," address to the Atlantic Council of the United States, 6 January 1992.
6. *Report on the Bottom-Up Review* (Department of Defense, October 1993), 13.
7. *Ibid.*, 19.
8. *Ibid.*, 30.
9. Five Reserve Division equivalents.
10. The force structure Secretary Aspin apparently foresaw supporting this strategy included ten active Army divisions, ten aircraft carriers, and twenty Air Force tactical wings. See "U.S. May Drop 2-War Capability; Aspin Envisions Smaller, High-Tech Military to 'Win-Hold-Win,'" *Washington Post*, 17 June 1993, A1.
11. Congress consistently resisted Pentagon efforts to reduce the force structure of the Army National Guard, so the current structure contains three additional National Guard divisions. The time required to train, ready and deploy those forces, however, is so great as to render them irrelevant to the calculations of fighting MRCs. In addition, the current Navy is some forty ships smaller than that envisioned by the Bottom-Up Review.
12. *Report of the Quadrennial Defense Review* (Department of Defense, May 1997), iii–iv.
13. *Ibid.*, 12.
14. *Ibid.*, 13.
15. *Ibid.*, 59.
16. *Ibid.*, 31.
17. For the best description of this crisis, see Don Oberdorfer, *The Two Koreas: A Contemporary History* (New York: Basic Books, 1997).
18. *Ibid.*, 324–25
19. Anthony Cordesman, *U.S. Forces in the Middle East: Resources and Capabilities* (Boulder, CO: Westview Press, 1997), 79.

20. *The Two Koreas*, 325–26.
21. Anthony Cordesman, *The Lessons and Non-Lessons of the Air and Missile War in Kosovo* (Washington, D.C.: Center for Strategic and International Studies, 1999), 18. Emphasis added.
22. *Ibid.*, 30.
23. The "heavy division equivalents" include heavy divisions and non-divisional maneuver brigades, with 3 brigades being counted as a division equivalent. In 1991, there were 9 heavy divisions and 7 light divisions, with 6 heavy and 2 light non-divisional maneuver brigades. The figure does not include the one heavy and one light division that were being deactivated during 1991. Today, there are 10 divisions: 6 heavy and 4 light, with 1 heavy and 1 light maneuver brigade.

Weapons Proliferation and Missile Defense: The Strategic Case

1. Quoted in Selig S. Harrison and Geoffrey Kemp, *India and America After the Cold War,* Carnegie Endowment for International Peace, 1993, 20.
2. "Executive Summary," *Report of the Commission to Assess the Ballistic Missile Threat to the United States* ["The Rumsfeld Commission Report"] (Washington, D.C.: Government Printing Office, July 1998), 5.
3. Herman Kahn, *On Thermonuclear War* (Princeton: Princeton University Press, 1960), 476. To a lesser extent than with nuclear weapons technology, information on American biological weapons work is being declassified, as well. Scientific and engineering information on how to weaponize dangerous biological substances is now publicly available. See, for example, Stephen Endicott and Edward Hagerman, *The United States and Biological Warfare: Secrets from the Early Cold War and Korea* (Bloomington, Indiana: Indiana University Press, 1998).
4. Useful overviews of Iraq's effort to build a bomb are A. J. Venter, "How Iraq's Saddam Almost Built his Bomb," *Jane's Intelligence Review* (December 1997); and David Kay, "Denial and Deception: The Lessons of Iraq," in *U.S. Intelligence at the Crossroads*, ed. Roy Godson, Ernest May and Gary Schmitt (Washington, D.C.: Brassey's, 1995), 109–27. Interestingly, Vannevar Bush proposed to President Roosevelt in 1942 that EMIS be used as a "short cut" to produce highly enriched uranium. An account of the decision to abandon EMIS is contained in Richard Rhodes, *The Making of the Atomic Bomb* (New York: Simon and Schuster, 1986), 406.

5. National Intelligence Council, *Emerging Missile Threat to North America during the Next 15 Years* (NIE 95-19), October 1995. For a useful commentary on the report, see General Accounting Office, *Foreign Missile Threats: The Analytic Soundness of Certain NIEs,* Report to the Chairman, Committee on National Security, U.S. House of Representatives, GAO/NSIAD-96-225, August 1996.
6. For a useful summary of Clinton administration statements, see Jack Spencer, *The Ballistic Missile Threat Handbook* (Washington, D.C.: The Heritage Foundation, 2000), ix.
7. As Secretary of Defense William S. Cohen said, "[T]here is a threat, and the threat is growing, and ... we expect it will soon pose a danger not only to our troops overseas but also to Americans here at home." News briefing, 20 January 1999.
8. On the question of whether the U.S. government is optimally organized to combat WMD proliferation, see the *Report of the Commission to Assess the Organization of the Federal Government to Combat the Proliferation of Weapons of Mass Destruction* ["The Deutsch-Specter Commission Report"] (Washington, D.C.: U.S. Government Printing Office, July 1999), 75.

Morality, Character and American Foreign Policy

1. Francis Bowen, trans., *Democracy in America,* bk. 2, chap. 14 (New York: Alfred A. Knopf, 1997), 242.
2. H. C. Lodge, *George Washington* (New York: Houghton Mifflin, 1917), 378, 379.

Statesmanship in the New Century

1. Patrick J. Buchanan, *A Republic Not an Empire: Reclaiming America's Destiny* (Washington, D.C.: Regnery, 1999), 9.
2. *Ibid.,* 10.
3. Winston S. Churchill, *The Second World War,* vol. 1, *The Gathering Storm* (New York: Houghton Mifflin, 1948), 283
4. Henry Kissinger, *Diplomacy* (New York: Touchstone, 1994), 579.
5. Jiang Minfan and Duan Zhaoxian, "Taiwan zhanlie diwei danxi" (The analysis of Taiwan's strategic position), *The Navy* 8 (1995), cited by You Ji, "Making Sense of War Games in the Taiwan Strait," *Journal of Contemporary China* 6, no. 15 (1997).
6. George P. Shultz, *Turmoil and Triumph: My Years as Secretary of State* (New York: Scribner, 1993), 382.

Strength and Will: A Historical Perspective

1. Paul Kennedy, *The Rise and Fall of the Great Powers: Economic Change and Military Conflict from 1500 to 2000* (New York: Random House, 1987), 536.
2. Winston S. Churchill, *Marlborough, His Life and Times* (London: G. G. Harrap, 1933), vol. 1, 427–28.
3. Paul M. Kennedy, "Tirpitz, England and the Second Naval Law of 1900: A Strategical Critique," *Militarische Mitteilungen* 2 (1970): 38.
4. L. C. F. Turner, "The Significance of the Schlieffen Plan," in *The War Plans of the Great Powers 1880–1914*, ed. Paul M. Kennedy (Boston, 1985), 204.
5. Niall Ferguson, *The Pity of War* (New York: Basic Books, 1999), 104.
6. Corelli Barnett, *The Collapse of British Power* (New York: Morrow, 1972), 277; Telford Taylor, *Munich: The Price of Peace* (Garden City, NJ: Doubleday, 1979), 201.
7. Brian Bond, *British Military Policy between the Two World Wars* (Oxford: Clarendon Press, 1980), 25
8. Paul M. Kennedy, *The Rise and Fall of British Naval Mastery* (London: A. Lane, 1976), 277.
9. A. J. P. Taylor, *English History, 1914–1945* (New York: Oxford University Press, 1965), 232.
10. Michael Howard, *The Continental Commitment* (London: Ashfield Press, 1989), 78.
11. Keith Robbins, *Appeasement* (Oxford: Blackwell, 1988), 30.
12. *Ibid.*, ix.
13. Barnett, *Collapse*, 250.
14. *Ibid.*, 274.
15. Leonard Mosley, *On Borrowed Time, How World War II Began* (London, 1969), 7. For the sources of the quotations see p. 477.
16. J. T. Emmerson, *The Rhineland Crisis* (London: Temple Smith, 1977), 246.
17. Arthur J. Marder, *From the Dardanelles to Oran: Studies of the Royal Navy in War and Peace, 1915–1940* (New York: Oxford University Press, 1974), 341.
18. *Ibid.*, 248.
19. Emmerson, *Rhineland*, 145.
20. *Ibid.*, 139.
21. A. J. P. Taylor, *The Origins of the Second World War*, 2nd ed. (New York: Atheneum, 1985), 97.
22. Paul Schmidt, *Hitler's Interpreter* (New York: Macmillan, 1951), 320.
23. T. Taylor, *Munich*, 576.
24. *Ibid.*, 617.

25. *Ibid.*, 794.
26. Donald Cameron Watt, *How War Came: The Immediate Origins of the Second World War, 1938–1939* (New York: Pantheon, 1989), 19.
27. T. Taylor, *Munich*, 208.
28. Barnett, *Collapse*, 301.
29. Charles Neu, *The Troubled Encounter: The United States and Japan* (New York: Wiley, 1975), 134.
30. *Ibid.*, 141.
31. *Ibid.*, 144.
32. *Ibid.*, 156.
33. *Ibid.*, 168.
34. Stephen E. Pelz, *Race to Pearl Harbor: The Failure of the Second London Naval Conference and the Onset of World War II* (Cambridge, MA: Harvard University Press, 1974), 226.
35. Neu, *Troubled Encounter*, 189.
36. *Ibid.*, 190.
37. Douglas A. Macgregor, *Breaking the Phalanx: A New Design for Landpower in the 21st Century* (Westport, CT: Praeger, 1997), 15.
38. *Ibid.*, 51.
39. *Ibid.*, 52.
40. *Ibid.*, 53.
41. *Ibid.*, 58.
42. *Ibid.*, 59.

Index

ICBMs, 55, 279; *see also* weapons
idealism, 22–24, 28–32, 36
ideology, 68, 237, 315, 317–18, 324
India: vs. China, 53, 58; nuclear
    weapons, 53, 212–13, 268, 272
Indonesia, 213–14, 320
Indyk, Martin, 119
intelligence gathering, 66, 72,
    273–75, 278–79; *see also* Central
    Intelligence Agency
International Atomic Energy
    Agency, 147, 153, 154, 253
internationalism: conservative,
    viii, 27–33, 38–43; liberal, 26,
    32–38
International Monetary Fund, 81,
    97, 171
Iran, 111–44, 237–38, 318, 319;
    anti-Americanism, 121, 122,
    140; broadcasting in, 112–13,
    143; civil society, 120–21;
    clerical factions, 125–27; consti-
    tution, 124, 128; corruption,
    121, 122; coup d'état (1953),
    114, 128, 140; democratic
    forces, 124–25, 127–31;
    diplomatic relations, 118–120,
    122–23, 140; economy, 127, 131,
    141–42; foreign investment,
    119, 140–42; fundamentalism,
    111, 114–16, 121–32, 135–37;
    human rights, 137–38, 143;
    intellectuals, 120, 127–31; and
    Israel, 134, 137; Jews in, 119,
    134, 137; media, 123–24;
    Ministry of Intelligence, 124,
    125; Ministry of Islamic
    Guidance, 111, 126;
    nationalism, 128–29; nuclear
    weapons, 88, 119, 138–39; oil,
    112, 141–41; power struggle,
    125–31; *rahbar* (revolutionary
    leader), 125; repression, 119,
    143; Revolutionary Guard
    Corps, 124, 130, 132; and
    Russia, 87–90; sanctions, 120,
    122–23, 136–37, 139–42;

secularism, 127–31; Special
    Clerical Court, 125, 128; student
    demonstrations (1999), 123,
    124, 130; terrorism, 112, 125,
    132–36, 143; universities, 128,
    129–31; U.S. visas, 143; Western
    culture, 116–25, 127, 130–31;
    women's rights, 120
Iranian expatriates, 119, 123–24,
    143
Iran-Iraq War, 102, 103, 115, 120,
    123, 138
Iran-Libyan Sanctions Act, 112
Iraq, 64, 99–110; Ba'athists, 103;
    bombing of, 108, 311;
    broadcasting, 109; crisis of
    1994, 254; no-fly zones, 105,
    109; oil, 91, 109; opposition in,
    99–105; 133; repression, 103–4;
    and Russia, 90–91; safe havens,
    104, 105, 108, 109; sanctions,
    90, 91, 100–1, 105, 106, 108;
    Shi'ites, 102, 109; Special
    Republic Guard, 105, 109, 254;
    Sunnis, 101, 102, 103; UN
    inspection, 100–1, 105–6, 270;
    U.S. aid, 115, 120; weapons
    development, 90, 102, 105–7,
    234–38, 270, 275–76, 298–99,
    301; *see also* Gulf War; Saddam
    Hussein
Iraqi National Congress, 100, 108,
    110, 133
Iraq Liberation Act, 99, 108,
    109–110
Iraq Policy Group, 102, 103
Iron Curtain, 11, 82, 113
Islam: in Central Asian republics,
    89; in China, 58; fundamental-
    ism, 89,111, 114–16, 121–32,
    135–37, 223, 318
Ismay, Lord Hastings Lionel, 180,
    311
isolationism: 10, 27–35, 38, 40,
    300, 310; and Gulf War, 27; and
    Kosovo, 28; and trade, 27–28
Israel, 137, 138, 221–40, 281, 282,

301; democracy, 234; and Egypt, 223; "land for peace," 221–22, 224, 228, 234; Gaza, 224; Golan, 235; Hebron, 226, 227–28; Jericho, 224; Jerusalem, 232, 233–34; and Jordan, 223; Labor party, 221, 222, 226; and Lebanon, 224, 235–36; Likud, 221, 222, 224; Oslo Accords, 222, 224–29, 232; Sinai, 234; and Syria, 224, 235–36; Temple Mount riots, 227–28; and Turkey, 237; UN partition, 232; U.S. presence, 235; West Bank, 224, 227; Wye River Accords, 228–29; *see also* Palestinian Authority
Italy, 338, 350–52
Ivanov, Igor, 91, 92

Jackson, Henry M. ("Scoop"), 308
James II of England, 340
Japan, 8, 11, 62, 198–99, 324; aggression, 338, 354–59; as ally, 70, 207–8, 282; appeasement of, 358–59; vs. Britain, 347–50; and China, 59, 63, 207, 355–57; democracy, 321; and Korea, 207, 210, 349; and Manchuria, 338, 346, 349, 350, 355–56; nationalism, 349; Pearl Harbor, 354; vs. Russia, 349; snubbing of, 52, 218; in WWI, 349; in WWII, 198, 354–59
Jay, John, 292
Jay Treaty, 296
Jefferson, Thomas, 296, 303
Jeremiah, David, 246
Jiang Zemin: and Clinton, 53, 56, 67; nationalism, 56; and Russia, 85–86; and Taiwan, 56, 70, 327
Johnson, Lyndon, 313
Joint Chiefs of Staff, 241, 242, 246
Jordan, 223

Kadivar, Mohsen, 128

Kahn, Herman, 274
Karrubi, Mehdi, 125
Kazakhstan, 58, 216
Kellogg-Briand Pact, 355
Kennan, George, 18, 24, 180, 307, 316
Kennedy, Edward, 309, 310
Kennedy, John F., 194, 313
Kerrey, Robert, 372
Khalilzad, Zalmay, 142
Khameneh'i, Ali, 111, 112, 118–20, 12, 124, 125, 134–35
Khatami, Mohammad, 111–23, 125–31, 138; civil society, 119, 120–21; CNN interview, 111–12, 118–20; "dialogue of civilizations," 116, 118–21; on history, 117; on liberty, 117, 121; as Minister of Islamic Guidance, 111, 126; as moderate, 111, 116; rule of law, 119, 121; and Western culture, 116–22; writings of, 116–17
Khobar Towers bombing, 112, 132–34
Kho'iniha, Mohammad Mosavi, 125
Khomeini, Ayatollah Ruhollah, 115, 120, 123, 124, 125, 128
Khosrokhavar, Farhad, 130
Khrushchev, Nikita, 322
Kim Dae Jung, 150–53, 159, 161–63, 321
Kim Il Sung, 147, 154
Kim Jong Il, 147, 153, 160, 162, 163, 164, 166
Kim Young Sam, 156
Kirkpatrick, Jeane, 9–10
Kiriyenko, Sergei, 79, 83
Kissinger, Henry, 13, 85, 94, 179, 322, 328
Kohl, Helmut, 188
Korea. *See* North Korea, South Korea
Korean War, 11, 145–46, 169, 262, 316, 322, 338, 360–61

Mubarak, Hosni, 223
multiculturalism, 32–35
multilateralism, 36, 184
multipolarity, 24, 82, 84–86, 91,
    202, 267
Munich Agreement (1938),
    312–13, 323–24
Murphy, Richard, 113
Muslims. *See* Islam
Mussolini, Benito, 346, 350–52
Myanmar, 56

NAFTA (North American Free
    Trade Agreement), 27–28
Nagano, Admiral Osami, 369
Naipaul, V. S., 117
Napoleon Bonaparte, 9, 264, 342
Nasser, Gamal Abdel, 313
Nateq Nuri, Ali Akbar, 127
National Defense Panel, 261
national interest, 13–14, 23–24,
    27, 38–40, 64, 72, 289–90
nationalism, 35–37, 289-93; Amer-
    ican, 23–24, 34, 37, 239–90,
    292–95; Chinese, 55–56, 68–69;
    European, 34, 36–37, 185, 187,
    189, 292; Nazi, 292, 292;
    Serbian, 34, 291–93
National Security Council, 102,
    112, 284, 330
NATO. *See* North Atlantic Treaty
    Organization.
Nazi party (National Socialist),
    291, 350; *see also* Hitler
Netanyahu, Benjamin, 221, 225–28
"new world order," 6
New York Times, 112, 113, 309–10
Nicaragua, 19, 33
Niebuhr, Reinhold, 24
Nixon, Richard, 3, 15, 85, 94
Noriega, Manuel, 14
North American Free Trade Agree-
    ment (NAFTA), 27–28
North Atlantic Treaty
    Organization (NATO), 20,
    179–96, 259–60, 262, 308, 333,
    360; American leadership,
189–91, 194; arms control, 273;
and Balkans, 86, 181–87, 362;
and EU, 188–89; expansion, 86,
90, 93, 96, 181, 190, 194–96,
310–11, 322; in Kosovo, 19,
179–80, 186–87, 190, 196, 299,
335; Strategic Concept, 181,
193, 196; and UN, 181
North Korea (Democratic People's
    Republic of Korea), 8, 18,
    145–175, 246–47; "Agreed
    Framework," 154–58, 173–74;
    appeasement of, 150, 154–57,
    159; biological weapons, 148;
    chemical weapons, 148;
    containment of, 159–60,
    169–70; crisis of 1994, 253–55;
    De-Militarized Zone, 146, 170;
    economy, 147, 163–68, 175, 255;
    "engagement" with, 150–53,
    159, 161, 165, 168–69; extortion,
    166–68, 281; famine, 147, 156,
    165, 172, 172; human rights,
    152, 172–73; international aid,
    156, 167, 172; and Japan, 167;
    negotiation with, 149–50,
    154–56, 159, 171; nuclear
    weapons, 6, 147–50, 153–55,
    157–58, 168, 173–74, 263, 272;
    reunification, 151, 162–63,
    174–75; sanctions, 159; self-
    reliance *(juche)*, 147, 164, 166,
    175; vs. S. Korea, 145–46,
    150–53, 156, 161–63, 173, 283,
    361; totalitarianism, 146–47;
    trade, 164–65, 175; treaty
    violation, 171; U.S. aid, 101,
    150, 156–57, 160, 272; weapons
    development, 147–50, 159,
    166–68, 272, 276–77, 301;
    weapons export, 139, 159, 167,
    276, 280; weapons inspection,
    153–55, 157, 253
nuclear freeze, 308
Nuclear Non-Proliferation Treaty,
    147, 153, 155, 171, 253, 268,
    269, 272